CW01086248

Money, Finance, Reality, Morality

A New Way to Address Old Problems

By

Edward Hadas

Money, Finance, Reality, Morality: A New Way to Address Old Problems

By Edward Hadas

This book first published 2022

Ethics International Press Ltd, UK

British Library Cataloguing in Publication Data

A catalogue record for this book is available from the British Library

Print Book ISBN: 978-1-80441-026-4

eBook ISBN: 978-1-80441-027-1

Contents

viii

Preface

What is different: This is a book about money and finance. It is also a book based on an understanding of economic activity in which finance, money, and even barter are completely optional. In turn, the understanding of the economy is based on a fundamental judgement about the right way to approach economics, the academic study of some parts of the human experience. I do not believe that a model of the economy can be valid unless it is fully applicable to all communities – not only the complex, money-filled national economies that economists typically study, but also much simpler ones, all the way down to the now vanished hunter-gatherers, who mostly laboured and consumed together and who had neither money nor more than minimal trading relations with other groups. The paradigm presented in Chapters One and Two satisfies my standard of validity.

My description of economies is quite different in several fundamental ways from those commonly taken for granted in university economics departments. The difference that is most relevant to this book is not actually that the professors generally approach the economy as a monetary thing, while I do not. It is that they assume that the study of economics is essentially numerical, while I do not. For them, the only good explanations and analyses are either abstractly mathematical, something like the laws of physics, or statistical, like the patterns discovered in biology or much contemporary sociology. For me, economics is primarily a moral, social, and qualitative discipline. I recognise that some economic numbers can be informative, but I have found that even the helpful ones often bring more false certainty than true understanding. In my judgement, it is almost self-evident that economic systems and the people who constitute them do not follow rigid mathematical laws, whether simple or complicated. People are just not like that. Their behaviour can sometimes be described statistically, but those patterns and tendencies generally conceal far more than they reveal.

How this book came to be: Considering my distrust of the conventional numerical approach to economics, the choice to write about the essentially numerical domains of money and finance may seem strange. It sometimes seems strange to me. Indeed, I was proud of having written a book on economic theory (Hadas, 2007) that hardly mentioned either money or finance. Before the 2008-2009 financial crisis, I firmly intended to continue to stay away from both. The crisis and the subsequent slow economic recovery changed my mind. At the time, I could not explain to my satisfaction why the world's financial system came so close to collapsing, why it was so hard for the global economy to recover from the damage done by a brief financial crisis, or why so little changed in the global financial system after governments rescued it from the results of its obvious errors.

After several years, I came to understand that my approach to economics, to study it as a moral discipline, was the hermeneutic key to the crisis. Several more years were required to grasp firmly that finance's ethical troubles sprung from a faulty popular (and professional) misunderstanding of its proper economic role. Delving into this misunderstanding, I thought more deeply about what money could and should do. Once this conceptual framing was clear, I set out to explain not only the 2008-2009 crisis, but the nature of the entire "financial exception" that I discuss in Chapter One. In effect, removing economists' numerical blinkers allowed a clearer vision of the underlying moral drama of this seemingly number-filled crisis. As a sort of grim bonus, the dozen or so years it took to think through these ideas and turn them into a book were enough for yet another possibly serious problem in the money-financial system to roll around, this time a sudden rise in consumer price inflation. The latest troubles support this book's basic thesis: the cavalcade of financial crises will continue until the system's rules and customs become reality-close and ethically sound.

No policy recommendations: This book lacks one of the common features of post-crisis books, a collection of pragmatic proposals for avoiding future troubles. An earlier draft did have a list of that sort, but I decided not to include it after noticing that none of my fifteen big suggestions could currently gain any significant political support. I decided that a collection of apparently unrealistic proposals was less likely to win over sceptical readers than to persuade waverers that I am a utopian dreamer. I am still confident that these proposals, or something like them, could work well in the real contemporary world of complex economies and the sempiternal world of morally weak humanity. However, nothing will work at all without a new, or perhaps a revived, social consensus about financial greed. That, I am sorry to say, looks like a distant prospect.

Not much visible philosophy: The book has few explicitly philosophical discussions, but my agenda is deeply philosophical. In the most general terms, I want to replace the naïve utilitarianism, reality-blind methodological individualism, and pseudo-non-normativity that underpin academic economics with a much more solid foundation, one drawn from the great Western traditions of philosophy, social thought, and philosophical anthropology. In more detail, the book includes a refinement of Aristotle's discussion of money, an almost scholastic effort to show that what we call "money" is actually two different substances, a firm rejection of the Locke-Hume-Smith effort to separate the money from government and the economy from society, an effort to demystify Karl Marx's claim to have demystified money, a Durkheimian identification of a dual sociology of finance, and an understanding of time that is influenced by both Augustine and Heidegger. Most important, the moral analysis of finance has been informed by a Thomistic understanding of the good life.

Not much Catholicism: Between my first book on economics and this one I published a book on Catholic Social Teaching (Hadas, 2020). The economic aspects of that teaching helped shape the current work. In particular, Pope John Paul II's encyclical on labour (John Paul II, 1981) is the foundation for the Great Exchange paradigm that I present in Chapter Two. More generally, the subsequent pope, Benedict XVI, summarised the moral framing that is the foundation of all my economic thinking: "The economic sphere is neither ethically neutral, nor inherently inhuman and opposed to society. It is part and parcel of human activity and precisely because it is human, it must be structured and governed in an ethical manner" (Benedict XVI, 2009: 36). Since quotations from papal texts are far more likely to repel than attract potential readers, that is the only one in the book.

Not much debate with economists: This book also includes a number of skirmishes with various conventional ideas about economics. As with philosophy and theology, I have avoided both polemics and details that would only interest specialists. I particularly want to spare readers who are unfamiliar with mainstream or Marxist economics from having to wade through detailed condemnations of unfamiliar bad ideas. Readers more versed in economic theory might have preferred more fighting words, but I do not think that knowledgeable and thoughtful doubters will be persuaded by being told that much of their thinking is crude, immoral, inaccurate, and incoherent (although I do think that those adjectives describe the basic principles of mainstream academic economics). I am humble enough to recognise that far more intelligence than I could ever hope to muster has gone into the many debates on, for example, capital theory, the effect of policy interest rates, and the quantification of investment risk. However, I am confident enough, or perhaps foolish or arrogant enough, not only to dismiss most of those efforts as fundamentally misguided, but largely to ignore them in presenting my own understanding. Still, I do provide a few detailed refutations, which readers with less economic training can skim over without great loss.

I have provided only schematic and geographically limited discussions of economic, financial, and monetary history. The justification for this undesirable brevity, as for the cursory discussions of the penumbra of symbolic and social meanings that surround money and finance, is that the alternative – careful and nuanced analysis – would have been even worse. I decided that the hundreds of pages, not to mention the years of study, needed to do justice to these topics, would have added more confusion than insight to an argument that is essentially conceptual.

Not many references: The decision to concentrate on my own ideas explains the paucity of references in the text. I have only sourced facts, quotes, and direct references to relatively obscure works. The intellectual self-centredness might excuse the relatively brief bibliography, which should be read as a sampling of the many broad thinkers and narrow specialists who have influenced and informed my thinking about the topics in this book. My hope is that the parsimonious approach to citations and sources, while rather unscholarly by today's academic standards, allows this book's novelties to stand out. I am arrogant enough to claim that much of what I say about money and finance in this book is in many ways new.

Summary: *Money, Finance, Reality, Morality* is a simple but accurate summary of this book. After a first, introductory chapter, there are single chapters on each of the title's words. There are a few wrinkles, though. I deal with monetary reality in Chapter Two, so Chapter Four is entirely dedicated to the mostly dangerous reality-distance of contemporary finance. The morality in Chapter Five is mostly limited to a single sin, greed, although there is an implicit sociology of the virtues of generosity and justice.

Both Chapters Two and Four have some fairly detailed discussions of financial instruments and practices. Less technically informed or interested readers are welcome to skim over those sections. More informed or interested readers can also look at the Appendix, which goes into further detail.

Acknowledgements: The gestation of this book took decades, the writing several years. Over that time several institutions and many people have helped me in various ways: with suggestions, debates, friendly support, and hard questions. I am in (non-financial) debt to more organisations and people than I can hope to list, but here are the ones that it would be shameful not to mention.

Institutions: Las Casas Institute at Blackfriars Hall of Oxford University, University of Dallas, The Institute of Human Ecology at Catholic University of America, Oxford University Department for Continuing Education, Reuters Breakingviews, Stanford University in Oxford, Telos Foundation.

People: Andrew Abela, Jan Benz (for enthusiasm), Philip Booth, Leonie Caldecott, Christine Desan, Hugo Dixon (for asking the first question), Father Richard Finn, Lauren Fishman and Katherine Silk (for wondering what I was on about), Paul Gait, Richard Gipps, Andrew Griffin, David Harrison, Sarah Lister, the Kelly family, Margaret McCarthy, Lucas Neo, Michael Pakaluk, Peter and Kinga Róna, David C. Schindler, Tim and Mary Ann Sheehy, Stephanie Solywoda, Russell Sparkes, Sarah Thomas, Lucy Traves.

Chapter 1. The problem with money and finance

In praise of the modern economy

The modern economy is a wonder of coordination. The diverse labours of billions of people are meshed together to provide an incredible range of goods and services to the same billions of people.

Each person contributes only a tiny portion of the labour required for the production of almost anything that is consumed. The assembly line worker depends on the other workers on the line, the product's designers, the factory builders, the maintenance experts, the contract-protecting lawyers, the driver who takes the product to the retailer. Builders, engineers, drivers, and retailers all have their own long chains of dependency, creating a myriad of interlocking contributions and relationships. The teacher who provides education directly in person is delivering a personal service, but she could not work without the labour of all the people who provide the books, the buildings, and the bureaucracies of a school. It is not just material that is passed through the economy. All workers also draw their own tiny portions from the modern world's great treasuries of knowledge, trust, and ethical expectations. Many workers also contribute little bits of the labour needed to keep those treasuries well-stocked.

Exactly as the modern economy unites the products of many people's labours, it divides the labour itself. Specialisation allows people to be more productive in their labour, largely by encouraging the exploitation and expansion of the just mentioned treasuries. The treasury of trust is especially important for the specialisation of labour. Expertise has no appeal without confidence that each sliver of expert labour will be fitted into the whole of the economy. This scale and density of economic trust is a wonder of the age. It is also relevant to the role of money in the economy.

I will come back to that role in the next chapter. For the moment, I want to point out that the complexity of the production system – the coordinated efforts of so many labourers engaged in so many diverse tasks – ensures that there are great distances of time and place between most people's actual labour and the ultimate, consumable fruits of their efforts. The result is the direct opposite of self-sufficiency. Each individual's labour is likely to have almost no direct ties with her consumption. Her job might contribute to the production of the clothes on her back, the electricity in her house, the schooling of her children, or the mobile phone in her pocket, but none of those would be possible without the labour of numerous strangers, many of them living and working in distant places.

This complex economic system has various disadvantages, but at least one great virtue. It is well on the way to accomplishing what was considered impossible for almost all of human history: the end of absolute poverty. There are richer and poorer people in every society, but fewer and fewer people who lack the necessities of life. Actually, the interdependent economy does far more than prevent the worst sort of deprivation. For most of the people in the world, and there are far more people than ever before, the complex mixing and allocating of modern labour and production also provides such basic economic goods as long lives, education, electricity, and mobile phones.

Where the economies are most developed, the range of goods and services produced and the division of labour used to produce them are tremendous. The labour in these economies is not all wonderful, far from it, but the specialisation has many advantages. In comparison to the largely agricultural past, far more labour now requires skill and imagination and a far higher proportion of the population has the opportunity to find a true vocation, a spiritual meaning, in their labour.

The good economic news is not likely to stop with the current accomplishments. With a bit more social and political work, the coordinated modern economic system can undoubtedly reduce the difference between the world's rich and poor. Everyone in the world should be able to consume roughly the same goods and services. It is more controversial to suggest that universal consumption prosperity can be maintained without destroying the environment or running out of raw materials, but at least some experts think that is possible. Over the last two centuries, technical innovations and social reorganisations have belied all pessimistic predictions about the limits to growth.

I am not claiming that modern prosperity has created a new paradise of labour or consumption, let alone of the human relationship with the natural world. There are numerous profound problems, from the persistence of dreadful poverty to the more spiritual disorder of consumerist frenzies. Still, among the many dramatically new things of the modern world – the unprecedented changes in families, sexual roles, religion, politics, social organisation, and art (just to name the most prominent) – the economy stands out for its accomplishments. From a moral perspective, the near-elimination of absolute poverty is probably the most significant mark of progress, but there are many others, from the increase in creature comforts to the decreases in the physical stresses and strains of the life of labour in the home, field, factory, and office, from the added years of education to the increased variety and time for leisure, from the shrinking of effective distances to the expansion of diets.

This is not a book about the whole economy, so there is not space for a full inventory of pluses and minuses. My point is simply to provide some background for the weaknesses of the money-financial system. That system's strengths and weaknesses should be compared to the economy which it is supposed to support.

One achievement of this modern economy is particularly relevant to the comparison with finance – its resilience. The labour-production-consumption system shifts fairly easily and quickly in response to many sorts of pressures. When tastes change or technology advances, the supply of newly desired goods and services quickly catches up with demand, often in no more than a few months. Not only are manmade economic calamities, such as exploding factories or mass poisonings, very rare, but when they do occur, they rarely disrupt the relevant parts of the economy for more than a few months. The same is true for natural disasters and lesser manmade difficulties, such as aeroplane crashes, tainted food, corporate chicanery, raw materials shortages, and faulty product designs. After such events, the return to normal rarely takes more than a few weeks. In general, as the economy has become more complex, it has become more resilient.

One basic reason for this resilience is the redundancy which economic complexity both allows and supports. When things go wrong, there are almost always alternative sources of whatever is wanted, inventories to be drawn down, factories that can be expanded without too much difficulty, and reasonably attractive alternative products. Even when the system slows down, as it did during the anti-Covid-19 restrictions on production and after war and sanctions reduced exports from Russia and Ukraine, the problems almost never last more than a few years.

The Berlin International Airport is a good example of the economy's resilience, redundancy, and helpful interdependence. By the standards of the modern economy, the project was a debacle (Airport Industry Review, 2020). Faulty design led to a multiplication of the initially planned time and hours of labour needed for construction. However, the delay did little noticeable damage to the Berlin economy and none to the regional, let alone the global, air transport system. The local airport authority managed to keep old airports working reasonably well. The difficulties created by the construction delays were divided into morsels so tiny that they were hardly noticed by the people who endured them. Without doubt, an "on time and under budget" airport would have provided much earlier improvements in transport and efficiency as well as allowing better uses for the labour and energy which was actually used to keep the old system going. However, the modern economy is astoundingly good at finding second-best solutions, even to relatively large problems.

Or consider the Covid-19 pandemic of 2020. The headlines described a gigantic recession in all developed economies, but almost the entire decline in activity was simply the mechanical result of official restrictions. As a whole, developed economies showed their usual resilience in response to unprecedented and largely unexpected challenges. With only a few glitches, food retailers were able to meet the additional demand created by the sudden ending of most institutional food service and restaurant meals. The telecommunications system absorbed a massive shift to working from home with equal ease. The medical systems were initially overwhelmed in several places, but within a few weeks all developed economies were able to deal with the shift in required services quite well. Research and knowledge were coordinated globally, and production of needed medical supplies and tests increased rapidly. New software was developed to track contacts, and massive numbers of skilled people were quickly given the resources needed to work on cures and vaccines. The damage to poorer economies were more severe, because the more developed a production economy is, the better it resists stress.

The financial exception

Now comes the comparison, the one glaring exception to the pervasive pattern of economic competence, redundancy, resilience, and trustworthiness. The systems of money and finance both play vital roles in the astounding economic coordination of labour, production, and consumption. However, unlike almost everything else in the economy, both are plagued with a daunting list of persistent and pervasive problems. The economies have to deal with an unstable supply of money, unwanted changes in prices, excessive financial gains, unevenly spread financial losses, political tensions over financial obligations, and recurrent financial crises. The money-finance problems and crises are not new. The money problems have been present for as long as money has played a central role in economies and the finance problems for as long as finance has existed. The money-finance troubles may be getting less severe, but if so, not at a very impressive rate. Although the financial crises in the 1920s in Europe and the 1930s in the United States remain the most economically destructive in the last century, in more recent years there has been a long series of similar, quite serious, and long-lasting crises in many countries around the world. Many of these financial breakdowns have caused years of serious economic difficulties.

The more recent the historical comparison with the rest of the global economy, the worse it looks for finance. Since the Second World War, extreme poverty has diminished sharply, average life expectancies have risen remarkably, rich countries have reduced pollution significantly, education has expanded dramatically in rich and poor countries, the introduction of computers and mobile telephones has created what can be called an industrial revolution … and the money and finance systems continue to generate cycles of boom and bust, often distorting and damaging the rest of the economy for prolonged periods. In other words, the money-finance exception has become even more glaring.

Professionals in the businesses of finance mostly admit that there is a serious problem. So do economists and regulators. This acknowledgement has led to recurrent actions, to what are called, again and again, vast efforts at reform. The waves of change have probably helped reduce the damage done by monetary and financial inadequacy. Still, the global financial crisis of 2008, an obvious and clearly destructive example of systemic failure, showed that something is still fundamentally wrong. In that crisis, the financial troubles were monumental, they infected the rest of the economy, and the economic damage was long-lasting. Arguably, the German economy recovered faster from the physical and psychological devastation of the Second World War than the developed world economy recovered from the financial crisis (Eichengreen and Ritschl, 2008).

Some of the economic problems and many of the subsequent distortions of the financial system have not been cleared up fully as I write, more than a full decade later. Also as I write, there are signs that the developed world may be entering into another period of serious monetary-financial disorder – uncomfortably high rates of retail price inflation without much reversal of the socially troubling results of years of price inflation of the financial assets that I will call money-things. Even if the worst is avoided, the flirtation with a new financial crisis before the mess from the last one has been fully cleared away is a sign of a badly functioning system. Meanwhile, I think it is safe to predict the economic effects of months of tight anti-pandemic restrictions and the economic effects of the first large war in Europe in decades will almost certainly be invisible in two or three years – or a decade if post-war reconstruction is included in the measure.

When an important system in the modern economy has so many persistent problems, it is safe to say that something is profoundly wrong. What is it with money, and especially with finance? Why is there this financial exception?

Perhaps such problems are unavoidable in capitalism, as Marxists claim. Perhaps it is foolish to dream of an economy in which money and the intertemporal monetary arrangements of finance work as smoothly as the production of coal, semiconductors, or education. Such dreams are not actually foolish, as I will explain shortly. The cause of this exception is a deep misunderstanding of how these monetary things do and should work. More profoundly, the problem is in what philosophers of science call the existing paradigm. A large part of the money-finance system is faulty because of the inadequacies of the basic operating model of how money works, what finance can and should do, and how the whole system does and should fit into the rest of the economy. More specifically, my list of mistaken ideas includes the generally accepted notions of what money is, how interest rates work, the role played by financial arrangements in the economy, the design of the most commonly used financial arrangements, the operation of banks, the monetary operations of government, the structure of financial markets, the pricing of commodities, the complexity of monetary policy and financial regulation, and the refusal to consider the social danger caused by the acceptance of financial greed. All of those claims will be justified in the course of the book (and all those terms will be explained). The last claim, about greed, may be the most surprising. It is, in my view, the most important.

Just as I am well aware that not everything in the real economy of labour, production, allocation, and consumption works well, I am well aware that not everything in the world of money and finance works badly. Indeed, for most people in most of the economy most of the time, the money system performs its primary tasks pretty effectively. It lubricates and helps to organise the almost incredibly complex chains of production and distribution that I described earlier. The money-transaction business has become more efficient, like a normal part of the economy. The finance business also sometimes helps the economy work well.

While the good done by the money-financial system is substantial, the overall judgement of it has to be overwhelmingly negative. The reasons for that judgement will be developed over the course of this book, as I explain what money is by nature, what finance is by nature, and why the current money-finance arrangements are inappropriate to these natures.

Why the failure is surprising, and what that means

I just said that the current money-finance system works unusually badly. I also proposed, and said I would reject, the possibility that any money system must struggle with some irreparable structural flaw. In fact, not only is there no such flaw, but this system should actually be easier to control than almost any other part of the economy. Consider the differences. It takes quite a lot of skill, material, and coordination to keep up the smooth operations of the clothing trade, the education business, the air transport industry, or any other non-monetary part of the economy. There are hundreds or thousands or millions of people whose labour must be developed, divided, assigned, and supervised. The workforce must master thousands of skills, and many workers must combine a high degree of consistency and precision with at least modest degrees of initiative and imagination. Specialised facilities and equipment must be constructed and maintained. Continuing success requires unrelenting effort to master the endless series of problems caused by recalcitrant parts of both the physical world and the human psyche. Frequent, numerous, delicate, and complex alterations in the existing systems are needed to satisfy or stimulate new desires and to respond to changes in the political, social, or technological environment. Serious troubles arise almost inevitably but unpredictably. The human skills and institutional structures must be passed on from generation to generation. With all these tangible challenges, it is amazing that these economic systems work at all, let alone that they keep on working without much apparent trouble.

Money is so much simpler, and so should be much more tractable. There are almost no physical challenges, past the operating of a few relatively simple factories to produce coins and notes and the construction of an extensive and expensive but easily standardised banking network. Paper and especially electronic or digital money can be made, distributed, and destroyed almost instantaneously and at almost no cost. Far from the seemingly infinite variety of most goods and services in the economy, money comes in very few varieties (currencies), and those are largely interchangeable. In the modern information-saturated economy, everything about the monetary system can be measured with ease. Money-control fits easily into the remit of modern governments – governments which are the best organised and most socially integrated political authorities ever seen. For example, each political authority in an advanced economy manages to follow the almost incredibly dense set of detailed rules which govern the collection of taxes and the payment of benefits to millions or tens of millions of people. It would seem that such competent governments should not have great struggles ensuring that socially desired quantities of money are steadily available at the right time to the right people.

Finance is a bit more complicated than money, basically because it involves, as I will explain, monetary promises that are far easier to make than to keep. Still, finance always exists under the tight control of custom, these days encoded into extensive laws and even more extensive regulations. The combined force of custom, law, and regulation could easily limit the terms of financial contracts to ensure they are plausible and flexible, and to limit the adverse effects of breaking them. Besides, there is no obvious reason that financial difficulties should harm the real economy of labour, production, distribution, and consumption. The breaking of financial contracts does no direct damage to people or things. Financial disorders might cause monetary strains, but, again, monetary remedies should be easy to find. After all – it is worth repeating this – money can be created, deployed, and destroyed instantaneously and at almost no cost. Again, a comparison might be helpful. The global economy supplies 1.4 billion new smartphones each year in several hundred political jurisdictions (IDC, 2022). It keeps more than seven billion mobile phones connected to each other at a cost so modest that all but the poorest fifth of the world's population has access to them (bankmycell, 2022). An economy that can do that should have no trouble organising successful monetary and financial systems.

Nor do the monetary and financial systems have to work especially well. People and organisations have shown themselves capable of adjusting well to fairly significant changes in prices, wages, and other money-numbers, to almost all levels of interest rates, and to large fluctuations in currency exchange rates. If the money and finance systems were nothing worse than fickle in these numbers, they would not be considered failures, although an impartial judge would certainly see room for improvement. However, the system does not reach even this minimum standard of competence. The monetary system often provides either too little or too much money for the good of the overall economy. When money is created, the process is cumbersome and the new funds often end up in the wrong hands for supporting the common economic good. The finance system is in far worse shape. It more often than not fails to do what it is supposed to do efficiently and justly, and it suffers from fairly regular crises which are severe enough to do lasting damage to the rest of the economy.

Once again, these failures raise the basic question: why are these systems in such a mess? I have already pointed to my answer, an erroneous paradigm. Psychology provides a useful analogy. Sometimes people cannot manage something which should be easy – say, an educated person who is petrified of flying or a competent professional who struggles to finish straightforward work assignments. These troubled people can sometimes be coaxed onto airplanes or bullied into working, but the recurring failure is generally a symptom of profoundly disordered thinking, of putting the facts of the matter into the wrong emotional or intellectual model. The more irrational the failure, the more wrong the person's operational paradigm must be. The central argument of this book is that something analogous is happening with the monetary and financial systems. The failures of these fairly simple and easily adjusted economic sub-systems are signs of a deep intellectual-emotional-moral pathology.

More specifically, I will argue in this book that the money-finance system, in particular the financial part, suffers from two basic errors: first, the acceptance of arrangements that are unnecessarily and dangerously detached from reality and, second, an anomalous, widespread, and unchecked enthusiasm for morally bad behaviour. Behind the bad behaviour is greed, a vice that is pervasive, promoted throughout the financial system, and deeply pernicious. The two problems are, in my view, intimately related. Greed excites the emotions and distorts judgements, so the relevant authorities and participants in the money-financial system tolerate or even encourage reality-distant arrangements and systemically disruptive behaviour. The results include an inefficient monetary system and financial arrangements and expectations that are clearly not in accord with the limits to human knowledge, the common good of society, or the most basic standards of justice. In other words, greed blinds the critical faculties that would otherwise tether money and especially finance more closely to reality and that would submit both to the standards of social justice.

Slaves to bad old ideas

Paradigm shifts are very difficult, because they require radical change in the thinking of people whose judgements, expectations, and instincts are well settled in a comfortable and apparently sensible routine. Shifts are especially hard when, as often happens, almost all respected experts reject the new analytic framework as senseless, trivial, incomprehensible, wrong, or reprehensible. Full conversion requires a total absorption of the new approach, training in new analytic instincts, experience with the results of the new thinking, and a deep cleansing of the residues of old ideas. In any academic discipline, the shift will almost certainly be gradual – one funeral at a time, as is said – so early adapters are likely to face years of professional snubs and bitter discord.

Despite these great difficulties, there have been many paradigm shifts in many fields of study, for example from Aristotelian to Newtonian and then to relativistic physics, from primarily trusting and theological to more sceptical historical-critical biblical exegesis, or from a Christian to a secular framing of history. I hope to encourage a similarly profound change in economics. I would love to see university departments and consulting firms hesitating to hire people who did not accept this book's paradigm. I can dream of a department chair or a recruiter explaining, "Oh, you think that the economy is fundamentally mathematical and that economic activity is not always deeply and self-consciously moral. You deny that this activity is fundamentally non-conflictual, non-optimising, non-utilitarian, non-individualistic, and non-materialist. I'm sorry, I'm not sure you would fit in here." I can dream …

I can dream, but the long road of evangelisation lies ahead of me. It is a hard road to travel. I can offer no experiments that can discredit the old approach, because both paradigms can provide explanations for everything. Numerical proofs cannot demonstrate that economics is essentially non-numerical. I have to rely on the traditional technique of intellectual evangelisation: trying simultaneously to uproot old assumptions and to sow the seeds of the new approach. The rest of this chapter is dedicated primarily to the first part of the mission – the turning over of the intellectual soil. I will discuss three widely held but deeply erroneous ideas about money. (Money comes before finance, because the latter cannot be understood without a firm understanding of the former.) The explanations of these confusions should also serve as a teaser for the next chapter's positive agenda, a more analytically rigorous description of what money really is and does.

Money is a scarce commodity

The first wrong belief is that money is essentially a durable and scarce commodity. Until less than a century ago, that statement would have been expressed slightly differently: money is essentially a tangible and scarce commodity. In practice, the tangible money-substance was usually gold or silver, but theoretically (according to this wrong theory) it could be anything that was fairly hard to obtain and that could be touched, stored indefinitely, and retrieved at any time without any change or decay. The more modern version of the belief eliminates the "touched", but retains the other features of durable value.

The revision was necessary, as I will explain, to deal with the evidence. However, it rather confuses the basic idea, so I will start with the older version of this credal claim – *pure* money is pure gold, silver, or some other scarce physical thing. If the gold is minted into coins, then the *true* value of gold-backed coins is thought to be *essentially* the value of the gold that the coins actually contain. Historically, this assumption of *fundamental* value was not altered by the steady debasement of coins (coins of the same numerical value were minted with less precious metal content or "clipped" after minting) or by the subsequent increased reliance on less tangible forms of money. The true value of notes or bills of "paper money" and of account balances of "bank-money" were thought *actually* and *ultimately* to be the value of the gold (or silver or whatever) real money for which these things being used as money could hypothetically be exchanged. The actual coins, paper, and account entries were only money in some tentative or imperfect sense. What was *really* money was the durable commodity that backed these tokens.

This definition portrayed real money as something that had transcended space and time. The precious commodity could be used everywhere that the monetary commodity was considered valuable and would last as long as that valuation did, which was likely to be forever. Until well into the 20th century, this definition of money as a tangible commodity was accepted unquestioningly by most users of money and by the vast majority of experts, both the all-purpose philosophers who wrote on the topic over the centuries and the professional economists who emerged during the 19th century with more detailed theories about the creation, circulation, purposes, and imbalances of money.

Until the development of the modern, money-saturated industrial economy, the definition appeared realistic. In practice, almost all forms of pre-modern money did rely for their value on the presence of, or some connection with, gold, silver, or some other quite concrete commodity in strictly limited supply. It seemed almost obvious that the *real* money was in fact the universal carrier of value, not the coins or other things that constituted a claim to obtain a promised amount of that *ultimate* value-carrier. These money-ish things were treated as mere substitutes for the *real* thing. Without the scarcity and the durability, how could money have any value or use?

However, over the course of the 19th and 20th centuries, the substitutes became the real thing. The history of the transition is instructive. From the invention of paper and bank-money until the 1970s, every money-issuing institution maintained the fiction that any money could be exchanged for a constant amount of gold. Even when the right to exchange for gold was suspended or limited, as it often was, the principle of a "gold standard" was maintained as sacrosanct. It had to be, because there was no alternative inside the tangible-money paradigm. Users and economists were persuaded that nothing could really be money without the promise of an eventual or potential golden exchange. However, the fiction of a purported gold value of this supposedly substitute-money eventually led to economic difficulties and banking crises. In response, the legal exchangeability principle was abolished in the 1970s, at first tentatively but after a few years quite definitively (Federal Reserve History, 2013). Since that time, no money in the world has had any connection, not even the most tenuous, with any sort of tangible commodity.

According to the tangible-money theory, the repudiation of the golden exchange would destroy the monetary system. When the change actually came, some true believers stored up gold in anticipation of a monetary collapse. However, the removal of the supposed gold backing had no obvious effects. The system continued to function about as well as when the gold-exchange promise was still thought to be at least hypothetically valid. The new arrangement was better in some ways and worse in others, but certainly not obviously inferior overall.

This may sound like positive proof that the old definition of money and the paradigm to which it belonged were simply wrong – money is clearly not gold or gold-reliant in the way that nearly everyone had thought it was. However, as historians of science understand well, established paradigms are remarkably resilient to contrary evidence (Kuhn 1970: Chapter 8). Both the general public and the economics profession were extremely reluctant to abandon the basic idea that money is *essentially* some sort of scarce commodity which stores value. They still are. The credulous enthusiasm for crypto-currencies, which remains great as I write this book, is based on the notion that a currency which holds its value only because of its strictly limited supply will inevitably replace a currency that is protected by the imprimatur and control of a powerful government.

Economists do mostly know better than to trust bitcoin and the like, but they have been less insightful in their discussions of the nature of normal money. Many of them have resorted to a trick familiar to historians of science, broadening the definition in question, hopefully making it wide enough to catch up with reality but not so wide that it loses all meaning. The chosen modification of the definition of money was mentioned at the beginning of this section: "durable" replaced "tangible". The redefinition has kept the old understanding of money alive (with perhaps a little tangible aid from the gold still kept in vaults controlled by governmental monetary authorities).

Many, probably most, economists still adhere to the old idea in its new form. They insist that while money may no longer need to be "made of" or "convertible into" something tangible and valuable, it is still *essentially* a durable commodity of some sort, a "thing" that can be treated as a long-lasting alternative to the things that it can buy. These economists believe that bank-money (or possibly only the money created by the government's monetary authorities) is *essentially* like any other commodity used in the economy. The money is no longer a claim on gold. Instead, it is a claim on something else, either the ability of the issuing government to raise taxes or the ability of the money-holding banks to stay profitable. These limits are supposed to ensure that the quantity of paper and bank-money available is also limited, so that, like gold, paper and bank-money are *structurally* in short supply. The limited quantity gives money *by nature* an intrinsic durable value. In the modified model, bank and paper money are no longer thought of as inferior substitutes for gold. Rather, they have become advanced successors to tangible commodities. There is no shift in the paradigm. *Conceptually*, money is still considered to be a convenient thing which has an enduring intrinsic value because it is in limited supply.

That view is wrong. As I will explain in much more detail in the next chapter, the conventional wisdom of economists and citizens remains almost exactly backwards from the truth. Money is money because it is believed to be money and is *actually* used as money. The real "moneyness" of all money, past and present, is *exactly* and *essentially* the acceptability as a medium of payment for wages, prices, taxes, and whatever else money is expected to pay for. The "moneyness" of gold coins, their *nature* as money, came not from the precious metal which they contained, but from something *essentially* intangible and not necessarily durable, the trustworthiness of the money's creator. The gold content supported the credibility, but it was the trustworthiness that mattered.

In a word, all money is *essentially* created out of nothing and has no substrate that provides its value. Far from being like a commodity that has something like a constant value, money *by nature* does not have any durable value. Further, scarcity is not a *natural* attribute of the money system. Rather, *fundamentally* the supply of money should be neither scarce nor excessive. Money should be in ample supply, relative to the size of the money-using economy.

In the preceding paragraphs, I have italicised the words concerned with nature and essence. My concern with such philosophical topics is completely practical. The *underlying, fundamental, essential, substantial, pure reality* of money can be quite different from the appearance. A pre-modern coin may look like it is stamped to authenticate the value of the gold it contains, but it is *really* the stamp, not the claimed or the actual amount of gold, which provides the value. Money may seem to be a commodity which can be exchanged for other commodities or for itself over time, but it is *really* and in its *nature* a token which organises current production and allocation. (These claims will be justified in Chapter Two.)

Money is individualistic

The second wrong belief is that money is essentially private: asocial or antisocial. This claim comes in several varieties. In the mild asocial version, money is considered to be a tool that is essentially separated from all other important social structures. Money should work without any connections to the state and its agencies, the justice system, the Churches, the various traditional aristocracies, the communities of the arts and of the mind, or even sporting sets. Of course, it is recognised that in practice money plays a role in all these other institutions and that the institutions which manage the money system are part of the governing establishment, but the theoretical separation of money from the rest of society is maintained. It has to be, because, according to this part of the paradigm, monetary thinking is typically antithetical to the good of institutions outside of the economy. Money is thought to be out of place in matters of the higher and common good of society. It seems obvious that there is something wrong with allowing "the best justice that money can buy"; politicians who are too interested in money are defined as "corrupt"; a fine sportsman or woman is supposed to look beyond monetary winnings; and so forth through all the non-monetary axes of social organisation. Money lowers the social tone or even profanes the sacred. In contrast, money is thought to be used rightly when it is limited to the asocial sphere of exclusively private economic relationships.

The more extreme, antisocial variety of this belief is associated with various sorts of anti-Establishment revolutionaries. In this thinking, money does something more powerful and more destructive than merely lower the social tone. It actively undermines the non-monetary foundations of society. Since, in this view, any reliance on money is directly opposed to the nature of all non-monetary structures, the arrival of a money-mentality destroys or depraves all existing structures. Money-guided universities are no longer the same as universities organised around social class, knowledge, or some other non-monetary standard. Money-guided churches necessarily forget the divine. Money-guided society is all about transactions, grasping, and greed, with no room for generosity, nobility, or even simple fun. When something is for sale, it is no longer valued as it should be.

Mostly, the asocial and antisocial understandings of money are used to criticise modern societies. There are many variations of William Wordsworth's famous line, "Getting and spending, we lay waste our powers" (Wordsworth, 1802) but they all express much the same sentiment: the very act of putting a price on something demeans it, the careful attention to higher and lower prices is a further degradation, and the rise of social groups which either did or still do pay such monetary attention demeans society.

Marxists are the most influential believers in antisocial money. Marx's own attitude to this clamed antisocial monetary force was two-sided. On one side, he praised the way the modern money economy was eliminating the primitive and oppressive relations of feudal society. On the other, he and his followers sharply criticised the cruelty and inhumanity of money-dominated bourgeois society. Somewhat ironically, the devoutly anti-Marxist enthusiasts for "free markets" agree with the Marxist description of money. They just reverse the Marxist judgement. Instead of condemning the rise of money and predicting a revolution of the money-oppressed, they argue that a system which relies on non-social money can be fairer, more honest, and more individually liberating than any available non-monetary social structures. The debates between Marxists and their opponents can be lively – debates within paradigms often are – but there is no need for me to adjudicate them, since the basic assumption shared by both sides about the nature of money is wrong.

A bit of intellectual history helps explain the error, because while the first monetary error, of tangibility, was based on a plausible but actually wrong empirical judgement, the asocial mistake is largely philosophical. The treatment of money as something which is by its nature either far from or actually hostile to normal social relations can be traced back to Aristotle, one of the fathers of Western philosophy. In his discussion of justice, he separated commutative justice, found in the private exchange of goods of equal monetary value, from necessarily social forms of justice, both the distributive justice of who should get what and the corrective justice of how punishments should be meted out. Aristotle's idea that the commutative justice of particular monetary matters required only the agreement of individuals became quite central to both modern political philosophy and the conventional monetary paradigm. From 17th century English philosopher John Locke onward, most writers on economics have argued or assumed that all monetary contracts create a justice or, for Marxists, an injustice that was distant from all normal social and political interactions. The historian Karl Polanyi described the rise of the monetary and contractual economy as a gradual "disembedding" of economic arrangements from society (Polanyi, 1944).

The modern economy and modern societies are certainly different in many ways from premodern ones, but not in their attitude towards money. The asocial–antisocial understanding of money is fundamentally wrong, always and everywhere. Indeed, the idea of asocial money is self-contradictory, because money is essentially a socially validated human artefact, which, as I just suggested and will explain in Chapter Two, must always be validated by some social–political authority. To maintain that social validation, money must be integrally entwined with all of a society's authority structures and guiding institutions. Money, the money economy, the financial system, and the practice of commutative justice within the economy are all firmly embedded in a particular society or polity. Money is one social institution among many, inextricably bound to many others, most notably the legal system and the networks of banks. The anthropological–historical evidence supports the philosophical logic.

Monetary institutions require a well-functioning society to work well, because they rely so extensively on other institutions. Far from being distant from or opposed to the organising rules of society, money is always an expression of a firmly shared social order.

Of course, societies are never perfectly harmonious. It does not take a great philosopher to recognise that societies are both united and divided, and that their governing institutions, including a well-functioning monetary system, can foment resentment as well as support order. Money can indeed be socially alienating, just as Marx claimed. However, modern social–economic alienation is not exclusively or even especially monetary. Money can also offer a degree of liberation within the social order, exactly as the neo-Lockeans declare. Again, there is nothing special about money in this regard. The social choice of the last centuries to rely more on money for managing the economy, and thus necessarily less on traditional social and political structures, is not in itself an indication of either social decay or increased individual autonomy. It is, rather, one of many interlocking, mutually supportive, and sometimes mutually antagonistic modern changes that have so greatly transformed societies and the normal experiences of their members. I will have more to say about the many social meanings of money in Chapter Two.

Money tells the exact truth about values

The third and last wrong idea is perhaps the most wrongheaded of the three, despite many loud claims that it is both empirically and philosophically justified. This is the idea that money precisely and consistently measures the value of the things that it pays for. The credal belief in the precisionist-consistency of money-numbers has become deeply woven into the fabric of contemporary economic thinking and expectations. In their research and in their judgements, professional economists almost unthinkingly assume that observed money-values (the prices and wages which are actually paid) are the base of an exact and reliable scale for comparing the real values of otherwise incommensurate things. The actual prices paid can only be a base, because the same numerical quantity of money can buy different collections of things at different times and places. However, economists are certain that all actual prices can be manipulated – through the application of an impartial scientific technique – to extract and express a constant, essential, and numerical value. These almost ironically named "real" numbers retain their value in all circumstances, so they can be compared across time and space. For example, it is considered perfectly reasonable to say that the typical French income in the 1600s was, say, 30 percent higher or lower than the typical Chinese income 500 years earlier or one tenth as high as the typical Chinese income today.

This perfectionist-consistency assumption certainly provides a paradigmatic satisfaction to the modern desire for impartial and universal numerical measures of everything and anything. The assumption also leads to a great deal of detailed labour for the economists who are charged with keeping the relations of the numerous imaginary-real prices consistent and plausible. The task is monumental, since the varieties and interactions of labour, consumption, and money actually vary greatly. The servants of these hypothetical "real" money-numbers should take into account many changes: in what is produced, in how much labour goes into production, in taxes, pension arrangements, property prices, and labour and consumption that is exchanged without money. A huge collection of fanciful conjectures and approximations are needed to ensure that economics is an empirical and quantitative science, a discipline based on observations and measurements.

The purified numerical observations serve as the foundation of a massive network of microeconomic theories about the economic behaviour of individuals and macroeconomic theories about the economic organisation of societies. Unfortunately, the foundation is anything but solid. While the numerical legerdemain is skilful and imaginative, it ultimately only reveals a tremendous professional dedication to a misguided cause. The arbitrariness of the "real" numbers is the sort of anomaly that should raise doubts about the whole quantitative paradigm of economics. The challenge disappears in the paradigm of economics as an essentially non-quantitative study of essentially non-quantitative human activities.

The precisionist-consistency assumption is dead wrong. Far from being either precise or consistent, the relations among money-numbers have no clear or constant non-monetary meaning and the numerical relations of those numbers can give little insight about anything outside of the monetary system. It is true, as I will explain Chapter Two, that prices are indeed generally based *roughly* on various economic facts and forces. However, a statement that a particular pie is *worth* ten dollars means only and exactly that what the person making the statement thinks is the right price – right now in this place, for this pie – is ten dollars. To say that a particular hour of labour assembling pies is worth ten dollars means exactly that ten dollars is considered to be the right hourly wage for this baker, here and now. Such statements indicate nothing about the true human value of pie or pie-making or about the likely price of similar pies or pie-making labour in another place or time. Without setting the price of the pie inside an elaborate social-psychological-ethical structure, the price-number can disclose nothing about the pie's actual or perceived goodness.

The roughness extends to monetary comparisons. These can be indicative and suggestive, but never precise. The only exact meaning of "That pie is worth twice as much as this one" is tautological – the money price is or should be exactly twice as high. The comparison does not mean that the pie is worth twice as much by any non-monetary standard. That sort of numerical comparison on its own does not even have any obvious human meaning. People can give no more meaning to "twice as valuable" in reference to pie than to "twice as tasty, beautiful, hungry or tired" in reference to any part of the human experience. After all, people are not the calculating creatures dreamed up by utilitarian philosophers. The uncertainties and imprecisions of the meanings of individual prices and wages are multiplied when the objects and efforts are combined. Monetary composites which combine the prices of large collections of economic objects have little meaning, as do monetary comparisons over long periods of time. In particular, the highly fetishised calculations of Gross Domestic Product (GDP) disclose little and precise GDP comparisons (for example, "up 2.3%") disclose less.

I suspect that for most readers the precisionist-consistency monetary myth is the least familiar of the three I have chosen to debunk. To make it more concrete, I will give three examples.

My first example is exactly a monetary comparison over time. Consider the apparently uncontroversial statement, "My current income is about 60 percent higher than my father's income was when he was my age". The crude numerical comparison can be in some nominal sense true, assuming it reflects accurate information on pay statements or tax returns. Indeed, as a statement of numerical truth the round number is unnecessarily approximate. A calculator will quickly determine that, "I am 58.453 percent better paid than ...". Further, thanks to the ready availability of nominal-to-real conversion tables, the effects of inflation, as measured on these official tables, can easily be removed. "In real terms, I am paid 12.275 percent more than...". However, while the numerical comparison sounds sophisticated and precise, it still has no meaning beyond the tautological – my income, as adjusted in this particular way, is indeed 12.275 percent higher than my father's comparably adjusted income.

All efforts to extract a precise numerical comparison of consumption lifestyles from that numerical statement are pointless, because it simply makes no sense to think that any number, let alone one precise to one part in 100,000, can meaningfully compare two people's lifestyles in two quite different social and economic milieus. It might be fair to say that my lifestyle with foreign holidays and the internet is more affluent than my father's back in the day, when he could only afford domestic breaks and had only landline phones and black-and-white TV. It might also be fair to draw the opposite conclusion, taking into account his secure pension and the more intrusive governments that I have to deal with. In any case, it is not meaningful to say that my spending is objectively worth a tenth or a fifth more, let alone precisely 12.27 percent more. The goods in question are simply not quantitatively comparable.

The second example is a traditional topic of discussion among economists, the so-called diamond-water paradox (White, 2022). Water, which is necessary for life, is objectively far more valuable than diamonds, which are merely decorative. However, a kilogram or a cubic metre of diamonds almost always costs much more money than the same quantity of water. The seeming paradox of values relies on the precisionist-consistency assumption. In reality, comparisons of monetary measures have no particular meaning, since price does not actually measure any constant, objective value. The relative prices of diamonds and water do not express any judgement on relative values. They may reflect the relative costs of production, the relative scarcity of the two objects, or some sort of relative social value, but the only thing they definitely express is a tautology – this is how much water and diamonds cost.

My final example is the precision presented in the standard accounting techniques of everyday business life. Imagine that a new machine for mixing peanut butter can stir 20 percent more litres each hour than the old model (taking up the same space and using the same quantity of energy). The numerical gain in output per hour can be measured precisely, perhaps even to one part in 10,000. It is quite different for the monetary question – how much does this investment reduce the cost of production? That can only be answered roughly, since much guesswork is required – most notably estimates of how long the new machine will last and of future maintenance expenses. The answer also requires an arbitrary calculation of what economists call the present value of these future costs. (This futile and faulty concept is discussed in the Appendix). The inevitable imprecision is far too great to conclude that, for example, the cost reduction is 1.46 percent. The most that can be said with anything like accuracy is that the new machine reduces overall monetary measures of mixing costs by roughly a few percentage points.

Prices, wages, and other money-numbers cannot be totally random and variable. However, to do their job – which is to help the economy function, as I will explain in Chapter Two – they need only to be precise and constant enough to perform their crucial but basically mechanical economic role. This bar is very low, and money measures generally cross it easily. When they do not, as in the tremendously inconsistent pricing of U.S. healthcare, there is usually something seriously wrong with the badly priced part of the economy.

Bad money-numbers rarely do much damage. Still, taking the precisionist-constancy myth as truth brings many unnecessary and undesired consequences. Most important, the assumption of mutually compatible monetary values leads to reliance on money as a supposedly solid quantitative anchor for economic analysis and planning. Money measures are not such an anchor. They cannot quantify the economic good and they cannot provide consistent, let alone precise, comparisons of economic welfare.

Also, belief in the precisionist-consistency fallacy often leads to a counterproductive prioritisation of the money-numbers in economic policies. Authorities who try to shift the economy around for the sake of protecting some purely monetary value have the wrong priorities, almost by definition. The most common traditional target was an exchange rate between currencies. More recently, inflation rates have been held sacred, along with GDP or the rate of increase in GDP. A too slavish devotion to any of these always leads to bad decisions and sometimes to real misery. It is much better to manipulate the numerical supply and value of money for the sake of the common economic good than the other way around.

Other profoundly wrong ideas from the current money-finance paradigm will emerge during the course of this book. Rather than provide a preview, though, I want to close this chapter with an observation that complements the fact that opened it. It is not only the persistent failures of the finance system that are extraordinary in the modern economy. The persistence of very old ideas about money and finance is almost as unusual.

I mentioned that some of these bad ideas can be traced back to Aristotle. That sort of long and lively intellectual legacy is expected and helpful in philosophy, literature, and other arts, but it is far from typical in anything connected with the modern economy. Almost all the knowledge needed to operate the world's machines was acquired after 1800, and much of it only since electricity was mastered late in the 19th century. Pre-modern theorising is equally irrelevant to the detailed regulation of modern industry, the design of modern cities, and the processing of modern quantities and types of information. The guiding beliefs of money and finance are different. While these beliefs may reinforce some strands of modern thinking, they are actually as obsolete as the physiology of humours and the physics of the four elements. They have been discredited by economic experience and superseded by the modern facts of sociology, group psychology, and anthropology.

There are, though, some really old ideas which really could help economists design a better money-finance system. Those come from the fields of study that do not make the kind of past-obliterating progress that is standard in most of the economy. Traditional moral psychology and philosophical ethics have much to offer money and especially finance. Money would be better understood if economists took seriously the implications of a fundamental principle of Immanuel Kant, that human worth (Würde, sometimes translated as "dignity") is "infinitely above any price, with which it cannot be balanced or compared at all without, as it were, violating its sanctity" (Kant, 2012:47). The financial system would work much better if it also took into account the fundamental moral reality of human nature as articulated by Christians and accepted in most traditional Western thinking – people always strive for the good but are always tempted by the bad (Thomas Aquinas, 1920: II.II. 61, 66).

Chapter 2. Money

My criticisms of the wrong answers at the end of the last chapter included hints of the right ones. Money is not a commodity; it is a token for exchanging labour with consumption. Money is not asocial; it is an organising institution that is deeply embedded in society. Money is not a precise or consistent measure of anything; it is a rough but convenient numerical tool that can be used as desired in different societies and social situations. In this chapter I will amplify and justify those descriptions.

The chapter is regrettably long. In theory, it could have been much shorter. Money is not fundamentally very complicated, and the technical details, whether of any actual monetary system or of some ideal one, do not change the basic, simple picture. However, a perusal of some of the extensive existing writings on money and discussions with potential readers persuaded me that the understanding of money which I am trying to present is so unusual that a mere description of the actual economic function of money would be more puzzling than illuminating. I could have multiplied the length of this chapter, as well as adding years to its writing, by entering into a detailed dialogue with other theories about the nature, history, and meanings of money. I chose instead to try to guide readers along, offering a coherent alternative and merely challenging some especially common preconceptions and assumptions. I have also addressed some complications of the money system, which I hope will deal with some common objections to my approach.

To help readers follow this long and fairly detailed argument, I have divided the chapter into ten sections. Here is a summary.

The initial two sections are preliminary. The first basically just catalogues and extends the comments in the first chapter about various social and cultural meanings of money. Many of these symbolic meanings of money are fascinating, but neither respect nor curiosity is my motivation for including them. I simply want to help readers recognise and put aside any fascinating ideas they have about money, because these can distract their attention from the mundane reality of money's economic role. The sociological, anthropological, political, semiotic, cultural, and psychological uses and meanings of money will inevitably colour what both economists and non-specialists think about money. I hope that awareness of this influence will encourage some intellectual wariness.

The second introductory section is a brief description of the actual, fundamental, ontological, real, and human nature and meaning of the economy itself. In most introductions to the academic discipline of economics, this topic is either ignored or breezily dismissed with a few ambiguous, meaningless, or simply wrong sentences. In the standard practice, any definitions are then set aside and economics turns out to be predominantly the study of various monetary matters, with all the discussions of the things that money pays for considered almost exclusively in monetary terms. That approach takes as given the actual role of money in the economy, so it is clearly inadequate for a discussion of that role. It merely begs such basic questions as *why* money is used to buy and sell particular things, *how* money relates to the things bought and sold, and *what* is really being exchanged for money. The place, advantages, and limits of money in the economy cannot really be addressed without addressing those fundamental questions, and those questions cannot really be addressed without understanding what the economy really is. This chapter's second section provides that understanding.

The third section then describes how money actually fits into the just-defined economy. Anyone who has studied economics will be relieved to find that my definition of the role of money is familiar – it is a medium of exchange. If they read my explanation carefully, though, they may become somewhat less comfortable.

The next five sections amplify the concept, explaining some of money's key characteristics: precisely how it fits into the rest of the economy, how well it describes economic reality, what it is made of, how and why it is created and destroyed, and the challenge of keeping the supply of money well aligned with paid-for economic activity. I could close the chapter there, but there are two related false ideas about money which are so commonly believed that I judged it best to deal with them directly. The first, that money's value is consistent over time, has already been introduced. The second, that money is a form of credit, might seem technical, but the seemingly abstruse difference in the definition of money has significant implications for finance.

1. Money as a symbol

Not all societies have used money, but for those that have, it is always an institution. In giving it that sociological or anthropological name, I mean that any monetary system has commonly understood rules, powerful traditions, complex relations with its users and with other social institutions, and an existence that is expected to continue indefinitely, long after the deaths of all current individual members (or users, in the case of money). Institutions are never merely functional, because people working together inevitably develop complex matrices of meanings for all their practices. The institution of money is typical. It is always meaningful as well as practical. Like other institutions, it is laden with a deep and subtle symbolism. All sorts of imaginative cultural observers, from pre-modern myth-makers to post-modern narratologists, have been fascinated by what I call symbol-money. Contemporary economists, however, miss almost all the excitement at least in their conscious thoughts. They are not much interested in such things as cultural meanings, signs, patterns, and rituals. They prefer to think of money as something straightforward, believing that their own analysis is straightforward. To them money is like a wall painted a single shade of white. In contrast, symbol-money is like a gorgeous painting by Veronese, filled with a mysterious panorama of vibrant colours.

There is no need to debate whether the true nature of money is dully functional, or deeply symbolic. It is always both. Money as an economic tool is functional, while money as a cultural institution is richly symbolic. Many of today's academic economists might prefer leaving all the brightly coloured meanings to frivolous intellectuals and wild-eyed poets, while they carry on with the serious work of watching money at work in the economy. Such an abdication would be a mistake. All of money's non-economic meanings can, and some of them definitely do, influence thinking – even their own – about money as an economic tool. To understand money, broader knowledge of the many variations of symbol-money definitely brings the needed wariness that I mentioned earlier.

These variations of meaning are so numerous that the symbolism of money is what psychologists and hermeneutic scholars sometimes call over-determined. In other words, money has many, not necessarily consistent symbolic meanings. As the list in this section will show, symbol-money both divides and unifies societies and polities. It debases and exalts social positions. It can be good or bad, powerful or impotent, noble or base, spiritual or secular, and so forth. The complexity and contradictions are not surprising. Important social institutions – think of marriage, the military, and eating practices – carry all sorts of attributes, some of which will inevitably overlap with, contradict, or seem irrelevant to each other.

To understand fully the multivalent institution of money would require a particularly complex exercise in what the anthropologist Clifford Geertz called (Geertz, 1973) 'thick descriptions', the open-ended and culturally sensitive analysis of all the features of money, their relations with each other, and the social tensions and desires which support, shape, and sometimes undermine them. Each society in every era would have its own quite thick description of symbol-money, and a full analysis would include an ultra-thick description of money's possible universal underlying symbolic meta-meanings. Continuing with my painting analogy, such a full description would be like a tour of a gigantic palace filled from top to bottom with complex and brightly painted Veronese canvases. The symbol-money guidebook would be a mighty project, probably requiring a studio of scholars. To understand the scale of this project, consider Georg Simmel's *Philosophy of Money* (Simmel, 1982). The book, first published in 1900, is probably the most complete available attempt to understand what money means in a particular society. It takes about 500 pages to discuss only a few of these meanings, and his discussions of the chosen themes are seriously inadequate.

I am certainly not trying to finish up what Simmel began! Rather, I offer only painfully brief descriptions of two dozen symbolic attributes of money – varieties of symbol-money. Some of these meanings build cultural or other significance on quite concrete foundations while others are almost entirely symbolic. I beg readers' indulgence for all errors and over-simplifications. As a partial excuse, I can point out that the presence of such mistakes only buttresses one of my basic arguments: symbol-money is a far more delicate and complicated "thing" than the money relevant to a narrowly economic analysis.

Money is:

1. *A sterile treasure*: Money sits in a treasury, safe-deposit box or bank account. It makes nothing, does nothing, contributes nothing. It is sterile, infertile. The uselessness may occasionally bother the owner, but more often the mere possession of money provides substantial comfort and satisfaction. Money is the purest form of property, a social thing-in-itself that is obviously desired because, according to the accepted standards of the culture, it is obviously desirable. The hoarding need not have any pragmatic justification, although owners of the hoarded or treasure-money sometimes say that they are storing up money for later use. The claim is not false, but the owners would usually much prefer to hold onto the money and what it stands for through their lifetimes and through the generations. Hoarded money need not be held in some ready-to-spend form. On the contrary, treasure-money is often held in forms that are ostentatiously unspendable (economically sterile) – ingots of metal, luxurious jewellery, fine art, unproductive land, or any other thing that can just sit there being valuable. In the modern world, monetary treasuries often include stocks, bonds, and more elaborate financial "instruments" that have overcome the inherent sterility of traditional treasures. That somewhat dubious accomplishment will be discussed at length in Chapter Three.

2. *A guarantee of safety*: Ask a despised refugee, a government leader dealing with famine, or a family flooded out of its home what money means and the answer is likely to be something about safety. Sewn in clothes, buried under ground, kept under lock and key, even held in some bank – secreted money provides the means to avert or soften many kinds of disaster. The reality of money-protected safety is surrounded by a penumbra of symbolic safety. A stash of money expresses the desire for and the feeling of safety for people who are not actually in danger. The comfort from monetary protection is strongest and most appreciated when governments are

weakest and prospects are most uncertain, so the safest money tends to be the hardest to spend, because it is held in a safe place far from home, or hoarded in the form of hidden gold.

3. *A promise of magic*: Money condenses potential power, action, and affluence into a tiny token, these days into the invisible token of a bank balance. Like the lamp of Aladdin, money is wonderful for the seemingly infinite variety of its future transformations. Like the fabled lamp, money can be taken anywhere and made to do almost anything. In some ways, other shows of wealth are drab and limited in comparison to the magic of money. While a large house or an expensive voyage will probably never quite live up to expectations, and often brings headaches and disappointment, money always remains the stuff of dreams. The wonder of potential in the imagination is always greater than any reality of the material world, so money almost inevitably loses some of its magic when it is actually spent.

4. *A token of social conflict*: Money is something to fight over and with. It encapsulates political authority, and the lack of it articulates social as well as political dependence. In most societies, the distribution of money is very unequal, with each of the rich few controlling some huge multiple of the money held by any of the far more numerous members of the un-rich classes. The most moneyed, the people and organisations with money to spare, tend to shape a society's laws and institutions. That shaping tends to favour the interests of the moneyed, and to punish and limit the almost-moneyless. The hostile tendencies are reciprocated. The almost-moneyless, often wretched, and sometimes desperate tend to be tempted to use politics or violence to demand a more equal distribution of money and money-purchased power. The divisions created by the vastly unequal distribution of money define at least some of the conflicts in every modern society. The rich usually win most of the battles, but money cannot always buy the strength and loyalty needed to win the social wars.

5. *A tool of economic and social oppression*: Money does not only divide, it conquers. It is a tool of power. Because money is so easy to accumulate, unlike more tangible assets, and because money is so easily exchangeable for money-earning assets, the rich tend to become more powerful in every

society. The more that societies rely on money in their economies (a topic I will discuss later in this chapter), the more the rich tend to be able to control the operations of banks, companies, the regulatory systems, and the legislatures. While the rich often isolate themselves from misery and the miserable, their distance does not led to benign indifference. On the contrary, their will is typically imposed on the poor. The will of the rich is generally two-fold, to retain their own economic and political control and to add ever more to their own collections of money.

6. *A form of social unity*: Money brings societies together like no other social institution. The tax system shares the money from all and gives the money to all. Commercial monetary exchanges turn occasional encounters into temporary communities. The flexibility of money allows new businesses to be created almost instantaneously, through the pooling of monetary contributions. Over wider spaces, money's portability and fungibility allow people to join social and economic communities easily in new places and to come together to form new groups, both small and large. Money is the life-blood of most employers, which are an important place of community in modern societies. In those organisations, money modulates relations among workers and creates a clear border between inside and outside.

7. *A source of individual alienation*: Money is a poor substitute for love, loyalty, and the dense networks of kinship, custom, friendship, and obligation that create strong communities. Money relations are always mean and calculating, so much so that even monetary generosity creates a numbered line that alienates donor from recipient. The reliance on monetary transactions brings an antisocial sort of freedom (the antisocial idea mentioned in Chapter One). A person with enough money can choose to be isolated, and often will make that choice, because non-monetary ties constrain and grate. The decision to use money to acquire everything that is wanted brings in its wake the great loneliness of not-needing and not-sharing, and the loneliness of being needed only for the sake of getting money.

8. *A tool of personal autonomy and fulfilment*: Money is the symbol and reality of personal freedom. Money allows its owner to move away, physically and spiritually, from many of the oppressive forces in life, including unpleasant

family, unwanted neighbours, and persecuting governments. Money allows its owners to choose among different possible types of education, employment, leisure activities, and all sorts of goods and services. Money may not be able to buy love, but the freedom to spend as desired for the sake of the beloved is a genuine freedom of expression that encourages genuine expressions of generosity. Money can be spent in large lumps, creating large and personally meaningful gestures that would otherwise be impossible.

9. *A tool for personal degradation*: Money expresses want and need. The poor are often afraid of not having enough of it, and the rich seem almost always to want more. The desire for money can entice people into undignified labours such as prostitution or exploitative finance, and the absence of money can lead to borrowing on exploitative terms and a descent towards monetary desperation. The actual lack of money is almost a shorthand for social exclusion and the perceived lack of money has become a sign and cause of social despair.

10. *A social solvent which debases true values*: Money allows and encourages rich people, especially the newly rich, to undermine, demolish, or work around the institutions that hold up a society and its ethical values (the Marxist idea mentioned in Chapter One). Since money is featureless and fungible, it easily shakes off all the weight of all traditions, including the traditions that provide the social ballast needed for what is sometimes called social reproduction, the transmission of customs, ethical standards, and knowledge from one generation to the next. When moneyed people buy honours and social status, the established non-monetary social order is stained and strained. When measured monetary transactions displace traditional interpersonal arrangements, the mutually respectful sharing and hierarchies of non-monetary social systems are debased and replaced by commodification, quantification, and a crude common standard of value. When money becomes the measure of all things, every hint of transcendental value and values is obliterated.

11. *A useful token in unifying social rituals*: Money is one of the ways that people express themselves as members of a society. From pocket money for children through payments for insurance policies, savings accounts, and

pension funds, various distinct sorts of money carry distinct social meanings. Many of these rituals of the monetary institution strengthen communities. Dowries and bride prices are less common than in the past, but gifts of money to newlyweds, to adult children, and to elderly parents are often deeply symbolic expressions of affection and obligation. The different names given to various types of money – wages, salaries, bonuses, rent, dividends, capital gains, premiums, etc. – create a system of values and meanings that express and enrich a shared social life.

12. *A mark of government authority*: In modern economies, governments are the ultimate providers or guarantors of money (as I will explain later in this chapter), so the more that the economy depends on monetary transactions, the more people are tied to their governments, for better and for worse. The tax and benefits systems create pervasive direct monetary ties between citizens and their governments. More indirectly, the legally-mandated records of money transactions inside the banking system allow the government to monitor, guide, and punish people and enterprises in and for their economic behaviour. Even the requirement to use only "legal tender" as a currency ties the people to the government that backs the relevant monetary authority. Governments that cannot print their own money (for example "sub-sovereigns" such as U.S. states and, to some extent, member states of the euro) often suffer from the lack of the political authority and popular respect that true monetary sovereignty brings.

13. *A political unifier*: The national currency is one of the key marks of the modern nation-state. For most people today, the ability to buy and sell in a single currency is the clearest practical sign of a shared political identity. Money is often far superior to such other political unifiers as land, blood, or history because, unlike them, it does not rely on largely imagined stories and does not exclude minority groups. The sharing of money in universal government benefits systems enhances the sense of political unity. The inevitable unity of money systems helps explain some European politicians' enthusiasm for the creation of a multinational currency. The euro's existence and persistence automatically increase regional unity by creating a "eurozone", a commercial unity whose participating governments are monetary sub-sovereigns.

14. *A psychological symbol*: Money is part of our psychological language. When traditional Freudian analysts look at the hoarding of money, they detect powerful psychological motivations lurking behind the conscious desires for future spending or for protection against potential disaster. They see a desire to control life, to gather up and increase the hoarder's substance in the face of a strange and hostile world. Pure Freudians see money as a substitute for, or a slightly more adult expression of, the impossible infantile desire to retain excrement inside the body. This "anal retentive" understanding of money is particularly applicable to the apparently irrational behaviour of misers, who just want to hoard more money, not to use any of the freedom that money can buy. Freudians explain that almost everyone has miserly tendencies, because infantile desires are never fully abandoned. Conversely, some depth psychologists see the extravagant enthusiasm for spending money, often seen in an extreme form in the manic phases of bipolar disorder, as the expression of primeval generosity, an enthusiastic embracing of the mysterious grandeur of the universe.

15. *A symbol of social position*: Money is often used to certify a person's power and position. Raw money is less important for this social symbolism than the things that money buys – land, houses, diplomas, gratitude for charitable contributions. Still, money itself is often a significant marker. The use of cash (without any borrowing) to buy a house or a car or to pay university tuition is a clear sign of socio-economic success. Money in the bank is believed to indicate wealth and excellence. A big balance in a savings account is often taken as a sign of respectability, for example when applying for residency rights in a foreign country. Companies sometimes glory in cash hoards, often against the counsel of their financial experts. The names of types of money-payments often carry distinct social meanings. Salaries denote higher status than wages, and investment income (tellingly known in some tax jurisdictions as "unearned" income) is higher still.

16. *A religious object*: Money and religion (Mammon and God) have a complex relationship. All the great religions theoretically scorn the love of money, but priests and other cultic leaders, as well as many believers, have often been ensnared in cults of cash accumulation. Many people pray for

more money and a hefty bank balance is sometimes interpreted as a sign of being right with the, or a, Mammon-friendly deity. Conversely, money often substitutes for or takes on religious purposes and connotations. Christians sometimes speak of an idolatrous awe of money, while Marx wrote of a capitalist "commodity fetish". The two traditions are describing roughly the same thing, the worship of and enslavement to what is sometimes called "the almighty dollar". The religious vocabulary is at most only slightly exaggerated. People certainly make huge sacrifices to gain those dollars or euros and then often expect the money to do quasi-spiritual things for them – to buy happiness for oneself, respect or even love from others, or favour with God.

17. *A counterfeit of immortality*: The rich and the poor are subject to the same fear and mystery of death. No amount of money can buy immortal life. Still, many people believe that their monetary fortunes create a legacy that transcends death. In pre-modern cultures, the legacy came mostly as potentially immortal things: physical monuments and commemorative poetry. These persist, but purely monetary memorials have become more common. There are Rhodes scholars and Nobel prizes, and a host of lesser-known eponymous fellowships, professorial chairs, and foundations. Money allows the name to endure through the years and, if there is enough of it, over the generations. At a more modest scale, middle class parents can be kept alive in memory by their monetary heritage – "this house was paid for by my late parents".

18. *A wordless language within a community*: Non-verbal communication contributes to the unity of different groups. People are united by shared "body languages" and commonly understood ritual movements of politeness and worship. Money also "talks" for particular groups. People show respect or superiority with tips and show random hope in buying lottery tickets. They measure their social standing in salaries. They express something about their character in choosing to hunt for bargains or to pay full price. They show recklessness or caution in their patterns of spending. They show prudence, greed, or a devil-may-care attitude in their approach towards hoarding money. How much money is kept in a wallet or shoved in a drawer? How often are bank statements studied? How frightening are

overdrafts or debts? The answers to these monetary questions help express who people are in their social context.

19. *A universal language between communities*: Like the gender-signs outside public toilets, money is a language which is understood virtually everywhere. Money is the world's surest and most universal communicator. A visitor in a strange country who understands nothing of the native language can easily use money to get through daily life and to express friendship, pride, humility, desires, and gratitude. Money vastly simplifies insertion into a new community, because anyone can buy the right clothes, food, and housing. Trade hardly works without money, and trade brings people and peoples together. Religion, learning, and marriage are also institutions that can bring unity across political and social lines, but they work more slowly than monetary exchanges and they are usually far more divisive when they go wrong.

20. *A token of financial investment*: Money is the language of financial arrangements. As will be discussed in Chapter Three, these agreements to exchange some sums of money now for other sums in the future both unify and divide society. They help tie together many organisations within the economy and they create both the single large social institution of the financial system and the numerous individual banks that constitute that system. They also increase the social distance between rich and poor. As I will also explain in Chapter Three, in economic terms money-hoarding is quite different from financing actual investments, but in social terms the two activities are merged together into "investments". These investments bring social status, political and economic power – and their own moral ambiguities.

21. *A bearer of "bad infinity"*: As Aristotle recognised, money transcends the limits of physical reality. In the physical world, I can only use and own a finite amount of anything. My ability to consume is finite, my lifespan is finite, and the number of farms, artworks, and energy in the universe is finite. Money, though, is in some way infinite. Just as it is always possible to add one to the largest number that I can write down or think of, it is always possible to create another euro, no matter how many are already in circulation. It is always possible to want more money, have that desire

satisfied, and then want still more money. This lurking infinity of desire
has, as Aristotle also recognised, something unnatural about it (Aristotle
1984: 1.9 (1257b-1258a)). While knowledge and goodness are infinite in a
good way, because they express something of the transcendent and divine,
our place in this world is constrained by physical limits, both our own and
those of the world. Money falsely and unnaturally promises, or threatens,
to break those worldly limits. It can only offer what the philosopher G. W.
F. Hegel called a bad or wrong infinity (Hegel, 1975: 94).

22. *The opposite of nature and hope*: The natural world of plants, animals,
physical reproduction, gradual growth, and gradual decay is 'supple, free,
living, fecund, non-interchangeable, non-homogenous, non-exchangeable,
non-buyable and sellable, non-countable and calculable' (Péguy, 2019: 191).
The French poet and writer Charles Péguy gives this characterisation of the
world in its natural state explicitly as a contrast to the nature of the
'counter-object' of money. Money can buy a kind of security, but only
through a 'mummification' of life's essential flux and freedom. It can only
'conserve through cold'. Money symbolises and expresses everything that
humans do to create a calculating, divided, and controlled world. The anti-
humanity of money complements an anti-divinity. Money claims to delimit
all the possibilities of the future, says Péguy. When people let the quantity
of money in their bank accounts guide their actions and expectations, then
hope, the human ability to trust in God's good intentions for us, is lost as a
theological category.

23. *A precise arbiter of relative values*: Economists typically do not consider
money-numbers to be symbolic. On the contrary, as discussed in Chapter
One, they generally think that monetary measures reflect, more or less
accurately, something, more or less tangible, about the value of things.
Economists often think that the establishment or discovery of what
(Foucault, 2008: lecture 2) calls 'true' prices is central to the success of any
economy. This reasoning rests on the often unspoken and sometimes even
denied assumption that money- numbers, and especially the ratios between
them, should and can disclose consistent and meaningful quantitative
values of something. However, as I will explain in the next section, to use
those money-numbers to form judgements of relative actual human or
objective values is to think symbolically, not empirically or pragmatically.

Although economists often think of themselves as "hard" scientists like physicists or biologists, their reliance on quantitative symbolism more resembles the work of astrologers and alchemists, who organised precise quantitative observations into supposedly meaningful cosmic and qualitative systems.

24. *A bearer of a curse on humanity*: The love of money is the root of all evils, says Saint Paul (1 Timothy 6:10). His pagan near-contemporary Ovid speaks (Ovid, 2020: 1.141) of the discovery of 'gold, which brings more injuries than iron' as a sign of the coming of the last, worst age of history. Lottery winners are often ruined by the money they coveted, and strict moralists have often described money as a bearer of some sort of contamination. The rhetoric may be exaggerated, but money's compactness, power, flexibility, and unlimited possible quantity all do inevitably encourage or even inspire greed. People need a firm resolve if they are to resist desiring more money at all times, whether only a little bit more, a lot more, or more without limit. The curse of King Midas is real enough – the preference for money over the things it can buy turns the world into a glittering heap of destruction. The desire to gamble money converts an almost religious awe in the face of Chance or Fortune into a crass and socially destructive manifestation of greed. However useful money may be, it is always morally dangerous.

Most of these broad and deep meanings of money are found in every money-using society, and at least some of them influence the ways that everyone, from the most sophisticated economists to the more ignorant consumer and the smallest child, thinks about any question that has even vaguely monetary implications. In other words, all money-thoughts are inevitably tinged with some consideration of the ostentatious, protective, magical, divisive, unifying, retentive, generous, enslaving, liberating, greedy, or debasing symbolic meanings of money. It is possible to keep analytic attention focused solely on the purely economic uses of money. I will try to do that through the rest of this book. However, retaining such a narrow perspective requires a recognition that symbol-money is a distinct type of money, essentially different from both what I will call the token-money of labour and consumption and what I will call the savings-money of present and future. I will explain those terms more carefully in the fourth section of this chapter.

Before delving into these plainer types of money, I want to reiterate my deep respect for symbol-money. Not only is it far more complex and intellectually interesting than either token-money or savings-money, but it is, at least arguably, far more important to the human condition. What we *make of* money in our minds discloses more about what we think about the world and our place in it than what we actually *do with* money. In other words, money's non-economic meanings are more significant than its economic functionality. That was almost certainly the case in pre-modern economies, when trade and manufacture were minimal and money was largely used to denote status (as treasure), embody political subjugation (as tribute), ratify social relations (as dowries or bride-prices) or as part of some cultic rituals (as offerings). In the thickly symbolic societies studied by various sorts of cultural anthropologists, money often has little of its modern quantitative signification. Instead, its movements and positions are understood as part of an interwoven system in which women, trophies, gifts, and blessings are also socially significant tokens (Söffner, 2020). The pre-eminence of money's symbolic meaning can be seen in the Christian understanding of money, Mammon, as a symbol and embodiment of the worldly kingdom which believers are asked to disregard in favour of the kingdom of God. In post-Christian societies, money may well have become even more symbolically important, both because there is more of it around and because of the decline of its most potent traditional rivals as symbolic structures: the forms of religious practice and other divine-human connections.

While I have no intention of synthesising all these symbols, I do have one piece of advice for contemporary social-economic planners. They should remember that symbol-money is potentially both unifying and alienating, so they should work to ensure that the actual use of money in society reinforces its unitive symbolism and counteracts its symbolism of separation. For example, it is probably good to ensure that some money is available to families and communities to provide a cushion of safety in a crisis. Similarly but conversely, it is probably good to remove money as much as possible from the experiences of education, healthcare, and other social systems, to minimise the alienating effect of money, created by, for example, the stigma of inadequacy and the confusion of misleading quantifications.

With some regret, I must now bid farewell to that line of thinking. However interesting and important these thick descriptions of symbol-money are for sociology, anthropology, psychology, or public policy, they are mostly irrelevant for the economy. Money, understood as a purely economic tool, has only one purpose. I will explain my understandings of the economy, money, and money's economic role in the next two sections. To close this one, I want to point out very briefly the two essentially non-economic understandings of symbol-money that have most blurred the conventional economic study of money and finance.

The first is an amalgam of the initial three items on my list: sterile treasure, token of wealth and guarantee of safety. They are all aspects of what economists call money's ability to store value. The idea that money holds potential spending power is certainly not wrong. When workers who have saved money in pension funds retire, for example, they can usually withdraw and spend money from those funds. However, the idea is also not right. As I will explain over the course of this chapter, when the coin, bill, or entry is saved, it has been moved outside of the economy of labour and consumption. It becomes savings-money, which is not money in a strictly economic sense (as I define economic).

The second especially dangerous intrusion of symbol-money on economic thinking comes from the last meaning on my list, the implacable curse of monetary greed. As I will also explain, there is nothing intrinsically greed-inspiring about money understood as a purely economic tool. However, greed is an insidious force in human psychology, one that easily manifests itself in people's thinking about money, especially about the savings-money that has been taken out of the actual economy. The temptation of greed can be welcomed or resisted. In the current financial system, there is far too much welcoming, which is morally wrong and economically counterproductive.

All this will be explained in some detail in Chapter Five, but it might be helpful to summarise the conclusion of that argument here, as it ties together the symbol-money idea of storing value with the symbol-money attribute of greed. Greed encourages the belief that money should at least retain its value in storage. Without this greedy belief, changes in the value of stored, saved, or invested money would cause no social stress. In those improved moral circumstances, the holders of these monetary treasures would never be consumed by the desire that they turn into ever larger fortunes, a desire that is both unjust and economically and socially disruptive. In short, the financial portion of the money-finance system often fails to serve the economic good largely because it does not discourage, let alone control, greed.

2. The Great Exchange

At the beginning of this chapter I said that economists should not simply take the existence of money for granted, let alone unquestioningly identify economic activity as everything actually or potentially monetary. They need a totally non-monetary definition of economic activity. In this section, I provide one.

Let me begin by restating the conventional, unquestioning view of money and economics. At least in my experience, when most people talk about "the economy" they talk about money – what is done to earn it, the things it is spent on, how it is distributed, and how various parts of the money-system operate. Monetary transactions are rarely *not* considered to be the standard unit of economic activity, and questions about the true meaning of monetary measures are even rarer.

If this perception of the common understanding of "the economy" is right, then the general public has much the same approach as professionals. In the two or three centuries that economics has been anything like an academic discipline, the study has been almost entirely limited to money and the material things and human activities that money pays for, the domain that I call the paid-for economy. Whether consciously or unconsciously, economists have taken for granted a teleological narrative in which the use of money is considered the most "rational" or "modern" social-economic arrangement. Some sociologists, historians and anthropologists have taken a more neutral view of the goodness of monetised society, but for the last few generations, economists have generally laboured in splendid isolation from other students of society. Even the experiments of game theory, a primitive attempt at psychological analysis that is much loved by economists, almost always involve monetary or quasi-monetary rewards and punishments.

This is all wrong. The economy is not actually "about" money. Rather, the essence of the economy is the human activities which money usually pays for.

A definition

More precisely, economic activity is the gift of human labour to the world in exchange for the receipt of the fruits of that labour as gifts from the world. More roughly, economics is the study of the relationships of the worldly human activities of labour and consumption. To my knowledge, this definition is novel in its completeness (encompassing labour, the allocation of labour, production, consumption, the distribution of consumption, and environmental responsibility), its universality (valid in all societies, whatever their spiritual and cultural values, and whatever their technological and intellectual sophistication) and its total independence from money.

Because this definition is so important to my thesis, I think a little genealogy is in order. The focus on the primary human activity (labour and consumption) is a modernised, that is individualised, version of the etymological meaning of "economy" – the law (*nomos*) of the household (*oikos*). The idea of economics as a study of exchanges can be traced back to Aristotle, who discussed the non-monetary exchanges of the household, which he approved of, and the monetary exchanges of merchants, which he found unnatural for roughly the same reasons that I will use in describing money as an artificial imposition on economic activity. The concept of the economy as encompassing all labour and consumptions without privileging the concerns of the government, the rich, the nobles, or the workers is an extension of the founding 18th century social assumption of modern economics, as (Rosanvallon, 1989) explains. The interest in labour as the core of the economy was introduced by Locke, developed by Smith and Marx, and re-developed by, among others, Pope John Paul II, who added an anthropological dimension to it. The notion of consumption as the correlative of labour is implicit in standard economic discussions of National Product and National Income, although the anthropological dimensions of the pairing are almost never noted. Finally, the importance of gift in human societies has been the subject of intense anthropological attention since the beginning of the 20th century (Douglas, 2002). (Benedict XVI, 2009: 36) implied that full commutative justice in economic activity requires a gift-mentality, taking up a well-established – and well-merited – disparagement of contractual thinking about economics. The combination of all these ideas is, I think, my own.

In this definition of economic activity, money and the economy overlap but are far from identical. On one side, money is not used solely within the economy as I have defined it. Money is also used in all the symbolic ways discussed in the preceding section. In particular, the symbolic use of money (or something that goes by that name) to "store value" overlaps with the real economy, but that social role has no direct connection to the primordial human economic activities of labour and consumption. The nature of this non-economic money will be discussed extensively in this book, starting in the next section. On the other side of the money-economy relations, there is a great deal of genuine economic activity that occurs without any use of money.

This definition of the economy might be disconcerting to readers accustomed to think of money at the centre of any reasonable economic theory. I hope that any intellectual discontent fades as the argument in this book is developed, because my understanding is actually in accord with what is commonly meant by "the economy", at least once the everyday meaning is thought through carefully.

Roughly speaking, economics deals with a particular two-sided human activity: labour, which is the transformation or humanisation of the world in which people find themselves, and consumption, which is the use of this humanised world to promote some of the goods of the human condition.

To understand how money fits into and with these economic things, five key terms in the definition of the economy are relevant – exchange, labour, consumption fruits of labour, gifts, and the humanised world. I explain them one by one.

Exchange

I start with *exchange*. Monetary exchanges are familiar to modern people – we get paid to work and we pay to buy stuff created by work, ours and that of other people. Students of nature are familiar with the most primitive non-monetary version of this basic metabolic exchange – all living things exchange a sort of labour, of getting nourishment, for the physical flourishing provided by the acquired food. However, the broader, nobler, and equally basic human economic exchange has received far less attention. In the economy, humans exchange many "labour-things", activities and efforts which often hold a great deal of meaning for them, for many quite different "consumption-things", goods and services which are also meaningful to them. This metabolic give and take – social, emotional, physical, moral, intellectual, and aesthetic – is an essential and often beautiful part of being human. The Great Exchange of labour and its fruits is built into the human condition. Every society is to some extent built around it.

The Great Exchange, the defining economic exchange of labour and its fruits, is central enough to all human experience to merit capitalisation. The greatness of this exchange is three-fold. Most trivially, the exchange is of greatly different things. Labour expresses one aspect of human nature, while use of the fruits of labour, the consumption of goods and services, express a quite different aspect. More significantly, this exchange is great because it is necessary, required for the continuation and the fullness of human life. People cannot live at all without some consumption and they cannot live a dignified life without both some sort of subjectively and objectively meaningful labour and some subjectively and socially meaningful collection of consumption goods and services.

Most important, the concept of the Great Exchange is great because it is all-encompassing. It expresses the essence of innumerable lesser economic exchanges – of this labour for these wages (money is involved in that lesser exchange), of these fruits of labour for those prices (again monetary), of this labour of producing food for the food that I have produced and will consume (no money is involved in this exchange), of this family's joint toil for this family's joint consumption (money not necessary), of this man's craftwork for that man's farm produce (money not necessary), of this pre-modern aristocrat's labour of warfare and aesthetic glory for those fruits of those peasants' servile labour (money is optional), of this mother's loving labours of care for the development of her child and the child's reciprocal loving consumption of that labour (no money), of each particular amount of money exchanged for specific goods and services through the long chains of production and distribution (money), of taxes paid for government services and benefits (a mix of monetary and non-monetary relations). Each and every individual economic exchange can only be understood fully as a small part of the one Great Exchange.

Labour

On one side of the exchange are people as they *labour*. Labour always utilises the labourer's own strength, skills, and character. It also almost always utilises some of the physical things of this world, either in their raw state of nature or, much more commonly, in some already transformed and partly humanised state. The various abilities of different people and the numerous resources of the world create many types of labour. People hunt, gather, and nurture. They plant, harvest, and grind. They mine, smelt, and forge. They study, teach, and experiment. They organise and train, command and carry out orders, provide entertainment and aid fitness, spread and retain information. They labour to keep the peace and they labour to fight in war.

People are, in their nature, "formed" for labour, in the same way that they are, in their nature, "formed" for thinking (the *sapiens* in *homo sapiens*), for living in communities, for using their hands and, some would say, for wonder at and worship of the divine. Like these other aspects of human nature, the human call to labour is universal – all people have it and should respond to it all their lives. (My "all people" includes everyone from infants to the terminally ill. I will discuss their labour shortly.)

The labourer is always motivated, at least in large part, by positive desires. Each person feels the need to labour – to strive for personal excellence by developing and using skills in labour, and to support the common good by contributing to the production of useful and desirable fruits. Like everything else in human nature, however, the will to labour well is also always, in least in some small part, flawed. All people find their labour burdensome, at least some of time. The negative judgement is reasonable, since labour always comes with some unwelcome toil and some unwished-for obligations. The burdens of labour ensure that the life of labour always has moments of shirking and minimising effort. Some combination of rewards for accomplishment and punishments for failure is needed to counter these natural human weaknesses. For most members of most societies, some of those rewards and punishments come in the form of great or lesser allocations of the fruits of that society's labour.

The existence of both a positive desire for excellence in labour and a negative pain of toil is hard to dispute. How the two are balanced is a far more controversial topic. At the highest level, the mix of human virtue and vice is the subject of a philosophical and theological debate that is unlikely to end any time soon. My own philosophical judgement is that in the economy as in the rest of the human condition the positive, the striving for good, is a far more basic and generally more powerful force in each person and in every society, but that the negative force is always formidable. I will not defend that optimistic judgement here, because it is not crucial to most of the arguments in this book. On the contrary, my focus on the danger of greed in finance would fit at least as well with a more pessimistic reading of the balance of good and evil in human economic nature.

Money must be removed from the understanding of the human nature of labour for the activity's moral and spiritual breadth and depth to be fully appreciated. Its breadth, the role in human life, is huge, especially in temporal terms. The full range of types of labour probably takes up most of most people's waking hours. As for the depth, the role in creating and supporting dignified human lives and thriving societies, the best way to present it is by mentioning a few of the more outstanding and underappreciated types of labour, along with their wondrous fruits. These labours often escape economists' notice because they are so often unpaid.

To be fair, the labours of personal and household care are no longer totally unappreciated by professional economists. Feminist economists now pay attention to what has traditionally been dismissed as mere "women's work". However, even they sometimes fail to give full praise to the labour required to bear and raise children, nurture families, tend the ill, and provide emotional and practical support to all people in any sort of need, not to mention to the many tasks involved in making homes as fine as possible. All these organised, purposeful, and generally quite practical efforts of love and concern are emotionally, psychologically, and physically challenging. Most of them are highly skilled. They are far more often unpaid than paid, and far more often undertaken by women than by men. They produce the wonderful and beautiful fruits of loved and cared-for human beings, people who can flourish in lovingly maintained domestic environments.

Fruitful labour, though, is not limited to the daily toil of healthy adult men and women, paid or unpaid. Infants and children also labour, putting effort into their natural, age-appropriate tasks. Infants labour to discover, understand, and participate in the wonder and woe of the human condition. As babies turn into children, they learn through their labours, including the labours of play and games, to meet the many challenges of growing up. In modern societies the child's daily labour generally includes the joys and pains of formal schooling, which is supposed to bear many distinct fruits: the skills needed for more productive labour in the future, the knowledge needed for virtuous and fulfilled lives and for strong societies, and the wisdom needed for spiritual peace. The many phases of child-labour eventually bear the most vital fruit, the next generation of adults.

While the young mostly labour to learn how to thrive, the ill and the weak must labour to survive. That hard toil is mostly, although certainly not always, left to old age. The work can seem pointless, but it is supposed to, and often actually does, produce the sometimes bitter but still terribly valuable fruit of lives lived out in accord with the natural dignity of human nature. The weakness of some also can, and often does, develop spiritual depths in others, the labourers who provide the weak with loving care.

Consumption

In the Great Exchange, people do not only give. They also receive. Exactly as everyone labours, everyone consumes. They consume the *fruits of labour*.

All labour bears some fruit. In other words, every labour brings something new into the human community, whether a transformation of some physical object, an addition to the knowledge of the labourer or the community, or a change in someone's body or soul. In itself, consumption is the use, and sometimes the using up, of these diverse fruits. In the economic exchange, it is the distinctly human reception of gifts, both from the physical world humanised by labour and from the human community set in that world.

Economists give "consumption" a broader meaning than it has in everyday speech. They do not limit consumption to using something up so thoroughly that it is no longer fit for its original purpose. Rather, they include in consumption the use of goods that decay slowly or not at all. My definition of consumption is broader yêt, as I include the receiving of the fruits of the various labours of love and care. In the Great Exchange, the infant consumes the parent's time and effort just as the customers of lawyers or architects consume those professionals' time and effort. I hasten to add that from a moral, psychological, spiritual, or cultural perspective, my purely economic treatment of love is unbecoming and dishonestly reductive. However, it is a realistic picture of the metabolism of labour and its fruits.

Consumption is conventionally divided into goods, the stuff of consumption that is primarily taken from the world, and services, the consumption stuff that is primarily created by human labour. The division is useful, but the boundary is often unclear. Anything in the natural world has to be extensively humanised by labour before it can be consumed, so consumption goods are inevitably a nature-human hybrid. Only with careful husbandry, cooking, and cutlery can plants and animals become meals. Ores need engineering knowledge and human craft to become cars. Houses are made of construction expertise as well as of wood or brick. Conversely, almost all services require some physical stuff to be delivered.

Architects and lawyers need paper and, these days, computers. Parents need food, clothes, and toys. Actors need theatres and equipment to turn drama into performances. Services are human–nature hybrids. Over the last few centuries, the human transformations of the world have become more extensive, so the human sides of these hybrids, both goods and services, have become more significant.

Whether close to or far from the non-humanised or pre-humanised world, consumption, like labour, is necessary for human dignity. Indeed, the well-ordered and joyful consumption of the many goods and services that meet human needs and desires is a noble expression of true humanity. Of course, reality falls short of such an idealised description. Like labour, consumption is always marred by the flaws of human nature. People are often greedy, wanting to consume more than is good for them or for the common good of their communities. People can also be proud, taking undue satisfaction in their own consumption. They can be jealous, coveting the consumption goods and services enjoyed by others. They can be careless, squandering the gifts of consumption. The two sides to human nature shown in consumption, the natural expression of nobility and the natural disorder of the desires, co-exist uneasily.

Gift

Philosophically, I argue that, as with labour, the good in consumption predominates over the bad, but as with labour, my philosophical-anthropological judgement is not directly relevant to the discussion of money and finance. However, the two positive evaluations do help explain my description of both sorts of economic activity as *gifts*. The claim may be surprising, since it directly contradicts the narrow understanding of commutative justice normally associated with money. When money is exchanged for labour or its fruits, the value of the two sides of the transaction is supposed to be precisely equal. The idea that both sides of economic activity are gifts also goes against the popular idea that a gift is only truly a gift if it is offered without any hope for a possible future recompense. Offerings made with the expectation of return offerings are commonly thought of as some sort of barter, not as a gift.

The objections are both unnecessarily reductive. The desire for purely monetary equivalence in particular exchanges misses the ongoing nature of the Great Exchange, as I explain later in this chapter. Similarly, the unilateral notion of gifts misses the communal and indeterminate nature of the "gift economy". Think of the rituals which surround gift-giving for Christmas and birthdays in many affluent societies. Even the most generous gifts are always given with the hope and expectation of some sort of reciprocation. The desired return may be an actual present now or in the future, or it could be something less tangible, perhaps gratitude for the giver's generosity or respect for her social status. In the gift economy, the offerings are inherently generous, socially meaningful, and made with some attention to and expectation of appropriate gifts in return.

Labour's offering in the Great Exchange must indeed be a gift, in this broad and nuanced understanding, if only because the reciprocation, in the form of fruits of this or other people's labour, cannot have the same value, in human terms, as the offering. This non-equivalence is unavoidable, as the third confusion discussed in Chapter One should have made clear. What is received in the Great Exchange is always essentially different from what is offered, so there can be no true equality between the two sides. More profoundly, labour is a gift because its fruits are always shared with and within some community. The size of the relevant community depends on the particular exchange. The group may be as small as the immediate family, as was typical in isolated pre-modern subsistence farming, or as large as the entire world, as is often the case in the contemporary hyper-connected global economy. Finally and most profoundly, labour is gift because the ultimate purpose of this open-ended offering is generous. People offer themselves in labour. They put to use some combination of their energy, strength, intelligence, skills, affections, and passions. It is easy to criticise the secondary and less essential purposes of the gifts of labour – to gain as high rewards as possible or to gain higher rewards than neighbours. However, the primary and essential purposes of the self-offering that is labour are the generous desires to make the physical world serve human society and to make that society more humane.

Just as people give the gift of labour to humanise the world, they receive the gift of consumption from that humanised world. The ultimate giver of this gift is hard to identify. Spiritually-minded people might say it is God, the bounty of Mother Nature, or some other conceptually similar force or entity. From the more limited perspective of the actual consumers, the donors are multiple. There are the labourers who humanise nature, the society that organises the labour and allocates its fruits, the actual physical world, and in a philosophical or even a mystical sense, the fact of that world's capacity to be humanised.

People like to receive these presents from the world. They like to consume, and rightly so. The gifts of consumption are good for them. The goodness starts with the infant's delight in the consumption of her mother's milk and loving attention. The simple pleasures of consuming food and love continue through life, embroidered and expanded. Other types of consumption are added later – the enjoyment of works of art, the calm and excitement of leisure activity, and the basking in and boasting about the comforts and luxuries of domestic life. Morally, the challenge of consumption is to receive the many gifts from the world with appropriate gratitude, with due respect for the various givers, and without undue coveting or worldly attachment. As with labour, there are many and inevitable failures, but the receiving of gifts of consumption can be as virtuous as the giving of gifts of labour.

The humanised world

In the Great Exchange, people are the donors of labour and the recipients of consumption. However, as I just explained, consumption goods and services are not made only from human labour. They are also made from the transformation of some non-human, physical materials. The original form of this to-be-transformed material is what I call the *world*. I am using that word in a philosophical sense – the non-human stuff in and among which humans live. Other words are also used to express the same concept. Scientists usually refer to the environment, ecosystem, or natural world, depending on their emphasis. Social theorists talk of the physical world or of nature, which they contrast with human societies and civilisations. Some religious people speak of Creation.

Whatever the name, this raw material of eventual consumption has two characteristics that are salient for economic activity. First, the raw, pre-humanised world is close to useless, because it can barely serve humanity. Second, the world is potentially useful, because many of its many parts can serve humanity by being transformed into consumption goods and services. The nature of the world – recalcitrant but potentially fruitful – helps explain many aspects of the Great Exchange: the toil of labour, the reliance on accumulated human knowledge, and the limits to the available quantity and quality of consumption goods and services.

The transformation of the world is one of the two basic tasks of labour. (The other is the fuller humanisation of human communities.) The only labours that do not in some way transform the physical world are the most direct forms of human-to-human caring labour and perhaps the most spiritual forms of human-to-divine labour. Other than such pure love and worship, everything that is consumed requires some humanisation of the world through labour. In my terminology, the gifts of labour fructify the various things of the world, transforming them into gifts for consumption.

Although the world is necessarily present throughout the Great Exchange, economic activity is always essentially human rather than material. However important the worldly parts of particular consumption goods may be, the economic value always comes from the human transformation, not from the worldly raw material.

The secondary role of the non-human world in the economy is often somewhat hidden by the widespread practice of assigning a social and often a monetary value to some parts of the world. Most significantly, land is often owned, bought, and sold. The control and lack of control of land often bring different degrees of social status. Also, gold, oil and other so-called commodities are often treated as having a monetary value that far exceeds the costs of the labour used for production. This practice of assigning human-style economic values to non-human things is accepted without question by most economists and by almost all economic actors, but they are wrong to be so blasé. Such attributions should be treated as essentially unnatural, for money is a human artefact that is only truly at home in the human Great Exchange. As the discussion in this chapter will make clear, the monetary values assigned to things rather than the people using them are part of the symbolic and social penumbra that surrounds the actual human economy. In particular, they are leading examples of the social-symbolic understanding of money as a store of value.

Money and the Great Exchange (preview)

The Great Exchange *is* economic reality. The economy is nothing other or more than this exchange: people transforming the world to serve people; the humanisation of the world by labour and the disposition of that humanised world in consumption; the exchange of the gifts of labouring people to the world for the gifts from the world to consuming people. Money, it should already be clear, can be nothing other or more than a useful tool or token in this Great Exchange. To treat money as if *it* were the economy or even pre-eminent in the economy is to insult the grandeur of the world and of the human efforts to transform it.

The next section explains how money actually does fit into the economy. As a transition, I will first introduce five features of the Great Exchange that will prove relevant. Some of them should already be familiar, as they are basically fuller explorations and rectifications of the false ideas discussed in Chapter One.

1) *The Great Exchange is essentially but not exclusively social*: The human transformation of the world is always and everywhere a group effort. Philosophically, there is no truth to the claim of some philosophers that individuals can, should, or do promote solely their own desires. Defending this dismissal would take me too far from the scope of this book, but it is worth stating, since standard economic models – from Adam Smith to game theory, including much of Marxism – are based on the opposite assumption, of universal and exclusive self-interest. Whatever the value of this "methodological individualism" for the understanding of psychology or morality (none whatsoever in my judgement), it is especially unhelpful in economics, since the Great Exchange is necessarily communal in practice and in motivation. No one can consume only the fruits of her own labour. In both labour and consumption, the almost seamlessly connected world must be shared.

In labour, the sharing always involves a relatively large group of people. The group includes the dead, since today's labourers always learned many of their skills and habits from parents or teachers, who in turn learned from theirs, and so forth. The community of labour also includes future generations, since an important motivation for excellence in labour is concern for the good of future generations. In the present, all labouring communities include both men and women, since the labours of continuing the human race require both sexes. Each community also includes people of all ages, since everyone spends childhood in need of the fruits of other people's labour and weakness and illness force many adults to spend time in similar need. The limits to human ability also constrain people to labour together. In pre-modern economies, farmers needed craftsmen, laymen called for priests and the ill for doctors, the strong laboured at dominating the weak, and soldiers joined each other in battle. As economies became more sophisticated, the labours became more specialised and skilled, so the communities of labour have grown larger and their structures and interdependencies have become more complex.

Consumption is also necessarily communal, in several dimensions. The fruits of all the different labours are pooled, so all can consume what all produce. Also, people live, eat, dress, work, study, play, travel, and so forth in groups, whether small or large. Their consumption takes place in places shared by groups: houses, neighbourhoods, cities and larger unified political entities, shops, schools, hospitals, highways, and so forth. As economies have become more interdependent, consumption, like labour, has become more deeply social. For example, mass production ties many people together through consuming identical products, and mass entertainment has allowed or forced millions of people to share identical experiences of leisure consumption.

There are two significant qualifications to this universal economic sociality. First, while the existence of communities of labour and consumption is inevitable, the fruits of any particular labour need not be shared by everyone in a particular society. The labour of the butcher has no direct effect on the consumption of his vegetarian neighbour, and the labour of yacht-makers does nothing, directly at least, for the consumption of nearby subsistence farmers.

Second, even in the most communal economic life, labour and consumption are also in some way totally personal. At the most basic level, the Great Exchange can sometimes take place primarily within one person – I as labourer may basically provide the fruits of labour for myself as consumer. More significantly, even when I labour and consume primarily as a member of one or more communities, I can and generally want to make personal choices, find personal satisfaction, and have my own approach to both sides of the Great Exchange.

The economic lesson: a tool which helps the economy work better (hint: think money) must be essentially social, shared by some community. It should also be sufficiently personal to help each member of the society have her own economic life, on both sides of the Great Exchange.

2) *Labour and consumption are too fundamentally different for meaningful comparisons*: As a human activity, all labour has an essential similarity. In every type of labour, people do much the same things. They apply many aspects of their selves – generally some selection of knowledge, instincts, intelligence, physical strength, emotions, and spiritual energy – to specific tasks in the world. Another commonality is the setting of all labour in social structures – each labourer is always guided by some collection of rules of practice and standards of excellence. The rules and standards are always present, whether they are written down, passed down, or merely internalised. The homemaker knows how and why to clean and cook, the child how and why to play and learn, the carer to give practical signs of love, the farmer to plough and harvest, the factory worker to accomplish his allotted tasks, the executive hers, and so forth.

The structural similarity of all types of labour explains the ease with which most people can change their lives of labour. Some of the changes are the normal experience of the human condition. The child's labour of learning yields almost seamlessly to the labour of the first adult toil and labour in an office can be followed without too much trouble by the labour of caring for an infant. Some changes in labour follow patterns which vary by society. In many modern economies, one job often naturally leads to another and one career sometimes leads to another. Of course, there are limits to this labour interchangeability. Not everyone has the intelligence, temperament, or physical characteristics required for some types of labour. Still, the differences in labour are small in comparison to those of consumption.

For the fruits of labour are truly diverse. Even in the simplest economies, the list includes such diverse goods and services as food, clothing, shelter, physical warmth, spiritual protection, and the many services provided by labours of love. In the modern economy, the variety of consumption is kaleidoscopic. A poem, a car, school lessons, toothpaste, aeroplane journeys, home-grown vegetables, and helpful love from a carer (economic sophistication hardly changes this human need and desire) – modern consumers are offered hundreds of thousands of different goods and services.

As well as being more variegated, the objects of consumption are far less interchangeable than the tasks of labour. On the labour side, the poet can fairly easily become a teacher, a car designer, an assembly line worker, or a farmer. She might well already sometimes labour in a hobby garden. On the consumption side, similar substitutability is quite rare. While one brand of toothpaste is much like another, a poem cannot replace toothpaste, a car, a lesson, or a cuddle. Sociological judgements sometimes amplify small distinctions in consumption goods. For example, luxury cars and entry-level vehicles are almost interchangeable when considered as useful machines or as products of labour. As consumers' social statements, they could hardly be more different.

The differences among the almost innumerable consumption goods and services are so great that there is no common scale on which they can be consistently compared. When water is scarce, it is more valuable than diamonds, but once there is enough water available, surplus water is generally much less valued than an additional diamond. That comparison is relatively straightforward. But is a car more valuable than a poem or a nice bed-sheet than a picture on the wall or than a well-learned lesson? Such questions are almost absurd. And even if a ranking could be devised – whether subjective, objective, or somehow contextual, it would not be numerical. Any attempt to measure on any scale just how much more valuable the picture is than the poem requires a further step into the land of conceptual absurdity. As discussed in Chapter One, it simply makes no sense to say that a poem is worth half as much, or twice as much, as a car.

The incomparable and incommensurate nature of different consumption goods and services is not a problem in itself, but it does complicate the organisation of the Great Exchange. There is, though, one seemingly simple solution to this consumption-valuation conundrum. The different consumption items could be valued in terms of the labour that goes into each of them. This approximation might succeed because, as I just said, one hour of labour is much the same as another. "Labour-hours needed for production" could provide a numerical standard value. In this system, if a car "contains" 2000 labour-hours and a poem contains 10 hours, then the car would be worth 200 times as much as the poem.

The idea of using labour-hours for the valuation of consumption goods and services may be appealing, but it has severe limits. The most important problem is conceptual. There is no reason to assume that the consumed item is actually *worth* the amount of labour required for producing it. The item's "subjective" value comes from the satisfaction *felt* by the consuming individual user or her society. There is no necessary relationship between consumption pleasure and hours of labour. Nor are those hours necessarily related to the item's "objective" value, which comes from the *actual good* provided to the individual consumer, to a particular society, or to the whole of current and future humanity. For example, in terms of either the labourer's satisfaction or the common good, an hour of a mother's loving labour may well be worth more than ten hours of labour in an advertising agency.

There are also daunting practical issues with this proposed comparative measure of consumption. The most important one is caused by the standard social practice of ignoring the near-identity, in human terms, of all labour. I mentioned the social differentiation of value for different types of cars. It is much the same with many types of labour. Objectively similar types of labour often have quite different social values. For example, aristocratic labour used to be high-status and peasant labour low-status. Now lawyers and bankers are high while manual labourers and carers are mostly low. The differences are expressed both in social standing, which is basically irrelevant to economics, and in rewards of consumption goods and services, which are extremely relevant, since they make up one side of the Great Exchange. The differences in assigned consumption-values for different types of labour make it impossible to use some crude temporal labour-unit or some sophisticated skill-adjusted-labour-units as the standard of value for consumption goods. After all, if labour contributions are valued in terms of the allotted rewards of consumption goods and services, it is impossible simultaneously to value those same consumption goods and services in terms of the contributing hours of labour.

Another practical issue is the inherently communal nature of labour. It is impossible to determine which hours of labour built a particular car. What portion comes from the factory worker, advertising writer, software engineer, and cleaning person at the manufacturer's executive offices? What portion came from the labours whose fruits are now part of the common patrimony of engineering knowledge? Does the car not also implicitly include at least some of the labour used to build the roads on which it will be driven and some of the labour used to create and enforce the laws that ensure that driving is safe? There is no undeniably correct answer to such questions.

All these qualifications and complications point to a simple truth. The Great Exchange is indeed an exchange, but no numerical system of valuation can offer a genuine, natural, absolute, and realistic equivalence between the different elements on the two sides. Indeed, without a common scale of value, equivalence is not so much impossible as meaningless. Any two elements of the labour-consumption exchange are too different in their nature and in the social esteem they receive for both of them to be given comparable numerical values which could be called true.

Only at the highest possible level can it be said that the value of labour and consumption are in some realistic way equal. Since all the labour in the world produces all the fruits of that labour, there is an ultimate labour-consumption identity (barring a few technical adjustments). However, that grand equality provides no guidance on how to pair up the individual items in a vast heap of socially differentiated contributory labour with the even more practically and socially differentiated items in the equally vast heap of consumption.

The economic lesson: if a tool can be created to help the economy work better (hint: think money) by reducing the individual items on the two sides of the Great Exchange to a common numerical standard, it can only provide a rough and ultimately somewhat arbitrary guide to subjective, objective, and sociological value. However, it might be very helpful in sorting out the two huge and diverse heaps of labour and consumption.

3) *The Great Exchange is essentially instantaneous*: Essentially, the two sides of economic activity always happen at the same time. Each is a human activity that always occurs in the always vanishing temporal point between past and future, so conceptually any economic community consumes exactly as and exactly what it produces. In practice, of course, there are reasons for a delay between any particular time spent in labour and consumption of the fruits of that particular labour – see the next observation for a discussion – but these adjustments do not change the true nature of the economic action, any more than friction invalidates the Newtonian laws of motion. The Great Exchange is always the gift of currently available labour and the consumption of the currently available fruits of labour.

That idea may be surprising, so I will try to provide a little philosophical context. The underlying issue is how economic activity fits into time. To what extent can actual labour and consumption (not some token which is said to represent them) be moved backwards or forwards in time? Very little. The labour which was done yesterday cannot be undone, the labour which was not done yesterday cannot generally be done today without delaying today's labour, and the labour which is not done today is basically lost forever. Consumption is similar. If I do not eat today, I am hungry today. Neither the memory nor the prospect of food changes my current hunger. Nor can memories or prospects soften today's homelessness, cold, or lack of clothing.

I exaggerate slightly. Human societies generally keep a reserve supply of most consumption goods (services are more difficult). Human physiology allows for some storage of energy. Human psychology allows for some storage of sentiment – persistent residues of the past and occasional intimations of the future. Still, the exceptions only slightly modify the stolid truth. The Great Exchange takes place in the present. The economy, understood as the exchanged fluxes of labour and consumption, is far more contemporaneous than beauty and holiness, which are thought to be timeless, than cultures, which always exist in some combination of past and present, and than politics, which take place in some combination of past, present, and future.

The economic lesson: A tool that helps the economy work better (hint: think money) has to be a tool which works essentially and primarily in the present. Any use of the tool over time is liable to distort the Great Exchange or to distract attention from it.

4) *The Great Exchange is often rather slow*: While both labour and consumption always and essentially take place in the present, production is different. Production is familiar – a factory produces cars, a farm produces wheat, an engineering firm produces designs, and a mother or carer produces loving care. In terms of the Great Exchange, production is the actual process of the humanisation of the world, its conversion of labour into labour's consumable fruits.

However production is thought about, it almost always takes place over a fair amount of time. Many years can elapse between the collection of the rawest materials from nature and the consumption of the finished goods and services. The train of economic causes and effects that led to the loaf of bread made into today's sandwiches can be traced back, perhaps over many centuries. The narrative of labour could start with the clearing of the fields that produced the wheat that produced the flour that produced the bread. Or the chain can be traced back to the excavation needed for the mines that produced the iron ore that produced the steel that is used in the wheat-harvesting ploughs and bread-baking ovens. Even without looking so far back, the flour was probably milled several months ago and the loaf itself was probably baked a day or two before it was eaten.

The bread example is typical. The goods portion of the essentially instantaneous Great Exchange of the human economy is backed by many time-consuming processes of production. Even the "production" of a parent's love (I repeat that this purely economic description is socially and morally inadequate) requires years of something like training, the time spent in growing into a loving and skilled adult.

I already mentioned the most fundamental reason that the transformations within the Exchange take time: raw nature, including raw human nature, is uncooperative. A great deal of labour is required to turn the unformed world and untrained humanity into the humanised world. Most of this labour of extraction, transformation, refinement, maturing, and training must be done in sequence, so much time is required.

There is an inevitable tension between the production from nature over time and the instantaneous human exchange of labour and its fruits. One of the accomplishments of the modern economy is the effective organisation and management of ever longer and more complicated chains of production. This requires remarkable feats of logistics, for example converting iron ore from Australia and manganese from South Africa to steel in China, which is then used to build a washing machine that will be sold in Iran as well as China, South Africa, and Australia. For such long and diffuse chains to work, the people who contribute labour at any point on them must be able to share instantaneously, and as it were in advance, the benefits of the final, consumable fruits of their labour. The mine worker in Australia wants to have some current claim on the washing machine that will, in some months or years, be in some small part the fruit of her labour.

Actually, she wants a claim on far more than a tiny portion of that washing machine and any other consumption goods containing the ore that her own labour has helped to wrest from the recalcitrant world. She wants, and to some extent needs, to claim some share of all the production in whatever parts of the Great Exchange are relevant to her – food, clothing, shelter, education, and so forth. Each of these consumption goods and services emerge from its own more or less long chains of production. While many of the chains overlap and interact, there is rarely a clear connection between the immediate fruits of any particular person's labour and much of that person's consumption. For the economy to work well, it is necessary to find a way to substitute a sampling of the total production of finished consumption goods and services for the incomplete and quite specific products of any particular person's labour. In a multi-chained economy, the necessary widespread substitution requires a remarkable degree of effective social organisation and mutual trust. Some system or mechanism, preferably one which is simple and flexible, would make this systemic substitution of the complete for the partial much easier.

The economic lesson: A tool which helps the economy work better (hint: think money) may be used and useful within the many long processes of humanising nature.

The exchange of the incomplete products of labour for finished consumption goods is one part of a larger challenge of coordinating labour and consumption in a complex economy. Before discussing that challenge, I want to add two observations about the difference between the Great Exchange and the intertemporal chains of production and distribution.

The first is a correction of a common economic misunderstanding. It is generally stated or assumed that the archetypical economic act is a monetary transaction that takes place somewhere along one of these chains – the component maker sells to the final producer, the farmer to the merchant, the clothmaker to the pedlar, or the Bangladeshi clothing factory to the Swedish retail chain. Notably, Adam Smith assumed that these intermediate actions and transactions, along with the emotions and desires which he thought promoted and perfected them, were the centre of successful economic activity. He described a 'certain propensity in human nature ... to truck, barter, and exchange one thing for another' (Smith, 2003:23). Karl Marx had a different view of society but a similar view of the centre of economics. In his model, all monetary transactions were "exchanges of commodities". That might be an accurate if superficial description of truck-and-barter transactions in the middle of the chains of production, but it definitionally reduces wages for labour into a systematic method of symbolic dehumanisation.

While the haggling of truck-and-barter exchanges undoubtedly takes place, Smith's psychological model and Marx's political-sociological one share a fundamental misunderstanding. Neither Smith nor Marx, generally considered the two founders of modern economic thought, fully recognised that the economy, which *is* the Great Exchange, is built out of much more communal and comprehensive aspects of human nature. The economy *is* the mutual interaction of the human need and orientation to labour with the human need for and receptivity to the goods and services of consumption, combined with the human loyalty to communities of shared economic effort and the world's potential for being humanised through labour. Chains of production are merely aspects of the Great Exchange. Contracts and the truck and barter of negotiations are – like bureaucratic structures, traditional practices, and administrative commands – merely ways of organising this Exchange. Wages, as I will explain, are a helpful tool. They are not inherently dehumanising.

Second, the rhythm of labour and the rhythm of consumption are slightly different, so in practice the economic "now", the instant of the instantaneous Great Exchange, can take some time. The two activities are rarely simultaneous during the course of the day – generally they alternate. Over a slightly longer time, most ready-to-consume goods are stored for some time in warehouses, shops, or cupboards at home. The expansion and shrinkage of these inventories prevents small unexpected shifts in either production or consumption from disrupting the overall economy. This helpful dampening stretches the instant of Exchange into a long-ish current moment.

5) *It is often hard to coordinate the Great Exchange*: In any economic community, the Great Exchange involves the differentiated labour of many people who produce many distinct and often distant items and the consumption of those items by the same people, that is everyone, who laboured to produce them. Numerous decisions are needed on both sides of the Exchange – about what which community members should labour on now, given the available collection of skills and parts of nature, and about what which members would like to and can consume now. Decisions are also needed on how much labour should be dedicated to continuing current production and how much to additions to and alterations of the

capacity to produce goods and services. The decisions made for the whole community are entwined with similar decisions made for and by groups and for and by individuals within the community. Who will labour at what and who will consume what? What labour will be associated with which consumption? How will all the labour be coordinated? How will all the stages of production be arranged? How will disputes over the allocation of labour and consumption be avoided and resolved?

The answers to these enquiries are mutually dependent and ever-changing, especially in modern economies with their extraordinarily wide range of capabilities. Economic desires shift steadily, in part under the influence of what is currently possible, while what is possible is steadily changed by the social and individual responses to those economic desires. Feelings about the present are influenced by the hopes and expectations for the future, while those hopes and expectations are influenced by the current situation. Decisions about the allocation of labour influence the allocation of consumption, and vice versa. Decisions about the labour and consumption of individuals and groups within a community influence the decisions for the whole community, and vice versa. To make matters more confusing, all the enquiries, considerations, and decisions take place under some difficult constraints of reality – limited knowledge, limited possibilities, and sometimes unreasonable or unrecognised desires.

The conclusion is clear. The coordination of labour and consumption is complicated.

The third observation on the Great Exchange – labour and consumption are fundamentally different – adds to the complexity. Indeed, the two activities that are exchanged are so different that there can be no objective equivalence of the human value of any individual's labour with any collection of consumption goods and services. The combination of a necessary labour-consumption exchange with the incommensurability of the two sides of that exchange adds greatly to the practical complexity of economic coordination. Since a natural objective equivalence is lacking, any decisions about what consumption goes with which labour will require human judgements. People and societies generally set ethical or social standards for comparing the two sides of the Exchange (we value brain more or less than brawn, men's work more or less than women's work, parents' work more or less than single people's), and translate those standards into actual allocations. Other social and ethical considerations may also be deemed relevant for allocation, for example the common dignity of all people, the special needs or non-labour-related merits of certain individuals, and inherited or assigned social status.

There are various ways to manage the complex practical and social tasks of coordination, allocation, and adjudication. One approach is to be guided by *rules*. Tradition is one source of rules. You do what your fathers and mothers did before you. You share a set portion of your labour or its fruits with a set community of people, you give a set portion of your labour or its fruits to your social superiors, or you receive a set tribute from your social inferiors. Traditions can be more or less flexible in response to peculiarities of character and natural events, and they can be more or less open to evolution as knowledge grows or circumstances and beliefs change. Decree is another source of rules. A dictator, committee or appointed expert can tell you what labour to do when and where, and can decide what goods and services you will be given to consume.

Pre-modern communities, which tended to be small and fairly simple, largely relied on traditional rules for the organisation of the Great Exchange. Rules still play an important role in economic organisations, but on their own they cannot deal very effectively with the complexities of the modern economy. The chains of production are far too long and integrated for most people to have either labour or fruits of labour that can easily be shared or offered. A medieval farmer could offer a third of his crop to the liege lord, but a software engineer cannot easily offer a third of her production to the government, or a tenth of her production to the supermarket that provides her with food. Hypothetically, a mega-mega-mega computer could perhaps assign everyone's labour and consumption with precision, excellence, respect for the desires of each person, and a clear understanding of the common economic good. However, in reality the complexities, interactions, incomplete knowledge, and mutual dependencies in the modern economy are far too great to allow such virtuous central planning.

What would be really helpful is an economic tool which can – even if only artificially, approximately, and temporarily – provide some rough numerical equivalences. Coordinating, allocating, and planning would all be easier if everyone involved could rely on commonly agreed numerical comparisons of one type of labour with another, of one type of consumption with another, and of all types of labour with all types of consumption. The tool could be some sort of token which stands for each of the individual morsels of the Great Exchange – this bit of labour, that particular consumption good or service.

Of course, the "standing for" of this countable token would be approximate. At best, it would be like a flat and monochromatic map of a beautiful mountainous landscape. Actually, it could not even achieve that degree of resemblance. The token would be quantitative, while the Great Exchange is essentially non-quantitative because it is essentially human. Still, a tractable token would help people follow traditions, set and obey rules, and organise the complex mutual dependencies of highly divided labour and highly diverse consumption.

Actually, there is no need for the conditional "would be". Such a tool already exists. It is the token called money.

The economic lesson: Money is a tool which helps the economy work better by creating artificial, rough, and socially sanctioned common scales of valuation for labour and consumption.

The modifying adjectives are crucial to understanding money. This tool has many significant limits.

3. Introduction to money

What money is

The definition of money follows directly from the previous discussion. It is a *communally recognised, quantitative token that is used within parts of the Great Exchange*. In simpler words, it is a token that consumers exchange for goods and services and that labourers receive in exchange for their labour.

Essentially, money is a mediator of the broad and universal human activities of labour and consumption. In practice, monetary mediation is closely connected with the details of production, which is the actual transformation of specific labour and particular things in the world into specific goods and services for consumption. As a broad generalisation, the more complex a production process is, the more likely money will be an effective way to connect all the relevant labour with all the relevant consumption. In modern economies, money-using producer organisations, for example companies and government agencies, often serve as mediators in the paid-for portion of the Great Exchange. Consumers typically pay prices to these organisations and labourers typically receive wages from them.

My definition of money corresponds reasonably well with two of the three standard descriptions. Money is a "medium of exchange" because it is a tool that aids the Great Exchange of labour and consumption. It is a "unit of account" because it is quantitative. As I have hinted, and as will be explained later in this chapter, I have serious problems with the other description, "store of value".

The basic flow of money in the economy can be seen as linear, either from consumers to producers or from producers to labourers. However, the two lines, person (consumer)-to-producer and producer-to-person (labourer), are clearly connected. Indeed, the money flow reflects the circular flow of the Great Exchange: the labouring person gives (labour) to the being-humanised world which gives (consumption goods and services) to the consuming person, who is also the labouring person. Money goes out from people and comes in to people. Like any circle, the money-cycle has neither beginning nor end. It is true that people first spend as consumers and that the spent money is then paid to them as labourers. It is equally true that they first earn and then spend. Money continually flows around in what (Smith, 2003: 368) called the "great wheel of circulation".

Along with being necessarily cyclical, money is also inherently social. It always flows from, through, and to the many. It comes from many consumers, is united by and passes through chains of many producers, and is divided among many labourers. For each individual, this triple multiplicity creates an automatic organisational and human interdependence. As a labourer, I depend on many consumers and producers. As a consumer, I depend on many labourers and producers.

Like the definition of the economy, the definition of money uses terms that might be confusing. However, none of them need be discussed here. I have already introduced the *Great Exchange* (in the last section) and the impossibility of assigning meaningful *quantitative* measures to either of the two sides of that exchange (in Chapter One). I will say more about the unreality of monetary numbers in this chapter's fifth section. In the fourth, next section I will discuss the importance of the limitation of money's use to *parts* of the economy and in the sixth section the nature and importance of *common* recognition of the value of monetary *tokens*.

In this section, I want to explore in a little more depth the workings of the money economy, identifying three functions that are particularly helpful in complex modern industrial economies.

The genius of monetary allocation (allocation itself)

Money does not directly organise or allocate labour and consumption. People do that: as individual labourers and consumers, through the organisations they construct, and by the sovereign power of their governments. Money is merely a tool that can be used to help the complex process of continuously exchanging an intricate and ever-changing network of labour for an equally intricate and ever-changing but entirely different network of consumption. Money is not the only tool that is used – I will discuss a few others in the next section of this chapter. Also, labour and consumption can take place without the use of any tool other than the basic human aid of intelligent choice.

However, money is a most useful and much used tool. In modern economies, prices, wages, and other money-numbers have a significant influence on how much consumers can buy and help them decide what to buy. They also influence the decisions that labourers make about what paid work they will do and how much dedication they will give to that work. Money-numbers help planners at organisations and governments make decisions and then implement them. In other words, money-strands are woven throughout the modern economic fabric.

Let me list a few of the ways the money is useful.

a) As explained in the last section, money assigns commensurate numerical values on each side of the Great Exchange economy, to distinctly different types of labour and to vastly different consumption goods.

b) Also as explained in the last section, money allows any and all labour and consumption to be compared, contrasted, and connected. Money can be used indifferently on both sides of the Great Exchange. The same money pays for both labour and consumption, so labour is automatically valued in terms of consumption, and consumption in terms of labour.

c) The combination of these two properties of money is synergistic, so much so that they are rarely understood as separate. The consumer who has tens of thousands of paid-for items to choose from can also be and often is a paid-for labourer who has thousands of potential careers or employers. The producer may have to coordinate thousands or even millions of employers, customers, and suppliers. A government collects taxes on money paying for both labour and consumption and pays money to people in consideration of both their labour and their consumption. Overall, money simplifies and generally, although by no means always, clarifies many economic decisions.

d) Money works well in the ignorance of the human condition. It might seem that it would be more efficient and more just to rely on the direct and carefully arranged management of labour and consumption than on a tool marred by crudeness, unreality, and indirectness. These practical considerations were hardly on the mind of the 19th century socialists who condemned money as oppressive. They were thinking exclusively of some sort of symbol-money. However, during the First World War, the German government's thinking was resolutely practical when it constructed a command economy with extensive production and consumption quotas and relatively little reliance on money. When the new Soviet government copied that model in the nascent U.S.S.R., its motivations were both practical and ideological.

The German experiment did not have time to fail, but the Soviet experiment had the time, and it failed massively. No central planner, no matter how powerful her computers, can know enough about everything in the economy to always make correct decisions. No planner, no matter how wise, can persuade consumers and labourers that its decisions are better than the individuals' own monetary choices. No authority, no matter how thoughtful, can outguess all the imaginative ways that people and organisations spend their money to improve the workings of the Great Exchange.

e) Money is effective at translating economic decisions into economic actions. An imagined and stylised but still typical example might help explain this subtle property. A taxpayer in Columbus, Ohio says, "Thanks to the higher taxes we are paying this year, the government will have enough money to widen the highway from here to Cincinnati, but the higher payments mean that we can no longer quite afford the trip to Spain we were planning. I guess that will be rough on the tourism business in Barcelona." The monetary meaning of both changes is quite clear. An additional hundred dollars of taxes collected from a million separate taxpayers will pay for the labour and materials needed to build the road, while a collection of hundred-dollar spending cuts will reduce the number of holidays Ohioans take in Barcelona, and thus the money available to pay wages to the people there who take care of tourists. The loss of money is likely to lead to a decline in the number of people working in the Catalan tourist trade.

In the real economy, however, the transfer is far from obvious. The direct monetary transfer is certainly not mirrored in the real economy. Spanish airline pilots, hotel keepers, and tour guides who are surplus to the new requirements at home will not suddenly be heading to Jeffersonville, Ohio to take up newly created jobs pouring concrete. The actual shifts in the use and organisation of economic resources will be far more indirect and complex than the shift in spending. There will be two waves of economic and monetary changes, both small and both then getting smaller, as they ripple and dissipate through the two distant economies. One wave starts in Ohio, where new economic resources will be dedicated to highway reconstruction. Since the needed resources are not lying around totally idle, the new configuration of labour will alter some old configurations. Some workers must change their labour, some factories must change their production, and so forth. Each individual shift in labour and production leads to a collection of further, smaller adjustments. The Ohio-wave continues to spread until the changes are too diffuse and small to be identified. On the other side of the Atlantic, the Spanish-wave starts with the lost pay and jobs in the tourist trade. The displaced workers will look for employment in different places or in different parts of the economy, creating another set of smaller changes, and so forth until, once again, the changes are too diffuse and small to be identified.

The money system guides and encourages the real economic changes throughout both these two steadily spreading and diminishing waves. The system generally works very well. With remarkable speed a new balance of prices, wages, labour, and consumption is created in large swathes of the Great Exchange, including many parts which might seem to have no relation to either tourism or highway construction.

Of course, the money system cannot work miracles. No amount of tax revenues will allow the government to buy, say, highways that float freely in the air. Less fantastically, if the number of skilled highway construction workers in the world is insufficient to build all the highways that governments decide to build, then no amount of money can instantaneously turn tour guides into tamping equipment operators. Money can, however, gradually help bring the necessary changes in the Great Exchange. Money can be used to train new skilled highway construction workers.

f) Money's non-material nature allows limitless divisibility (there is no smallest unit of money) and total ubiquity (money can move at the speed of light throughout its domain). These monetary properties are beneficial for the operation of the Great Exchange. While the labour and objects that money pays for can only be divided to a limited extent, and often cannot be transported easily, money can, always in theory and increasingly in practice, be moved around almost instantaneously in as small units as desired.

The non-materiality brings numerous concrete economic advantages. With virtual money, there is no problem arranging for five people to share ownership of a single car, for five million people scattered around the world to share a financial relationship with a single enterprise, and for one person to transfer the equivalent consumption-value of three minutes or three milliseconds of her labour to a business, person, government, or charity thousands of kilometres away. The automatic divisibility of money also keeps transaction costs to a minimum. It costs almost nothing to divide a single wage, received for a unified offering of labour, into hundreds of tiny purchases of diverse consumption goods and services.

g) Money-numbers can have no real human meaning, since people are not numerical, but they still help people make decisions. Money helps consumers choose between similar goods and services by providing commensurate prices as a clear base for evaluating incommensurate qualitative comparisons. Money also aids comparisons of quite different types of labour and quite different consumption lifestyles.

h) Money can be spent anywhere it is accepted, facilitating monetary trade over long distances.

i) Shared money revenues and payrolls naturally tie together the labourers inside an organisation, supporting a sense of community.

j) Gifts of money are a remarkably simple way for people to transfer consumption from themselves to distant loved ones.

k) Money makes it relatively easy for people to move from place to place or job to job, to return defective or unwanted products, and to try new ones.

l) Money provides clear markers of status – salaries can be compared far more universally than lifestyles.

The genius of monetary allocation (balance)

Unlike command economies, money-based allocations are essentially self-balancing. With money, there is no need for a central authority to ensure that the desired labour is used, that all the production is consumed, and that promises of particular allocations can be kept. On the contrary, the basic structure of a money system inside the essentially balanced Great Exchange ensures that, at least in principle, everything produced is automatically consumed. The two-sided money system is fully aligned with the primitive, non-monetary fundamental equivalence of labour and consumption. In the monetary economy, this value-balance is maintained almost automatically. Because money circulates endlessly through the cycle of labour and consumption, the total quantity of wages and other payments to people as labourers is basically defined to be equal to the total quantity of prices and other payments by the same people as consumers.

A caution is required. The equivalence of pay for labour and paid-for goods and services is rough rather than exact, for reasons that I will discuss later in this chapter. The imperfections receive a great deal of attention from economists, but that attention easily obscures the overall power of the basic conceptual symmetry of labour and consumption and the resulting arithmetical symmetry of the money-numbers of wages and prices.

This fundamental equivalence should be the centre of economic analysis and the starting point of monetary analysis. Unfortunately, it is often slighted by economists. They are trained to think of "markets", the "places" where Smith's truck and barter take place, as the centre of economic activity. However, markets do not differentiate between labour and consumption. Indeed, they are often used to break the fundamental human tie of wages with prices (for example in the pricing of commodities and the justification of high profit margins). In effect, market-based analysis is fundamentally uneconomic, if economics is understood correctly as the study of the human activities of labour and consumption.

I will go through the monetary expression of fundamental economic equivalence with a minimal amount of algebra. Person A receives wages of x. She is probably unaware that the fundamental equivalence ensures that in her economy the total of all incomes, the sum of everyone's x, which I will call X, equals Y, the total value of all prices paid. Y is the sum of all the individual prices, each of which I will call y. Person A probably knows whether her income x is relatively high or low in her economy, but she need not think that her share of total wages is a specific, very small fraction, x

divided by X. She also knows that she pays a price, y, for each consumption good or service that she buys, and that the total money she personally spends on consumption, which I call y*, will be (roughly) equal to her income, x, but she does not have to worry that her share of total spending on consumption, y* divided by Y, is equal to x divided by X.

In other words, the system works without the need for any conscious knowledge of the actual fractions x/X and y*/Y. Each person's proportion of the economy's total wages (her own x/X) is necessarily identical to that person's proportion of prices paid (her own y*/Y). When the proportions on both sides of the economy are added up, the entirety of labour income has necessarily paid the entirety of the consumption prices.

These basic monetary facts can be represented in two equations:

$$\sum_{n=1}^{N} x_n = X = \sum_{m=1}^{M} y_m = \sum_{n=1}^{N} y_n^* = Y \quad (1)$$

$$\frac{x_n}{X} = \frac{y_n^*}{Y} \quad (2)$$

where N = number of paid labourers-consumers; x_n= wages of labourer n; M= number of consumption goods and services sold; y_m= price of item m; y_n^* = total consumption spending of consumer n.

The balances represented by these fundamental monetary equalities make a major contribution to one of the remarkable accomplishments of modern economies – the very extensive utilisation of the available resources of labour, raw materials, and productive capacity.

The genius of monetary allocation (flexibility)

Money systems are vastly more flexible than anything in the real economy – the production system, the skills of labourers, or the tastes of consumers. However money is used – as wages, prices, taxes, contributions, premiums, benefits, savings, or various types of financial money-flows (the last two are not actually money as tokens in the Great Exchange) – the amount of money paid or demanded for anything can be changed almost instantaneously. As I will discuss later, this quality of nearly unlimited flexibility even extends to the total available supply of money.

Monetary flexibility can create trouble, for example when sudden price increases unnecessarily deprive poor people of necessities. For the most part, though, the flexibility of money-numbers is a great aid to economic management, in particular to adjusting to the sort of changes I described in the tourism-to-construction example above. There are many reasons for adjustments, besides changes in production such as tourism-to-highways. There can be changes in technology or in the availability of raw stuff, for example crops and ores, from the semi-humanised world. The population alters constantly. Each labourer learns as she grows older and time brings an ever-shifting collection of labourers into the economy. Simultaneously, consumers change in age, tastes, and desires, while organisations and governments alter practices and rules.

In theory (always) and in practice (quite often), money-numbers change in response to all these economic shifts. There is a common pattern. The money-numbers will rise if something – whether labour, a raw material, an intermediate good, the supply available to consumers – becomes scarcer, either absolutely or relative to a change in the demand for the thing. They will fall if the supply of the thing becomes more abundant, especially relative to the desire to buy the thing. In theory (always) and in practice (fairly often), people change their behaviour in response to the changed money values. The behavioural changes, which can be in several directions, help to bring production and consumption back into balance. Suppose the cost of producing beef stays the same but the price of beef rises relative to other prices. That is a sign for everyone that there was probably something like a shortage at the old price. The higher price might end the scarcity by dissuading less keen or poorer potential purchasers from buying beef. Alternatively or in addition, a higher price might also both encourage beef producers to increase their supply and provide them with at least some of the money needed to pay for additional livestock, feed, and barns. The same higher price might also encourage consumers to buy more pork as a substitute for beef, creating an increase in demand that could also increase the price of pork and induce more pork production. The chain of interactions of prices and real economic behaviour continues until the whole paid-for economy is once again working at as full capacity as possible. X (total wages) once again equals Y (total spending on consumption).

The monetary push towards what economists call equilibrium, or the balance of supply and demand, rarely works as smoothly as might be suggested by the idealised examples that I have presented in this section, of more highway construction and less tourism and of higher beef prices and less beef consumption or more beef and pork production. This money-tool is powerful and flexible, but its workings are far from mechanical or "perfect" (a word that is central to naïve neoclassical models of supply and demand). The limitations to the balancing effects of money-numbers spring largely from the many uses of these quantitative tools. Sometimes changes in money-numbers express social, political, and economic power-relations. Sometimes the changes are caused by shifts in laws, regulations, and psychological factors. Sometimes, the people who decide on prices and wages choose to limit the flexibility of money-numbers or to prevent changes in one money-number from influencing either other money-numbers or the quantities or quality of production. For example, producers may simply pocket the gains from higher beef prices as profits, that is (roughly speaking) revenue in excess of wages and other operating costs. More generally, producers sometimes fail to change prices when real economic imbalances suggest they should, and sometimes they do change them without any justification related to shortages or excesses at the current price.

Even when price changes are informative, their message is often cryptic. One producer cannot always tell whether the ability to charge a higher price is the economy's way of asking for more production, the economy's way of saying that production is becoming more expensive for other suppliers, or just a sign that the old balance between the overall supply of money and the total supply of paid-for items has been lost.

These qualifications to the reality and usefulness of monetary flexibility are significant, but they should not be exaggerated. Not only is the money system far more helpfully flexible than any alternative system of labour allocation, consumption distribution, and generalised information-transfer could be, but price changes provide helpful information cheaply, without any need for additional analytic labour.

Four complications

I have drawn what I hope is an appealingly simple picture of the splendour of the monetary system. Much of the rest of this chapter is dedicated to making it more complicated, and perhaps a bit less splendid. To start, I will list four ways in which the use of money either apparently or actually does not precisely mirror activity in the Great Exchange.

Paying for things instead of paying people: I have emphasised that the economy, the Great Exchange, is a two-sided *human* activity. If money is, as I claim, a useful token in this human interchange, then it should be essentially human and totally economic, a tool used only by and for people and only to pay for labour and consumption. My definition would be violated by the existence of other sorts of payments: payments to people but not for labour and consumption or payments for things other than those that are consumed. In fact, many transfers of money – perhaps most transactions – appear to violate the definition. Taxes, benefits, and other monetary transfers are almost defined by their disconnection from wages (of labour) and prices (of consumption). Also, producer organisations buy things all the time from other producer organisations, things that are not consumed by individual people but are put to further use in the process of production.

The numerous exceptions do not actually violate or invalidate the human-centred definition. The government's money is all ultimately generated by the economic activity – by labour and consumption – in the paid-for (monetary) economy. The government merely extracts and then distributes some of the money going around the cycle of the Great Exchange. A significant portion of the benefits that it pays out can be considered wages for labour of care that would otherwise be unpaid, but that consideration is not required to see that the governments' transfer systems are inseparable from the money-cycle of labour and consumption. The same unity of transfer and Great Exchange is essential to all other transfers, from car insurance to protection rackets, from religious donations to lotteries. As is fitting for these essentially social activities undertaken by individuals, the final monetary allocations to individuals are determined by a social as well as an individual logic.

The human connection is more hidden when producer organisations buy components or some other non-human thing from other producer organisations. Even then, though, the monetary detachment from the human Great Exchange is only apparent. The monetary exchanges of producer organisations are not essentially money-for-things. They are summaries and simplifications of numerous payments for labour. More precisely, the always instantaneous money flows to and from people are temporarily *congealed* in things during the course of production of consumption goods and services. (I am using the word from (Marx, 2009), but not its Marxist symbol-money interpretation.) The congealed labour of "raw" materials, components, and partially finished products can be called production-things. (The scare-quotes on "raw" are a reminder that these materials are only raw relative to their further treatment – they have already been humanised through the labour of extraction or harvesting.)

The process of monetising production-things runs in parallel with the process of combining the numerous labours of production. The chains of production, which run from the non-humanised world to the final consumable product are typically divided by numerous pricing-points. At the initial imposition of a monetary value, the price of this first production-thing is, in rough terms, the sum of all the wages that were paid to make it. In both economic and monetary terms, the production-thing can be described as the labour that is congealed in it. The pattern continues recursively through all subsequent pricing-points. The price of each production-thing represents, still in very rough terms, the total prices of the relevant production-things at their last pricing-points, plus the subsequent wages of the labour involved in transforming or combining those production-things. As the chains of production advance, the production-things add more layers of congealed labour, both economically and in their prices.

An example might help clarify my meaning. A car is a material thing produced from numerous types of labour and numerous things taken from the non-humanised world. The production of cars typically involves thousands of pricing points, as suppliers sell production-things to other suppliers further along the chain of production. When the consumer finally pays for the car, she is basically paying for all the many types of labour along the chain of production. She pays for the labour used to extract the ore made into steel made into the engine block, the labour used to collect the silica made into glass made into windows, and so forth for scores of raw materials and thousands of intermediate production-things. The consumer is also paying for some portion of the labour used to construct the various tools needed in the various stages of production, from the milling machines dedicated to producing car parts to the roads on which inventory is transported, as well as some portion of the labour used to provide services such as design and human resources management. All these labour costs are accumulated or congealed over the various chains of production through numerous apparently money-for-thing money-flows.

The producer organisations along the many contributing chains of production often debate about which organisation should pay for what. The disputes can be lively, but they do not remove the essentially human nature of monetary transactions. The monetary exchanges all ultimately mirror, mediate, or modulate the human action of the Great Exchange. In the simplest terms, almost all the wages paid to labourers are eventually paid for by consumers and almost all the money paid by consumers eventually goes to labourers.

Money-things: In monetary terms, production-things are basically temporarily congealed labour. In them, the monetary cycle which mirrors the unbroken Great Exchange is paused but not fundamentally altered. However, sometimes money does leave the Great Exchange entirely, when it is placed in some "receptacle" from which it can potentially be removed and put back into the Exchange. I will have much more to say about the various types of these "money-things", from loans and land to shares and savings accounts.

Governments: In modern economies, the political authorities and their agencies play three distinct monetary roles. In all of them, the money-flows can appear to be distant from the Great Exchange. The appearances are largely deceptive.

One governmental monetary role is the production and distribution of certain goods and services. They do this in two essentially different ways. When state-controlled producer organisations sell their products at prices that are close to the total cost of the wages congealed in those wares, then the government is, in monetary terms, not substantially different from "private" companies producing the same items. Such businesses can be and often have been "privatised" without significant changes in their operations. They need no special monetary attention.

Such attention is required for the other type of governmental money-flows. These concern the organisations that provide numerous consumption services and goods at no or low monetary cost to the actual consumers. Most notably, residents of developed economies expect to pay nothing or next to nothing directly for their government's provision of armed forces, police services, healthcare, education, roads, and various types of parks and recreation. This free and cheap consumption is quite expensive. In rich countries, the governments pay, directly and indirectly, about a fifth of all wages.

How does this work? As the wage bill demonstrates, the rewards for current and congealed labour are fully in the paid-for economy. Labourers receive normal money-wages and suppliers are paid normal money-prices. On the side of consumption, however, the operations are not at all or not fully monetary, since consumers pay nothing or relatively little for the goods and services that they receive. Money collected as taxes is used to close the inevitable monetary gap.

Those taxes are part of the government's second monetary role: the collection of money from the governed and the distribution (or redistribution) of money to them. The monetary distributions, which I will call benefits, go to the old, the ill, the young, and the unemployed, and to any other individuals, groups, and organisations that are deemed worthy of the government's monetary support. As the length of the list suggests, benefits systems are now significant parts of paid-for economies. In rich countries, governments distribute about as much money in benefits as they pay out in wages and purchases.

In every country, the purely monetary governmental transfer-system supplements and interacts with the non-governmental wage-price system, but the two systems follow different "logics". Roughly speaking, the transfer-system calibrates payments to need, justice, and the common good, while the wage-price system aims to promote efficiency by rewarding skill, effort, and status. The description and analysis of these logics are important for understanding the operations and interactions of economies and societies, but the social-economic reasoning is irrelevant to money and finance, the subjects of this book. What is relevant is the possibility that the giant governmental money-transfer systems, along with the indirect payments for government-provided services and goods, threaten or even invalidate my claim that there is a fundamental monetary equivalence of wages and prices in the paid-for economy.

In other words, does the government's monetary role distort my basic economic picture of mirroring equivalences, between prices and wages in the paid-for economy and labour and consumption in the Great Exchange itself? A distortion would not discredit my paradigm (remember that paradigms can always deal with apparent exceptions and deviations), but it would create some difficulties.

Fortunately for my understanding, the governmental flows of money actually only break the wage-price balance in a trivial way, by removing the perfect equivalence of wages and prices that is found in my first equation and that would be found in some hypothetical government-free world. In the real world, the equivalence is merely changed: to post-governmental wages with post-governmental prices. In other words, total wages, calculated after-tax and after-benefit, equal total prices, also calculated after-tax and after-benefits. This equivalence holds for individuals, for companies, and for the economy as a whole.

Since government benefits can sometimes be described as either additions to income or reductions of prices, the exact counts of government-adjusted wages and prices will always be subject to debate. That imprecision might embolden critics of my approach. They could also object that I am confusing benefits with wages. I would counter that the debates about classification are trivial and that government benefits are best understood as quasi-wages which are paid to compensate people for their otherwise unpaid labours of care and being. I find such controversies interesting, but they are irrelevant to the central monetary and human equivalence: the money received in return for labour equals the money paid out for the fruits of labour (consumption goods and services).

As I have said, the equivalence is rough. The deviations are important (they will be discussed later in this chapter), but they do not change the basic picture of money moving around the labour-consumption circle. The consideration of government merely adds a complication to this endless circular flow, turning the primal wage-price circle into a post-governmental wage-price circle. My first balancing equation can easily be modified to include this complication:

$$\sum_{n=1}^{N} x_n + g_n = X = \sum_{m=1}^{M} y_m + g'_n = \sum_{n=1}^{N} y_n^* = Y \quad (3)$$

Where g_n is the tax flow between government and labourer x (e.g. income taxes and pension payments) and g'_n is the tax flow between government and consumers (e.g. sales taxes and subsidies).

The final interaction of government and money is quite different from the previous two. Those are both *within* the monetary system, but governments also operate so to speak *above* the system. More precisely, in modern economies governments are ultimately responsible for the operation *of* the money-system. Governments often delegate the actual management to other entities. In particular, banks are currently responsible for most of the creation and destruction of money in the Great Exchange and for ensuring that the money, old and new, moves smoothly around the middle section of the Triptych.

Other redistributive intermediaries: Other organisations have distributive or redistributive monetary characteristics that are similar to those of governments. Some charities receive money donations from some people and make money payments to others. Insurers take small amounts of money from a large number of people and give large amounts of money to a small number of people. Lotteries and other gambling operations, gangs, and religious groups also do something similar, with various justifications.

The non-wage, non-price monetary transfers between organisations are complemented by similar transfers between individuals. People sometimes give money directly to family members, friends, or other people whom they judge to be worthy. Less generously, people sometimes agree to make and receive monetary payments as part of inter-personal financial arrangements. All these individual payments, like the organisationally mediated ones, are ultimately part of the Great Exchange. After they are taken into account, payments for labour, now including governmental and private transfers, still equal payments for the fruits of labour, now including governmental and private transfers. These non-governmental payments can easily be added to the already modified fundamental equation:

$$\sum_{n=1}^{N} x_n + g_n + p_n = X = \sum_{m=1}^{M} y_m + g'_n = \sum_{n=1}^{N} y_n^* = Y \ (4)$$

Where p_n is the non-wage and non-tax money flow of labourer x.

Theories of steady monetary value

I have said that money provides useful but necessarily untrue measures in the essentially non-measurable economic life of labour and consumption. Money-numbers are quite different from measures such as yards of cloth, degrees of temperature or numbers of people. All of these have a clear and concrete meaning, because they are tied to something definite and genuinely measurable in the physical world. Money measures can have no such objective correlatives, because economic activity cannot be reduced to quantitative units. Money-numbers are definitely related to and vaguely correlated with the real things of actual labour and actual consumption, but no numbers can have a firm or consistent relationship with non-numerical human activities.

The lack of a close real anchor leaves money somewhat adrift. Tautologically, one euro is always worth one euro, but the euro's value in terms of actual labour and consumption is necessarily somewhere in the range between inconstant and incoherent. The same euro will always pay for different collections of labour and consumption at the same time in different places and at different times in the same place.

This indeterminacy can be disconcerting for economic actors. For many of the economists who believe that money is the essential unit of economic analysis, the indeterminacy is worse than disconcerting. It is a professional embarrassment. To them, it just seems wrong that economic things cannot be measured meaningfully in precise monetary terms and that money cannot be valued consistently in economic terms. These economists would much prefer that actual paid wages and prices, the declared monetary "exchange values" of paid-for labour and consumption goods and services, were in some way based on a true numerical value that was in some way built into the real economy, or perhaps into the psychology of consumers or labourers.

Indeed, economists do more than wish for consistent values. They typically attribute a real value to money-numbers that is based on *something* consistent and quantifiable. The nature of that "something" has been hotly debated. I identify five leading proposals.

Gold and taxes: The first and most traditional approach, introduced as false in Chapter One, is to claim that money has a consistent value in itself. The value is created by the gold or other precious material which the money either contains or for which it can, at least in theory, be exchanged. In this understanding, money has no human meaning at all. Rather, human economic activities have a monetary meaning, as do all money-things, exactly because they can be exchanged for money. In this approach, money is not considered to be essentially or merely a token used in some parts of the Great Exchange. Rather, it is supposed to be a commodity which is exchanged, and which can be saved just as well as spent.

There are practical problems with this idea. The available quantities of gold, silver and the like cannot be divided finely enough to provide a useful token, especially if large quantities of the precious material are saved, taking them out of the Great Exchange. To compensate, something else must be actually used as money, typically paper or ledger numbers. The ersatz-money comes with an unreliable promise of convertibility to real "hard money". Looked at realistically, such "gold standards" are merely polite fictions. Economists have also suggested alternative, more readily available "backings" for hard money, in particular future tax receipts and loans which create new money. These have the opposite practical weakness – their supply is too large and uncertain to provide a solid value.

These practical problems are substantial, but the conceptual weakness of the commodity money theory – the assumption that money can and should be separated from economic activity – is even more serious. In effect, the economy is treated as a servant of money rather than keeping money in its proper place as a servant of the necessarily human economic good. Commodity-money is not necessarily cruel, but it becomes so when the constraints on its supply distort or limit economic activity. In 1896, the United States Presidential candidate William Jennings Bryan was basically right to call for an end to the Gold Standard that impoverished indebted farmers and debtors by limiting the supply of money. In his stirring words, "You shall not press down upon the brow of labour this crown of thorns. You shall not crucify mankind upon a cross of gold" (Bryan, 1896).

Labour value: The most plausible claimed objective standard for monetary value is as a measure of accumulated labour-time. As discussed earlier, the approach is alluring. Labour-value can in some ways be approximated by time, time can be measured directly and objectively, and time spent is certainly one of the ways people evaluate their lives of labour. However, time-spent is far from the only way in which people and societies value labour, so labour-hours cannot serve as a standard for monetary value.

"Real" money: I mentioned in Chapter One that economists have created a quasi-monetary unit which they claim has a constant, objective value. With great professional hubris, they give the name "real" money, as in Real Gross Domestic Product, to this bundle of dubious assumptions and inappropriate simplifications. The "real" quasi-money measure can be useful for specific purposes. However, it is far too rigid and arbitrary to be considered a comprehensive or objective measure of the real (as compared to the "real") economy.

Barter-money: Economists often speak dreamily of past societies in which there was trade but no money. Such societies are mere thought experiments about a world of "once upon a time", since in real history pre-monetary economies traded little and their rare exchanges of goods were far more marked by ritual than by numerical calculations. In this narrative, commodity-money is merely a simplification of an otherwise endless collection of transitive exchange values. Money becomes the middle term of all exchanges: Pears are no longer exchanged for nails, but for money, and money is then used to buy nails. Money could be made of anything, but the tired-of-barter money-inventors always choose something fairly compact and quite rare – usually silver or gold.

The barter-replacement narrative of money is highly individualistic. Individual agreements guide the creation of all money and set all money-prices. This trade-money has no social guardian, no total balance, and no ambiguity. That independence from authority may appeal to many economists, but the barter explanation of the nature of money is unhelpful, incoherent, and incomplete. It is unhelpful because the assumption that exchanges of real or abstract commodities sit at the base of money-numbers adds no information to the very limited information contained in relative prices described as portions of the total supply of money. It is incoherent because as soon as money enters into the putative barter-economy, the absolute prices depend on the supply of money, so the supposed barter-history is immediately irrelevant to the workings and values of the money system. It is incomplete because individual commodity exchange ratios do not capture the systematic mutual causality of monetary values – prices influence wages and wages influence prices.

Utility: For almost two centuries, many economists have postulated that quantities of money are somehow related to quantities of what they consider to be the crucial, universal, and subjective good of the human condition. This putative non-monetary but money-related quantitative good has been given several names, including happiness, pleasure, and utility. The last is most favoured by economists, who rarely claim that money is the sole key to all sorts of human happiness or pleasure. However, they do believe that there is a correspondence between money-numbers and units of the putative utility, and that this correspondence holds throughout the economic realm (which for them is basically the realm of money). In the partial-equilibrium model that is at the conceptual heart of neoclassical microeconomics, the price of anything is set at the point that demand, which is expressed as the expected utility at a given price, intersects with supply, which is assumed to increase in a fairly steady way as the price increases.

The basic intuition behind this model, that earning or spending more money is always better than earning or spending less money, is certainly not always true, but it at least is more or less plausible, all things being equal. Economists, however, generally assume far more than a rough and general correspondence between utility and money. The model implies that actual wages and prices provide a fairly accurate index of relative utility. With a few additional implausible assumptions (these pile up quickly in neoclassical models), the correspondence between money and utility turns out to be monotonic. In other words, the degree of difference in prices or wages represents exactly the degree of difference in the utility provided. For example, if one item costs a third more than another, the first item must provide a third more utility.

Utility is much loved by economists, especially when they are teaching introductory courses, but it cannot actually add any solidity to the value of money. Even if a numerical scale of utility did exist and even if utility could be measured by some money-dependent formula – two highly implausible possibilities – the actual, real units of money spent could not be translated into consistent units of utility. That transformation would have to rely on the artificial "real" units that I just discussed. The putative translation into utility would only add another layer of arbitrary or imaginary adjustments to the original, unquestionably observable but undoubtedly inconstant monetary measure.

What money-numbers do mean

I have just effectively dismissed five suggested precise meanings of money-numbers: the commodity value of gold or something somewhat like it, the labour value of labour-hours (or labour power), an objective value standardised by "real" adjustments, the exchange value of barter-based appraisals, and the subjective value of utility. My negativity may sound unlimited, but I do recognise that money-numbers must mean *something*. They cannot be picked out of thin air or assigned randomly. They are, rather, given to things and actions by people, who always have reasons for such choices. There must, then, be reasons for assigning particular numbers to each otherwise non-numerical or not obviously numerical economic act (of labour or consumption). So, what do money-numbers mean in general? And what does any particular money-number tell us?

The answer to both questions is simple but frustrating. The meaning of every money-number is a highly variable agglomeration of some or all of the totalising meanings that I just dismissed, and perhaps of other meanings that I have not considered. Money-numbers are indeed meaningful, but their precise, true meaning can never be determined, because there are too many shifting forces at work, on each one of them and on the entire collection of them, to permit anything more than the roughest interpretation. In mathematical language, there are always simply too many variables for any causal equations of meaning to be solvable.

Consider, for example, how a particular employee's wage is established. The number relies on numerous comparisons, motivations, and interactions. The assumed or desired social status of the position, the pay of comparable workers, the employer's competitive position and pricing flexibility, the psychological situation of employer's managers and of the employee, the cost of living where the employee lives, the levels of taxes and benefits, the family situation of the employee, the general business environment, the sense of fairness and justice of both employer and employee, the availability of money in the monetary system, the system of taxes and benefits, and a collection of legal requirements – all these and probably other factors play a role in setting each and every wage in modern economies. The process is similar for setting prices, with the additional considerations involved in establishing profits. Taxes are also money-numbers, and their determination is also extremely complex, with the addition of politics and, it might be hoped, an extra dose of ethical considerations.

In addition to all this, it is impossible to know exactly what should be or is paid for in any particular money-number. Consider a mobile phone. Should or does the price include some of the wages paid for the labour of the engineers and teachers who maintain the intellectual infrastructure which supports the sophisticated technology, or a fee to the governments and companies which create the physical infrastructure that makes the phones useful? Alternatively, should telephones be relatively inexpensive and university tuition fees and taxes relatively expensive?

Or consider a car. As it stands, the price includes the car itself, a contribution to the cost of some car-related activities from research to lobbying, and the first few years of specified repairs. That choice is arbitrary. There is, for example, a good argument that what is being purchased is the privilege of using the entire automotive transportation complex. In that case, the most appropriate price might be an annual usage fee, which paid not only for manufacturing the car but also for keeping the road and fuel delivery systems in order.

A question that is relevant to finance is whether the price of anything should include a contribution to the payments needed to maintain or increase total production. A question that is relevant to public policy is where in the price-wage-tax system to assign the payments needed to provide such public services as pollution abatement, medical care, and law enforcement. There are no true or false answers to such questions. There are only answers which have emerged over time, generally through some combination of social choices and historic accidents, and which shift over time, for reasons that are sometimes clear and sometimes hard to fathom.

The merits of various choices of how to allocate costs and benefits in the money-system is beyond the scope of this book, but the practical conclusion is simple and clear. Any division of the seamless web of the economy is arbitrary. Economists recognise the seriousness of the issue in their discussions of internalising positive and negative externalities. However, the division between internal and external implied in their category of "externalities" is misleading. There is no clear boundary between what is included in a thing and what is external to it.

In sum, so much is going on that all money-numbers are surrounded by an ineradicable uncertainty. They can have no clear economic meaning.

The fog of ambiguity limits but does not eliminate the usefulness of discussions of *fair or just prices and wages*. This concept has been dear to some Christian thinkers and many Socialists. They reason that since money-numbers are set by human decisions, which always aim at some good or goods, it is appropriate for them to aim at the good of justice. It is then also appropriate to criticise particular money-numbers for failing to reach that target. The good intentions cannot cover up the fundamental flaw in the argument. A particular money-number cannot be either just or unjust absolutely.

Consider two fairly uncontroversial understandings of economic injustice. If enough food is available in the real economy for everyone to have a well-balanced diet, it is unjust if the relevant part of the money-system, the combination of food prices with food-buyers' wages and monetary benefits, does not allocate everyone enough to eat, after considering the access to food acquired without money. Similarly, if there is not quite enough food to go around, money-numbers that end up allocating an excess to some and a severe deficiency to others are unjust.

In either situation, what is unjust is not the price of food, the wages of the hungry, the lack of access to gardens for grow-your-own, or the inadequacy of government payments to farmers or consumers. What is unjust is the situation: the unnecessarily inadequate food allocated to some people. The situation would be unjust if wages were higher but prices were also higher. Conversely, even lower wages or even higher prices could be just, if government programmes ensured the distribution of adequate food to everyone. Single prices and wages cannot be judged as just or unjust, because moral judgements require the analysis of the results of a fairly large collection of money-numbers, plus an analysis of any relevant non-monetary economic arrangements.

Of course, some money-numbers may be so extreme that they are unlikely to be part of a just economic arrangement. However, the morality is still located only in the real arrangements of the Great Exchange. The numbers themselves are essentially morally neutral tools. They can be judged for their efficiency in achieving particular results, but not for their intrinsic justice.

More generally, any effort to solidify the value of money and to give a single clear meaning to money-numbers will be unsuccessful. The problem is fundament: the whole quest is based on a false understanding of the nature of money. Money is *not* a measure of value, whether subjective or objective. It is *not* a clear reference to a specific part of the real world. It is a simple tool, really a simplistic, oversimplifying tool that happens to be enormously useful. It is a device that helps people organise their economic lives and helps each society organise its economy in accord with its will. (I will not try to answer the very pertinent questions of who speaks for a "society" and how this "society" wills and decides.) Money is a crude tool that attaches numbers to things and to relations that cannot actually be quantified. There is no reason to expect such a tool to provide any sort of absolute, timeless, or true knowledge.

Once this understanding of money has been fully absorbed, it is clear that the intense and arcane debate among economists over what sort of value prices and wages actually represent – use value, exchange value, equilibrium value, or some adjusted labour value – is almost totally pointless. Various prices and wages certainly bear some relation to some or all of these claimed values at some times, but the essential purpose of the money system is not to represent or express any sort of consistent values. It is to help the Great Exchange operate smoothly and efficiently.

Of course, to see money as an arbitrary tool two mental steps are necessary: to stop thinking that money is at the centre of economics and to recognise that the actual economy is simply not susceptible to the kind of meaningful numerical scaling that money appears to offer. Economists, in my experience of them, find both these steps very difficult to take. I claim that the effort to suspend and then abandon the numerical paradigm is worth making, because it will enable economists to see that economic numbers often hide more than they reveal.

Adding information to money

Money is flexible, efficient, consistent, and informative, but the information it gives is limited. Money-numbers (prices, wages, taxes, and so forth) are just numbers. They cannot provide any details about what was paid for, when and where transactions took place, or the identity of either the spender or the recipient of money. They can neither tell tax authorities about the taxes that are or should be connected to particular payments, nor help merchants and producers follow individual customers, nor inform the police and political authorities about potentially criminal or insurrectionist purchases.

These inabilities are unavoidable, because money is in its nature or essence an anonymous and uniform commodity. However, money can only exist in some material form: as a coin, note, cheque, or electronic record. All those forms are individuated – each euro note or coin is unique, as is each cheque and every entry on an electronic register of money-flows. The individual bits of money can carry various types of information. In particular, the records attached to electronic transactions can be very thorough.

This information has become more readily available and more widely used as the costs of all data processing – including the monitoring, aggregating, and searching of bank data – have fallen. The most visible manifestation of this use of money's information is the rise of "cashless" transactions, for which banks routinely approve, execute, and register all the details, and do so more quickly and accurately than cashiers can deal with payments in notes and coins. Central monetary authorities want to advance this trend further by introducing government-issued "digital currencies". At least conceivably, these could connect transactions directly to the people who make them, rather than, as happens now, to their bank accounts.

Since essences are unchanging by definition, the essence of money is not changed by attaching information to it. However, when essentially anonymous money becomes inseparable from a large packet of information, then a new thing has been created with its own compound nature. This compound of information and money, informing-money, has many benefits, relative to plain money. Informing-money adds convenience and discourages fraud by allowing banks, and perhaps eventually governments, to keep detailed track of the spending of people and organisations. Money-users can also watch their account balances.

However, some applications of informing-money are more controversial. Many advocates of privacy are opposed to banks selling their monetary information. Critics of manipulative business practices do not want the information in informing-money to be used to attract and evaluate actual and potential customers. Perhaps most significantly, the prospect of controls that limit politically unacceptable transactions frightens and angers actual and potential dissidents, as well as believers in the goodness of various sorts of commercial and political freedom.

For some economists, there is a painful irony in such possibilities. In particular, the mid-20th century Austrian economist Friedrich Hayek warmly praised the price system for providing enough information to allow the economy to function well without any stifling central controls (Hayek, 1945). In his thinking, economic centralisation was a significant and dangerous step on the road to political enslavement. Hayek would be appalled to find that the technological progress which he generally welcomed could lead to a money-system in which his cherished indications of supply and demand cannot be separated from a useful tool for the authoritarian governments that he dreaded. If the fears of Hayek are even halfway justified, then money as a source of political oppression could easily become a 25th social meaning.

4. The Triptych

The institution of money is set in both the economy, the Great Exchange of labour and consumption in the world, and society, the network of institutions which guide social relations. In modern economies, money plays a crucial role, but it is only one crucial institution on a long list. It is certainly no more important than what might be called the Republic of Technology (which expands the vast store of modern knowledge and keeps it readily available), the factory system of mass and skilled production (which translates that knowledge into consumption goods), the legal, administrative, and regulatory bureaucracies that are both effective and extensive (which establish goals and keep order in numerous dimensions of the economy), the government-guided and government-mandated systems for managing incomes (which make possible the massiveness of mass production), and limited and regulated competition (which spurs innovation and combats self-serving lethargy). In modern societies, the institution of money plays a very important but probably not crucial role. It is generally subservient to such institutions as political systems, class relationships, family structures, and the not terribly monetary healthcare and education complexes.

In this section, I will place money in these two contexts, economic and social. My guide is a simple tripartite division, which is illustrated in the following diagram. It is important enough for my argument that its name, the Triptych, is capitalised and its three sections are identified throughout this book simply by their location in the illustration: left, middle and right.

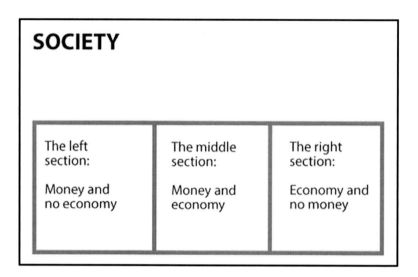

The left section of the Triptych represents the social uses of money, those that take place outside of the Great Exchange of labour and consumption. (I will have a great deal to say about how or whether this money, used outside of the economy, is "money" in the same sense as the money used to modulate or mediate parts of the Great Exchange.) The middle section is where money is used as the prime mediator of that Exchange. It is populated by all paid-for labour and paid-for consumption and includes many taxes and other non-price, non-thing payments. Finally, the right section represents the part of the Great Exchange in which the institution of money is not directly present. All three sections are set entirely within the larger rectangle of society. The Triptych can also be portrayed as a Venn Diagram, seen below, with one oblong including all uses of money and the other including all the actions, paid-for or not, in the Great Exchange. The space of intersection is the paid-for economy, the middle section of the Triptych. I have chosen to refer to the Triptych, because that image emphases the borders between the sections, which are very important in understanding the nature of finance. It is also less likely to lead to the inaccurate idea that money is much the same inside and outside of the Great Exchange. On the other hand, it loses the Venn Diagram's clarity in showing the unity of the economic activity in the paid-for middle and the unpaid-for right sections.

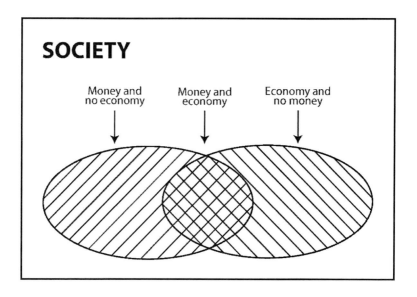

The relative sizes of the three sections in the illustrations of the Triptych and Diagram are not meant to be indicative of their relative importance. Indeed, the right section cannot be measured at all, and neither of the other two sections can be quantified meaningfully by any non-monetary measure. The left and middle sections are both clearly numerical, but whether their money-numbers are truly commensurate turns out to be a non-trivial question. Still, while quantification of the sections is impossible, a rough impression is possible. I would say that economists almost invariably overestimate the importance of the middle section, too often misunderstand the nature, and exaggerate the importance, of the left, and pay far too little attention to the right.

The left section (non-economic money)

The money of the left section, money which has no correlative in the Great Exchange, has already been mentioned several times. Here I will summarise and unify the explanations, starting with the introduction of a specialised vocabulary. When writing about pre-modern economies (by which I mean pre-industrial), I usually call the money held in and exchanged within that section "treasure-money". In modern economies, the monetary and near-monetary "treasures" are typically intangible and the "treasuries" which hold them are often legal claims rather than physical spaces. In respect for this transition, *savings-money* is my name for the modern form of this non-economic money in the Triptych's left-section.

In principle, treasure-money or savings-money can always be converted into the monetary tokens used in the middle section. That potential is why savings-money is commonly considered to be actual money or near-money. In modern economies, there is generally a fairly lively two-way flow between savings-money and the money in the real economy. The latter, however, is the only real money, according to my definition of money as an economic tool, because only the money used in the middle section is actually and directly relevant to the Great Exchange. For the sake of clarity, however, I will refer specifically to *token-money* when the difference between the circulating money in the paid-for economy and economically inert savings-money is relevant.

Along with the savings-money, the left section also contains the physical and conceptual repositories in which this potential and past token-money is stored. The different types of pre-modern treasure-money were often stored in a literal treasury, but the meaning of that word has shifted along with the shifts of the typical forms of savings-money. I give all those different containers for savings-money a common name: the ugly but clear neologism of *money-things*. (Money-things should not be confused with money-numbers. The things are all in the left section of the Triptych, while the numbers are in both the middle and the left sections.)

This new monetary vocabulary may confuse some readers. It is designed, however, with exactly the opposite intention – to mark clearly a distinction that is blurred over in such standard monetary categories as "savings", "real assets" and "financial assets". I am trying to bring out the monetary border-line that divides the left from the middle section of the Triptych. On one side of the border, in the middle section, the money is token-money, the numerical tool which helps organise, allocate, and socially place the economic activities of labour and consumption. On the other side of the border, in the left section, the money is the non-economic savings-money, which has various actual social "meanings" and various potential economic powers that I will discuss in this section throughout the rest of the book. Expressed differently, I am drawing a line between the monetary aspects of a particular economy's Great Exchange and the monetary aspects of the legal, social, and cultural arrangements in which that economy is embedded.

The stark difference is worth reiterating. Token-money is primarily used to make payments that are directly or indirectly dependent on the economic activities of labour and consumption. In contrast, savings-money *never* pays for labour and consumption. It can usually be moved across the border of the Triptych into the middle section, in which case it is converted into token-money. However, as long as it remains in the left section, it cannot buy labour or consumption. It can only bring psychological satisfaction, economic and political power, potential future consumption, and legally valid claims on steady flows of other people's token-money, in the form of rents, interest payments and dividends.

The last, the claims on other people's token-money, are at the core of finance, but savings-money is not always used in the financial system. In its simplest form, savings-money is nothing more than token-money rendered inert by being removed from the Great Exchange. Traditional treasuries often held economically inert coins, as did mattresses, piggy-banks, and other receptacles. The modern equivalents to this neutered token-money are banknotes held in a safe place and the far more typical balances held in bank savings accounts. The account is a money-thing and its value is a quantity of savings-money.

Economically inert coins were not the only type of money-thing in pre-modern economies. On the contrary, treasure-money was commonly held in non-monetary form – the ingots, artworks, and jewels mentioned in the first section of this chapter. These treasures primarily served social purposes: to demonstrate such perceived goods as the nation's grandeur, the favour received by the ruler from the gods, or the dedication of the people to the divine powers. Only secondarily were these treasures viewed as "money", i.e. as potential token-money. Indeed, while they were in fact a store of value which could be "cashed in" (otherwise they would not be money in any sense), the reconversion from treasure to token was typically undesired and relatively infrequent.

Stored coins hardly feature as modern savings-money, but jewels, jewellery, and other precious objects are still part of some people's collections of money-things (generally known as portfolios). Of the pre-modern treasures, gold is the one which has passed most thoroughly into the era of money-things. Many governments keep supplies of it, perhaps in a lingering confusion about the nature of money or maybe as a signal of some sort of political solidity. Some individuals also own gold, often in a lingering confusion about the nature of money. Artworks without any precious materials have been added to the list of tangible and economically non-functional money-things owned by individuals, as has a motley list of collectibles and so-called antiques. Comic books, playing cards and miscellaneous bric-a-brac which were once useless old junk are now sometimes treated as money-things.

The current price of most money-things can be estimated with reasonable precision. (Since they are mostly quite distant from the real economy, they are to some extent exempt from the precisionist-consistency fallacy.) National inventories of money-things suggest that the entertaining new categories account for a small portion of the total value of tangible money-things. Land, or more precisely the ownership claim on physical land, remains pre-eminent in that category. Confusingly, this important type of money thing is almost never solely a money-thing. The land, which is part of the non-humanised world, cannot be separated from the labours of humanisation that allow the land to hold buildings, roads, and other elements in the Great Exchange. Conceptually, the price paid of any parcel of land includes both savings-money that pays for the land itself and token-money that compensates for the improvements on the land. In practice, the division between the two types of money is difficult to determine, a difficulty that contributes to the border problems in one currency that I will discuss a little later. There are similarly difficult and potentially problematic divisions between token-money and savings-money in the prices of commodities such as oil, wheat, and gold.

Land has been a money-thing for as long as it could be bought and sold (actually not that long in many societies), but in industrial economies land has lost significance relative to intangible money-things. I have already mentioned one of them, simple bank account balances. More significant, both in absolute quantity and in economic influence, are financial money-things. Finance is the subject of much of the rest of the book, so here I will only point out that all financial "securities" (stocks or shares, bonds and loans, derivative securities, etc.) are money-things, but not all money-things are financial.

Before leaving this brief introduction to the left section of the Triptych, I will make two general comments. First, the rules and nature of token-money have to be quite different from those of money-things, because the two types of money have such different relations to the economy. The ties of anything in the left section to the Great Exchange are at best tenuous, while all money in the middle section is intimately connected. Until remarkably recently, these differences were only dimly understood by economists, and even now they are often ignored or forgotten, at some cost to society and the economy.

Second, one reason that economists have had trouble telling savings-money apart from token-money is that, except in this book, they are almost always given the same name, money. As I will point out in Chapter Three, finance is full of poorly defined terms, but the confusion about "money" is more basic than any of those. The two money-words are related, rather as conscience and consciousness are related (in French, the same *conscience* is used for both those English words), but they have not been clearly separated because the thinking about money is philosophically and economically confused. Of course, the linguistic homophones only reinforce that confusion.

The middle section

The entire previous section of this chapter was dedicated to the middle section of the Triptych, the paid-for portion of the economy. It showed how money is a remarkably good tool for economic organising and allocations. Having discussed money's economic strengths, I should also go over some of its weaknesses. The subsequent four sections introduce some ways in which the token-money system can fail to be a helpful economic tool. In this subsection, I simply make two critical observations about how that tool actually works, one descriptive and one contextual.

The descriptive observation is that money never comes in the generic form of "simply money" or "money-in-itself". It always comes as a particular kind of money, typically called a currency in modern economies. Each currency has its own specific legal, institutional, and political arrangements. Many variations of those arrangements have been tried out or imagined, but the standard modern arrangement is to have only one legally valid currency in every politically defined nation, and, at least usually, for each nation's currency to be valid only within its own borders. Some countries do use several currencies, more or less legally, and there are several currencies that are shared by more than one country. However, these practices are considered exceptional.

Underlying all currency arrangements is the principle or desire that a currency should pay for as many different things as is practically and politically possible. This desire for universality is theoretically justified, since the moneyness of money is exactly the ability to intermediate between any elements of Great Exchange for which quantitative mediation is desired. The more that a currency can pay for, the closer that currency approaches to the essence of money. However, the essential universality of money cannot be realised in the current global political order, because it conflicts with the political and governmental practicalities of money that I will describe later in this chapter. In short, a truly universal modern currency is almost inconceivable without a single global monetary authority to control its supply. That will not happen any time soon, since the money-supply has become too politically significant for most nation-states to be willing to abandon all their power over it.

One result of this non-universality of money is the creation of currency borders. These create economic frictions, some of which I will discuss later in this chapter. Here I will simply state that neither of the leading current lubricants for that friction, active markets for exchanging currencies and governmental guarantees of the "exchange rate" between currencies, has worked very well. On the contrary, "foreign exchange" crises remain a recurring problem in modern economies. The crises and the various limits to cross-currency spending are examples of the special incompetence of the money-financial system that I discussed in Chapter One.

The contextual observation is that the monetary tool is not the only, and generally not the most significant, organising tool in any economy, even when the middle section is large and well organised. Money does all the fine things described in the last section, but even quite simple economies cannot run well relying solely on that collection of fine things for organising its operations. In addition to money, economies must and do rely on traditions, rules, regulations, and laws. Then there are the numerous economic organisations, each with its own administrative structures, principles of unity, and disciplinary arrangements. In advanced economies, these organisations are largely structured as more or less rigid hierarchical bureaucracies, with their own rules and cultures. At the top of all modern economies are governments, which always have significant economic power and responsibilities. More complex economies always go together with more complex political-administrative governments, because to operate smoothly those economies need both more extensive regulatory systems and bigger governments to set and enforce these regulations.

The observation that money is only one of many organising institutions in economies should be so obvious that it is not worth making. Conceptually, it takes a sort of wilful naïveté even to consider that something as simple and numerical as money-numbers could be the sole or even the primary organising principle of something as complex and human as an economy. Practically, it takes remarkably blinkered vision not to see that money has a fairly modest role in the actual guidance of contemporary economic life.

Unfortunately, there are enough blinkers and blindness around that I do need to relativise the importance of money. The assumption that money is what makes the economy a system is built into economists' standard professional paradigm, much like and related to the assumption that the desire to and practice of "truck and barter" are the core of economic psychology and reality. In contrast, money does not have a privileged position in the Great Exchange paradigm that I am promoting. On the contrary, in that paradigm money is basically mistrusted, because money suffers from the profound conceptual weakness of being a purely numerical tool that is applied to things that are both essentially non-numerical and too different to be commensurate in even non-numerical ways. It is remarkable that a tool as flawed as money can do as much as it can, but it is obviously going to be less important than less conceptually distorted institutions.

The right section (economy without money)

I have already said that the right section of the Triptych was the predominant section in pre-modern economies and continues to play a far more important role in industrial economies than money-focused economists usually notice. Those are the principal characteristics that are relevant to a book that is distinctly *not* about the non-monetary economy. However, I do have seven further explanatory and hortatory comments.

1) *Where money is not used*: To start, it might be helpful to identify some typical non-uses of money in the economy. I have already mentioned the most important area in the modern world, the relations within a *family*. Parents do not generally pay their children for their labour, and children almost never pay parents for theirs. Nor do adults expect their weak elderly parents to pay them for any care provided. Familial non-monetary exchanges often include care and support inside extended families and what can reasonably be considered enlarged families: for example, the exchange of gifts and hospitality, pot-luck dinners, and mutual dinner invitations in a neighbourhood or among a group of friends, and the labour of kindly souls who help the neighbour's kids *gratis* with their homework.

Money is often found on the edge of these family arrangements. For example, in one-income families, various household members typically spend the wage of the paid labourer on consumption goods and services for the benefit of all or some of the members. However, the economy within such families is essentially non-monetary. The allocations of labour and consumption, including the goods and services that have been paid for, are guided by some combination of established rules, aspirational principles, intermittent negotiations, and shifting power-relations.

In pre-industrial economies, money could be relatively scarce because allocations that were not familial were very often *customary*. In other words, obligations to people outside of the familial group that would now typically be monetary were often set by custom: this proportion of a crop or that many days of labour was owed to the feudal lord or local priest. The lords, kings, or communities might also be owed unpaid communal labour, for example for clearing waterways or fighting in armies. *Compulsion* was often mixed with custom in the provision of unpaid pre-modern communal labour. There is little of that in the modern world – soldiers and even prisoners are usually paid something for their labour. However, in advanced economies the absence of money is central to the nature of *voluntary* labour and to consumption-sharing in times of disaster. "I want to give something to those who need" is a conscious effort to avoid some types of symbol-money. Socially and psychologically, volunteers are set apart from people paid to labour at the same tasks: caring for the sick, visiting the lonely, tidying up neighbourhoods. Finally, there are several non-monetary types of *rationing*. Non-monetary criteria for rationing include the willingness to wait in a queue, residence within a certain zone, scores on tests, and degrees of illness.

2) *Why money is not used*: Considering the optional role of money in the Great Exchange, it is its use, not its absence, that requires explanation. However, I have pointed out that money really is useful, so useful some of these advantages might seem to be pertinent to economic domains in which money is not currently used. There are several possible reasons for that non-use.

Sometimes money-numbers add more complexity than clarity. This is often the case within large producing organisations. It is often more efficient *not* to create pricing-points on the long chain of production. It can be more efficient to rely on administrative procedures, systems analysis, and the

communal spirit of labour. Money is always in the background, but
generally as an adjunct, and sometimes even an impediment, to the
organisation of the central economic activity. At a much smaller scale,
feuding families that try to insert money into disputed questions of internal
allocation – "I'm going to charge you for your meals from now on, you lazy
monster of a husband" – rarely find that money clarifies the justice of the
conflicting claims.

More often, however, money is not avoided because token-money is
working badly, but because some sort of symbol-money is working too
well. Symbolic meanings can make money inappropriate to particular
types of labour or consumption. This symbolic aversion is widespread
within families and is common when judging sexual relations, although
"sex work" is now sometimes considered a normal sort of paid-for labour.
More generally, the idea that money is too inherently calculating and
separating to "buy" anything like the unmeasurable and inherently
unifying relations of love has become more widespread in recent decades.
In Western countries, longstanding traditions of monetary dowries and
bride-prices have largely been abandoned, while the established social
taboos on thinking about the love of children, parents, and relatives in
monetary terms have been strengthened.

Popular attitudes towards monetary and non-monetary gifts provide good
examples of the nuances of symbol-money. In the preceding section, I
included efficiency in giving presents as one of money's advantages, but
efficiency and giving are uneasy partners. Monetary gifts are often felt to
be inappropriate within a loving relationship or even within a mutually
respectful business exchange of tokens of friendship. The rules for business
presents sometimes call for either the stronger or needier partner to make
the more valuable gift, but the expression of the different values is almost
never supposed to take the form of exchanging different amounts of
money. In personal relations, it would seem weird or rude to say, "I didn't
have time to buy you a bottle of wine, but here's the fifteen euros I would
have spent".

I just mentioned that volunteering is defined by its non-use of money. The
reasoning is similar to the logic of family love. There is thought to be

something noble and good about labouring without monetary rewards and something socially unifying and perhaps morally ennobling about being allowed or encouraged to consume without paying. Of course, human motives are often morally mixed, so volunteering has often been associated with demonstrations of social status: "She can afford to do all that without pay". Even then, the understanding that the decision to forgo pay is a sign of social status relies on a negative judgement of the use of money, the same basic judgement that led many landed aristocrats in the 19th century to disdain newly enriched and sometimes ennobled industrialists as "money-grubbing".

When governments eschew mediation by money in using their power, they are sending a message of strength and ruthlessness. They are spurning the symbolic understanding of money as an open-ended and two-sided tool. To levy a monetary fine or force a landowner to sell her property for some price is to inevitably enter into a sort of negotiation between the government and the governed. Simply to seize goods and dispossess an owner is unilateral declaration of total control.

Rationing is sometimes preferred to the use of money because it is seen as more just. In this case, it is a sociological symbol-money that is being rejected. Money carries the meaning of bringing social division, not in the fact of its quantification but in the unevenness of its distribution. However, when consumption goods and services are rationed by professionally determined need, there is also a hint of disdain for the quantification that is inherent to money: "Money is no object". Even when monetary calculations encircle the non-monetary allocations – the total wages of doctors or the total payments for building schools – it is considered inappropriate for the patient or the student to have to think in monetary terms.

3) *The money frontier*: Many types of labour and consumption take place without any money, but there is a good deal of variation in what might be considered their distance from the border with the middle, monetary-economic section of the Triptych. Activity that could be paid for without causing much social or economic disruption can be thought of as sitting towards the left of the non-monetary section. Some types of labour are so

close that they are sometimes in and sometimes out of the money economy, even in the same society at the same time. In modern economies, besides the just mentioned volunteering, the domestic and caring labours of housecleaning and childcare are the leading examples of sometimes-paid activities. These are often performed within families or communities without any pay: Mama takes care of the baby while Papa works at the shop or as a public relations consultant. Sometimes, however, the labour is paid-for: "We hire a nanny". More rarely, pay fully replaces unpaid labour within the family: "I pay my sister to watch the little ones".

Directly economic considerations have some influence on the social and personal decisions about which section of the Triptych a particular labour offering will fall into. Most notably, people often compare different types of labour (childcare against public relations) in part by calculating the likely effects on their allocation of consumption goods and services (wages in public relations minus cost of childcare brings more or less spending money than "stay at home" labour). However, other considerations – sociological, psychological, technological, and moral – are usually at least as significant. Those considerations are often related to varieties of symbol-money. For example, the appeal of traditional domestic service, labouring as a butler or housemaid in a single family, has been reduced by a sociological development, the rise of bourgeois classes, and by a psychological shift, from acceptance to rejection of being paid by household masters. Also, technological developments such as automatic washing machines and effective detergent have reduced both the toil and the skill of housework, perhaps changing feelings about paying people to perform it. On the other hand, the opening up of socially prestigious and intellectually challenging paid labour to women has increased the appeal of paying for other people to provide the traditionally feminine labours of caring and cleaning, at least for the women who can afford such services. Simultaneously, the new standard expectation that women should labour for pay may have increased the willingness of some women to take on paid domestic labour.

4) *The confusion of imputed wages*: The comments about paid and unpaid labour may have already taken me too far from my functionalist approach to money. Nonetheless, I will add one further comment: the assignment of

hypothetical monetary values to non-monetary economic activity can falsify the nature of the unpaid activity in significant ways. Sexual activity in an obvious example. Paid-for and unpaid sexual relations are so different that imputing a monetary value to the latter falsifies its nature. What is purchased from a prostitute is essentially different from what is given in (something like) love. For the same reasons, although to a much lesser extent, it is wrong to impute a monetary value for unpaid housework or childcare. The many symbolic meanings of money ensure that housework done without pay is in some basic ways different from paid housework. The nature of the differences can certainly be disputed. Paid arrangements may be more or less oppressive, loving, or appropriate than unpaid arrangements. However, since all of these descriptive adjectives are non-monetary, none of them can be priced in any meaningful way. Similarly, imputed monetary values of volunteering or hobbies will never capture the value to the persons and to the society created by placing this labour in the right section of the Triptych.

5) *Paying for being human*: Traditionally, what might be called the bare labours of being – growing up, schooling, being ill, and growing old – were on the farthest right part of the non-money section of the Triptych. They were so far from the paid-for economy that economists rarely considered them to be labour at all. That choice was based on an incorrect understanding of what the economy is. These labours are clearly part of the universal and unceasing human Great Exchange. They are gifts of humanity to the world, contributing enough to the individual and common good to be deemed worthy of reciprocal gifts of consumption goods and services. The neglect of unpaid caring labour deprives the academic discipline of economics of its full human dimensions, by ignoring some of the most important types of labour and implicitly denigrating the labourers who perform them. Economics without unpaid labour is like sociology without religion, anthropology without social hierarchy, or modern politics without bureaucracy.

In more mundane terms, the error of ignoring such labour now distorts economists' understanding of the middle section of the Triptych, since the development of child, old age, illness, and disability benefits of government welfare programmes have moved these labours there, or at least much closer to it.

6) *The shrinking or non-shrinking right section*: I said earlier that some economists simply ignore the right section of the Triptych, while almost all the rest underestimate its importance. That underestimation has declined, in part because feminist economists have brought "women's work" closer to the academic mainstream, but more significantly because the middle section has expanded at the expense of the right. This shift started with the decline of largely unpaid agricultural labour and the rise of paid farm-work. That was followed by increasing paid employment in industry, and in recent decades by a decline in unpaid women's work and an increase in the hours and years women spend labouring in the paid-for economy. Still more recently, the just mentioned government payments for being human have moved the traditionally unpaid labours of illness and old age into or at least closer to the middle section.

This trend of shrinkage in the Triptych's right section in terms of labour has to be set against the expansion of that section in term of consumption: of healthcare, education, and other free-to-user services. More speculatively, increased prosperity in developed economies, which allows more people to buy more things without much thought about the cost, might be thought to have moved such consumption towards the right side of the middle section. While money continues to do the same organisational work in producing and allocating basic foodstuffs and mobile phone services, more consumers are becoming increasingly "price insensitive" – the money-numbers involved are too small to be worth worrying about.

7) *The right section of the Triptych is not economically inferior to the middle one*: In the Great Exchange paradigm of economics, paid and unpaid labour are equally labour. One type is associated with the useful tool of money, and the other is not. The monetary connection does not create any economic superiority. Indeed, the expansion of unpaid and barely-paid consumption suggests that in the popular and political imagination some economic activities that were formerly monetary are better accomplished at some distance from the money-system.

The conceptual equality of paid and unpaid economic activity is literally inconceivable in the conventional economists' paradigm, because in it money is the only accurate or meaningful marker of economic activity. The exclusion of the right section of the Triptych is an even more substantial intellectual error, in my judgement, than the non-separation of the left section from the middle one. Whatever their relative seriousness, the twin errors influence public policy and attitudes in unhelpful ways. For example, economists have encouraged the political focus on Gross Domestic Product, a money-number that is used as if it were an accurate measure of a nation's entire economy. However, GDP and changes in GDP are actually poor indicators to the overall economic good, especially in advanced economies. Both the goal of quantification and the necessary lack of qualitative analysis needed to make the quantification possible encourage crude efforts to maximise money-numbers indiscriminately.

5. Money and economic reality

I now return to the token-money economy, the middle section of the Triptych. I start in this section with a discussion of realism: how well does the use of money correspond to the reality of the relevant activity in the Great Exchange? That question is rarely asked, because the precisionist-consistency fallacy leads economists simply to assume that money-numbers are highly realistic, in some sense. The professionals disagree about precisely what sense – which values the numbers actually reveal – but they are all confident that some money-numbers do somehow provide clear indices of what is really going on in the economy. That presupposition is, as I hope I have made clear, wrong. However useful money is, it is a shifting and crude thing with attributes that are in many ways profoundly different from the non-quantitative reality of human economic activity. It is by no means obvious that the token-money system will correspond at all closely with the economic reality of labour, production, and consumption.

I see two basic ways of thinking about the reality-closeness of the token-money system. I mentioned earlier in this chapter that money provides a sort of map of the paid-for economy. The token-money system might be like a good map, one that captures many of the terrain's essential attributes without producing great distortions in anything significant. Alternatively, this system may be more like an ill-fitting and unattractive garment, something that usefully keeps the wearer warm and decent, but does not express much of the body's form, dignity, or beauty.

The case for the map analogy is quite strong. Fundamentally, just as the lines on an accurate map represent roads in the real world, most if not all movements of token-money within the middle portion of the Triptych (i.e. excluding transactions which involve non-economic savings-money) represent actual movements of labour, production, and consumption. Particular acts of labour are directly rewarded with money in wages, while particular stages of production and particular acts of consumption are directly paid for in prices. In addition, the transfers of taxes, benefits, donations, and other secondary movements of token-money indirectly change the ultimate allocations of consumption goods and services, by reducing the consumption allocations of those paying money into this secondary economy while increasing the allocations of those receiving from it.

There is one important way in which the map analogy for money is quite misleading. On geographical maps, it is not only the lines and markings that correspond with geographical features in the real physical world. The distances also correspond, because maps are scaled: one centimetre on paper or screen always equals, say, one kilometre on the road or field. The putative money-map cannot be scaled in that way, because the reality it describes is not scaled. There are, as I keep repeating, no humanly meaningful and consistent economic numbers. The numbers in the money-map correspond at best very roughly with anything in the actual Great Exchange. They inevitably falsify, distort, or confuse much of what is going on.

Despite the lack of a meaningful scalar correspondence, the money-map has what might be called a fairly close topological correspondence with reality. In mathematics, topological spaces need not have consistent metrics. In a non-metric space, a large square cannot be differentiated from a small one, or necessarily from a circle (depending on the rules of the chosen topology). A non-metric topological map would capture something about the shape of something, and money-numbers do capture some of the shape of economic activity.

While the token-money map is not scalar, it is, like a good map, scalable. By that I mean that money is equally useful for understanding and arranging the smallest and the largest economic transactions. Money can be used in almost exactly the same way to pay for a granola bar and to build and operate a fleet of commercial aircraft. Again like a good map, the token-money system is unbiased. It records prices and facilitates the conversion of all paid-for labour into all paid-for consumption, without favouring particular parts of that section of the economy.

Finally, two of the more unrealistic aspects of money, its easy divisibility and transportability (discussed earlier in this chapter), provide helpful representations of the deep interdependence of the various parts of the economy. For example, the 500-euro tax payment which moves from the labourer or consumer to the government may originally have been tied to a particular period of labour or a particular consumed item, but its representation as money turns it into something generic – a token of a roughly specified quantity of a totally non-specified mix of economic action or output. The movement of this small bundle of indeterminate potential consumption and labour around the economy may not seem to map reality, since there is no way to take, say, 1.2 percent of the output of one person's labour, pass it to the government and then spread it around the entire society. However, conceptually, the flowing of token-money through the tax and benefit systems represents quite effectively the shared nature of all economic activity.

While the case for money as a good economic map is strong, so is the case for it being no better than an ugly garment that does little more than preserve decency, or, in the case of money, economic efficiency.

The most obvious problem is that money-numbers are numbers. As two centuries of professional economics has clearly shown, the digits themselves create an insidious temptation, leading ever so easily to the imposition of an ill-fitting, unrealistic numerical uniformity and claimed commensurability on the middle section of the Triptych. The great functionality of these numbers is inseparable from the allure of the precisionist-consistency fallacy.

Another serious discrepancy between money and reality emerges in the way money is typically used, in a series of discrete and concrete transactions. There are some exceptions, but it is considered normal to use measured amounts of money to pay for measured amounts of labour or consumption. I am paid precisely this much in direct compensation for precisely this specific past or future labour, and I pay precisely that much in direct compensation for this particular consumption good or service. The money-transfer system has equally clear divisions.

This specificity belies the temporally open-ended nature of all economic activity and relationships. The Great Exchange is a continuous as well as an instantaneous exchange of labour and production. Just as we labour now and consume now, we labour and consume steadily and without meaningful interruptions from birth until death, always doing both economic activities with a memory of the past and an anticipation of the future. To divide labour by time, as money does, is effectively to ignore how any particular moments come seamlessly out of the past of a person, a community, and indeed a civilisation. Periodic salaries, set by the month or year, show some recognition of this seamlessness, but money would lose its usefulness if it were paid out in the way that labour actually performed, steadily over many interlocking lifetimes. Similarly, to divide consumption into discrete units is effectively to ignore or at least to underappreciate the joint and continuing efforts which lie behind each item. A car is a specific machine, but the factories and expertise that produce the car are ongoing. Once again, money-numbers, in this case accountants' allowances for depreciation, show some recognition of this seamlessness, but, as with labour, money would lose its usefulness if it were paid out realistically, that is continuously and through the entire society.

I hinted at a related weakness of the token-money system when I mentioned its inability to capture the gifts inherent in both labour and consumption. The forced and contrived numerical equality of the two sides of every monetary transaction describes a durably utilitarian economic fabric – I always give, or should give, exactly as much as I get, by whatever standard "as much as" is judged and measured. In the actual, non-monetary Great Exchange, the reality of commutative justice is quite different. The warp of labour and the weft of consumption are of equal value as they together weave the fabric of economic life. Commutative justice is provided in cloths of many different colours and patterns, occasionally rough and ugly but more often exuberant, beautiful, and extravagant. Less poetically, money is structurally incapable of capturing more than a small portion of the many standards of actual commutative justice, the balancing of the toil, genius, and traditions of labour with the beauty, efficiency, elegance, pleasure, status, suitability, wisdom and who knows what else of consumption.

Nor can token-money describe how little things come together to create or harm the single common good which is greater than all its parts. When money-numbers are used to attempt to express the uncountable human accomplishments in humanising the world, the uncountable damage humanity has wrought on the natural world, or the diverse bounty provided by the many consumption gifts from that humanised world, the quantification is like turning a fine ball-gown into a rough burlap sack. While the monetary measures of such things rarely give totally false signals, they provide just about the greyest and flattest imaginable perspective on the economy.

So token-money is both a good map and bad clothing. The answer to the initial question in this section, which it resembles more, depends on what is expected. If money is regarded, as it should be, as a functional but limited tool, then it is more like a map. It does what it is supposed to do quite well. The inherent distortions and inadequacies of money measures do not introduce distortions so dangerous that money cannot perform its economic duty. When the precision-consistency illusions of money are allowed too much sway, however, then money looks like an ill-fitting garment. If what is desired is a universal economic measure, a full and articulate language of making and consuming, then money does not come close. It distorts too much, misses too much, debases too much, and distracts too much from the generous shared imagination that guides the whole economy, paid-for and non-monetary alike. From that perspective, token-money is no more than a utilitarian scheme to make the human condition look duller than it is.

6. What gives money its value

Essentially, token-money is a totally intangible token which simplifies, standardises, and unifies, somewhat roughly but very usefully, some activities on the two sides of the Great Exchange. This functionality is helpful, remarkably so in modern industrial economies, but readers who are either philosophically inclined or knowledgeable about the history of monetary theory will be puzzled. The intangibility of something that organises so many tangible things is peculiar philosophically. The ability for everyone in an economy to rely on numbers that have neither tangible base nor genuine quantitative meaning is equally peculiar both philosophically and historically. The puzzle can be expressed in three different but interlinked questions. First, how did abstract tokens come to symbolise these concrete economic actions? Second, more concretely and currently, what gives money its value? Third, in even more basic language, what is money really made of?

The simplest answer to the last question is "nothing". Money is what economists refer to as fiat. That Latin word simply means "let it be made", but the monetary meaning has a specific connotation, taken from the beginning of the Bible. When God created the universe and all it contains out of nothing, "fiat" was the word used in the leading Latin translation to express the divine command. Like the world, money is made *ex nihilo*, from nothing at all. The philosopher John Searle provides a more modern and more descriptive term, calling money "baseless" (Searle, 2017). In particular, it is not made from or reliant on a base of gold, pieces of paper which represent gold, computer ledger entries which represent pieces of paper, future taxes, hypothetical units of standardised labour, or anything else.

Searle's formulation is superior to the traditional "fiat" because, unlike divine creation, money essentially stays nothing. It does not really or essentially become anything concrete. When the monetary fiat is said (I will discuss who or what can say it soon), a purely conceptual number-thing is created to intermediate the Great Exchange. This number-thing does always have some worldly substrate or, to use a description used in Aristotelian philosophy, some material accident, but the material – metal, paper, data record, or legal claim – only represents the money. The money *is* what the people believe it is.

This belief provides the answer to the second formulation of the question. Money gets its value from users' shared belief in its value. The answer is circular, but shared beliefs always are. When we participate in a particular monetary system, we are giving our assent to the already shared belief in the value of this currency. Our participation widens, deepens, and maintains the circle of trust, allowing money to be used to pay for labour, consumption, tax liabilities, money-things (subject to limitations I will discuss later), and whatever else money-users are willing to pay and accept money for. A particular currency works as a token only because, and only as long as, people continue to believe that this particular token-money can actually be exchanged for whatever money is expected to pay for, most notably labour, the consumable fruits of labour, and the obligations to governments. When people or their organisations lose this trust, they stop accepting that currency as a token. For them, this type of money has lost its value. Shared mistrust reverses the fiat of money, leaving behind only valueless pieces of metal or paper, or economically meaningless electronic records.

The recognition that money is a sort of quantification and reification of social trust helps answer the first, more historical formulation of the basic ontological money-question. Money came to hold value through the shared belief in the trustworthiness of the creator or backer of the money: the person, institution or authority that declares that this coin, bill, or computer record actually is money. The history of money can be told as a saga of trust, of users' confidence mostly gained over the centuries, and sometimes disastrously lost. This history has involved several types of issuing institutions – religious temples, goldsmiths, groups of merchants, large companies, individual banks, consortiums of banks and governments, government-delegated monetary authorities, and central governments. There have been some dramatic moments during these institutions' rises and falls, but there is no suspense about the overall direction. At the end of the story, money is always created or firmly backed by some legitimate government.

Philosophers of history under the influence of G. W. F. Hegel might describe this ultimate usurpation of monetary authority as part of the State's ineluctable destiny to take up an ever more domineering role in society. More pragmatic observers can note that political authorities are the only social institutions in contemporary societies that can enforce and deserve monetary trust through indefinite quantities of time and space. In the most concrete terms, only governments can reliably be expected to punish counterfeiters, restrain any authorised creators of money from excess, force payment of taxes in a preferred currency, and force individuals and institutions to disclose the information needed to manage a monetary system. Enforcement relies on fear, but trust is ultimately a positive quality. It is deserved when money-users accept that despite all the things that their government does wrong, in some fundamental way this government and its policies overall, especially those dealing with money, aim to promote a good, prosperous, and just society. In general, modern governments receive and deserve full monetary trust.

Of course, governments have often exercised their monetary authority cruelly, insidiously, foolishly, for the benefit of some elite, or to inflict unjust punishments, just as they have sometimes exercised their military, penal, and legal authority cruelly, insidiously, foolishly, for the benefit of some elite, or to inflict unjust punishments. No matter how badly governments fail, however, in the modern world there is no realistic monetary alternative. Even after a failure of government-backed money, people are almost always more willing to give the sovereign political authorities another chance than to trust any other less powerful or less inclusive institution to run the money system.

Today's elected governments do not actually create most of the money-supply directly. They rely on two intermediaries or "fronts". First, largely for political reasons, they usually claim that there is a clear separation between the political governments that collect taxes and the central monetary authorities (misleadingly known as central banks) that are responsible for managing the money-supply. These authorities are almost always portrayed as technocratic and ultimately non-political. This is a myth. Institutions that have substantial power over how and to whom newly created money is distributed must make political decisions. Second, for largely historical reasons, until quite recently the central monetary authorities created very modest amounts of new money directly. The bulk of the creation has been done by banks, operating as something like subcontractors to the political-monetary authorities. The operating details of the system are quite complicated, but the basic pattern is straightforward. Governmental authorities, often a rather messy collection of them, set rules about money-creation for the banks, the banks generally follow but sometimes abuse those rules, and the government takes over when disaster strikes. The frequency of such disasters is one of the main reasons for the disastrous financial exception discussed in Chapter One.

I should probably note that there is a great deal of mystification around the management of the money-supply. For what I consider largely ideological reasons, many economists would rather not accept the importance of trust, regulation, central authorities, and ultimately political power in the creation and maintenance of the value of money. So-called Chartalist (state-based) monetary analysis is now nearly universal in practice, but still often rejected in theory, largely because economists wish to understand money as individualistic and contractual rather than social and authoritative. This desire leads them to turn to other explanations of the source of money's value: usually either some sort of inaccurate historical narrative based on the substitution of a commodity for barter (discussed earlier in this chapter) or a more accurate historical narrative based on private lending arrangements (to be discussed later in this chapter).

Returning to reality, baselessness makes money inherently fragile. If governments take too much advantage of their monetary power, they can destroy the trust that maintains the value. To avoid the possible sapping of confidence, the monetary authorities sometimes pretend (or honestly but falsely claim) that there really is some tangible or valuable backing to money. The gold standard and silver-backed U.S. dollars are long gone, not to mention the French Revolution's supposedly land-backed assignats. These days, countries are more likely to declare that something like the "full faith and credit" of the issuing government stands behind their money. The post-modern extreme is probably British banknotes, which cryptically state that the Bank of England will pay the bearer of the note the value of the note. Such declarations may comfort users, but they are all nonsense. Money is always essentially baseless.

The idea that money has economic meaning only because users agree that it does can perhaps be made less strange if the definition of token-money as a literal token is taken seriously, not a token of some tangible thing but as a token of meaning. Such tokens belong in the domain of semiotics – the study of the many signs, symbols and intangible systems that hold people together in communities and societies. As (Geertz, 1973: 5) says, "Man is an animal suspended in webs of significance he himself has spun". Token-money is one of those webs. Savings-money is another. As a sign-system, token-money is fairly simple – perhaps more complicated than the system of standardised signage on public toilets and no-smoking zones, but much less complicated than any natural, spoken language. Like any semiotic system, money is both self-contained and reliant on a common understanding of meanings. Considered in this way, the desire for money to be "backed" by something tangible or almost tangible is basically a sign of semiotic insecurity – of a lack of trust in the system's consistency or coherence. As long as there is trust, the semiotic system works perfectly well without any backing. To misuse a comment of Gertrude Stein, there does not have to be any 'there there' in money.

Semiotic insecurity explains why coins traditionally were made entirely or partly of gold. The precious metal was deployed to support the value-meaning of money, because a tangible token of fidelity helped buttress money-users' confidence in relatively weak and unreliable governments or in opaque bankers. The social semiotics of gold and silver is certainly worthy of cultural study, but from the perspective of monetary economics, the reliance on material support for essentially conceptual money is simply a wasteful manifestation of the monetary creator's untrustworthiness.

As money-issuing governments became more trustworthy and powerful, they abandoned their reliance on gold, first in reality and finally even the pretence. The departure was a pure economic gain. It freed up the substantial resources needed to extract and refine the metals and to mint, store, and transport coins. It also removed some of the unmerited wealth that had accrued to gold miners or their governments. The economic advantages of truly baseless money required and reflected one of the most significant political shifts in history, the expansion of the authority and competence of central governments into the everyday lives of all citizens and subjects. Governments can now create or back money without relying on gold in exactly the same way that they can maintain domestic order without posting gun-toting soldiers or citizen militias on every corner.

7. The shifting Central Monetary Ratio

There are two sorts of monetary balance – wages with prices and money-numbers with the middle section of the Triptych. The first is basically although not entirely built into the money system, because the two totals, of money paid in wages to people-as-labourers and of money paid as prices by people-as-consumers, refer to exactly the same money and the same people. The balance between token-money and the paid-for economy is much trickier.

The Central Monetary Ratio

The second balance can be thought of as a ratio or fraction: money-to-things. I call it the Central Monetary Ratio, which can be defined as the quantitative relationship of circulating token-money to the size of the money-using middle section of the Triptych. Conceptually, this Central Ratio describes the overall level of prices and wages. Economists generally refer to it as the price level, which is accurate but inadequate, since there is no theoretical reason to favour prices over incomes. The two sides of the Great Exchange are conceptually identical and in practice almost equal numerically.

Whichever side the calculation of the Central Ratio starts with, it will at best be, like almost everything connected to money, a helpful but arbitrary and unrealistic construction. For largely practical reasons, the monetary numerator of the fraction can only be approximated. For definitional reasons, the real economy denominator can only be postulated. I will explain.

The numerator (money-supply): The active token-money-supply consists of the sum of money that is currently being spent, or circulated, in the paid-for Great Exchange. This money-supply, formerly known as the "quantity of money", cannot be calculated precisely, because current spending takes place over an only roughly defined long now. Wages and other income are never translated instantaneously into consumption spending. The wages for personal services might linger for a few days before becoming the prices for consumption. For complex manufactured products, parts of the now can last for years. Even if the appropriate monetary data could all be collected and sorted, the classification would be somewhat arbitrary. The monetary border, between the token-money that is currently in circulation in the middle section of the Triptych and the savings-money that is lying inert in the left section, is fuzzy. Consumers generally have a significant, shifting, but inherently uncertain amount of money that might or might not be in circulation. Besides the variable-sized "cushions" of extra funds in checking or current accounts, there are savings that can be liquidated for big or unexpected purchases as well as unspent loan proceeds that have been received or could be "drawn down". The quantity of this money straddling the border between the two sections of the Triptych is large enough to preclude an exact measure of the money-supply, which is the token-money that is actively moving around the wage-price circle, or making a detour through the transfer system.

Monetary economists are well aware of this ambiguity, which they describe in terms of different "velocities of money". The more of what I call savings-money is included in their count of the money-supply, the slower is their measure of monetary velocity. In the model I am proposing, actual token-money, which is the only money that matters in the Great Exchange, is *definitionally* engaged in the instantaneous buying and selling of the middle section of the Triptych. It does not have a variable "velocity".

This ambiguity and several others have led the statisticians estimating the current Central Monetary Ratio to ignore the money-supply. Instead, they create a tiny sample of the paid-for economy, a little circle within the middle section of the Triptych. This circle, known as a basket, is a selection of supposedly typical consumption goods and services. The sum of the prices of all the items in the basket is the numerator in the calculation of the Central Monetary Ratio. Since wages equal prices, the statisticians could also choose and use a basket of jobs, but it turns out to be harder to keep a basket of nearly identical jobs than one of nearly identical consumption goods and services. Consumption consistency is elusive enough. Even a casual study of the composition of price indices shows the statisticians' efforts to find a typical, consistent, and reasonably comprehensive basket has brought in a distressingly high number of more or less arbitrary and more or less political choices and adjustments. A more detailed study demonstrates an unseemly reliance on the precisionist-consistency fallacy.

The denominator (total paid-for consumption or labour): The numerator of the Central Monetary Ratio is clearly a number, whether it is the conceptually clear but in practice incalculable sum of all current prices or wages or the more tractable sum of a basket of prices or wages. The denominator, the collection of things that money buys in this economy, clearly cannot be expressed as a number. To think otherwise is to fall headlong into the quicksand of the precisionist side of the precisionist-consistency fallacy.

This incommensurability would not present any difficulties in the calculation of changes in the Central Monetary Ratio if the real denominator remained constant. In an economy which always produced one thing at the same pace, say a tonne of steel every day, the Central Ratio would be exactly the price of that tonne of steel. That would be the price level. If the supply of token-money doubled, then by definition (because token-money is defined as being spent now) the price level, the price of the tonne of steel, would double.

This super-reduced model is super-misleading, since one great practical advantage of money is its ability to pay for shifting collections of goods and services, and of labour. The calculation of changes in the Central Ratio's denominator requires numerical adjustments for the relevant shifts. Here the calculation gets ensnared in the consistency side of the precisionist-consistency fallacy. The only consistent numbers that are readily available to compare different goods and services over time are their prices, but the goal of keeping track of the Central Ratio is exactly to calculate how much prices of typical things have risen (or fallen). To get to this ratio, we need to create a non-price number-system to put a number on the changes in the collection of goods and services in the middle section of the Triptych. Calculations of the Central Monetary Ratio necessarily rely on the totally artificial numbers that economists have craftily called "real" (discussed earlier in this chapter. Since the mix, quality, and patterns of consumption change quite significantly and rapidly in contemporary dynamic economies, the adjustments needed to keep a constant denominator in the Central Ratio are little short of heroic, or ridiculous.

In sum, the Central Monetary Ratio is a comparison of an unknown number to a heap of non-numerical things. What is said of sausages and legislation is true for price indices: it is best not to see them being made. However, blind trust in the precisionist-consistency fallacy has imbued the calculated ratios, generally called price indexes and generally expressed with a totally spurious precision (units of one in a thousand), with a totally undeserved respect.

Still, even rough numbers show patterns. I will mention three of them for the Central Monetary Ratio.

First, this ratio is always changing. Like everything to do with money, the ultimate balance of token-money and paid-for activity is too rough to allow for anything like a steady equilibrium. Leaving aside the impossibility of true constancy – what does it even mean to say that a necessarily hypothetical number-to-thing ratio remains the same? – both the numerator and the denominator of the Central Ratio are necessarily unstable and necessarily not coordinated in their changes. The numerator, overall prices and wages, shifts as its component money-numbers perform their economic task of responding to and guiding changes in economic activity. The denominator, things purchased or labour paid for, changes as patterns of labour, production, and consumption change. The lack of precise coordination springs from the only indirectly related flexibility of both money and economic activity.

Second, the Central Ratio *usually* changes sufficiently slowly, slightly, and steadily that the changes have little or no effect on the economic decisions of either individuals or production organisations. Total indifference is known by economists as monetary neutrality. The concept refers to changes in the Ratio, not to changes in its denominator. For example, economic decisions are indeed likely to be influenced by a decline in the available array of paid-for goods and services. Monetary neutrality exists when the behavioural changes are the same if the decline is experienced as lower wages and steady prices, steady wages and higher prices, or higher wages and even higher prices.

Strict monetary neutrality, like so many generalised economic claims, is impossible to demonstrate, since every situation is different. There are situations where a more rapidly rising Central Monetary Ratio has a different economic effect than a more stable one would. (I will discuss one of them, hyperinflation, soon.) However, the key point is that the Central Ratio does not often change very much. This outcome should not be surprising in modern economies. The volatility of the Ratio's denominator is constrained by the physical, psychological, and sociological limits to the pace and size of changes in the labour and consumption of large groups of people. The numerator is under human control and the controllers – the banks, the government-controlled monetary authorities, and the political governments – generally share a desire to promote overall prosperity, a goal which they recognise tends to be harder to reach when there are sudden and uneconomic changes in the token-money-supply. After several generations of fumbling, these controllers have developed techniques of monetary control which, while far from ideal, are usually sufficiently powerful and accurate to keep the Central Ratio from moving too far too fast.

The third observed characteristic of the Central Ratio is the reverse of the second. *Sometimes* the Central Ratio changes so significantly and quickly that the overall paid-for economy is disrupted. I introduced the fact of occasional severe monetary (and financial) failures in Chapter One. There I merely pointed out that the persistence of such failures needed to be explained, because failures of the same magnitude and with similarly long-lasting consequences are so much rarer in every other part of modern economies. As I suggested there, this exception is especially galling because it is actually relatively easy for even modestly attentive monetary authorities to keep the Central Monetary Ratio relatively stable, and these authorities are motivated to do so.

Why do the economically damaging sharp deviations of the Central Monetary Ratio keep recurring? One reason is the noxious effects of greedy, reality-distant finance, a topic that takes up most of the rest of this book. In this section, I will merely look at the most common immediate causes of serious monetary problems, dividing them into four groups.

Local problems

The entire money system can be thrown out of balance by a major disruption in the price structure of some large and crucial part of the paid-for economy. These disruptions are rare, because, under normal circumstances, prices and wages are roughly equal in individual organisations and industries, just as they are in the middle section of the Triptych as a whole. Localised imbalances and gradual changes are fairly common, but the scale of disorder is generally modest, because wages in one organisation rarely deviate far from wages in comparable organisations and prices rarely deviate very far from the relevant wages and transfers.

Rapid and economically disruptive price changes are much harder to avoid when prices are not closely connected to the transfer-adjusted wages connected with production. In economic theory, this disconnect is a desirable attribute of what are known as markets. In reality, prices that are set without the anchor of wages are often disruptively volatile. In particular, dramatic price moves in "traded commodities" have often spread woe through much of the paid-for economy. At one extreme, the prices for wheat or oil can fall so low that growers and producers are threatened with penury. At the other, prices can rise so high that growers and producers have more money than they can easily spend.

I will start with excessively low prices, which can cause what I call tractor problems. Consider the effect of a severe drought on tractor production.

The lack of rain has no effect on the possible production of tractors. They can be produced at the same pace in bad crop years as in good ones. The drought also has little effect on the wear and tear on old tractors, so the desire for new vehicles remains almost constant. However, the drought does tend to have a significant negative effect on the incomes of potential tractor-buyers. The market price of a tonne of wheat is likely to rise, but not by enough to compensate for the reduced number of tonnes produced by the typical farmer. As a result, many farmers who would be happy to buy a new tractor will not have enough money to pay for one. In response to this shortage of money, fewer tractors are produced. Since the total wages and total revenues in the tractor factories and at their suppliers *are* closely related, the lower farm revenues will bring lower wages for everyone labouring in the long chain of tractor-production. As these labourers are forced to cut back on their paid-for consumption, they spread waves of decline through the economy – less money, less production, and less employment. In sum, the money system tends to transmit and amplify what should and presumably could be a sectoral issue of smaller wheat crops into a general economic retreat.

In the early years of the modern economy, varieties of this tractor-problem helped cause many broad economic declines. The culprit was almost always agriculture, for several reasons. Economically unhelpful market pricing was typical in that sector, as were large and unpredictable variations of output. Also, the role of agriculture in economies remained sufficiently important through the 19th century that the monetary waves that started from lost farm revenues could be strong enough to do widespread economic damage. In addition, poorly designed monetary and financial arrangements tended to magnify the original monetary losses. Finally, governments were too small and unimaginative to offer much help.

In recent decades, the effects of agricultural misfortune have been mitigated by the reversal of all those factors. The sector's share of the money-flows in the middle-section of the Triptych has declined. Increasingly global distribution for crops has reduced the amplitude of price swings in local markets. Both the financial system and governments are more competent and active. Similar trends have kept most other traded commodities from causing general monetary trouble.

However, a 10-fold increase in the nominal price of oil in 1973 created a
wave of disruptions in the global economy and money-system, in the
opposite direction from the traditional agriculture-induced decline. Oil was
crucial to the industrial economy, the price increase was large and fast, and
the monetary response was inept. The direct results were a fairly sharp
increase in the numerator of the Central Ratio in many countries, as money
was created to pay more for oil, and a fairly sharp decline in the
denominator, as the higher price of oil disrupted industrial patterns around
the world. Also, despite extravagant additional consumption in many oil-
producing nations, much of the additional token-money received for oil
was converted into savings-money (a process economists misleadingly
called "recycling"), with sad results. Subsequent gyrations in the oil price
seem to have been less disruptive to both the economy and the money-
economy balance, although both the truth of that claim and causes of the
claimed improvement are contested.

Border problems in one currency

A full discussion of financial carnage must await the broader discussion of
finance in Chapter Three. Here, I can point out that troubles caused by oil
revenues crossing the border between the middle and left sections of the
Triptych are not unusual. Sudden changes in the relations between the two
sections are a common source of economically disruptive monetary
imbalances. For the last century these token-savings shocks have been
much more disruptive than commodity-market price shocks.

The border crossings, known to economists as savings (money flows from
the middle to the left section) and dissaving (from the left to the middle),
are usually not problematic, because the quantity of flows in and out of
token-money are usually sufficiently similar to have little effect on the
numerator of the Central Ratio. For example, nothing at all changes in the
euro area monetary economy if Monsieur Dupont takes 100 euros out of
circulation in the eurozone's Great Exchange and uses it to buy a money-
thing from Frau Schmidt, as long as Schmidt converts her newly acquired
100 euros of savings-money into token-money. The transactions of the
multitude of Duponts and Schmidts in the whole economy typically come
close to balancing each other out.

However, sometimes the flow becomes disruptively unbalanced. Since the 1930s, economists have mostly focused on one type of excess, the paradox of thrift. The problem typically starts when some current event, perhaps a drought or, much more frequently, trouble in the left section of the Triptych, leads many paid labourers and business organisations to worry about the imminent loss of some of their incomes and revenues respectively. The businesses are worried about the consumers, who are making a large number of individual decisions to spend less token-money so as to convert more of it into savings-money. Each saver expects to bring the hoarded money back into the middle section later, when it will be more needed or more valuable. The businesses which cut back on their spending both respond to and amplify the consumers' caution. The common purpose is virtuous prudence, but, paradoxically, the shared result is monetary imprudence. The net withdrawal of token-money from the middle section reduces the Central Ratio, with the deflationary effects to be discussed in the next section – falling prices, production, and paid employment.

Economists call this sudden decline of token-money a "demand shock". That is accurate enough, although the problem is at least as much monetary as practical or psychological. As I will explain later in this chapter, the belief that money which is not spent stores value is confused. With a more accurate understanding of the difference between token-money and savings-money, it would be easier to discourage and limit unhelpful crossings of the savings-token monetary border, preventing foolish and disruptive rushes from one side to the other.

In practice, the border-problems almost always come from excessive saving, or, more accurately, from unnecessary restraint in consumption spending. In theory, though, excess flows can move in the other direction, from savings-money into transaction money. If some campaigners against grand fortunes had their way, they could demonstrate the problem. Consider the frequently made claim that all of the world's hungry people could be fed if only all of the world's billionaires gave up their wealth. The thinking is confused. The hungry can only be fed by changes in the actual Great Exchange – the arrangements of labour, production, and allocation. No amount of money moving from the left into the middle section of the Triptych can have any direct effect on food production. A large and poorly managed money-flow could, however, have an undesired effect on allocation. A sudden increase in the quantity of token-money paying for food might increase the Central Monetary Ratio in this part of the Great Exchange. In other words, food prices might increase. Without compensating monetary adjustments, the increased price would disproportionally hurt people who can currently barely afford enough to eat. If effect, a massive dissaving would make food less affordable for some of the people who most need it to be inexpensive. That would be a paradox of anti-thrift.

Border problems across currencies

Money is always a communal project, one which must be tied to some authoritative communal structure. In the modern world, the ultimate monetary authorities are always political. As a result, currencies are mostly strictly national. The only current exceptions are the multinational euro and a few countries that have "dollarised" their monetary system. Neither works very well. There are persistent tensions between the European Central Bank, which controls the euro, and the eurozone's national politicians, who have ultimate monetary responsibility, while dollarisation is politically difficult to sustain. The exceptions basically support the rule: national money-borders are normally required in the middle section of the Triptych.

Money-borders, however, are economically inefficient. They reduce two related and important advantages of money, the full commensurability of money-numbers with each other and the ability to use the same money to pay for many different things. Indeed, the economic logic of token-money points unequivocally towards a single world-currency. That would presumably require a single world government to protect the integrity of the monetary system and keep the global Central Monetary Ratio under control.

Over at least the last three centuries, the inherent tension between the two monetary logics, the domestic political and the international economic, has frequently created domestic and sometimes global problems – political and economic as well as monetary. In particular, cross-border monetary considerations have often left or threatened to leave national economies with either more or less token-money than is needed to keep the domestic paid-for economy running smoothly. Many techniques for avoiding or mitigating cross-currency monetary tensions have been tried, including fixed and floating currency exchange rates, limited and unlimited movements of money between currencies, and various sorts of tariffs and trade restrictions. None of them have worked well consistently, presumably because monetary stability requires more dynamic integration into economies and societies than is possible when many jurisdictions are involved.

Cross-currency money-flows can be quite simple, even if the currency of X-country cannot be spent in Y-country. There is no monetary problem if trade is monetarily balanced, that is residents of Y-country use *all* the X-currency they receive from selling their labour, goods, or services to residents of X-country to pay for labour, goods, or services from X-country. The complications mount quickly, however, when *some* X-currency gets stuck, so to speak, in a "no man's land" between the two political authorities and currency zones. This will occur if the residents of Y do not actually spend all the X-currency they receive. The unspent money becomes savings-money, held in country-Y but valued in X-currency. The complex and politically untethered multi-currency monetary system can expand massively if the varying national regulations allow money to move easily from one country or currency to another without any contrary flow of goods and services.

The details can be fiendish, but the three most important sources of money-economy imbalance are fairly easy to identify. First, if companies or banks in country X have to earn revenues in X-currency to make payments in Y-currency, then changes in the X-Y currency exchange rate can vastly increase the difficulty of finding the needed money. Establishing this sort of cross-currency obligation has been called the original sin of international finance. Second, if the economy of country X has become reliant on the willingness of sellers of goods and services from country Y to hold onto significant quantities of currency X, then a decline in that willingness can be disruptive to the monetary balance and economic organisations in country X. Third, if businesses and governments in country X have become reliant on money from financial investors in country Y, then a withdrawal of money by those investors can destabilise the monetary system and economy in country X.

Before economies became very industrial, cross-border trade accounted for a fairly significant proportion of the use of money, so dislocations in currency relations could create monetary imbalances fairly easily. The leading manifestation of such imbalances was the net export of gold and silver. That could be problematic, but pre-modern monetary imbalances rarely had much effect on the overall economy, which was dominated by economic activity, mostly agricultural production and domestic labour, in the right section of the Triptych.

The situation is reversed in most modern economies. Unbalanced monetary flows across currencies rarely account for more than a modest portion of the token-money in circulation, so the potential damage from sudden shifts in behaviour or values in cross-border money-flows is usually limited. However, countries can maintain chronically uneven monetary relationships with other countries for as long as banks, financial speculators, or residents in one country are willing to hold savings-money in a foreign currency. That willingness can evaporate slowly or disappear suddenly. The move from one currency relationship to another almost certainly causes changes in currency exchange rates. It can also shift at least one country's Central Monetary Ratio, and even disrupt entire economies, which no longer have large non-monetary right sections to stabilise them. Most of the countries that are most vulnerable to currency-shocks are relatively small and poor, but some economists believe that cross-currency monetary imbalances in the United States helped bring about the 2008 financial crisis and subsequent recession there.

Money creation problem

In modern economies, token-money is constantly created and destroyed, in large part because of the two-way flow of money across the token-savings border. In addition to this bi-directional flux, there is the unidirectional flow of money creation (money destruction of any scale has not been seen for almost a century). This is the fiat of additional baseless money. It comes in two forms.

First and most directly, governments create token-money. Traditionally, they did this by minting new coins. Later, they printed notes (confusingly sometimes called banknotes). In theory, they could now simply increase the balances in the bank accounts of individuals or organisations. That mode of creation has rarely been used, however, largely because of a basically ideological unwillingness to admit the predominant role of governments in modern monetary systems. In order to pretend that there is an important conceptual difference between money directly created by governments (confusingly sometimes known as outside money) and money created by banks (confusingly sometimes known as inside money), governments drag banks into most of their money-creation. They do this by borrowing newly-created savings-money from banks, leaving the banks with loans to the government. The government spreads the money into the middle section of the Triptych by distributing benefits and by paying actual and congealed wages.

The bank-lending part of governments' money-creation is a tribute to the second, predominant, and quite indirect modern method of money-creation. Token-money is mostly created when people or organisations borrow money from banks. These financial arrangements will be discussed at length in Chapter Three, but the monetary point is simple. Since the loaned money usually increases the borrower's spending while subtracting little if anything from anyone else's spending, the sum of money in circulation increases by roughly the amount of money that was borrowed. Conversely, when the quantity of debts is reduced, money is destroyed.

The reliance on bank lending for money creation would help keep the Central Monetary Ratio more or less constant, under two conditions: first, the government is not simultaneously creating money directly without any corresponding economic activity, and second, the proceeds of all bank loans are used as token-money, to pay for activity in the middle section of the Triptych. In reality, only the first of these two conditions is regularly fulfilled. Governments are usually fairly responsible monetary actors. Their token-money-creation is generally modest enough that the bulk of the additional supply of token-money is spent, either by the government or by recipients of government benefits, on additional economic activity. In the standard vocabulary, additional government spending through fiscal deficits is not inflationary. Banks are much less reliable. The money they create in lending can be used as either token-money or savings-money, so lending can encourage the sort of one-currency border problems discussed earlier in this section.

Additional money, whether created by banks or by governments, can easily be used to pay higher wages and prices that do not correspond to any increase in the quality or quantity of production. In that case, the newly made money increases the Central Monetary Ratio. In other words, it is inflationary. Inflationary money-creation has probably been the leading source of money-economy imbalances in both pre-industrial and industrial economies.

Governments have generally been directly responsible for the most extreme inflationary episodes. When they have lacked the political authority needed to increase taxes explicitly, they have often resorted to paying their bills with newly debased coins, thus making more money out of the same amount of gold, or, in more recent centuries, with newly created token-money. In calmer modern economies, however, the banks that are directly responsible for most of the money creation also do most of the inflationary work. However, governments are still indirectly responsible, since they have total regulatory control over these monetary subcontractors.

The monetary process of creating the token-money that "pays for" inflation is now fairly well understood, but the underlying dynamics of generalised price and wage increases are still controversial. Various economists have seen the prime causes in one or more items on a list that includes governments, central banks, regular banks, non-bank financial institutions, psychology, interest rates, demographics, labour unions, unemployment, competitive market conditions, and the dynamics of capitalism. Many of the theories are ingenious and persuasive, but after watching four decades of almost totally unexpected increases in the stability of the Central Monetary Ratios around the world, that is of steadily declining inflation rates, I do not believe that the interplay of influences on that Ratio are well understood. Indeed, even the most basic question of causality – whether the push towards higher prices comes primarily from the supply of money or from something more psychological – remains unanswered.

Denominator problems

In modern economies, much effort is dedicated to diagnosing and correcting problems in the paid-for economy, that is in the denominator of the Central Monetary Ratio. The extensive critical attention can easily give the impression that these economies suffer from the chronic illness of inadequate paid-for labour and production. The incessant attention to economic shortcomings also encourages seeing these denominator problems as causes of frequent numerator problems in the Central Ratio. It is argued, or simply assumed, that the lack of economic activity leads to a shortfall in the money-supply, relative to what is needed for full employment and full consumption. Both of those judgements, of chronic economic illness and of frequent economy-caused monetary-problems, are more wrong than right.

First, as I pointed out in Chapter One, the paid-for portions of modern economies are rarely very ill. On the contrary, they are almost always remarkably healthy and stable. Economies around the world have shown a great ability to keep going much as they have been – in normal times, after natural disasters, and during periods of rapid economic change. The inadequacies that receive so much attention are almost always better understood as like modest imperfections in a professional athlete's performance than as like symptoms of a serious or chronic illness. The problems deserve steady and calm attention, but not dramatic economic and monetary countermeasures.

Second, in the last two centuries, very few of the serious problems in the Central Monetary Ratio have been caused by shifts in the denominator. On the contrary, these disorders have almost always been originally and predominantly numerator problems: shocks within the money-finance system. Also, when there is a direction of causality in Ratio problems, it is far more likely to be from the top to the bottom of the fraction than the other way around. Numerator problems, that is money-finance dysfunctions, were at the centre of the rolling economic depressions of the late 19th century, the Great Depression of the 1930s, the crises in many developing economies following the largely financial "oil crisis" of 1973, the steep national recessions known as the 1997 Asian Crisis, and the Great Recession that followed the 2008 Financial Crisis. However, it should be noted that while the numerator of the Central Monetary Ratio is much more prone to serious and, so to speak, contagious instability than the denominator, the purely monetary part of the money-finance system has been much less economically disruptive than the financial one.

There have been exceptions to this pattern of numerator-foremost problems in the Central Ratio. Most notably, the economic shifts before, during, and after the 20th century's First and Second World Wars were denominator problems that led to some large and economically and politically disruptive changes in the Central Ratio. Smaller wars and more localised political-economic crises have also led to monetary disruptions, for example the hyperinflation after disastrous economic policies in Zimbabwe and the sanction-caused high inflation in Iran. However, such denominator-caused monetary disruptions, which were never frequent, have become rarer over the decades. The world's monetary authorities have become less incompetent in their responses to economic challenges.

Still, denominator problems in the Central Monetary Ratio have not been eliminated. The most recent example is the dramatic economic response to the 2020 Covid-19 pandemic. In many countries, the almost instantaneous forced unemployment of about a quarter of the paid workforce presented monetary policymakers with shifts in employment and consumption that were arguably both larger and more sudden than those created by moving into and out of war economies. The policymakers responded to the "lockdown" challenge by creating and distributing enough new money to keep the middle section of the Triptych as active as was legally possible. In developed economies, the money-floods worked as planned. Consumption and employment were resilient, both during and after the few months of severe economic restrictions. However, the policy of potentially increasing the numerator of the Central Monetary Ratio while the denominator was definitely decreasing was an invitation to an unwanted rise in the Ratio.

At first, this invitation was declined. Consumers and businesses treated most of the newly distributed money as savings-money, so the Central (token-) Monetary Ratio was quite stable. However, the newly created savings-money did not go away. It was hoarded in banks and held in money-things, primed to be added to the numerator of the Central Ratio. The potential significant conversion from savings-money to token-money started to become an actual one about a year after most of the economic restrictions had ended. This money-push was a response to some relatively small denominator problems: clogged supply chains and intermittent shortages of components. Those problems caused far smaller declines in denominators of Central Monetary Ratios than the anti-Covid-19 restrictions had, but this time the numerators started to increase. The result was a collection of the "border problems in one currency" that I discussed earlier in this section. As I write in mid-2022, the problems persist. Inflation rates in most currencies are increasing at a faster pace than during any extended period over the last four decades.

The pattern is all too typical. The original denominator problem, the anti-Covid-19 shutdowns, was serious, but it disappeared quickly. Economies responded with their usual alacrity and flexibility to the additional requirements and then to dwindling restrictions. The supply chains got clogged up later, but they soon stated to unclog. The first set of component shortages were also temporary. The Russia-Ukraine war and renewed Chinese anti-Covid restrictions caused new denominator problems in 2022, but there is no reason to doubt that the global economy will cope with the latest challenges fairly quickly and quite well.

The money-finance systems are different. While they worked well during the shutdowns, from then onward they were neither flexible nor resilient. Two years after the first economic restrictions, the central monetary authorities were still struggling to manage a possibly serious numerator problem, one that was caused by their original response to the denominator problem. As I write, there is a substantial risk that the poor or incomplete monetary response to a past economic problem will end up seriously disturbing the denominator as well as the numerator of the Central Ratio.

8. Managing the supply of money

The Central Monetary Ratio changes constantly. Some large or sudden changes in that ratio have a significant negative effect on the actual Great Exchange. These observations raise three obvious questions. When is active control of the money-supply helpful? How can the money-supply be controlled? How large should monetary adjustments be? I will try to answer each of them in this section.

When is active control of the money-supply helpful?

In theory, labourers, producers, governments, and every other organisation can deal with any degree of change in the Central Monetary Ratio. In theory, people and organisations can use past monetary information and future monetary expectations to adjust for current changes in the Central Ratio. In simpler words, they can keep up with changes in prices, incomes, and transfers. In practice, however, keeping up requires a fair amount of work and guesswork. Not only does that effort reduce the time and concentration available for other types of labour, but inaccurate guesses can create new problems, often followed by new policies and then by new errors and uncertainty. The scale of the potential problems and the difficulty of finding just and effective solutions are both magnified by the complex interactions of token-money and savings-money. In the language of information theory, large changes in the Central Ratio can create enough monetary noise to create significant difficulties in understanding monetary signals. The result, as the historical record makes clear, can be monetarily-induced inefficiency in the organisation of the economy.

The problems can come from Ratio changes in either direction.

Sharp *decreases* in the Central Ratio, known as price deflation, can lead to shortages of token-money among both producers and consumers. The shortages are theoretically unnecessary, but in practice, some adjustments of money-numbers tend to proceed faster than others. The typical pattern is that some incomes – whether of wages, company revenues, or tax receipts – fall faster than the corresponding expenses. Economic actors respond to this imbalance by reducing expenses: buying less, reducing the number of employees, or cutting back on benefit programs. The lower spending further reduces the token-money-supply, creating a new imbalance and new reductions of spending. The spiral eventually stops and then reverses, when some money-numbers are judged to be low enough to lure new savings-money across the one-currency border. However, the declines in spending can do significant damage to the Great Exchange before the bargains become irresistible. Unbalanced deflationary episodes were common in the 19th century. At the time, economists cruelly described them as gluts of production, as if consumers were quite content with consuming less than in the past. Keynes changed the discourse, explaining that deflations are caused by an inadequate supply of token-money. The nearly universal application of Keynes' cure, for governments to bring about an increase in the token-money-supply, has effectively eliminated disruptive declines in the Central Monetary Ratio.

At the other extreme, sharp *increases* in the Central Ratio can lead to hyperinflation, extremely high rates of inflation. Episodes of uncontrolled spirals of higher wages and prices – measured at 10% or more in a month, a week, or a day – are rare, because they require an extraordinary combination of self-destructive political stubbornness and unlimited monetary authority. Typically, they come when a politically insecure government creates new money in an effort to keep economically unrealistic and politically popular promises of allocation to its supporters or creditors. The effort is vain, because the additional money quickly works its way through the entire paid-for economy, pushing up all prices and wages. The political promises remain largely unkept. In response, the government creates yet more money and the process continues until the government or its replacement finds a new, economically realistic political settlement, one that eliminates the need to attempt monetary magic.

In hyperinflation, token-money loses its neutrality, because money-numbers change their economic meaning so fast that the life of consumption and the organising of production are both largely reduced to spending token-money as fast as it arrives. However, purely monetary analysis cannot really explain the direction of hyperinflation's monetary non-neutrality. Monetary systems only collapse into uncontrolled inflation when economies, societies, or political systems – generally all three – are badly dysfunctional.

These gargantuan changes in the Central Monetary Ratio are clearly very bad for the economy. Does this imply that smaller changes in the Ratio are bad but less so, and that the money system works best when the Central Ratio is stable? The plausible conventional wisdom of economists is that the effects of inflation are not scaled in this way. Rather, small variation in the Central Ratio do little or no harm, because people can adjust to them fully and fairly easily. Less plausibly, it is often argued that a steady but low rate of inflation actually has an economically helpful psychological effect on consumers or producers. The current conventional wisdom replaced a quite different assumption: that any inflation is a clear threat to economic health, besides being something like a gateway drug that often eventually leads to the monetary addiction of hyperinflation.

The changing dogma is a reminder of economists' imperfect understanding of the dynamics of the Central Monetary Ratio. Admittedly, the historical evidence is unclear. On one side, economies seem to function reasonably well with reported annual inflation rates as high as 10% or even 20%. On the other side, there is no way to know if the affected economies would have done better, let alone how much better, with lower reported inflation rates. It is also unclear whether or to what extent there is a difference in the economic responses to different patterns and levels of inflation. Other unsettled issues include the different effects of fairly uniform and quite varied increases in prices and wages, the importance or even the conceptual correctness of discussing inflation in the left section of the Triptych ("asset price inflation"), and the relevance of currency exchange rates to the Central Monetary Ratio.

In the midst of such intellectual obscurity, I endorse uncertainty: it is not clear whether or under what conditions any or a little inflation or deflation is helpful or harmful. I can only draw one not very impressive conclusion. Considering the economic damage done by large changes in the Central Ratio. it is likely that money generally performs its economic missions most effectively when changes in the numerator of the Central Ratio are reasonably modest.

How can the money-supply be controlled?

In current reality, laws and customs generally restrict the ability of monetary authorities to create and destroy money when and how they think best. In this subsection, I will ignore these actual restrictions, so that I can discuss how the monetary authorities could work if laws and customs were aligned with the actual nature of money.

The most serious challenges in managing the numerator of the Central Ratio are not technical. Monetary authorities can easily mint and distribute more coins, print and distribute more notes, or create additional bank-money by sending out some electronic signals. For a decrease, the physical processes can be reversed and the electronic signals can change signs. Today's powerful, intrusive, and well-informed governments, working in today's largely "dematerialised" monetary system, are well placed to design effective and inexpensive systems of money-supply management. The government's direct creation of bank-money would presumably be widely welcomed, as people would see their bank balances increase. The direct reduction of bank balances might require more delicacy, but the amount of token-money actually in circulation can be restrained by more psychologically tolerable regulations. For example, increasing minimum balances in current accounts effectively converts some token-money to inert savings-money.

The most serious challenges to money-supply-management are intellectual. I see three of them.

The first is the *interpretation of reality*. For example, an increase in the number of people who register as unemployed fairly clearly indicates an undesired shortage of paid employment. However, the cause of the shortage is rarely very clear. It might be a sign that the supply of token-money is not large enough to pay all the workers who should have jobs. In that case, the best cure is simply to create more token-money. However, the primary hindrance to additional paid-employment could well be non-monetary, perhaps poorly designed labour laws, transformations in technologies or tastes, or an inadequate education system. If the problem is wrongly diagnosed as monetary, then the additions to the money-supply that would cure a money-shortage could actually lead to undesirable monetary excess. More generally, since the Central Monetary Ratio can at best be estimated very roughly, there can be no certain, let alone simple, way to determine whether or by how much the current money-economy relationship is changing. Policymakers must interpret the runes produced by surveys of actual wages and prices, adjusting as best they can for any number of possibly relevant factors. With so much uncertainty, the maintenance of a fairly stable Central Monetary Ratio requires monetary authorities with wisdom, flexibility, and humility.

The second challenge in money-supply management is *the resolution of political conflicts*. The monetary authority and the other parts of the government must decide which bank account balances should be increased or decreased. Any choice of how much money goes to or comes from different bank accounts has social, economic, and ethical implications. This non-neutrality of monetary choices ensures that the arrangement of the money-supply is inextricable from politics. The challenges involved are too great, too complex, and too contingent to allow for simple, absolute, or apolitical rules of monetary allocation. Goals such as efficiency and justice can play helpful roles in the debate, but they cannot be considered self-evident guides for actual decisions.

For example, consider one universal extreme rule, allocating additional money in proportion to current income or current bank account balances. This choice is just in the sense of being consistent, but it increases the monetary gap between rich and poor, since x percent of a higher number is larger than the same x percent of a smaller one. As the already rich tend already to spend all the money they want to, a proportionate allocation is also likely to increase the amount of token-money that is converted into savings-money. At another universal extreme, the same nominal amount of new money (y euros rather than x percent) can be added to each person's account. This choice is also consistent, but might be seen as unfairly favouring the poor or even as rewarding the feckless. At a third, non-universal extreme, the government can distribute new money directly through paying for goods and services and through paying out benefits. This choice will be as just as the relevant policies are.

Since the 2008-2009 financial crisis, governments have put large quantities of newly created saving-money into the left section of the Triptych. One of the goals of this "quantitative easing" was to increase the creation of token-money by banks, but the method tends to favour the wealth of people who already own money-things over that of their poorer compatriots. In 2020 and 2021, the distribution of newly created money to individuals and enterprises to compensate for revenues and income lost because of the anti-Covid-19 policies was based on need and past activity. Many other criteria for the allocation of new money can be imagined, from religious tests to hereditary privileges, from industrial development to environmental protections. Each would bring its own practical and ethical advantages and difficulties, as would any mix of criteria.

The third challenge is to *maintain public trust* through all changes in the quantity and value of money. The challenge was not too difficult as long as money was covered with a golden aura, since gold gave coin-money a comforting tradition of value along with undeniable scarcity and allure. Now, however, more is required. Baseless monies are neither scarce nor alluring and their traditions are brief and not always happy. Success is probably the surest way to protect success. Fortunately, as just mentioned, trust-destroying extreme deflation is now almost unheard of and trust-destroying hyperinflation has been rare. However, uncomfortably high rates of inflation and serious troubles in the money-finance system have been uncomfortably common. The threat of lost trust has not disappeared.

How large should monetary adjustments be?

The flexibility of the supply of token-money is theoretically unlimited, but large changes are only called for when the money-economy relationship has become deeply disordered. This can happen when inflation rates are far too high, when paid-for economic activity is suddenly curtailed (as with the anti-Covid-19 restrictions) or, in the other direction, when too many people are supplementing token-money with such substitutes such as barter arrangements or informal promises to pay later. All of those extreme circumstances are fairly rare.

The normal economic situation of continuous but modest fluxes in the real economy requires only relatively modest "fine-tuning" adjustments to the money-supply. How modest? In typical years in most countries, "real" GDP, the common proxy for the denominator of the central ratio, expands by far less than five percent each year. In normal times, the money-supply should expand at a roughly comparable rate. The rate of expansion for token-money could be faster in developing countries with more rapid expansion of production and significant economic moves of economic activity from the right to middle sections of the Triptych. In either case, the rate is slow enough that the fine-tuning does not have to be very refined. Modest government token-money creation – whether through running a fiscal deficit (payments exceed tax receipts) or the provision of a regular "bonus" distribution of token-money to bank accounts – is likely to be enough to keep the supply of money from disrupting the economy.

9. Money is not really a store of value

Having described what money is and how it relates to the economy I can now come back to something that money, understood as the token-money circulating in the middle section of the Triptych, basically is not: a "store of value". In the first section of this Chapter I said the claim that money could store value was neither exactly right nor exactly wrong. I will now explain why it is more wrong than right.

Obviously, there is something right about this description of money. In its everyday use, money does something that can reasonably be described as storing value. I can slip a twenty euro note in my wallet or deposit three hundred euros in a bank account. The money sits unused the whole time that I wait to spend it, whether for a few hours or a few weeks or months. In some sense, the value of those euros is being stored. I can also keep ten thousand euros in some sort of bank savings account, or stuffed in a mattress, with no particular intention to spend the money right away. I can expect to be able to withdraw the money and spend it many months or years from now. In the interim, the money is, in some sense, stored and I am storing the money's value.

The historical record also supports the idea that money is a store of value. Stored money and stored money-things, for example the potential-money of gold held as ingots or turned into ornaments, have been around for as long as token-money. Indeed, in pre-modern economies such treasure-money probably seemed to have more of the symbolic meanings that were then thought to constitute "moneyness" than actual token-money had. It was the hoarded gold more than its purchasing power that inspired greed, showed divine favour, reinforced political power, symbolised psychological control, and provided for tangible safety in adversity. Physically as well as symbolically, pre-modern money was far better suited for storage than for transactions. Coins were expensive to produce, bulky to transport, hard to protect, easy to debase, and difficult to assay, but they almost reeked of value in a way that paper or an entry in a book never can. Besides, the precious metal in coins was easily transformed into lovely, valuable objects which could, if needed, be melted and minted back into token-money.

The greater importance of storage than transactions also fits with the techniques typically used for organising the Great Exchange in these pre-modern economies. Chains of production were mostly short, local, and limited to people who knew each other. They were entwined with non-economic relations and obligations. Under the circumstances, there was relatively little need or desire for token-money's advantages, discussed earlier in this chapter. Indeed, the anonymity of monetary transactions tended, as critics of the modern economy have long noted, to dissolve the economic foundations and manifestations of the largely non-monetary social order.

In denying that money serves as a store of value, I am not only arguing against everyday practice and the historical record. I also stand against the nearly unanimous judgement of economists. "Store of value" is on every list of the essential attributes of money and the tension between value-storing money held in savings accounts and spending-money held in current accounts is fundamental to any economic model of monetary policy.

I am confident that a close study of that tension would lead to accepting the conclusion that I am explaining and defending. The money in the savings account is indeed storing something that can be called value, but it cannot *also simultaneously* have the other attribute of money: to act as a medium of exchange. However, I will not follow the intellectual journey needed to show that the reality of separation undermines the appearance of dual functionality. I will start with what the economy is, the Great Exchange.

The basic argument is simple. In the Great Exchange, the mutual gifts of labour and consumption and the active humanisation of the world have nothing to with value or with storing value, so the token-money working in the Great Exchange can have nothing to do with storing value, whatever is meant by storage and value. Money that is storing value cannot be token-money, which is defined by its use in the instantaneous coordination of labour and consumption. Money that is defined as storing value must be something else: savings-money (or treasure-money).

I will make the argument more complicated by advancing three claims. First, when something called money is stored, the token-money used in the Great Exchange is not what is being stored. Second, storage is not what is actually happening to the not-really-money. Third, in the not-really-storage of not-really money, either value is not preserved or what is preserved is not value. I will discuss each claim in turn.

Money is not what is stored. I have defined money as a token in the Great Exchange, and noted that the two sides of this exchange, labour and consumption, are always essentially current activities. Labour, which money sometimes represents, cannot be stored in any meaningful sense. At most, a labourer might be able to rest one day to store up energy for the next. Consumption services, which money also sometimes represents, are similar. The piano lesson, an hour of a lawyer's time, or a mother's hug that was not consumed today is lost, not stored. Consumption goods, which money also sometimes represents, sometimes can be stored, but storage is considered an expense to be minimised. In sum, none of the things that money represents are actually suitable for storage.

It is, then, misleading to say that money, the token which represents those things, is what is stored. Whatever is actually stored in the wallet, mattress or the reserve account is not the same token-money that is used to balance and allocate current paid-for labour and current paid-for consumption. When money moves out of the middle section of the Triptych, it changes its function and nature.

Philosophers might say that the problem rests in the multiple meanings of the word "money". It is used equivocally, to mean different things. I discussed what might be called symbol-money in the first section of this chapter. The second and third sections introduced economic money, which I call token-money, and the fourth added an introduction to savings-money. The meanings are close enough that they can all refer to the same physical or quasi–physical thing, whether a coin, banknote, or book entry. However, token-money and savings-money are essentially different, because they serve two completely different economic purposes. More precisely, token-money serves several economic purposes (allocation, organisation, and information) while savings-money does not actually belong in the economy, the human interchange of labour and consumption, at all. It is still a token, but of a social relationship that I will describe shortly.

The essential difference between these two things called money is shown clearly by the need for a recalibration of the token-money system when token-money is appropriated for savings (or vice versa, when savings-money is converted into token-money). To provide a dramatic example, imagine that all consumers and producers in an economy decide together one night to hoard half their current supply of token-money. If nothing else in the real and monetary economies changes in response, then the price of everything will double the next day, because the Central Monetary Ratio has halved. Clearly, in economic terms the newly removed money is no longer what it was when it was still token-money in the middle section of the Triptych. This "money" has become something else, savings-money, and it resides in a new place, the left section.

Savings-money is commonly treated as if it was actually token-money in some potential state. Holders generally believe they should be able to exchange any amount of savings-money at any time with no loss of value. Since, however, the two types of money are not actually the same, an unquestioning expectation of maintained value and effortless conversion necessarily strains the money-economy relationship. The treatment of a verbal overlap of two different things as if it were really a conceptual identity is an invitation to trouble. The dates on a calendar are not edible and the money tucked away in a mattress is not automatically spendable, certainly not with any assurance about what it will pay for.

Storage is not what is happening to the not-really-money. In the physical world, storage always brings transformation over time. When a bushel of wheat or a nice new shirt is stored, the thing that went into storage is changed when it comes out. The alteration is typically a decay. Let enough time pass and the wheat will probably be infested and the shirt will probably be less fashionable. Occasionally, as for fine wine and whiskey, there can be an improvement, but *some* change is almost inevitable. Real-world storage also comes with the possibility of damage or destruction and the costs of maintaining a place for storage.

The expectations for savings-money are quite different. It is not supposed to be changed at all, and its storage is supposed to be risk-free and almost cost-free. In particular, the savings-money is expected to maintain its value within the Great Exchange when it is converted back into token-money. This expectation is basically never met, as I will explain shortly. However, the idea that time not only possibly could be transcended in the left section of the Triptych, but definitely should be, shows that this activity belongs in a different social category from storage. Savings-money is best understood as *a marker of enduring social claims.*

Such claims are commonplace in any functioning society. Whenever a citizen walks into a government office, she can expect respectful treatment from the bureaucrats on duty. If I send an email to a work colleague, I can expect to be understood and answered. Adults may expect children to give them their seats on a bus. Saving-money embodies a similar sort of social claim. Having *this* amount of hoarded or saved money is effectively a socially condoned expectation that at some future time other people or institutions will sell the holder of the hoarded-money *that* amount of labour, goods, or services.

Such a social token, unlike any labour or consumption within the Great Exchange, can exist outside of time. Indeed, by its nature the social-token of savings-money is expected to be outside of the ebb and flow of economic circumstances. This value of the social-token must, however, depend on the social rules that validate and specify the expectations that it carries. Savings-money will be worth whatever the society in which it is converted into token-money decides it is worth at the time of conversion. The amount of wheat that hoarded gold coins could purchase in a pre-modern famine was only knowable when the gold was actually offered. Similarly, the holder of money in modern savings accounts cannot know the future worth of her claim. She should not even be too surprised if the claim is declared valueless. Savings-money claims are relations between people and within societies, which can change dramatically and quickly.

Either value is not preserved or what is preserved is not value. The only thing that is certain about the future value of savings-money is that it will not be the same as it is now. The ceaseless and shifting flows of labour and consumption ensure that today's economy is always different from yesterday's. The pre-Socratic philosopher Heraclitus said that a person cannot step into the same river twice. Similarly, the saver cannot put her money back into the same economy from which it came – that economy no longer exists. The goods and services which the one hundred euros of token-money could have purchased when they were taken out of the Great Exchange and turned into one hundred euros of savings-money will necessarily be different from those available in the future when the savings-money is transformed into a different hundred euros of token-money.

Of course, under normal circumstances, the saved money will itself be preserved. Unless the social rules which surround such tokens are changed dramatically, the saved one hundred euro note can be taken from the mattress and spent, and the hoarded one thousand euro bank deposit can be withdrawn. The renewed euros will be able to buy whatever that quantity of euros can then buy. This continuity, while often used as a justification for describing money as a store of value, is actually trivial. It is little more than a monetary tautology to say that because I had one hundred euros then and I have one hundred euros now I have stored the value of one hundred euros. What has been stored or preserved is a piece of paper, a claim to obtain a piece of paper, or a claim on a bank's book-entry. The value of the paper or claim has not been preserved.

These three observations are severe enough to justify my initial claim that the description of money as a store of value is more wrong than right. If gentler language is desired, it can be said that the description is more misleading than helpful for understanding the role of different species of money in the economy and society. Economists should impose conceptual clarity on the equivocation of everyday language by clearly separating savings-money from token-money.

While the difference between the two species of money is clear, the practical border between them can be fuzzy. For example, the money in the wallet that is spent over a few days and the balance in a bank account that declines to zero from one payday to another might be considered unstable hybrids. They are mostly instantaneous tokens which can last through the rather long instants of the Great Exchange. However, some of the unspent balance may well have different economic purposes. It may be part of a balance built up for several months or years to afford a large purchase, for example of a holiday or a car, in which case it is token-money caught in a particularly long instant. Alternatively, it may be kept as a ready reserve for unexpected needs or desires, in which case the sum is no longer token-money in suspense, but actually savings-money. There are also prices that contain a mixture of savings-money and token-money, most notably the costs of houses, physical commodities, and other consumption goods that are thought to be, to some extent, money-things.

These ambiguities should not be surprising. As I said in Chapter One, money is a rough tool. The imprecisions are not limited to value. They extend to the relations of different types of money.

There is a long tradition of considering almost any movement of money from the middle section of the Triptych into the left as virtuous. Putting something away for a rainy day, saving for retirement, and living below one's means are often treated as obviously good things to do with money. Whatever the psychological or ethical attributes of thrift, as a practical economic claim this is all nonsense. Movements of savings-money into and out of the middle section can at best have no effect on the real economy of labour and consumption. At worst, they can create trouble in the Central Monetary Ratio. However, the moral judgement could be reasonable when savings-money is understood as a social sign. The willingness to take less than the fully allotted share of consumption goods and services at one time might demonstrate self-restraint, which is considered virtuous in most spiritual traditions. There is also an intertemporal commutative justice in consuming less than the current flow of token-money would allow at one time and more than it would allow at another.

The traditional folk judgements in favour of savings merit respect, but thrift in itself does not merit adulation. Even leaving aside the practical difficulties caused by the paradox of thrift, savings deserves a mixed moral judgement. Virtuous self-control of spending is good, but in another folk moral tradition, at least as justified as the pro-thrift narrative, unneighbourly miserliness is considered bad. In the languages of symbol-money, an excessive desire to keep money in the left section of the Triptych suggests either some sort of greed, which is never desirable (I will have much to say about that in Chapter Five), or some disbelief in the goodwill of the community, a psychological state which often either expresses or encourages unjust enmity towards neighbours and governments.

The rethinking of savings-money in this section has significant implications for understanding and evaluating finance. If money were actually a store of value, then the intertemporal claims of financial arrangements (these will be explained in Chapter Three) would basically be implicit in the nature of money. I have explained why what is stored is actually not the value of the token-money used in the Great Exchange but a sort of sociological "credit" or claim. For the same reasons, financial claims for money over time are essentially sociological, not economic. As social constructions which are quite distant from the Great Exchange, they have to meet the same standards of effectiveness and justice as any other social arrangement.

10. Money is not intertemporal credit

In this section, I will discuss the most extreme form of the claim that money can store value. This is the claim that what is exchanged when money changes hands is not, as I have argued, ultimately labour and consumption, but what might be described as a sort of basket of future value, an intertemporal obligation, or a claim on some future collection of economic things. Economists who support this understanding of money often summarise this understanding by saying that "money is credit".

Intertemporal monetary commitments undoubtedly exist. Indeed, financial arrangements are exactly two-way intertemporal monetary commitments – a lender or investor provides something that is called money to a borrower or investee at one time, and the borrower or investee pays some sort of money to the lender or investor at different times. Such arrangements are the subject of most of the rest of the book. The question here is whether money is itself basically or essentially one of these intertemporal arrangements. When I discuss finance in Chapter Three, I simply assume that token-money is actually, in its nature or essence, an instantaneous token. With that assumption, credit relations, that is promises to provide economic value in the future, are necessarily and essentially different from money. In this section I discuss the common counter-assumption, that money is actually, by nature and essentially, a form of intertemporal credit, even if it sometimes appears to be an instantaneous token. The discussion is merited, because the counter-assumption is not obviously wrong. My definitions of money and finance could well be faulty or inadequate.

Like the broader ideas that money is a store of value or is based on some commodity, and unlike the ideas that money is a development of barter and that money is always and entirely a creature of the state, the idea that money is a form of credit has a good deal of history on its side. Much of the money that was created as a supplement and eventually a substitute for gold-containing coins was indeed credit-money. When tangible coins were not available to pay for something, the seller would often accept a written promise to provide what was considered real money, that is coins, at some later time. The seller was offering intertemporal credit: goods now in exchange for money later.

Originally, these promises usually had terms that would be familiar to contemporary lenders and borrowers, along the lines of "A promises to give X quantity of gold coins to B on date Y". As with today's loans, the amount X would generally be more than the amount that B would have accepted if A had coins right now. I will give the excess, known as interest payments, a great deal of attention in Chapter Three. Leaving them aside for the moment, the promise from A to B starts to look like money when B can use it as a sort of base for a promise to C: "B promises to pay X amount of gold, received from A on date Y, to C on date Z". Such specific "endorsements" were complicated but useful enough to become fairly common in the early years of the modern trading and industrial economy. However, the promises quickly became less complicated, totally impersonal, and much more useful as payments: "A promises to pay the bearer of this note X amount of gold at a date of the bearer's choice". The "notes" or "bills" which recorded these promises were treated as money.

In my explanation of how these supposedly gold-backed notes work, in Chapter One, I treated the promise of future gold as nothing more than a psychologically helpful fiction. I said that the money-ness of these notes is in the paper, not the promise. For proponents of the money-is-credit thesis, it is the credit, the claim on the future delivery of gold, that actually provided the value. For them, gold-backed money is essentially a loan of the value of the gold.

These economists still see credit when governments create money without gold backing. They generally argue that the government's banknotes are actually claims on future tax receipts. In effect, they say, the users of money are actually making a sort of loan to the government, whether the government expects to repay its obligations in the future with gold, tally sticks, paper money, or additions to bank account balances. In my judgement, that claim stretches credibility. Perhaps government-created money originally had a loan-like quality, even when the gold backing was largely hypothetical. That quality is no longer present when government-created money is the only acceptable currency.

Most token-money today is not created directly by governments. Rather, it is made by banks through loans. In the credit-money view, the central fact in these transactions is that the new bank-made money cannot come into being without a corresponding future obligation of repayment. In this paradigm, money is merely a convenient current abbreviation for the economic substance of the arrangement, the promise to repay the loan over time. The trust that the repayment will occur ("credit" comes from the Latin word for belief) gives the money its value.

In the credit view, the fundamental credit-nature of money is only obscured by the tendency of contemporary governments to guarantee the value of all or many bank-account balances. Many proponents of this theory argue that the real nature of money is found in the debts that originally created these balances, not in the government's commitment to protect the value of the bank balances if the original corresponding debts are not repaid. Other proponents see the guarantees as potentially changing the credit which creates the money from a private loan to a government obligation. There are also rival interpretations of the credit-related meanings of government-created money, banknotes, and the accounting niceties of central monetary authorities.

All of these versions of the theory are easily discredited, in a superficial way. While most money these days is indeed backed by or created out of loans, it is perfectly possible to create money backed by, or made out of, nothing other than trust in the creator's integrity and competence. Several fairly distinguished economists have proposed that most or all money should be created as simply and explicitly baseless, without any reference to a loan. If it is possible to create money without credit, then money can be baseless; it does not *have to be* credit. If money does not have to be credit, then it follows logically that money can only be credit empirically or contingently, but not essentially.

This discrediting of the credit-view is only superficial. In the social sciences, a rule is not falsified by apparent violations, even when there seem to be more such exceptions than examples of the rule being followed. In this case, the actual or potential absence of what looks like credit-based money does not disqualify the claim that money is always essentially credit. I would be rash to make that claim, since it would suggest that the empirical non-existence of what looks like baseless money through most of history disqualifies my own claim that money is always essentially a current fiat token. Historical and current experience can provide evidence, but they cannot decide where moneyness lies. That decision is ultimately conceptual.

It might seem that the distinction is mere philosophical hair-splitting. After all, while the two proposed concepts of money, intertemporal credit and instantaneous token, are directly opposed, the differences are rarely apparent in day-to-day transactions. The particular units of money which are traded for labour or consumption will function in the same way whether they are actually condensed credit or actually current tokens. However, the two visions lead to quite different recommendations for creating, destroying, monitoring, and regulating the supply of money. The implications are even more starkly different for the interpretation of the nature of the financial relationships to be discussed in Chapter Three. Credit-money believers often see money as a slightly unnatural extension and simplification of finance. To them, financial relationships are natural and basically virtuous. In my paradigm, however, intertemporal finance often introduces an unnatural and potentially harmful and unjust distortion into the essentially instantaneous token-money system.

Before defending my understanding of money, I will summarise the conceptual debate. I say that money allows me to exchange my current paid-for labour with some collection of *currently* available paid-for goods and services. The money in my wallet or current account is an *essentially* temporary token to be moved along and around in the extended now of the Great Exchange. They, the believers in credit-money, say that my pay is *essentially* a promise to provide me with a selection of goods and services to be chosen out of *future* production. They see money as essentially a temporal bridge, from the labour I performed or the government benefit I claimed in the past to the consumption I will purchase in the future.

In my understanding, the value of my token-money income is subject to little doubt. It is worth exactly what it can buy now, which is my proportion of the total current paid-for production (y^*/Y). In their understanding, the value of my credit-money is subject to the vagaries of fortune. My current income (current x) has no sure relationship with future production (future Y). When my credit-money is "cashed in", it may buy more or less than was expected when it was received.

The purposes of the two types of money are also quite different. My token-money is primarily a technical tool for the current organisation of labour and allocation of consumption. It is deeply embedded in society. The token-money system is a social construction which must be operated by a socially legitimate authority and which is always subject to social judgements of its distributive justice (a fair deal for everyone) and its service to the common good. In contrast, their credit-money is primarily an individualistic tool for tying past individual efforts to future individual rewards. The individualism remains even when the money moves to and from the artificial legal persons known as corporations. The essential fact, in this view, is that money is created through private contracts. These contracts should promote commutative justice (a fair deal to both sides), but have no responsibility to protect or advance the common good.

The current and intertemporal orientations of the two approaches to money lead to different social roles for money. In a token-money world, money is a pragmatic tool that encourages cooperation. Money is spent as it comes in, and it has no power to change the economy, as long as the relations between token-money and the paid-for economy are reasonably consistent. It is quite different in a credit-money world. Uncertainty, delay, and strife are built in, because the unavoidable temporal gap between all money-getting and money-spending creates hopes and fears about the future value of the currently held money. These emotions encourage conflict. The current holders of money are likely to have a quite different understanding of a just monetary value in the paid-for economy from that of the money's future recipients.

With token-money, there is no structural delay between receiving and spending. Like the two sides of the Great Exchange (labour and consumption), the two sides of the monetary exchange are considered as happening at the same time. As a whole, the economy consumes now what it produces now. In the credit-money worldview, money is created exactly to overcome the delay between today's labour and the harvesting of its final fruits. The initial receipt of credit-money brings the ability to buy things before the recipient has fully produced the equivalent of the things being purchased, while the provider of money has temporarily given away some ability to buy things.

These advances and delays of spending-power in the credit-money system suggest that if there are no adjustments the spender will tend to gain more purchasing power than is just, while the non-spender loses out. Justice requires compensating adjustments, compensation from the debtors for the value of the credit they received when they received not-truly-earned money. (Remember, there is no imbalance in the token-money approach.) According to the credit-money believers, the lack of compensation connected to everyday money is a mere matter of convenience. Normal monetary arrangements are, as mentioned, merely special cases of the financial arrangements to be discussed in Chapter Three. Money is a loan, just one that is non-interest bearing and everlasting. In a world of credit-money, there is no left section of the Triptych, because money-things are actually at the very centre of the paid-for economy.

Which view is right, token-money or credit-money? Obviously, I have taken a side in this debate, but the philosophy of social science tells me that neither view can be either proven or disproven. "The facts" cannot decide between these conflicting claims about the deep structure of monetary reality, since any collection of monetary practices always includes apparent exceptions to either model, with each deviation having more or less plausible explanations in the logic used to explain the chosen model. Nor can logical deductions provide an unassailable conclusion, since close analysis of logical chains which purport to demonstrate the truth of one or the other opposing monetary vision will always show that the conclusion was hidden somewhere in the assumptions. Finally, no brilliant experiment can definitively disqualify either claim, because undesired results can always be explained away.

As I discussed in Chapter One, what actually kills off old paradigms and nurtures new ones in the social sciences is something more nebulous, an amorphous and gradually gathered collection of plausible and ultimately persuasive new concepts, facts, arguments, and historical experiments. One of the purposes of this book is to expound this still fairly new monetary paradigm, the model based on the Great Exchange and the baseless units of token-money. One part of my propaganda is aimed against the legitimate opposition, in this case the credit-money paradigm. Here are three conceptual arguments against it.

The first argument was implicit in my earlier description of the economy as a continuous, intimate, and socially all-encompassing Great Exchange of gifts, the human offering of labour in exchange for the human receipt of the fruits of this labour. If money is, as seems plausible, a tool that both is shaped by this economy and is used to help guide it, then money must be as close as possible to the economy, which *is* this continuous exchange. Token-money is very close. It directly ties labour with consumption. More indirectly, through taxes, benefits, and other payments, it ties both these individual activities with the shared economic life of the entire community. In contrast, credit-money has only an indirect relationship with the Great Exchange, and its focus on the delay between labour and consumption misses the continuous and comprehensive relationship of the two sides of the economic cycle.

Second, the credit-money approach is built on the necessary delays in the cycle of economic activity. Since it is centred on paying in advance for the lengthy and largely physical process of production, credit-money is naturally connected to the long lives of mines, machines, and factories and to the shorter journeys from raw material to finished goods. In this perspective, the constant and continuous coming and going of actual people's current labour and consumption is a secondary factor. In contrast, token-money is a rough quantitative token that is primordially attached to the basic human activities of labour and consumption. It expresses a human-centred understanding of their actual relationship. With token-money, the labours involved in constructing long-lasting physical assets – the digging of mines, the building of factories and the gathering of inventories – are nothing special. Such labours are conceptually no different from the labours of actual current production, of personal service, or even of being. In my judgement, this token-money vision is more realistic than the credit-money alternative. It is certainly far more humane, as it treats human activity as central and the creation and accumulation of things as secondary.

Indeed, token-money almost automatically smooths over the delays in the long chains of production, the delays which, in the credit-money paradigm, explain the centrality of credit. With token-money, it is natural that the workers whose labour contributes to only the beginning of the chain of production can spend as they work. They are simply allocated a share of the total current production of consumption goods and services. The eventual expected contribution of the direct fruits of their labour to the consumption side of the economy may be relevant to the decision of how much they should be allocated now, but the delay between the labour and the harvest of its fruits is basically irrelevant.

Third, token-money is socially unifying, while credit-money is individualistic and divisive. Token-money is essentially a communal project. The central monetary authority is always a creature of the entire community of money-users. It is always supposed to control the money-supply in the interest of the common good. In contrast, credit-money is always created to promote the individual goods of particular borrowers and lenders. Some lenders may be motivated by some more communal purpose, but noble motives are certainly not necessary for the operation of a technically well-functioning credit-money system. In any case, credit-money is by nature imperfectly socialised. In its pure form, without government backing of banks, it can even be antisocial. The problem is that credit money can be destroyed when banks fail. The losses impose unjust punishments on innocent savers. They suffer for the sins of lenders or for other economic failings. More historically, credit has often amplified the sharp social division between the poor and the rich, because many loans create what I will describe in Chapter Three as poor-to-rich monetary transfers. The idea that money is a form of credit seems almost to sanctify unjust power-relationships.

As just mentioned, the two understandings of money provide directly opposed interpretations of finance, which consists in the arrangements of monetary exchanges over time. If the credit-view is right, the financial system is a natural part of any money economy. It is quite different in the token-money approach of this book. In the next chapter I will explain the implications of that approach – financial arrangements are never natural, often ineffective, and frequently unjust.

Are my three arguments persuasive? I think so, of course, but I have been thinking about money in this way for decades. Tempted but more sceptical readers will naturally want to try out the two approaches. Finance provides the best test case. In Chapter Three I present finance as it is seen when token-money is assumed to be instantaneous. If that description seems plausible or fitting, readers might want to question the credit view of money more profoundly.

Chapter 3. Introduction to finance

Having just alluded to finance, the principal subject of this book, it is time for a more formal introduction. As with my discussion of money, I will start with a cultural prelude, mentioning but not attempting to analyse some of the deep and often inconsistent psychological, sociological, and moral connotations that accompany these intertemporal monetary commitments. Almost all of the rest of the chapter is an attempt to put finance into its economic place. Much as money solves various economic problems, finance is one solution to one monetary problem. I explain that in the second section. In the third section, I show that finance is also the modern embodiment of a pre-modern social-economic relationship. That is followed by four sections that set finance and its components in a realistic social and moral framework and finally two sections to clear up some common confusions.

Before getting started, it might be helpful to have a somewhat clearer idea of the final destination. The point of this chapter and the following two is to put finance in its proper place – in the economy, in society, and in individual psychology. That intention is relevant because finance is currently in some improper places. Indeed, while token-money is often misunderstood and sometimes misused, as I hope I have made clear in the first two chapters, the abuses and distortions of finance are much more prevalent. As I will explain in this and the following two chapters, the fundamental problem is conceptual. Finance is too often used badly because it is almost always badly misunderstood. At best, I will argue, finance can be, and sometimes actually is, a quite useful and potentially just social tool. At worst, it is a tool that supports social injustice, economic inefficiency, international discord, and personal moral decay. All too often, its worst aspects predominate in the contemporary economy. There is too much finance of any sort and too many financial arrangements are unjust to the participants, unhelpful to the economy, and harmful to the social fabric.

1. Finance as a symbol

Any of the reader's temporarily suspected pre-existing or latent beliefs about finance are likely to be connected, more or less closely, to the ideas listed in this section. As with the ideas about money in the first section of Chapter Two, the concepts provided here constitute an outline of a "thick description". Each one is neither simply right nor completely wrong. Rather, they are all right and wrong, mutually supporting and mutually contradictory, shallow and profound. The two conceptual universes, of money and finance, are of course related, since finance is something that is done with money. However, the two are also quite different. The cultural connotations of money are, as it were, much thicker than those of finance. The numerical difference is indicative – 24 ideas about money and only ten about finance. The gap should not be surprising. Money is old and widespread. It has been around for millennia in some form and is by now deeply entrenched in all reasonably complex societies. Finance is also old, but it has been a significant axis of economic and social organisations for less than two centuries.

Finance has become especially significant culturally in recent years. At least among a certain political set, the word "financialisation" has become a metonym for a particular vision of economic organisation. The word is used primarily for criticism, but sometime for praise. I discuss it in the seventh section of this chapter.

Also like the parallel discussion of the cultural connotations of money, the following descriptions of the connotations of finance are too cursory to be anything more than suggestive. I regret having neither the space nor the expertise needed to provide more profound analysis. However, such ruminations would be quite distant from the topic of this book, which is not how people think about finance but how finance actually works in the economy and, to some extent, in society. Still, the concepts I am about to list are relevant to actual practices, as they inevitably swirl around in people's minds as they consider whether to use finance to address an economic problem or to establish a social relationship and what financial arrangements to use. It is impossible to understand fully how finance does and should work without allowing for those incursions from a more symbolic and perhaps more psychologically resonant universe. Readers, too, cannot permanently discard and should not ever totally disregard these ideas. While the real world of finance is basically built up as I describe in all but this section of the book, from the Great Exchange upward, that real world also expresses some downward projections from the thickly meaningful universe of archetypes, myths, and concepts.

Finance is:

1. *The ever-more of finance*: "Compound interest is often called the eighth wonder of the world, because it seems to possess magical powers, like turning a penny into $5 million" (Morningstar, ND). So says a leading website for investors, describing the exponential increase of value supposedly inherent to any financial arrangement. If the size of the hoard of money increased by 10 percent each year, the initial penny would need a mere 211 years to reach the five million dollar mark. (Marx, 1894: vol. 3, Chap. 24) described such faith in compounding as the belief that it is "a property of money to generate value and yield interest, much as it is an attribute of pear-trees to bear pears". The founder of Communism understood this purported financial property of money to be a central part of what less materialist social observers might call the Capitalist mythical imagination. The dream that money can multiply with neither effort from nor possible losses for its owner takes the Midas story to another dimension, both positively and negatively. Compounding is the magic force which turns a modest degree of monetary prudence into unbounded wealth. It is also the magic force which preserves and amplifies the power of the owning-class or the economic elite over the working masses.

Financial compounding has a further magic power. It overrules the second law of thermodynamics. In everything else, entropy is inevitable. Emotions, memories, and physical strength, not to mention buildings and machines – all of them naturally wane over time. With compounding, money always waxes, expanding and strengthening for ever and ever. Compounding money is on an automatic journey towards the infinite, in particular towards the monetary bad infinity mentioned in Chapter One. (The much more modest economic reality of compounding will be discussed at the end of this chapter.)

2. *The lure of justly unearned wealth*: In the middle section of the Triptych, prosperity always requires steady human labour and almost always involves a laborious and energetic transformation of the real world. Prosperity is sure to be lost if the labourers' efforts stop or if the relevant portion of the world's resources is used up. Finance promises everyone and anyone something much more appealing, gains which come with little toil and which never cease. The landlord, bondholder, or financial investor expects to harvest labour's fruits with only a single cast of her monetary seeds into the friendly and fertile financial ground. There is no need to plough, fertilise, or reap. Better still, the beneficiaries of this financial harvest rarely see any social or personal injustice in their perpetual, labour-free income. On the contrary, they usually see something like a law of nature. Compounding is the way the world works. Money not only holds its value as surely as a magnet holds its charge. It accrues more money with the same physical certainty that a magnet gathers iron filings.

In respectable society, the young are encouraged to aspire to these legitimate and wonderful financial gains, while the labour of extracting as much of them as possible constitutes both a respectable hobby for the investing class and a respected profession for the members of any nation's elite. The social judgement demonstrated by pay in the financial business is clear – it is sweet to make a fortune from almost nothing, sweeter to turn a small fortune into a larger one, and sweetest of all to make the very rich even richer.

3. *The guilt of debt*: In German, the same word (*Schuld*) refers equally to unpaid moral and monetary obligations. In the Greek text of the Lord's Prayer, Christians ask God to forgive their debts. While Jesus presumably is using the word as a symbol for the trespass of the divine law (as in the traditional English translation) or of sin (as in similar Biblical texts), the moral connotation of financial obligations is clear. The shame of owing money is common, even in cultures and languages that do not express the connection automatically. Households and governments which borrow money so that they can spend more than they earn have long been considered irresponsible. Public attitudes have recently softened – that is a key sign of the financialisation of societies – but it is still generally thought best not to fall into debt. Indeed, to choose to borrow, or even to be forced

to, is still commonly considered a mark of weak economic character, automatically punished by the debtor's undesirable dependency on his or her creditors. In the popular imagination, the weakness becomes vice if the debt contract is broken. The only way to restore the moral balance created by the guilt-obligation of debt is to make all the agreed payments.

4. *The slavery of debt*: In some parts of the Bible and in many pre-modern societies, it was assumed that otherwise unpayable debts can only be discharged by agreeing to enter some sort of slavery to the erstwhile creditor. Times have changed. Defaults on debt no longer deprive a person of all social freedom. However, extreme debts, paid or unpaid, still create a sort of financial slavery. The creditor effectively controls where the heavily indebted person can live and work, and the worry and monetary drain of interest payments create something close to a master–slave relationship, even if the financial master is more likely to be an anonymous institution that exercises its authority with bailiff's orders than a slaveholder who sends out a foreman with a whip. The physical softening has not erased the moral taint. There is something repulsively unjust about the endurance of debt-slavery. It seems cruel that the shackles imposed by some ancient receipt of money can endure for years, perhaps decades, long after whatever good was produced by the original loan has been exhausted. However, in the supposedly principled logic of finance, no circumstance is grave enough to merit removing the chains of financial obligations. As with traditional chattel slavery, the immutable laws of property and finance are more powerful and more absolute in debt slavery than any commandments of love or any adjustments to the actual conditions of the world.

5. *The evil of usury*: In one symbolic language of social relations, financial arrangements unjustly favour the provider of money over the recipient, at least until proven otherwise. The recipient of money ends up poorer, because more must be returned than was received, and, with equal certainty, the provider ends up richer. This transfer of money from those in need to those who already have is given the name "usury" (that, at least, is one reasonable conceptual summary of a much-disputed term). With that understanding, financial relations are necessarily usurious, and always stink of injustice, greed, and cruelty. Obviously, when it comes to sniffing out this usury, the olfactory capacity of the lenders is otherwise engaged,

presumably enjoying the floral bouquet of their gains. Moral teachers have not been so distracted. For most of history, they have firmly condemned usury whenever finance was present. They have often disagreed about when the evil of usury was actually present, but often enough they included any claim to gain from lending, especially from lending to the poor. Even as intellectuals and moralists came to accept some interest payments as licit, they and the less sophisticated public frequently treated money-lending and money-lenders as impure, as if touching the monetary gains of finance was like touching a corpse.

The stated reasons for the strong rejection vary. In the Aristotelian tradition, money is a sterile counting-thing, which cannot also be fertile, so there is something fraudulent about expecting it to multiply without any apparent effort. In socialist sociology, usury is an abuse of weak, relatively poor people by the rich and powerful. In egalitarian economic thinking, usury amounts to unjustly generous rewards for the relatively minor economic service of providing money, an injustice which is amplified when there are alternative ways to provide money with lower or no rewards to the provider. In literature and the popular imagination, the usurer is the embodiment of petty cruelty – coercing the desperate to accept harsh terms, pitiless in the face of calamity, and miserly in temperament.

6. *The community of credit*: In another symbolic language of social relations, finance strengthens communities and helps them promote the common good. All the members contribute money for financial investments when and as they can. These investments produce steady monetary gains for all the investors, besides being useful to everyone in the community. With finance, everything is shared. The gains from many bank loans are distributed among many depositors, as are any losses. For individuals, the voluntary commitments and negotiated terms of loans create a world of freedom, opportunity, and justice. Lenders can freely decide which people or enterprises to support, borrowers can freely choose what useful or pleasing things to buy with their newly available money, and the mutual agreement ensures that commutative justice is maintained. All this is built on trust – in the goodwill of the other party to the financial arrangement, in the beneficence of economic developments, and in the capacity of some legal systems to promulgate restorative justice if some other type of trust

proves misplaced. The etymology of credit – from the Latin for "to believe" – is apt.

Finance also bridges the generations. The young first borrow money from the middle-aged to build or buy houses or to found enterprises. As the new generation ages, its interest payments support the old in their retirement, until eventually the borrowers become lenders, supporting and then supported by the next generation. All live in healthy mutual dependence. Such claims of shared commitment and fairly allocated sacrifice may sound ridiculously idyllic, but they were appealing enough, and perhaps true enough, to encourage the creation and maintenance of many successful community- and user-controlled banks in most industrialising countries well into the 20th century. Subsequent trends have weakened the resonance of this symbolic communal meaning, but defenders of finance and would-be ethical investors still assume that finance either naturally supports the common good or can be guided to do so if it is properly organised.

7. *The security of financial wealth*: Finance does not only promise wealth beyond measure. It also promises measured wealth. The peaceful pensioner living off her annuity, the unruly heir living off his trust fund, the respectable widow scraping by on the income from her late husband's portfolio (carefully hoarding the principal so she will have something to pass on to the children), the manual worker who scrimped and saved to buy a few apartments and can now enjoy a more comfortable retirement thanks to their rental income – these are all finance-funded models of careful bourgeois respectability. Small numbers matter in this sort of finance – "Yields are up from 2% to 2.1% – that will take the grandchildren to Disney World this year" – and the accompanying smallness of the financial mind has become a cultural stereotype, both attacked as petty and praised as prudent. The seeming self-reliance of a man with his own income produced the smug confidence of the 19th century rentier. This type was sufficiently socially significant to inspire not only mocking portrayals by essayists and novelists, but the development of government systems which mimicked the rentiers' financial security by providing tax-funded systems of income creation.

8. *The peace of (debt) forgiveness*: Debts are meant to be paid, but debts are also meant to be forgiven. The writing off of the great debt of sin is the founding financial image of salvation in Christianity, perfecting the possibly symbolic scheduling of jubilees of debt forgiveness in the Old Testament (Anderson, 2009) (Sanders, 2020). Revolutionary governments have generally erased debts, eliminated many private financial obligations, and torn up private rental contracts. In modern business, banks forgive or write off debts all the time, although they do not court publicity for these business decisions. Campaigners for social justice often argue for a more joyful liberation from debt, a revival of the old jubilee, but these days even charities are more likely to count on investment income to do their good works than to abandon that income for the sake of forgiving the debts of others. The fading of this social symbol of finance – as offering the potential for forgiveness – is probably culturally significant, especially as it coincides with the increase of financialisation, which arguably has increased both the need for and virtue of forgiveness.

9. *The wicked lords of finance*: Evil financiers living in luxurious mansions are puppet-masters who pull the strings of kings and elected leaders. The bankers have no patriotism, because they and their money cross borders without noticing. They search only for their own good and they serve only their own God, Mammon. Many of these conniving masters of the universe are cosmopolitans, Jews, or Freemasons, members of some inherently international and obviously evil conspiracy. They often work with small-time lenders, men who are so callous that they will reduce neighbours to destitution and squeeze the poor for pennies. Their cruelty is only a small version of the inhumanity of the great houses of finance, which will sell a people into slavery or arms to the enemy, merely to earn a few extra dollars. The puppet-strings of finance are not always visible. Companies seem to do what their own managers and boards of directors decide. However, even the seemingly most powerful among them cannot move without the approval of their financial masters. Financiers may pose as concerned citizens. They may even support charitable works, but the gifts are merely a ruse to distract attention from their greed and power.

And so forth. The myths of wicked finance have propelled Christian anti-Semitism, Socialist anti-Capitalism, and populist anti-banking. The wicked

Shylock and his pound of flesh became the Rothschilds, followed by the Goldman Sachs and Morgan Stanley of today. For conspiratorial thinkers, the mingling of the political, corporate, cultural, and financial elites at the World Economic Forum in Davos is proof positive that finance is the hidden ruling class. As with the magic of compounding, the truth is much less lurid than the stories. I will present a more realistic story later in this chapter.

10. *The quasi-spiritual essence of the monetary economy*: In the thinking of a narrow circle of academic economists, finance plays a role which they consider realistic and economic but which an outside observer would be more likely to consider fictional and symbolic. The core to the economists' analysis will be presented, and rejected (I am one of those outside observers) in the ninth section of this chapter.

Basically, in this story, finance is the nervous system of the contemporary economy, and its management is a, or the, key technocratic task of economic management. In a turn towards a mystical or numerological understanding of reality, a single number – *the* interest rate – is believed to be the master-switch that controls the whole economic mechanism. The approach moves from the mystical to an almost religious understanding when it assigns high priests, known as central bankers, to determine the settings of this master-switch. Like other priestly authorities, they claim something like divine authority, although their oracles are not found in dreams or the flights of birds but in the runes of data and the arcane lineaments of elaborate and almost totally fictitious "models". Like their more conventional priestly counterparts, the central bankers resent and resist all political interferences, typically claiming that their deity, the financial system, can only be harmed by the grubby concerns and impaired vision of voters and their representatives.

The deeper meanings of finance are, as I said at the beginning of this section, mutually contradictory, but there is a clear imbalance to the negative. In the popular cultural imagination, the cruel misers who lend, the struggling victims who borrow, and the injustice of repayment far outweigh finance's community-building collaboration and individual protection. The cultural imagination has certainly not absorbed the economists' quasi-religion. Perhaps if it had, the overall judgement would be changed, although I doubt it. The negative impression could certainly be undeserved, unbalanced, out of date, or incomplete. At the very least, though, the ugly image raises a serious question – what is it about finance which makes it so corrupting in the cultural legends? I hope the rest of the chapter will provide an answer. It should become clear that unlike money, which is an ethically neutral social institution that can and to a large extent does achieve its purely economic goals with great efficiency, financial arrangements are often not the best social institution for reaching the one economic goal they can serve. Worse, without a strong moral framework, a financial system will, as the list of social meanings suggests, easily slide away from the common good and into injustice and even oppression.

2. Economic finance

What is finance, actually? Perhaps surprisingly, that question is not easy to answer. One problem is that the word is used to mean several different things, which I will discuss later. However, a puzzle remains even after narrowing the scope of finance to what I call pure-finance: agreed, intertemporal, two-way monetary flows. The definition is clear enough, at least after some explanation of the terms, but it does not capture what pure-finance is in any ontological sense. What is the definition of this limited set of monetary arrangements that corresponds to the definition of money as a numerical tool used for organising essentially non-numerical economic activity?

My answer to this ontological question might be confusing. Pure-finance has two distinct, although sometimes overlapping, essential functions. It has an economic purpose, to be a solution to what I call no-money-now problems. It also has a sociological purpose, to transfer token-money from relatively poor to relatively rich people. I discuss the economic function in this section and sociological one in the next.

The antecedents of economic finance were introduced in Chapter Two, where I mentioned that monetary imbalances can arise within the middle section of the Triptych. Although the simple system of monetary circulation is remarkably effective at paying for helpful labour, consumption, and transfers, sometimes people and organisations find themselves without the token-money needed to pay for labour, consumption, or transfers that are appropriate, helpful, required, or merely desired. They have a no-money-now problem. The "now" in the name is significant. Finance, which is one possible solution to this problem, relies on the expectation that money will be available later.

By the scale of the entire economy, no-money-now problems occur quite rarely. Overall, the components of the monetary cycle are quite well coordinated and calibrated with the components of the Great Exchange. However, for various reasons, both broadly social and more narrowly economic, the harmony is sometimes broken.

The most familiar no-money-now problem occurs within families. One parent works for pay, the other labours at childcare, and the children labour at growing up. Neither the "stay at home" parent nor the children typically receive any money from the wage economy in exchange for their toil. In the modern economy, where the middle section of the Triptych is so large, the effects of this non-pay can be dire. Neither carer nor offspring can thrive, or perhaps even survive, without a solution to their no-money-now problem. The most traditional solution is sharing, or what I call yoking. When the unpaid members of the family share the paid members' wages, the wage-earner and the non-wage-earners are yoked together into a consumption team. The more modern solution is for the government to pay token-money benefits, or to extract less token-money as taxes from the household, to ensure that this group of the unpaid obtain what the society has decided will be their appropriate share of the total consumption in a polity. It is relevant to the imminent discussion of finance that both these approaches, sharing-yoking and benefit-tax, are contemporaneous. The money needed for the consumption of the carer and the children is taken from other people's current pay, either as part of a voluntary community effort within the family or as taxes mandated and extracted by the government from the much larger community of the nation.

Free-to-user schools are another example of the no-money-now problem. The schools lack revenues, but teachers must be paid with token-money. The government's ability to raise taxes solves the school's no-money-now problem, effectively forcing the whole community to contribute some of the fruits of its total current labour to the public good of educating the community's young. The unpaid-for education also helps resolve the just discussed no-money-now problem of individual families – children do not have to pay directly for their education.

A type of no-money-now problems that is traditionally closely connected to finance occurs within modern economies' long chains of production. The labour that builds factories, plants trees, and designs new products does not generally produce any currently saleable fruits. Indeed, it may take years before this labour is converted into a consumption good or service in the paid-for economy. Even when the temporal gap is much smaller, for example the months needed for finished fabric to become paid-for clothing, the labourers involved in sewing, shipping, and selling the clothes might starve to death while waiting to be paid by the purchasers of the ultimate fruits of their labour. Finance, that is loans of the money to these labourers or, more often, to their employer provides one solution to such no-money-now problems.

What I called the tractor-problem in the seventh section of Chapter Two is another traditional example of money not being available when it is wanted, needed, or socially and economically advantageous. It is helpful to everyone if some technique can be found to pay for tractors during the years in which farmers' incomes are insufficient. Economists describe the provision of token-money for such economically sensible purchases as "intertemporal smoothing". Loans are a smoothing technique, as are government grants and communal drought insurance.

Finance has appeared as a possible solution in some of these preliminary examples of no-money-now problems. It could conceivably be used in all of them. Banks could lend money to growing children and to their carers, with repayments delayed until the next generation entered the paid workforce. A small portion of university students currently solve their no-money-now problems with loans, but *all* the money to pay all teachers could conceivably come from loans to the future earners who are currently attending schools. As with the putative family-care loans, the primary-school loans could be repaid many years later. Conversely, the examples suggest that the intertemporal two-sided contracts of finance are not the only solution to no-money-now problems. I divide the possible solutions into six families.

Yoking

A person who is not producing anything that can currently be sold is allocated some of the money received by some other person, group, or organisation. The yoke that ties the money-having person or organisation to the money-short labourer can be psychological, broadly organisational, or narrowly legal. In the modern economy, these monetary yokes range from intimate and indefinite to contractual and time-limited.

I have already mentioned the most intimate type of yoking, connections among family members. Economic and social changes have reduced the use of this traditional yoking. Still, the practice of paid labourers sharing their wages with unpaid family members is far from dead. Many wage-earners are expected to use some of their money income to support young and old "dependents", sometimes at a great distance. Socially, family money-sharing sometimes causes discord, but more often it is a sign and a reinforcement of unity. The desire for monetary solidarity is often strong enough for households with more than one income to yoke all the members' wages into a single common fund.

The least intimate form of modern yoking is found in business organisations. Companies and other organisations engaged in some economic activity divide up most of the money received from selling goods and services among all their employees, both those directly responsible for production and those with little or no direct tie to the paid-for goods and services. As long as the customers are willing, or can be forced, to pay for otherwise non-sellable labour, the firm's payroll can include any number of people whose contribution to current revenues is unclear or non-existent. These paid yoked labourers may be researchers, builders of new factories, community liaison officers, poets, soothsayers, paid sexual partners for the organisation's leaders or, as in China, political supervisors. For all of these people, the yoking to the company's revenue stream solves the no-money-now problem, because their wages will be included as a "cost of doing business" when calculating the price of the products sold.

To understand finance, it is important to note that corporate yoking typically extends to pay for labour that is expected to produce revenue sometime in the future. When a customer buys shoes, phones, computers, and so forth, the price is usually high enough to pay the costs of designing new product lines, creating and applying new technology, and constructing new factories. In other words, the labourers concerned with future production are yoked to those responsible for current output. In well-established corporations, this yoking of customer payments to future-oriented labour is by far the most common source of the token-money needed to pay for large new projects. Accountants describe this practice as paying for investments "out of operating cash flow".

Unfortunately, most economists seem to misunderstand the nature of the practice. Using the fanciful concoction of an implicit "cost of equity", they analyse the future-oriented portion of company revenues as a hidden type of finance. This convoluted treatment is necessary to support their purely financial view of companies, but it is redundant – and ridiculous – if finance is considered just one of several ways of solving a no-money-now problem. The yoking of current sales revenues with expenses that will bear fruit only in the long term is not a kind of pure-finance. Rather, this yoking is a distinct and often superior alternative to any financial arrangement.

Giving

If one person does not have money, then someone else can voluntarily provide it. Donations may come as gifts of money to otherwise non-yoked family members and friends, or as monetary contributions to good causes. Within communities, especially tightly knit ones, giving is often used to support families or individuals deemed in special need, and to provide wages for some of the labourers who work on projects and buildings for common use. Giving can work by crossing the border between the middle and right sections of the Triptych, with donations "in kind" of labour or of consumption goods. The motivations for contributions often include some combination of generosity, duty, and the expectation of non-monetary gain. For example, when churchgoers put money in the collection plate, they generally feel that they want to do so, that they should contribute, and that the ministers' prayers, words, and work will provide them with some spiritual benefit.

Gifts, especially totally or apparently gratuitous ones, fit in poorly with most economists' initial anthropological assumption that calculating self-interest is the sole or dominant motivation in human decisions. In reality (a condition often quite distant from economists' analysis), the gift economies described in the second section of Chapter Two are implicit throughout the Great Exchange, even in many apparently finely calculated individual decisions, so it is hardly surprising that giving is an appealing solution to some no-money-now problems. Indeed, an anthropologically more realistic "gaze" often discerns something like a gift-mentality in many apparently monetary solutions to no-money-now problems, especially small ones that occur in close groups. For example, buying rounds at the pub, or restaurant meals for friends or business contacts, is often best understood as gift-behaviour. The recipients are expected to "repay" in due course, although not necessarily in the monetary economy. Similarly, money sent from parents to their impecunious adult children are gifts that are usually made with no or quite open-ended expectations of reciprocity.

Pooling

Pooling is an organised communal solution to no-money-now problems. In pooled arrangements, each member of a fairly large group of people steadily pays relatively small amounts of token-money into a common fund. The process, like combining many drops of water to create a large pool, ensures there is enough money to pay a few members of the group relatively large amounts of money under certain circumstances. Insurance systems are essentially such share-and-distribute pooling arrangements. Token-money is received as "premiums" and simultaneously paid out in "claims" or "benefits". The latter are justified by some carefully defined event, typically one that causes a no-money-now problem. Insurers help with the costs of disease, death, retirement from paid labour, illness, and damage to property or business. With a diverse enough pool, pooling can help solve tractor-problems by transferring the combination of small proportions of the income of many farmers who are not affected by drought to each of the smaller number of farmers who are affected. In most communities in affluent economies, pooling, especially through insurance, plays a far more significant role than generosity of giving in helping people cope with setbacks.

Insurers often combine and entwine pooling with financial arrangements. However, the two parts to the no-money-now solutions are conceptually and practically distinct. Finance, like anything connected with savings-money, relies on intertemporal claims on economic resources. Pooling represents a direct sharing of current resources: the many each consume a little less so the approved few can consume a lot more.

Pooling is not limited to insurance plans. The method is sometimes also used to address other, less traumatic no-money-now problems. For example, in some communities, a group of families can create shared wedding or education funds, which dole out payments as children of various ages reach these milestones. Small toll payments on highways are sometimes pooled and disbursed for large repair or construction expenses. Lotteries and most sorts of betting arrangements also work by pooling, but they do not obviously solve no-money-now problems. Quite the contrary, such pools with random beneficiaries tend to create no-money-now problems among compulsive gamblers.

Socially, pools have many benefits. They create or reinforce communities of interest, they build shared commitments over time, and they can support the just allocation of consumption.

Taxing (governmental allocation)

Governments take money in taxes and give it out in various forms. Under the name of pensions or benefits, money is allocated to people who might otherwise suffer from no-money-now problems: the weak, the sick and the old. Of course, sometimes the problems they solve are better described as "not enough money now" than no-money-now, since many recipients have some other sources of income. Like insurance pools, government pension plans are often described as a combination of pools and financial arrangements, but both the monetary flows and the economic reality are much better understood as part of the organisation of the middle section of the Triptych. The payments into state systems are a current tax, reducing the consumption of the taxpayers, and the payments out are current benefits, increasing the consumption of recipients. There may be some pretence of the benefits being funded by past contributions, but the current payments, in and out, are the only ones that matter in the essentially instantaneous Great Exchange, and they are always determined as part of the current political settlement.

Besides helping with these "not enough money now" challenges, governmental welfare states solve many two-sided no-money-problems. On one side, the government uses its power to control economic resources to pay the wages of labourers who would otherwise be stuck in no-money-now labour, because they are providing goods and services which the social consensus deems should be available to consumers at low or no costs. I already mentioned schools, but governments are also directly responsible for the provision of police, courts, prisons, roads, industry regulation, and a substantial portion of healthcare. On the other side, the free-to-user services solve the potential no-money-now problems of poorer users by putting these activities, from their perspective, mostly or entirely in the right section of the Triptych.

This sort of government funding can be considered a very large form of yoked financing, with the recipients yoked not to a specific company but to the entire body politic. However, the governments are widely perceived as different in essence and not merely in size from other organisations, so the tax-benefit money-flow is best considered to be a different category from the revenue-pay flow of yoking. Also unlike yoked financing, but like the traded commodities discussed in Chapter Two, the separation of benefits from costs paid from tax revenues can lead to undesired increases in the Central Monetary Ratio, if governments rely on excessive money creation to pay benefits.

Changing

Sometimes the most direct way to deal with a no-money-now problem is not to find token-money to solve it but to stop it from occurring, by changing something about the organisation of the economy. The most obvious example of this approach has even inspired a new word, pre-distribution. The neologism is used as a contrast to the redistribution of the welfare state. For example, instead of using the proceeds of taxes on people with high incomes to pay benefits that solve the current no-money and not-enough-money problems of some poor people, why not duplicate and simplify the after-tax solution by lowering the pre-tax incomes of the rich and increasing the pre-benefit wages of the poor? Changing wage structures, for example by increasing minimum wages, could also be a substitute for giving and finance as solutions to some no-money-now problems.

Increasing spending-power through pre-distribution of incomes is not the only kind of changing that pre-empts no-money-now problems. The reduction of consumption desires can have a similar effect. Consider a middle-class family with the no-money-now problem of not having enough token-money to pay for an expensive holiday. As it stands, they might be tempted to turn to finance (to borrow money) to solve their problem. An alternative would be to avoid the problem by changing desires. They can decide to forgo the holiday.

Governments have what might be described as no-money-now problems when taxpayers are unwilling to pay for the goods, services, and monetary distributions that they expect the government to provide them. One way to solve that problem is through changing the political settlement, from an unrealistic to a realistic popular understanding of how much the government can afford to spend.

Individual purchasers of property are another group which generally have a no-money-now problem, ultimately because the price of *owning* the consumption good of housing includes both the token-money cost of consumption and the savings-money cost of the money-thing, the land that cannot be separated from the consumption good. While current wages can pay for current housing consumption, some sort of finance is generally required to convert wages received over a long time into a payment for the money-thing. Such housing loans entwine the left and middle sections of the Triptych in complicated and sometimes unhelpful ways. Change is rarely considered an alternative solution to the no-money-now problem of housing, but it arguably could be. A combination of a different ownership system for existing housing and pooling arrangements for paying for new construction might be able both to keep many houses as private property and to ensure that enough housing is constructed to satisfy the needs or desires of a community.

Finance

Financial arrangements are the sixth and final solution to the no-money-now problem. Like the other five families of solutions, economic finance involves a change in the allocation of token-money. Unlike most types of changing, but like yoking, giving, taxing, and pooling, finance involves a transfer of money from one set of persons or institutions to another. Finance differs from the last four solutions in the timing and directions of money-flows. Those four have a one-time, one-way flow. In financial arrangements, the flow is always over time and in two directions.

All financial arrangements involve two parties, a financial investor who (or which) has savings-money and an investee who (or which) has a no-money-now problem. The first stage of all financial arrangements is an immediate transfer of savings-money from the investor to the investee (some of whom are also known as borrowers). In economic finance, the investee generally converts the investor's savings money, the financial investment, into token-money, which is then spent in the Great Exchange. This is the solution to the no-money-now problem. In the second stage of the financial arrangement, the money-flows go in the opposite direction. Over time and in various quantities, the investee pays money, generally token-money, to the investor. The investor may either spend the received money right away or convert it into savings-money. The timing and quantity (or the rules for determining the quantity) of these "return" payments are agreed at the beginning of the arrangements. I will discuss the principal varieties of financial arrangements later in this chapter.

An investor may be a single person or an organisation which gathers savings-money from many people and organisations. Some of these collecting organisations make many different financial investments with their gathered savings-money. I call all these large-scale aggregators banks, since investing is one of the principal tasks of banks. I will discuss alternative names for monetary and financial institutions later.

Investees can also be either individuals or organisations. Because of finance's two-way money-flows, the investee must have some sort of durability, whether a continuing legal personality, a physical life expected to last long enough to meet the obligations of a particular arrangement, or some way to pass on financial obligations after a corporate or physical person's death. To make economic finance work well, investees should also be likely to be willing and able to make the agreed payments in the future. In the archetypical economic financial arrangement. the investee is a business which needs money to construct or maintain some revenue-generating operation.

3. Post-aristocratic finance

Post-aristocratic finance describes two-way intertemporal money-flows which have a primarily sociological purpose or result: to transfer token-money from relatively poor members of a society to relatively rich financial investors. Unlike economic finance, the essential goal of post-aristocratic finance is not to solve no-money-now problems, although post-aristocratic arrangements might incidentally do that. Also unlike economic finance, the first part of the post-aristocratic money-flow, from investor to investee, is not primarily a source of token-money to be spent in ways that are supposed to generate the return money-flow from investee to investor. The primary orientation is simply to create a long-lasting poor-to-rich monetary obligation.

The sociological orientation of post-aristocratic finance can be described in Marxist class terms: these arrangements help the rich and powerful class retain and increase its wealth and power, while retaining and amplifying the economic and political disadvantages of the various poor and powerless classes. I will not talk of classes, but I am Marxist enough to believe that the functioning of the left section of the Triptych cannot be explained without some sort of economic sociology. Sociology is very helpful for understanding why and when economic finance is preferred over simpler alternatives. Sociology is essential for making any sense of post-aristocratic finance.

Traditional land rents

What is this essential sociology? And why do I call this finance "post-aristocratic"? I will answer those questions with some very simplified sociology and economic history.

The sociology is no more than the very basic observation that in almost every society, everywhere and at all times, a very small proportion of the people possess or control a large proportion of everything that confers social status. Until well into the 19th century, this vast social inequality was accepted as some combination of just, natural, or inevitable by almost all philosophers, religious leaders, and rulers, and indeed by most of the ruled. In the last two centuries, the same inequality has increasingly been rejected as unjust, unnatural, and avoidable. Instead, the goodness of egalitarian societies has increasingly been promoted by leading philosophers, identified as religious truth, and become a political truism. The now dominant egalitarian ideal has greatly influenced societies and economies. In rich countries, the spread of universal services, the near-elimination of destitution, and the rise of the middle classes have significantly levelled economic hierarchies, at least from some perspectives. Still, for any perspective, fully egalitarian societies and economies remain much more of an aspiration than a description.

The sociological relations of the bottom and middle groups to the elite have many components, most of which are not very relevant to either economics or finance. However, the elite–rest division of consumption bears directly on many financial arrangements and on the social role of finance, because finance can help provide members of the elite with many more consumption goods and services than members of lower social groups.

The financial contribution to economic hierarchies, like the use of finance to solve no-money-now-problems, is optional. Consumption hierarchies can be, and have been, maintained without any recourse to finance. Pre-modern peasants and craftsmen provided some combination of labour and its fruits to their elite lords and masters. In contemporary economies, very large differences in wages produce a sharply unequal allocation. However, finance is an effective tool for creating and especially for reinforcing and perpetuating social-economic inequality. It has been used for that purpose, or at least with that result, since it was first developed. Indeed, such sociological finance was widespread long before economic finance became significant.

The stylised history of the sociological finance starts with the social understanding that much of the land in predominantly agricultural pre-modern economies was owned by aristocrats and other land-lords. Despite the claims of many philosophers, there is nothing obviously true about either the basic understanding that land can be owned outright by a person or any claim about the social rights and responsibilities that come with this possession of property. However, in practice, ownership was often thought to justify requiring users of the land to compensate owners. The obligations of such tenants, which can be called rents, were a poor-to-rich transfer that can be described as aristocratic proto-finance. The arrangements were only "proto" and not actually financial because the aristocrat-investor provided land rather than money to the user-investee and the user did not necessarily provide money in return. However, there was something close to a finance-style two-way intertemporal flow. On one side was a socially hypothesised and certified flow of economic resources from rich owners to poorer users. On the other side was a quite concrete flow of labour and consumption goods and services from relatively poor users to aristocrats.

As money became more prevalent, more of these lower-to-higher return obligations came to be expressed in monetary terms rather than "in kind". Also, tenanted land became a money-thing that an aristocratic or country gentleman could purchase as a financial investment. The new owner would give savings-money to the old owner in exchange for a future flow of token-money rents from tenants. This aristocratic understanding of the justice of rents on agricultural land has remained well accepted in most of the world, despite land reform and complaints from both socialists and some capitalist economists.

Today's agricultural land rents are direct post-aristocratic successors to the feudal dues of aristocratic proto-finance. However, post-aristocratic financial arrangements go far beyond land rents in the modern economy, which is much more complicated than its pre-modern predecessors. I will discuss briefly the four most significant types of poor-to-rich financial transfers.

Modern land rents

The first is the urban and suburban extension of traditional aristocratic land-rents. The newer arrangements are sociologically different from the old ones in several ways. The increase in economic importance of things done in buildings, relative to stuff produced directly from the ground, has reduced the social, political, and economic power connected with owning land. Perhaps as a result, land has lost some of its special social and economic status. Even the land which a person calls home is increasingly treated as a money-thing, conceptually interchangeable with any other repository of savings-money.

Also, the labour needed to keep land economically useful has increased greatly, because moderns can neither live nor labour without expensive constructions and numerous utilities. This change has substantially increased the proportion of payments from land-users to land-owners that is better characterised as token-money wages and congealed wages than the pure tribute to ownership that economists call rent. The division between congealed wages and financial tribute is murky, because the labour of "improving" land is generally compensated indirectly and slowly (and without any explicit financial-style arrangements) and the portion of property prices that is best described as economic rent can only be calculated as a residual from this imprecise payment. However, in rough terms these rents, the payments in excess of the rewards for labour involved in the creation and maintenance of buildings and other improvements, still probably account for more than half of all land-related token-money-flows in developed economies.

Another pre-modern-to-modern discontinuity in the treatment of land is found in the expectation of the duration of proto-financial and actual financial arrangements. Pre-modern user-to-aristocrat transfers for the use of land were expected to continue forever, while today's economic rents, especially for residential property, are often paid through mortgages that gradually shift effective control of the rental money-flows from one owner to another. In most countries, constant nominal mortgage payments contain steadily diminishing and eventually ceasing economic rents.

While these discontinuities are significant, there is a far greater continuity. Economic rents on land remain largely payments from poorer people to richer ones. The tribute of poor, landless user to landlord has been modernised but not fundamentally changed by becoming the rental and mortgage payments from user to landlord or lender. The literal landed aristocrats have lost much of their economic importance, but the aristocratic economic pattern persists. This is post-aristocratic land finance.

I am simplifying the situation. Modern rents are not always post-aristocratic payments. Some contemporary renters have more income and higher social status than their land-lords. Some mortgage borrowers are very affluent and the rental portions of many residential mortgage payments are often transfers between people of similar economic and social status. Still, poor-to-rich flows predominate in modern residential, commercial, and industrial rents, just as they did when the tribute of peasant tenants supported the luxurious lifestyles and military adventures of their landlords. Often, contemporary money-flows represent or express an aristocratic-like configuration of labour. The rents from today's hard-working users of real estate make possible the luxurious lifestyles and social adventures of modern rentiers.

Government debt

Government debt is the next important type of modern post-aristocratic finance, but the history of governments' borrowing arrangements shows much less sociological continuity than the history of land rents. There is an obvious formal continuity. Modern government debts take almost the same financial form as the obligations agreed to by the late pre-modern European political elite with no-money-now problems. Then, when kings wanted money to pay for their military adventures and aristocrats had lifestyle or architectural expectations that exceeded their monetary means, they found financial solutions that were generally not aristocratic. Rather, the ambitious kings and status-seeking aristocrats tended to become investees for commoners who had accumulated substantial quantities of savings-money through some sort of commerce. Although it was the poorer subjects who would ultimately provide the returns to these early bankers, the immediate relationship was anti-aristocratic: loans moved the control of economic resources from kings and grand titled families to money-grubbing traders.

The modern situation is quite different. Thanks to the vast expansion of tax systems and the spread of democratically or bureaucratically controlled spending, modern governments, at least in developed economies, rarely face serious no-money-now problems. However, when the political authorities decide to spend somewhat more token-money than they choose to gather in taxes, that is to run fiscal deficits, they typically usually obtain the money needed for "deficit spending" (the money not provided by taxes) through finance. The political authorities are the investees (borrowers) and the investors (lenders) are a collection of individuals, banks, and other organisations. The financial obligations are called government debt. In developed economies, the vast majority of government debt is sold to taxpayers.

Most economists would now agree that much or even nearly all of the money that these taxpayers use to buy this government debt was created by banks specifically to be loaned to governments. In economic-monetary terms, the choice to let banks do this money-creation is puzzling. Governments that control baseless currencies can create all the extra token-money they want on their own, without any help from banks and without creating any financial obligations. I will leave that puzzle aside for now. I will just point out that whether governments borrow the additional money or create it directly, their deficit spending is, in political-economic terms, a tax. The government-spent new money increases the portion of the Central Monetary Ratio's numerator under government control (relative to what the share would be without the newly created money), just as it does when tax revenues are increased. The only difference between the two methods is that money-creation increases both the total quantity on the Ratio's numerator and the government's share of it, while additional taxes only increase the government's share. ("Seigniorage" is the economists' term for the use of money-creation to increase the portion of paid-for economic resources under a government's control.)

Leaving political economy aside, government debt is not economic finance. It neither solves specific no-money-now problems – such as paying for wars or new palaces – nor clearly generates the revenues needed to provide investors' returns. In sociological terms, government finance is predominantly post-aristocratic. Most of the return payments go to people who sit fairly high up on their nation's social-economic pyramid, while most of those payments ultimately come from the bulk of taxpayers who sit much lower. As with modern land-rents, the money-flows of government debts are not sociologically uniform. Many relatively poor people own some government debt and a significant portion of the tax revenues that provide the returns come from the rich people. However, also as with modern land-rents, the post-aristocratic pattern predominates.

Like any other type of post-aristocratic finance, the poor-to-rich money-flows of government finance do not support the widespread claims that modern societies strive for increased economic equality. The irony is particularly great for contemporary governments, since their taxing and spending policies are not only explicitly designed to take more from the relatively rich and to give more to the relatively poor, they also provide the best evidence of the authenticity of those claims. The counter-example of government debt can be explained in various ways, including as a historical accident or as a sign of the hypocrisy of the egalitarian rhetoric. I also see a sociological compromise between egalitarian aspirations and political-sociological considerations. Debt-owners whose returns depend on the stability and monetary solvency of the political system are likely to be especially supportive of extensive and intrusive modern governments.

Excessive business income

Excessive business income provides a third new form of modern rental income. The "excessive" is crucial for understanding this category, as most business income is not post-aristocratic. The bulk of any company's revenues (or income) go to pay, directly or indirectly, for labour in the Great Exchange. A smaller portion provides a fair – but not excessive – return to financial investors. I will have much to say about the meaning, quantity, and indeed the existence of such fair or just returns later. For now, I will just state that returns to financial investors can be, and often are, unfairly or unjustly high. By definition, these excess returns are not part of economic finance, because they are not necessary or appropriate compensation for solving no-money-now problems. Sociologically, these excess returns are predominantly post-aristocratic. They come from the prices paid by a business's customers, who are overall poorer and less socially privileged than the business's financial investors, who receive the money.

Consumer lending

Consumer lending generates the fourth type of post-aristocratic financial returns. This business is the successor to a common form of aristocratic proto-finance in close-to-subsistence agricultural economies: between-harvest loans of seed, food, and later money to impoverished tenants and small farmers. When harvests were large enough to repay the loans and provide fair returns to lenders, the loans were economic finance. However, harvests were often too small, or the returns demanded were excessively high, so over time such loans created permanent debts. These financial obligations helped reinforce and expand aristocratic social and economic structures, sometimes to the point of turning investees into serfs or slaves.

Debt-slavery is no longer legal in most of the world, although finance is still widely used to oppress farmers in some poor countries. In both poorer and richer countries, finance is used to satisfy some consumers' desires and needs when their wages, benefits, and savings-money are inadequate. Although such financial arrangements do solve no-money-now problems, they are not really economic finance, as the investee's newly acquired money will not be spent on goods and services that can produce returns for investors. Rather, such consumer loans are largely post-aristocratic finance. Overall, such lending ends up making the poor poorer and the rich richer.

Finance itself

The spread of economic finance and the multiplication of post-aristocratic financial arrangements has helped make the finance business a post-aristocratic enterprise. Members of the social elite often labour at senior and mid-level roles in the management of pure-finance and the broader range of savings-money activities that I will call general-finance later in this chapter. Financial professionals' confidence in the justice of their privileged social position is strikingly reminiscent of the self-righteous social claims of pre-financial aristocrats. In societies without titled nobility, the professional successors of the providers of anti-aristocratic government finance have become self-entitled social aristocrats.

The sociological pattern of the money-flows is typically modern. There are some rich-to-rich flows from affluent investors to affluent professionals, but the quantity of post-aristocratic flows – from relatively poor investors and investees to relatively rich intermediaries – is greater.

4. Six general observations on finance

Finance is much more complicated than token-money. Token-money is about as simple a tool as can be imagined. It is socially and morally neutral. Money-numbers are tractable. Each economic thing (labour, consumption, and everything in between) has a single money-number at any time and place. These numbers are connected by simple arithmetic, their mathematical relationships are clear and direct, and their pragmatic meaning is unproblematic, once the precisionist-consistency fallacy is recognised. Finance and finance-numbers could hardly be more different. The activities are socially and morally charged. The numbers always come in groups. The relations and meaning of finance-numbers are mathematically complex and empirically unclear. The precisionist-consistency fallacy always lurks in financial arrangements, which always rely on exact numbers that are supposed to retain their economic meaning over time.

The rest of this chapter is dedicated to unravelling some, although certainly not all, of these intricate ambiguities. I start with six general observations.

First, finance *fits uneasily with modern economies*. Chapter Four will provide an extensive discussion of the economically unrealistic aspects and manifestations of finance. Here I will just make a simple point. The modern economy is essentially a communal or social project. Globally, it requires the cooperation and mutual trust of billions of people, both in the present and looking into the indefinite future. At the scale of a nation or company, economic success is built on even closer cooperation and greater trust, although from smaller numbers of people. Also, economies are continuous in time and geography, without clearly marked beginnings, ends, or borders.

The features of token-money, a social institution that operates continuously and instantaneously, are reasonably suitable for this complex and communal economy. The features of finance are not. Financial arrangements always require an arbitrary separation of two parties from the rest of the economy. The desire to fulfil the terms of these arrangements, a desire that is essential to the success of the financial system, can easily encourage efforts that undermine the cooperative essence of economic activity. Financial arrangements always have fixed beginnings and often claim to have fixed ends, creating uneconomic temporal divisions.

Second, finance will necessarily *struggle to live up to its ethical responsibilities*. The morality of finance in general is the subject of the eighth section of this chapter and the justice of the current financial system is the subject of Chapter Five. Here I will only point out that both the history and structure of financial arrangements do not suggest that finance is well oriented towards contemporary standards of social justice. Historically, the aristocratic proto-finance from which much of current finance descended was designed exclusively to support social privilege, often in the most extreme ways. The inequality in these proto-financial relationships was often so great that it led to literal debt-slavery, a result that almost no one today would defend. Little effort has been made to purify financial arrangements and expectations of this distinctly pre-modern inheritance. The legacy shapes post-aristocratic finance, and it has set a poor ethical tone for economic finance. Also, as a collection of separate bilateral contracts, finance is poorly arranged to promote distributive or social justice, which is widely considered to be an important good in modern societies. The best it can offer is commutative justice, and even that is challenged by the unequal power relationships that are almost inherent in no-money-now problems and are likely whenever post-aristocratic finance flourishes.

Third, along with not necessarily being just, *financial arrangements are not necessarily efficient*. The constituents and goodness of economic efficiency are controversial matters, but finance has several features that make it unattractively inefficient by most standards. Most notably, the arrangements of economic finance are effectively promises, which are always easier to make than to keep. Because the economy and society change, kept financial promises often have a different economic, sociological, or even political meaning when they are fulfilled than was intended when they were made. Such doubtful promises are inherently brittle and liable to create discord and disarray. See my fifth observation below. Such troubles create economic and social inefficiencies. Also inefficient is the fairly extensive legal and administrative labour required to supervise the keeping of financial promises and the responses to the breaking of promises. Post-aristocratic finance is not even designed to increase economic efficiency. On the contrary, it is oriented to paying for and protecting the privileges of the privileged, a goal that is generally considered economically inefficient in a society with any sort of egalitarian understanding of the social and economic good.

With all these disadvantages, it is hardly surprising that modern economies, in which efficiency is prized, have often turned away from finance, towards yoking, pooling, and taxes. The contrary trend towards financialisation, discussed in the seventh section of this chapter, is more surprising.

Fourth, financial arrangements are always characterised by what I call a *temporal-ontological asymmetry*. In less fancy words, finance involves an exchange of a certain current money-flow (to the investee) for an uncertain future flow (to the investor). In the plainest possible words, the investee receives actual payments of money now while the investor starts with only the promise and the potential of future payments. This asymmetry extends the inherent incommensurability of the elements of the Great Exchange in two ways. First, just as there is no clear way to relate the value of a car to that of a poem, there is no clear way to relate the *value of money* now to the value of money later, especially to an uncertain future amount of money. The value part of the monetary asymmetry is inherent in the nature of time. Second, future return payments are uncertain, creating an asymmetry between *expectation and reality*. This asymmetry is inherent in the human experience of the world. Since the future course of events is unknowable, it is impossible to guarantee any commitment, even the most specific financial promise.

Fifth, the temporal-ontological asymmetry inevitably, but with unpredictable frequency, sometimes leads to disappointments for one or both sides of financial arrangements. There are basically two possible *types of error in financial judgement*: intellectual and psychological. In the former case, the most plausible expectations of the future course of events turn out to be wrong. In the latter, the combined expectations of the two parties were always different from those plausible expectations. The distinction between the two types of error is somewhat arbitrary – one person's rational judgement is another's irrational hope or fear. However, the distinction is helpful because moods and mood-influenced actions have a significant effect in the left section of the Triptych, far more than in the middle section. I will propose a psychological explanation of this pattern in Chapter Four and a moral one in Chapter Five.

Finally, *finance has complex relations with the markets discussed by most economists*. I am referring to the supposed market mechanism described in the fourth section of Chapter Two. On one side, finance has many of these markets. Indeed, the concept of markets is more applicable in the left section of the Triptych than in the middle one. In the middle section, the abstract, inhuman, and fluctuating mechanism of competitive markets is quite distant from the reality of economic activity, which is centred on the entirely human and quite concrete Great Exchange, and which is buttressed by a complex collection of reasonably stable institutions and human organisations. The reality-distance of markets ensures that market-oriented analysis provides a distorted framing for the central monetary activity in that section, the flow of token-money that allocates and balances labour and consumption. In contrast, markets can flourish in the left section, where the currency is savings-money. Savings-money is as baseless as token-money, but unlike token-money it has little or no anchor in the hard and hard-to-change reality of human labour and consumption, social positions, factories, trusted trading relations, shared expertise, and so forth. In the absence of such constraints, market mechanisms can do what economists say they do, set prices. "Financial markets", in which specific financial securities are bought and sold, can thrive.

On the other side, however, the market paradigm misses several central features of actual finance. As was explained in the last section, post-aristocratic financial arrangements are predominantly sociological, providing a mechanism for post-aristocratic poor-to-rich monetary transfers. Market-oriented analysis will miss this central feature of the financial system. Similarly, market-based analysis has no term to discuss the distance from economic reality of much finance, the subject of Chapter Four. Furthermore, as will be explained in Chapter Five, much finance is marred by greed, another category not easily recognised in market-based analysis. These three non-market features – sociology, reality-distance, and greed – are so central to finance that purely market-based analysis of financial arrangements will always be deeply inadequate. A full understanding of what is essential in finance requires the sort of super-financial explanations that my model of no-money-now problems, economic power-relations, and moral sociology attempt to provide.

5. Two types of financial arrangement

There are no obvious economic or social reasons to favour particular patterns of money-flows in either economic or post-aristocratic financial arrangements. Indeed, the timing, quantity, and certainty of money-flows in both directions could possibly take many different forms that would be fair and economically helpful under various circumstances. In practice, however, the terms of almost all financial arrangements follow one of two patterns. *Debt* has hardly changed since ancient Sumer, although the mathematical calculations surrounding it have become much more sophisticated in the last few decades (Homer and Sylla, 2005). *Equities* are much more recent, but they have not altered much since they took on their current form in the middle of the 19th century. I will explain later why debt is very poorly suited to the modern economy and how equity should be rearranged. For now, I will only describe and analyse the two types of money-things.

Debt

First, a brief note on the vocabulary of debt. The investor is known as the lender, and is sometimes called a creditor. The initial financial investment (the money-flow from investor to investee) is often called a loan, and the money that is loaned is sometimes called the loan's principal or the investee's debt. The investee is known as a borrower or a debtor. The terminology of lending and borrowing obviously denotes a temporary arrangement – a thing that is loaned or borrowed is supposed to be returned. As I will explain later in this section, this model of temporary transfer is economically misleading, but I will sometimes use these familiar words.

In debt, the return money-flows are agreed in advance, almost always in precise monetary quantities, although occasionally in quantities to be calculated by a precisely specified formula. The advance specification explains why debt is sometimes referred to as *"fixed* income". The investee's agreed payments to the investor are almost always divided into two parts. The first is what I call the investors' *return*, a series of relatively small regular token-money money-flows known as interest payments. The interest payments start soon after the loan is received and continue until the arrival of the second part of the investee-investor money-flow, which I will call the Large Payment. In crude quantitative terms, that is before any consideration of the precisionist-consistency fallacy, this sum of token-money or savings-money is either identical or closely related to the amount originally provided by the investor.

The Large Payment is usually made at a fixed date, known as the maturity of the debt. Sometimes, however, for example in most domestic mortgages and some student loans, there is no Large Payment, only an agreed number of smaller payments. To keep this description as simple and economically relevant as possible, I will largely ignore these and many other small variations of debt structures.

The quantities of the two types of payment are mathematically related. The basic connection is very clear, although there are some wrinkles and variations. The size of each interest payment is basically the product of a number known as the interest rate and the size of the loan. The Large Payment is typically the same quantity of money that was originally loaned.

Investees do not always keep the agreed terms of debt money-things. The responses to such breaches vary. Sometimes, the investor simply receives no further payments. Lenders compensate for these occasional defaults by charging higher interest rates to borrowers. Sometimes the original contract includes specific penalties for non-payment, so investors eventually receive more than was originally promised. Sometimes the money-thing's terms are renegotiated so that the investor receives something, but less than originally agreed.

The maturity of loans typically comes long before the borrowed money has helped the investee generate enough profits for the Large Payment. It is expected that the borrower will typically "refinance" the loan by using the money provided by a new loan to provide the Large Payment of the maturing loan. Investees are generally so confident that they can refinance their debts that they frequently choose very short maturities, a few months or even days. These imminent maturities are basically fictions, since refinancing is not only expected but necessary to avoid a default. The confidence sometimes proves unjustified and refinancing is not available. Then the investee and investor both have a problem. I will discuss refinancing in slightly more detail in Chapter Four.

I have just presented the mathematics of debt without any intertemporal sociological fictions. The standard treatment is quite different. The Large

Payment is called a "repayment" of the original investment. That choice of vocabulary comes from the conventional debt story in which the investee is paying a just or fair fee for the temporary use of the investor's money. Eventually, when the money is returned, the fees stop. To anyone who has made or taken out a loan, this picture probably looks reasonable. However, there are three fairly serious problems with this narrative.

First, a comparison with other modes of solving the no-money-now problem suggests that these arrangements are not self-evidently just or fair. Consider yoking, which is currently far more commonly used than finance to solve, or more typically to prevent, companies' no-money-now problems. In yoking, shoe-buyers pay more than is necessary for the labour that is congealed in the current purchase. The higher-than-necessary price of the shoes provides the shoemaker with the money required to pay for building a new shoe factory. The company does not need to borrow money because the customers are making what a financially oriented analyst might call a quasi-loan. These current customers, though, do not expect to receive future interest payments on their yoked contribution and do not expect any sort of repayment of their quasi-loaned money. They do not expect a reduction on the price of shoes bought in the future as compensation for the current additional payment. If there is an injustice in this arrangement, it is one that has almost never been noticed. However, if this non-financial solution to an actual or potential no-money-now problem is not obviously unfair, then the financial solution to the same problem cannot be obviously fair.

Taxing is similar to yoking. Taxpayers do not expect to receive any monetary returns on their tax payments or any direct compensation from the government for any consumption that taxes effectively transferred, via the government, to others. However, if the same taxpayers provide the same money in a loan to the government, they do expect such a return. That return may be justified or justifiable, but it is not obviously just or fair.

The second problem with the conventional debt narrative is the description of the Large Payment as returning or repaying the principal of the loan. This image comes directly from the erroneous idea that money stores value without any alteration. The investor thinks the savings-money which has been taken out of one money-thing and lent to an investee is merely being used temporarily by the investee. When the debt is "repaid", it can be returned to storage in a mattress or whatever other money-thing the investor might choose. In reality, though, in economic finance the investee spends the principal of the loan, typically on actual or congealed labour. The principal of savings-money has disappeared into the token-money economy. It cannot be returned. The so-called return of the principal is actually the payment of some different money, representing different claims, in a new moment in the Great Exchange. The numerical monetary value of the original investment and the Large Payment may be the same, but such a tautological identity has no economic meaning, as long as the economy is understood to be the human activity of the Great Exchange.

The third issue with the conventional narrative concerns the division of the investee-investor money flow into two distinct categories. From the perspective of this book, interest payments and principal repayments are indistinguishable. Both are payments without any direct connection to the Great Exchange. The custom of ceasing interest payments after the Large Payment is made also has nothing to do with the working of the Great Exchange.

Equities

Equities, also known as shares and stocks (stocks as in "stocks and bonds", not as in the synonym for "inventories"), are open-ended financial arrangements. The easiest way to introduce them is by comparing them to debts. While borrowers are supposed to repay their debts, the shares that are "issued" by an investee carry no promise of a future Large Payment. While investees of debts pay carefully calculated interest payments, investees of shares (companies) are expected to pay equity investors (shareholders) an undetermined portion of the company's profits as dividends. Unlike debts, which are extinguished by the Large Payment, equities generally continue paying dividends indefinitely. Debts can be taken on by any economic actor – not only profit-seeking companies but also non-profit enterprises, money-issuing governments, and money-wanting individuals. In contrast, the dependence of dividends on profits limits equities to profit-seeking corporations.

Equities owners often search for "exchanges" or other arrangements for easily selling and buying shares. The reason is simple. Since equity investors have no Large Payment to wait for, the only way they can convert the value of their shares, a money-thing, from saving-money to token-money is to exchange the shares for token-money. Relatively open stock exchanges have traditionally been the most common type of institution for organising all sorts of money-for-share exchanges, both for issuing new shares and for shareholders buying and selling shares from each other. In these financial markets, prices are generally disclosed openly. More secretive arrangements for issuing and trading equities, including intra-family sales of family-owned business and so-called "private equity" transactions, are also fairly common.

Equity investments require far more trust than debt. Both debt and equity investors must trust that the government or some private enforcement organisation will compel the investee to conform to the agreed terms, but equity investors also have to rely on the investee's goodwill and dedication to fairness in setting dividends. The cultural foundations, legal or communal reinforcements, and prudential judgements required for successful equity finance are substantial. In pre-industrial forms of equity, the culture, reinforcements, and judgements were provided by interweaving the obligation to pay dividends with other social obligations. It was worthwhile to be honest and fair about sharing the proceeds of fishing or trading ventures with equity investors when fair payments brought honour in the clan and dishonesty and unfairness were punished by being shunned or murdered by unhappy partners, who were also clan-members. Such tight social-economic corporate systems still exist, for example in parts of the diamond trade, but shareholding in modern economies is usually anonymous. In these companies, trust relies on much more impersonal social systems.

The most important such system is legal. The law in all countries with share-issuing companies strongly supports the unenlightened self-interest of equity investors. They are generally considered to be the "owners" of far more than a particular financial investment. The entire "shareholder-owned corporation" is defined as their property. In economic and social terms, the description of shareholders as owners is obviously an exaggeration. The shareholders do not have anything like the degree of control over a company that an individual has over her own wardrobe, car, or house. However, the connection of equity with property rights is more than merely rhetorical. In corporate governance, the interests of shareholders, whether long-term or short-term, are generally given precedence over everything else. The equity-supporting corporate legal and organisational structures are set in equity-supporting national legal and regulatory systems, which are encouraged by an equity-supporting consensus among the ruling classes. In turn, the financial trust of equity finance is one element of the tremendous trust required in contemporary economies, which require basic confidence in the integrity of millions or even billions of unknown contributors to the labours of production and distributions.

The conventional narrative of the money-flows in equity finance is probably even more dubious than the comparable debt narrative. The equity investor's original financial investment in a company is supposed to create a permanent claim on the investee company. The investee cannot normally cancel the equity investment with a Large Payment, as it can with a debt. The dividends continue for as long as the investee continues to exist. In practice, this structure has been very rewarding for equity investors.

I will close this introduction with a final ethical-linguistic observation. In the first section of this chapter I pointed out that the language of finance is often morally charged. There I mentioned some negative associations: the debts of sin in the New Testament and the German "Schuld", which refers to both "guilt" and debts. In English, there are also the criminals who "pay off their debts to society". In positive contrast, in English "equity" connotes fairness and "shares" suggest collaborative participation. The different linguistic associations are basically historical accidents. The French word for shares, "actions", comes from a different historical path and has no pleasing ethical associations. Still, as I will explain in Chapter Four, the English-language accidents are indicative of reality. Shares are basically more ethically appealing than debts.

6. Ten economic uses of finance

Financial arrangements and the financial system as a whole demand three distinct sets of evaluations – economic, social, and moral. This section provides some economic judgements, and the following two address social and ethical issues respectively. The analyses in all three are meant to be more suggestive than definitive. They are complemented, although certainly not completed, by the discussions in Chapter Four and Five, which explore, respectively, finance's biggest practical and ethical problems.

In the current section, I will identify ten actual economic uses of finance, three basically supportive of the common good, four of doubtful effect, and three mostly or even entirely harmful. The categories are not in any way commensurate, so their importance cannot be ranked. Nor can they be quantified or combined into a single numerical expression of the overall economic value, whether positive or negative, of finance. However, I am willing to make a rough overall judgement – the strengths of finance are valuable, especially the potential strengths of a well-controlled and carefully designed financial system, but the inherent weaknesses of finance are also significant. Financial arrangements and financial thinking should neither be condemned absolutely nor welcomed unquestioningly.

1. Helpful financial selection

Economic finance helps put economic resources to good use. Financial arrangements often help new and socially valuable economic operations get started and help established firms become larger and better. This good effect of finance is particularly substantial in relatively poor countries, where yoking, which basically provides money to already successful companies, is often not a realistic alternative. However, even in rich countries, economic dynamism is hard to maintain without the discipline and imagination of financial investors.

The financial system's selection mechanism has four economically helpful features. First, competition among finance professionals, both actual investors and their agents, can sharpen their skills and encourage them to find and nurture good investees. Second, individual finance professionals can have many different specialised interests and expertise, leading to a socially beneficial diversity of investments. Third, having put up their own money, the self-interest of financial investors motivates them to help struggling investees get through difficult times. Finally, the personal connection which sometimes exists between investors and investees can contribute to a shared and durable commitment to the whole society.

The praise is especially merited for what might be called the sweet-spot of finance – building up relatively small businesses that have a reasonably high probability of later generating enough money to be self-sustaining. Finance is often the best solution for such no-money-now problems. In comparison to donors, financial investors have stronger motivations to encourage success. Relative to yoking arrangements, financial investors tend to provide more expertise, control, and willingness to change or challenge accepted practices. The same flexibility gives finance an advantage over often centralised, stolid, and excessively supervised governments. Relative to pooling arrangements, finance can typically draw on a larger group of money-suppliers, and the money can be allocated is a less constrained way.

However, the praise of financial selection is far from unconditional. To start, any service to the common good through financial allocation is almost accidental. Financial investors and their agents are looking for high, good, or fair monetary returns for themselves, not for some sort of "social return". If their judgements are poor, finance will fail both society and the investors themselves. If too many investments are profitable but not socially helpful, the investors will do well monetarily but society will be failed. Loan losses demonstrate the first problem, while monetarily successful financial investments in pornography and gambling demonstrate the second.

In addition, even when finance is a good method of allocating resources, yoking and taxing may sometimes be better ones. Both of the latter techniques collect their money under something like compulsion, while finance requires persuading investors that their money will provide a good return. Also, both these alternatives generally require less labour to operate than finance and both avoid the uncertainty and complexities which inevitably accompany finance's intertemporal asymmetry. Taxing has the additional advantage of providing almost any quantity of money to socially beneficial or economically promising ventures without any pressure to produce profits at some fixed time. These advantages help explain why yoking is so often used instead of finance for the expansion of established enterprises and taxing for many of the largest and most complicated economic undertakings.

2. Helpful financial unification

In most descriptions of the financial system, the just discussed economic virtue of selecting of good investments is paired with the virtue of uniting a large number of people by gathering money from them to invest throughout the economy. The most notable example of this social unification through finance is the banking system, or at least an idealised portrait of some of the banking system.

What might be called ideal-banks collect deposits from many investors (savers), sometimes from millions of them. They also make loans, generally to some smaller but still large number of investees (borrowers). (A technical note is needed here. In the modern theory of banking (Bank of England, 2014), the loans are said to create savings and other deposits, but in the traditional practice and theory of ideal-banks, it was more accurate to say that deposits "funded" the loans. In any case, the two are tied together in the monetary structure of each bank.) In the idealised version of banking, the communal participation has a sort of basic justice. The investors give up on some current consumption to allow economically helpful current spending by investees. Investors and investees alike share the ups and downs of the overall economy. A similar although less extreme communality is also typically found in financial markets for debt and equity. Investors frequently invest through pension funds or mutual funds, each of which brings together money from thousands or even millions of individual investors. These common funds typically have dozens or even hundreds of different investments at any time, enough to ensure that the investors are broadly exposed to the overall economy. Even individual companies often have hundreds or thousands of shareholders, who are brought together by a common concern.

The two wide spreads of ideal-banking, of investors for each investee and of investments for each investor, are quite distant from the aristocratic pre-origins and the bourgeois origins of finance. At their best, the two-way gathering and mutual dependence of ideal-banking can support social unity by creating a common purpose and, if necessary, by sharing pain (as discussed in the first section of this chapter). This idyllic picture of ideal-banks, with their many little savers and many shared investments, is not merely fantasy. In the 19th and early 20th centuries, the many "popular" banks did in fact gather the pennies of the poor, helping to create a socially stable working class. At their best, the investments of these institutions (each country had its own systems with their own names) also promoted local businesses, a communal economic approach, and, eventually, a socially responsible middle class.

However, most of the current system of gathering money for financial arrangements is quite far from this ideal. The communal aspects have not entirely disappeared, but any praise must be seriously qualified, because relatively few individual investors are members of anything like the masses. Rather, most investors are relatively prosperous and they accumulate and spend savings-money without any meaningful sacrifice of consumption. In contrast, the financial returns these investors receive, the interest and dividend payments, ultimately come predominantly from relatively poor people, whether consumer borrowers, taxpayers, or customers of investee-companies. (The theoretical shift from thinking of bank loans as created by deposits to creating them can be interpreted as a sign of the shift in banks' predominant social role from unifying economic finance to a more post-aristocratic model.)

3. Helpful financial smoothing

Finance can reduce the inefficiencies of production created by temporary monetary imbalances. For example, loans to farmers can break the unnecessary connection between an occasional bad harvest and sales of tractors. Arguably, finance can do even more than steady the purchasing power of the affected farmers and others. The obligations of interest payments might encourage sensible restraint among investees and the prospect of losses could encourage sensible restraint among investors.

In reality, though, the frequent bitter complaints of heavily indebted farmers suggest that the desperation of borrowers and the opportunism of lenders often overcome any tendency towards sensible restraint. The prevalence of unwanted social effects from financial intertemporal smoothing helps explain why other solutions are often preferred. Taxes, seen in government agricultural support programmes, and pooling, for example in farmer-owned cooperatives, are both common.

Government borrowing to "finance" fiscal deficits is often presented as a helpful type of smoothing, for the entire economy rather than for a particular section. Leaving aside the virtue of such "fiscal stabilisers", a question beyond the scope of this book, the choice to use finance rather than direct money-creation to find the relevant token-money is dubious. Only if the economic case for fiscal deficits is persuasive and the more direct method of paying for them is closed off for legal or cultural reasons (as it is in many jurisdictions), can government debt then be described as economically helpful finance. However, the alternative solution, direct money-creation, is definitely simpler and arguably more efficient.

4. Doubtful financial principle of corporate organisation

Equity shareholders are often considered the legal owners of profit-seeking corporations. The legal system and cultural expectations that flow from this "ownership" undoubtedly protect the shareholders' claims for just returns. However, similar protection could probably be provided without categorising these complex social organisations as property. More significantly, the monetary framing of these organisations generally serves the common good when the primary challenges facing them are monetary – basically generating a large and steady enough stream of revenues to stay in business. However, the continuing of this shareholder-oriented arrangement is harder to justify once the company has achieved durable monetary self-sufficiency.

Various aspects of the justice of this arrangement will be discussed in Chapter Five. For now, I only note that there is something to be justified. Profit-seeking corporations are far from the only organisations in modern societies which generate substantial continuing flows of token-money.

Government agencies, hospitals, schools, universities, not-for-profit enterprises, churches, and sporting clubs also all run significant budgets. However, only profit-seeking corporations are defined, legally and culturally, as being built solely on a financial foundation.

There are at least three reasons to doubt that this is always a wise choice. First, it is factually incorrect. Outside shareholders can only have indirect control, and even their delegates on boards of directors may well not always favour shareholders' interests. Second, the reason for directors' mixed loyalties is that corporations have many significant responsibilities which have little or nothing to do with shareholders. Corporate managers must, or at least should, consider the interests of employees, customers, and the whole of society. Those at the top of the corporate hierarchy, who generally own only a tiny proportion of the shares, are also supposed to develop, maintain, and purify one or more "corporate cultures". Third, financial investors generally lack the vision, knowledge, and motivation needed to take on these diverse responsibilities.

5. Doubtful financial intertemporal transfers

In some rich countries, most notably the United States, finance plays an important role in addressing the no-money-now problems of people deemed too old to labour for pay. The relevant financial process is generally presented as a transfer over time, saving while young ("investing for a pension") and dissaving when old ("receiving a pension"). I explained in Chapter Two that this intertemporal pension model is an economic fiction. The Great Exchange always happens now, so allocation arrangements, both of token-money and of the resources which this money pays for, are always current arrangements. Pension payments are not an exception. They are always current transfers of token-money through the financial system. On one side, pensioners use the money received from financial arrangements – selling some financial securities and receiving dividends and interest payments on others – as token-money. On the other side, non-pensioners use some of their token-money to purchase financial securities from pensioners and to pay the higher prices and taxes that investee companies and governments need to provide pensioners with their returns. In effect, there is a transfer of both token-money and economic resources from non-pensioners to pensioners.

The intertemporal fiction of finance-based pensions may sometimes be both just and socially valuable. However, the ties between past contributions and present pensions are never either obvious or obviously just. If the goal is communal support for the aged, then compulsory and clearly contemporaneous tax-and-benefit systems are both simpler and more efficient than investment-based pension arrangements.

Finance also plays a role in inheritances, the transfers from dead people to their designated beneficiaries. These transfers are usually directly intergenerational, from parents to children, but the recipients can also be non-relatives or charitable organisations. Before the advent of financial money-things, the monetary portion of inheritances was largely limited to rents from land. Now, however, legacies of financial money-things are widespread. Both the soon-to-die donors and the generally younger recipients are usually pleased with this use of finance. In societies with a claimed commitment to equality of opportunity, however, the ready inheritance of financial privilege looks like post-aristocratic finance.

6. Doubtful streams of financial income

I have already mentioned the relatively prosperous rentiers who benefit from these poor-to-rich transfers. One strand of the current debate on economic inequality amounts to a discussion of how large this group of rentiers should be and what proportion of total token-money should flow to them in the form of rental-tributes. Additional questions are raised by institutions such as churches, universities, and charities that rely extensively on the rents received from their "endowments" (portfolios of largely financial money-things). Another complication comes from the pension funds that distribute financial money-flows to their beneficiaries, who become temporary and vicarious rentiers.

I will participate in that debate in Chapter Five, when I talk about both the personal vice of greed and social issues of justice. Here I will only say that while there may well be a fairly straightforward argument for the justice of any particular financial returns, the social justice of any large rentier income is far from obvious for anyone who is not firmly committed to an aristocratic view of the world.

7. Doubtful promises

One of the advantages often claimed for the current financial system is its ability to manage some fundamental asymmetries of desires. First, investees want token-money which they will not have to "repay" for a long time, perhaps ever, while investors want to be able to withdraw "their" money when they want. Second, investees want their return-payments to be flexible, changing along with economic circumstances, while investors want either a precisely or roughly predictable flow of return-payments. Banks try to satisfy both investors and investees by pooling and then dividing the money coming in and out. Simplifying somewhat, many deposits are united and then divided into many loans, which provide interest income that is united and turned into many payments to depositors. The distribution of loans and the quantity and division of payments are chosen to satisfy as fully as possible the conflicting desires, based on the expectation that investors and investees will continue to behave roughly as they have in the past.

The pooling-separation technique works quite well almost all of the time. Investors get both ease of withdrawals of savings-money and a fairly predictable flow of token-money, investees get token-money to spend and some flexibility about their interest payments, and the banks get rewarded with profits for satisfying both sides. However, things sometimes go wrong, occasionally badly wrong, either because the future turns out to be more different from the past than reasonably could have been expected or because greedy bankers established unreasonably narrow margins of safety. Regulators set various types of rules and standards in their efforts to minimise both mistakes and the damage they cause. Over time, this intersection of history, prophecy, greed, and caution has often created a cyclical pattern: bad results at banks generate fear and increased regulation; cautious management at banks then generates good results, which lead to complacency and decreased regulation; then come bad results and a new round of the cycle.

For economists praising the financial system, the two-faced arrangements are an excellent example of its ingenuity. What a clever system this is! It is able to support simultaneously almost contradictory desires! Similarly, for financiers who defend the size and complexity of their system, not to mention the same financiers when they beg governments for monetary help in a crisis, the value of "borrowing short and safe while lending long and expecting some losses" is obvious. It is great enough that it deserves to be well rewarded in normal times and protected when things go wrong.

These claims have enough validity to classify the commitment to a double-transformation as doubtful rather than bad. However, from the perspective of this book, the primary result of offering economically fictitious promises to investors and investees is "reality-distance". In other words, they lead to financial arrangements with terms which are quite distant from the actual ebb and flow, as well as the genuine causes and effects, in the Great Exchange. Reality-distance is so endemic to finance that I dedicate all of Chapter Four to it.

8. Bad financial social power

If everyone in a society controlled roughly the same amount of savings-money, then finance would not amplify social divisions. However, today's financial system often continues the social divisions and monetary flows of its almost purely aristocratic ancestor. Money-things are generally distributed more unequally than incomes, and the inequality is far greater for money-things that are not connected to personal residences. The transfers of token-money from non-holders to holders of financial money-things work to widen the gaps in spending and social status between financial investors and financial non-investors.

This tendency will be discussed in several contexts later in this book. For now, I will only note that the observation of poor-to-rich financial practice probably helps explain both the longstanding Jewish, Christian, and Moslem condemnations of usury and the Biblical praise of forgiving financial debts. To the extent that the social and moral values that were connected to those religious teachings remain widely shared, financial solutions to no-money-now problems and financial arrangements that express social and economic power will always be ethically suspect.

9. Bad financial activity in companies

Companies often engage in what bankers sometimes call corporate activity – changing their financial relationships and legal boundaries through divisions, combinations, and the cancelling and issuing of various financial money-things. In the last half-century, the logic of finance has been increasingly used to justify economically pointless corporate activity and the tools of finance have facilitated the trend. The corporate activity occasionally serves the common good, but more often it presents noxious examples of financialisation, a concept I will discuss in the next section. Organisations that are coherent and basically well-functioning are too often torn apart or forced together solely because some financial investors hope that these manoeuvres will provide them with higher dividends and interest payments. The disruption to both human ties and well-established operating systems caused by this purely financial approach are clear, while the social gains are scarce.

10. Bad financial speculation

I pointed out earlier that the prices paid for money-things are far more closely connected to the amount of money in the left section of the Triptych and to the psychology of the people buying and selling these money-things than to any solid anchor in the real economy. The waves of savings-money and mood are strong, while the forces of economic reality that can resist them are weak. The result is pointlessly volatile prices of all money-things, including financial ones. The volatility of financial prices attracts, and is usually amplified by, people who see the potential to increase their supply of savings-money quickly and without much labour. In their "speculative" fervour to "buy low" and "sell high", they all but ignore the real economy. The desire for financial speculation is so great that these "traders" often eschew genuine financial investments, preferring to trade derivative securities that are based on them but are designed to have more volatile prices.

I will discuss financial speculation in Chapters Four and Five, but can summarise the conclusions here. Speculation squanders human talents and social resources while amplifying many of finance's inherent weaknesses. Its increased prevalence and respectability belong on the list of regrettable signs and effects of financialisation.

7. Topics in finance and society

While token-money is a narrowly functional economic tool, savings-money and especially finance have broad social meanings and ethical implications. The money-things of the left section of the Triptych embody, demarcate, and symbolise various economic aspects of social positions and relationships. In finance, the token-money return payments are connected to the savings-money money-things, so financial arrangements are both social and economic, straddling the two sections of the Triptych. A book about economics is not the place for a full sociological analysis of finance. Still, I will make three social-economic observations.

Sharp judgements, duller reality

The first observation is about the value judgements that surround finance. For much of history, finance has been unpopular with many leading thinkers and much of the population. In the first section of this chapter, I mentioned the most extreme criticism, the cultural narrative of the malignant lords of finance. Less conspiratorial critics make three other arguments, which I will paraphrase. First, post-aristocratic finance undermines the egalitarian norms of contemporary society. Second, professional financiers serve themselves much more faithfully than they serve the common good. In particular, banks too often fail to support helpful businesses and too often support economically pointless and socially corrosive financial speculation. Third, financial markets frequently fan mass psychological excesses of both hope and fear, creating unnecessary and disruptive alterations in the economy.

In recent decades, the criticism of finance has become less intense, as I will discuss in the next subsection, while enthusiasm has increased. There is no widely told positive narrative that matches the extremes of the lords of finance, although some of the bankers attending the World Economic Forum conferences might contentedly think that they are benign or even beneficent masters of the universe. More modestly, some economists describe finance as something like the backbone of successful modern economies, mostly because economic finance aids the production and distribution of many valuable goods and services. Finance enthusiasts also praise the helpful discipline provided by mandated return payments and the information and expertise spread by well-placed financiers. Pro-finance historians point out that sustained economic development has always been accompanied by an equally sustained expansion of an increasingly effective financial system. Further, financial markets are said to provide an effective check on various kinds of governmental and private excess. Pro-finance macroeconomists sometimes argue that bank lending does, or at least can, keep the economy moving in times of adversity and popular fear.

In my judgement, much of the specific analysis used to support these negative and positive social-economic claims about finance is somewhere between plausible and persuasive, but the emotional intensity of many critics and enthusiasts is unmerited. The roles of finance and financiers are both duller and more mixed than either side might want to admit. I will provide a few examples of the need to avoid oversimplification and exaggeration.

Financiers: The leaders of finance probably do have an inappropriately large role in local, national, and global elites. However, the story of the lords of finance is total nonsense. Leading financiers are much less malevolent than they are incompetent, arrogant, and excessively conventional in their thinking. Also, the actual power of financiers is easily exaggerated. Their decisions do create and destroy some paid jobs, as well as help and hinder some industrial investments. However, they are always constrained and often overruled by regulatory, political, business, and other social authorities. The countervailing powers could certainly do much more to control financiers, but societies, governments, and economies with humbled bankers would not look or feel much different from how they do now.

Post-aristocratic tendencies: Much finance is structurally post-aristocratic. However, the potential power of modern financial systems to concentrate incomes and wealth is far less than both the power of wage differentials to promote economic and social inequality and the power of modern tax systems to negate or amplify any monetary concentrations.

Intertemporal smoothing: Finance deserves some praise for solving what I have called tractor-problems, by countering the ups and downs of incomes with the ups and downs of loans. However, such tractor-problems are fairly rare in today's predominantly industrial economies. When they do arrive, they are mostly caused by financial excesses. It is odd to praise the financial system for solving problems that it largely caused. Also, taxing, pooling, and the hoarding of monetary savings are often at least as effective as finance at solving tractor-problems.

Booms and busts: Finance's most obvious weakness is the just-mentioned tendency to excess. The financial disruptions to the paid-for economy and to social relations are undoubtedly too great and too frequent – that is one of the central theses of this book. However, the losses from financial collapses seem to be on a declining trend. The economic damage after the 2008 Global Financial Crisis was all unnecessary, but it was much less than the damage caused by the financially induced Great Depression of the 1930s, or the grief brought by some of the rolling financially-induced crises in the preceding century. It is too early to tell how much economic and social damage will be done by the monetary and financial response to the anti-Covid-19 restrictions, but moderate optimism is appropriate, in my judgement. Over the last few decades, finance has become less rigid, temperate governments have taken more control of the supply of money away from unhelpful banks, and the regulatory responses to financial challenges and failures have become somewhat less clumsy.

Helping development: Finance really has helped economic development, through the controlled lending of banks, the token-money provided by foreigners through the global banking system, and governments' use of domestic financial systems to support or guide economic choices. However, a strong financial system is not one of the principal spurs of increased prosperity and a weak one is not one of the principal impediments. Finance is much less important than the education and attitudes of labourers, the competence and priorities of governments, the qualities of a country's institutions and laws, and the availability of natural resources. Even within the money-finance system, good management of the money-supply contributes much more to development than does a strong financial system, because effective and efficient alternatives to finance are so often available. Also, while cross-border financial investments have sometimes helped the development of some economies, purely financial money-flows have often done more economic harm than good. It is not clear whether the overall balance is positive or negative.

Overall, the dull truth about finance is that it rarely plays a crucial role in the real economy or in society. In comparison to money, let alone to technology, bureaucracy, class relations, and the modern spirit of enterprise, finance is only a secondary player in current economic and social dramas. It is excessively excoriated by its enemies and too lavishly praised by its supporters. The exaggerations are mostly caused by confusing cause with effect, in my judgement. The rise of unhelpful finance is usually more a sign of deeper social problems than a source of them, and the helpful uses of finance are more manifestations than causes of economically successful social arrangements.

Financialisation

While the social and economic importance of finance, for good or evil, is easily exaggerated, that importance has been increasing – more for evil than for good, in my judgement – for several decades, especially in developed economies. This trend is commonly known as financialisation. It can be described technically as an increase in the ratio of the total value of financial arrangements in an economy to the numerator of the economy's Central Monetary Ratio. Less technically, financialisation is an expansion of the left section of the Triptych, relative to the middle section.

This trend has only a modest direct effect on the actual economy, since most of the additional financial activity is quite distant from wages, prices, and production. The largest contributor to financialisation is purely financial debts, loans of savings-money that is used to buy money-things. Such debts, which are said to increase the economy's "financial leverage", serve no economic purpose.

Additional government debt is another substantial contributor to financialisation. These loans have no direct economic effect, as long as they are made by actual or potential taxpayers of the borrowing government. The token-money taken through taxpayers' loans has the same economic effects as the same money taken through direct taxes or the appropriately adjusted quantity of money taken by the government through the indirect tax of token-money-creation. Domestically held government debts can have political or social effects, but only to the extent that the governments do not use the tax system to compensate for the flows of token-money and savings-money connected with the additional money-things.

The rise in consumer lending, a smaller but still often significant contributor to financialisation, does increase an economy's reliance on finance. That increase, though, is probably balanced by the significant economic de-financialisation created by the turn from finance to yoking among businesses facing no-money-now problems.

Financialisation affects the economy much more as a way of thinking than as a way of paying for things. The trend is best understood as an increased reliance on financial standards for making socially relevant economic decisions. Signs of this cultural financialisation include the warm welcome given to increases in financial debts, the increased popular focus on prices in financial markets, the increased social tolerance of speculation in those markets, and the increased political and journalistic reliance on the expertise of economists trained by and under the influence of banks. In these increasingly financialised economies, financial measures have become more prominent guides to business decisions. The interests and thought patterns of financial investors have become more influential, relative to concerns for the welfare of workers, customers, and communities.

Financialisation sometimes takes a negative form – the refusal to eliminate or modify unnecessary or even harmful finance. Most notably, if economic efficiency were the guiding standard for deciding how to create the money needed to run government deficits, then the widespread recognition that governments are always ultimately responsible for the creation and destruction of money would have led to the separation of finance from money-creation. Similarly, the failures of the 2008 financial crisis would have led to separating the institutions that manage token-money transactions from those that mediate economic and post-aristocratic finance. There has been little support for and no practice of such separations, either of fiscal deficits from debt or of banking from finance. The unnecessary continuation of these economic irrationalities is a negative practical sign of financialisation.

Finally, a decline in anti-financial social sentiment amounts to an ideological negative financialisation. In politics, while finance-hate still flourishes in the fringes, even leaders who are described as populist have mostly abandoned the traditional villainisation of bankers. Both old workers' parties and new centrists eagerly cultivate support in the financial community. Among the elite, careers in finance have lost almost all of their once prevalent moral and social taint, to the point that professional financial speculators, once considered little more than social parasites, are now sometimes considered pillars of society. At a lower social level, the resistance of community or mutual banks to what I will describe in Chapter Five as greedy finance has melted away, along with almost all of these once flourishing institutions.

What lies behind this increasing financialisation? There is certainly no economic rationale for this change. On the contrary, the larger economic roles of governments and various sorts of corporate and regulatory bureaucracies would seem to fit better with a de-financialisation than with a greater reliance on financial thinking. Since the best explanation for financialisation is not economic, it has to be social or cultural. In other words, there seems to be some sort of social appetite for financial thinking. I think that any substantial analysis of the causes of that hunger requires some heavy-duty cultural theorising. That sort of labour is well beyond the scope of this book.

Implications of the precisionist-consistency fallacy

The modern taste for numerical precision and consistency is a cultural phenomenon that is only tangentially related to finance, but it may have contributed to the trend of financialisation. In Chapter One, I tried to show the falseness of two common and intimately related beliefs about token-money – that it provides precise measures of anything and that it can retain an identical value in any meaningful way over either time or space. Finance is more susceptible than money to this precisionist-consistency fallacy, because it is both filled with many very precisely specified numbers and relies on numerous numerical intertemporal and interspatial relationships.

The plethora of numbers in finance is indisputable. While a token-money price or wage is always a single exact number, even the simplest and most straightforward debt money-thing comes with three exact numbers – a quantity of money, a percentage interest rate, and a maturity date. If this money-thing is bought and sold, then many more numbers are attached to it – a current price, a discount or premium to par value, a duration, a current yield, and a yield to maturity. (Explanations of the meanings of these terms are readily available on the internet, thanks to the popular fascination with finance.) With their variable dividends, equities have fewer precise numbers than debts do. When shares are not easily bought and sold, there is only one such number, the current dividend. When shares are readily traded, however, buyers and sellers often discuss another number, the current share-price, with references to a plethora of numbers and calculations. These start with officially certified but largely arbitrary values such as shareholders' equity, annual or quarterly profits for shareholders and cash flow. In addition, specialists have devised an array of esoteric analytic calculations – delicately adjusted ratios, percentage changes, and endless comparisons with more or less truly comparable alternative financial investments. Composite and derivative securities, for example collections of loans and rights to buy shares or collections of shares at a particular price, come with an almost uncountable number of numbers.

The large quantity of numbers in finance does not lead to much quality. On the contrary, none of finance's precise numbers, not even the most basic ones, have any clear or consistent economic meaning. The problem cannot be avoided, because financial numbers are always based in part on future values, which are based on the inherently unknowable future. Any precision in the number exists only inside the left section of the Triptych. The economic meaning, in the centre section, can only be known imprecisely. For example, it is exactly true that an investee who borrows one thousand euros at an annual interest rate of five percent with a maturity of five years is expected to pay the investor fifty euros every year and one thousand euros after five years. However, it is impossible to know the value in the Great Exchange of those monetary commitments.

Such an impossibility is unacceptable to the many finance professionals who think that knowledge of what will happen to savings-money is something close to a right. They cannot create knowledge, but they can utter predictive oracles of precise numerical pseudo-knowledge. Some of these predictions may well turn out to be accurate, but there is no way to identify the correct ones in advance. The partial accuracy is more tantalising than helpful.

Increasing the degree of claimed precision only intensifies the denial of reality. It may be plausible to argue that the price of a particular money-thing is much more likely to be higher than lower two years from now. It is, however, absurd to predict that the price will be twenty-eight percent higher, as financial professionals often do.

The precisionism of finance is worse than foolish. It has an antisocial tendency. To see the problem, consider how flexibility helps non-financial parts of the economy cope with unexpected challenges. Survival, let alone thriving, often relies on changing plans and rearranging economic relationships in response to events. Token-money is also helpfully flexible. Prices and wages are changed easily and often, whenever they are no longer well suited for the arrangements of labour and consumption. In contrast, inflexible financial numbers can be obstacles to helpful changes. The legal requirement to pay interest and the commitment of corporate boards of directors to pay dividends can divert token-money, and crucially the labour and other economic resources which the money represents, away from more socially helpful uses. More psychologically, the commitment to precise payments distracts both investors and investees from the inherent fluidity and unity of the Great Exchange.

The antisocial tendencies of debt become more potent as the maturities lengthen, as terms become more rigid or unrealistic, and as investors and investees are more separated in culture or location. A flexible line of credit supervised by a sympathetic loan officer at a community bank is probably more pro-social than antisocial. (A line of credit is a promise to lend as much money as needed, up to an agreed maximum amount.) The antisocial extreme might be represented by a debt security maturing in 30 years that has been divided into many sub-securities, each with its own expected range of losses, and those sub-securities sold to multiple investors in many countries.

Equities, with their variable dividends, are structurally far closer to social reality than debt is (an advantage I will come back to in Chapter Four). Unfortunately, in contemporary financial practice the equity advantage is often reduced by the tendency of investors to think of debt and equity as basically interchangeable alternatives. That tendency is encouraged by financial theory, an intellectual construction based mostly on premises that are either doubtful or simply wrong. This theory injects a great deal of precisionist poison into what should be equities' admirable imprecision. (I discuss financial theory in the Appendix.)

8. Topics in financial morality

Economists generally think of their discipline as morally value-free. This claim is both empirically ridiculous and intellectually irresponsible. Empirically, economic analysis is always permeated with moral judgements, from assuming that unemployment and crime are basically bad to judging that rapid or steady growth in some quantitative measure of output is basically good. Intellectually, all purposeful human acts, both individual and social, have a moral dimension – the human desire is always for something that is apprehended as being good, as Thomas Aquinas puts it (Thomas Aquinas, 1920: II.I.8) – so a full analysis of any particular manifestation of any part of the human condition requires a reasonably full moral study. This requirement certainly applies to everything in the Great

Exchange, everything concerned with monetary arrangements, and everything concerned with finance. This section introduces some important moral issues in finance. In Chapter Five I will approach financial morality from a different perspective, introducing greed as finance's besetting sin.

The inherent justice of non-aristocratic finance

I have already alluded to one philosophical argument for the goodness of finance, the consequentialist claim that it benefits the economy as a whole. My judgement is mixed. Economic finance clearly does some good (accepting a fairly conventional idea of the goodness of ample and widely spread prosperity), but other solutions to no-money-now problems can be superior. Post-aristocratic finance does little if any economic good and is directly opposed to the claimed egalitarian social and economic ideals of modern societies. In this sub-section I look at two other, less consequentialist claims for the goodness of finance: that individual financial agreements are guided by commutative justice and that the use of finance to solve no-money-now problems promotes distributive justice.

At the *individual* level of commutative justice, defenders describe financial arrangements, the mutually agreed two-way flows of money over time, as fair and just exchanges of things of equal value. The claim of justice is sometimes subjective, that the *perceived* value of the two money flows is equal, and sometimes objective, that their *actual* value is equal.

The subjective argument seems simple enough. The agreements require the mutual consent of the parties involved, consent implies approval, and joint approval indicates fairness. In reality, though, consent in finance is often not a simple thing. The investee's consent is often coerced or confused, even when law and regulations prohibit some sorts of deception. When there is genuinely free and informed consent of both parties, the subjective concord may be based on truly shared but still deeply mistaken estimations of future values. If we agree that I will pay you 100 euros for a bottle of what you and I believe to be fine champagne, the arrangement is not just if it turns out that the bottle contains only unfermented grape juice. Such disappointments are fairly rare and relatively easily avoidable in current monetary transactions. They are more common and harder to avoid in arrangements that deal with the necessarily unknown future. If the champagne is not delivered five years after the money is delivered and spent on a failed fermentation process, the commutative justice of the arrangement is at best doubtful.

The objective argument for commutative financial justice is best expressed as an analogy. Just as current exchange rates between currencies are accepted as fair, so exchange rates between money now and money later can be fair. The precisionist-consistency fallacy of money casts severe doubt on the analogy. To start, the analogy is not persuasive. Currency exchange rates actually do often seem unfair, because the supposedly equivalent amounts of two different currencies buy such diverse collections of labour and consumption. That objection is multiplied when uncertain future results are part of the supposed equivalence. Even by the rough standards of money, claims that this amount of money now is worth the same as those amounts of money later are very ambitious.

In sum, it is hard to tell whether financial arrangements, either in particular or in general, qualify as following commutative justice, either subjectively or objectively. In any case, in the deeply interwoven economic and monetary relations of modern economies, it is impossible to opine on the justice or fairness of individual financial arrangements without considering the complex web of economic and social ties in which particular financial relationships are set. The question of individual commutative justice should be integrated with the *social* questions of distributive justice.

The most plausible argument that finance promotes just allocation starts with a schematic claim about what financial investment actually does. In this picture, finance makes it possible for investees to improve the world in some way, for example by a company increasing the production of something or improving the distribution network for something, or by an individual getting a higher education or going on a holiday earlier than would otherwise be possible. While the gains primarily accrue to the investee, their positive effects ripple through the economy. One less polluting car reduces the average level of pollution and one new house improves the average quality of residences.

The argument for justice is that the financial investors who contributed to this gain for the community can justly claim a portion of the overall economic gain for themselves. Their returns provide them with that just reward. Defenders of finance understand that the use of finance may well increase the overall share of the token-money in the Great Exchange received by financial investors, but the defenders argue that this relative increase comes from a justly allocated participation in a widely shared social gain. In short, investors get more because they have helped the whole society get more.

This claim for the distributive justice of finance is not totally invalid, but in practice it comes with four fairly serious limitations. First, the actual rewards of financial investing may not be modest enough to be just. Financial investors' returns often account for a relatively high portion of the total social gains from the investment. Second, financial investors tend to be relatively affluent, so their becoming even more relatively affluent fails any egalitarian standard of distributive justice. Third, post-aristocratic financial arrangements do not offer significant support for any activity in the middle section of the Triptych, so the rewards that they bring to financial investors can only support distributive justice if increasing economic inequality is considered just.

Finally, even when the financial "take" from the communal gains of expansion and innovation is just, other means of paying for these gains may be more just. For example, it may be just for the shareholders of Google, the search-engine near-monopolist, to receive a share of the broad economic benefits that the company provides, but other arrangements might have been or might be more just. In the very early phases of the company's development, when it faced a no-money-now problem, taxes, or more precisely token-money from the government, might have been more a more suitable solution than finance. Search engines could be considered a universal service of the sort that governments often support. Now, when the search engine generates enormous profits, the common good might be better served if Google were run as a not-for-profit utility, with no further returns to shareholders.

The concentration of financial power

I have said that post-aristocratic finance always reinforces the power of the rich and that economic finance tends to do the same. This description suggests that the social-economic role of finance should be a topic in moral debates over how societies should distribute and use power and influence. Any moral judgement of the claimed financial reinforcement of the established social hierarchy rests on the answers to four wide-ranging questions of practical philosophy.

First, is finance as clearly post-aristocratic as I have claimed? Even if financial arrangements as a whole produce poor-to-rich money-flows, there are clearly numerous individual and institutional exceptions. They might deserve more weight than I have given them. Also, I may have too easily dismissed the social value of the availability of or potential to establish non-aristocratic financial relationships. Certainly, it is much more realistic for a relatively poor person to hope to become a financial investor in contemporary economies than was the case in any actual aristocratic society. These realistic hopes may make the system less post-aristocratic than measures of the actual rich-poor distribution of financial money-things suggest.

Second, am I right to describe modern economies and societies as hierarchical? There are obviously wide gaps in incomes within all modern societies (and also between them), and even wider gaps in the ownership of money-things. However, such monetary measures may not capture what is ethically most important in considering economic equality and inequality. In terms of actual consumption of all necessities and some readily available comforts, most countries (and the world as a whole) have become much more equal in the last century. Increased production, the philosophy of mass production, and extensive governments ensure that the basic economic goods – desired and dignified labour, electricity, education, healthcare, internet services, transport – are more universally and equally available than at any time in the past. In the shadow of decreasing inequality of economic essentials, the financial system's reinforcement of the concentrated economic power of the rich might be best considered ethically insignificant.

Third, are almost all modern political philosophers right to assume or claim that more egalitarian societies are always better than less egalitarian ones? If the universal conclusion is correct, then the anti-egalitarian tendency of finance looks a problem that needs serious attention. However, some nuance might lead to a less firm judgement. If societies should be egalitarian, what sorts of equality should they strive for? Should people be equally free to enter into any sort of financial contract or to be able to lend or borrow? In that case, the inequality inherently promoted by post-aristocratic finance would raise no moral issues. If, however, people should be equally free from monetary and financial coercion, even economic finance would often be questionable.

Finally, are social and economic hierarchies good, as most pre-modern political philosophers argued? This question is not merely a reversal of the last one. Distributive economic justice looks very different if social hierarchies are positively good than if they are merely not necessarily bad. If such hierarchies support the common good, then a thick net of poor-to-rich financial obligations might be a just and effective way to ensure a desirable certainty and persistence in social relations.

Some moral questions

In this subsection, I will pose some important moral questions connected with finance. In the interest of brevity, I will not try to ask all the important moral questions, or try to answer any of them.

The central moral question for financial *investors* is how to ensure that their financial activity promotes the common good. This single general challenge can be divided into a large number of more specific queries. Here is a sample. Which financial investments solve no-money-problems in ways that support the common good? Does the investors' use of their return support that good? Do members of the "investing class" behave shamefully as idle aristocrats, diligently as skilled professionals, or nobly as a virtuous leisure class? The last concept may be unfamiliar in, or inappropriate to, the modern age. However, in line with their aristocratic ancestors, today's "investing class" might also have the responsibility to dedicate some of their time and energy to unpaid or poorly paid spiritual, political, intellectual, cultural, or military labour.

The most important moral question for *investees* is whether they have true freedom to enter into just financial arrangements. Once again, this central question is expressed in many particular ways. Does a financial obligation support a just commitment to the common good by requiring sober effort to keep up the agreed payments? Or does it put unjust pressure on the investee's consumption and unjustly force her to make undesired and economically unnecessary decisions about her labour? Does mortgage borrowing create more of a free and just commitment to the future of communities, an unjust quasi-slavery to lenders, or an unjust desire for speculative gains? Are business investees justly tied to helpful investors, or unjustly beholden to irresponsible and exploitative ones? Are consumer loans taken out freely and justly, after rational judgements of current and likely future incomes, expenditures, and likely desires? Or are they encouraged by unjust initial allocations of money incomes and by unjust pressure on the borrowers' psychology? Are borrowing governments freely engaging in fair negotiations with affluent lenders, or are they unjustly pressured by the investor elite to issue debt when simply creating money or extracting taxes would have the same monetary and economic effect?

The moral challenges related to *those excluded from voluntary financial relationships* are easily ignored, but they are real. The underlying moral question is whether the exclusion creates injustice. Many people who are too poor to make financial investments and who have chosen not to borrow (become investees) are nonetheless forced to participate in the financial system. They have to behave as if they were investees, because they must pay the higher prices needed to provide equity investors with their financial income. Is this combination of compulsion and exclusion just? More generally, does the inability to become investees or, much more rarely, to participate in the financial system as investors deprive the financially excluded from just participation in the economy and in society? Is their exclusion a just response to their own irresponsibility, unreliability, or foreignness, or is it an unjust response to their race, religion, nationality, or social class (assuming that such exclusions are not only illegal, as they are in most jurisdictions, but also unjust)? Is exclusion likely to lead them into unnecessary and unjust precariousness? Is compulsory renting of residence (as compared to borrowing to buy) a reasonable and just form of possession of shelter or an unjust marginalisation from communities of homeowners, who are generally both investees with mortgages and investors in a housing money-thing? Are government benefits programs morally just substitutes for unavailable financial arrangements, or does the lack of dignified alternatives increase the injustice of financial exclusion?

The central questions of *individual* justice in finance are similar to the social ones. For each particular financial arrangement, the analysis of its justice must take into account the situations of the actual and potential investors and investees. As discussed earlier, the stated willingness of the two parties to agree on terms is by no means a sufficient criterion for justice. Nor are subsequent good-faith expressions of satisfaction with the agreed terms. Ignorance is another problem. At least one party in these agreements often does not understand the implications of what has actually been agreed. Moral confusion and factual misunderstanding sometimes exist simultaneously. For example, a lender may understand very well the terms of a payday loan with an effective annual interest rate of one thousand percent. However, his confused consciousness and conscience may well allow him to believe that the arrangement is just: "that is the rate necessary for me to earn a decent return". The borrower may also believe the arrangement is just: "I only have to pay a very affordable fifty dollars per week". The borrower, however, is merely ignorant. He does not understand interest rates. Despite the mutual subjective endorsements, the ultra-high interest rate is likely to fail a more objective test of justice.

In addition to the questions about social groups and individuals within and outside of the financial system, each *type of financial arrangement* has its own social implications, each of which raises its own moral questions. For example, does the social decision to create a large amount of government debt support a just social anchor of a solid debt-owning bourgeoisie, or does it perpetuate the unjust elite of a debt-owning rentier class? Do the increases in the price of land created by mortgage loans justly encourage a responsible core of socially committed homeowners, or do they unjustly lead to a grasping commitment to the protection of home prices at the expense of the common good? Do loans to consumers and students justly spread consumption more equally through society, or do they merely turn financial investors into exploiters of human weakness and social injustice?

None of these questions can be answered without thorough sociological and moral analyses. The actual effects of specific financial arrangements, and of alternatives, in particular social-economic situations must be understood, and those effects then set against some postulated, proven, or agreed standard of the good. That is hard work, but is part of the labour required for building a good society.

Dividing gain and pain and keeping promises

The ontological-temporal asymmetry of finance ensures that the future does not always turn out as was expected when the terms of a financial arrangement were agreed. Commitments which seemed fair when they were made can turn out to be unfair, either to the investor or the investee. Such changes bring with them the moral question of how best to respond justly to unexpected developments. Debt investees have a legal commitment to pay certain amounts of token-money and equity investees have a less precise implicit agreement to give equity investors a fair share of the available money. Under what circumstances should those obligations be softened or waived?

Even when the investee's financial commitment is not legally binding, there is an implicit promise, and, as any child knows, it is unfair and unjust to break promises. Of course, as any contract lawyer knows, some promises cannot justly be kept. The list of reasons for nullifying contracts includes promises which should never have been made, for example to perform an illegal act, promises which have become impossible to keep, for example after a natural disaster or the outbreak of war, and promises which can only be kept by doing serious harm, for example when it is discovered that fulfilling the terms of a labour contract is likely to kill the employee. Those conditions can all be relevant to financial obligations.

Consider loans to poor consumers, or to the governments of poor countries, with terms that are so unrealistic, in relation to the borrower's prospects, that the investor does not actually expect them to be fully kept. Instead, the lender calculates the payments demanded from a group of such investees, fully expecting that many or even all of them will pay only a small portion of what they have promised. In effect, the investor's goal is merely to extract as much money as possible from as many investees as possible. The typical borrower, however, is not fully aware of the expectation of widespread non-payment. Rather, she or it is incessantly told that she personally must pay everything that she has promised.

These extortionate loans are an extreme example of the standard technique for loan pricing. Interest rates always include what amounts to insurance payments on policies to guarantee the lenders against non-payment. (I will say more about this later.) In effect, a large group of borrowers agrees to compensate the lender for the members of the borrowers' group that end up paying much less than initially promised. This sort of pooling is not obviously or inevitably unjust. However, the composition of the pools raises ethical questions. It is far from obvious which investees should be bound together.

Even assuming the initial debt terms are just, a new moral question arises when the borrowers find that they are struggling to make the promised payments. How much effort is it just to expect them to make to keep all the terms? What goods can they justly be asked to sacrifice? Should consumer debtors sell themselves into slavery (a widely approved pre-modern solution)? Should corporate debtors cut wages, stop investments, or renege on paying taxes before they fail to make their interest payments? Should governments reduce spending? Should graduates with onerous student loans give up on dreams and take up more lucrative careers? Or is it sometimes just for debtors simply to break their promises? If it is sometimes just, then under what circumstances?

The value of forgiveness

Theologians sometimes say that God's mercy is part of his justice. The law of the Old Testament Israelites required the regular forgiveness of debts and Christians are taught that divine justice requires them to forgive their (moral) debtors. In contemporary finance, however, forgiveness is almost never considered to be part of justice. It sometimes happens that the debt slate is wiped clean, but that forgiveness is inevitably treated as an undesired last resort, and it always comes with the lender's deep regret.

I believe that the conventional separation of financial justice from financial mercy is based on the common misunderstanding of the nature of finance. Once finance's two-way money flows are understood as I have presented them, as one of six possible solutions to no-money-problems, then the return flows will be considered far less important than the initial problem-solving provision of money. The investors' money could well have reached the investee though taxing, pooling, or giving, or the investee could have solved its no-money-now problem in some other non-financial way. With so many often plausible alternatives, a monetary return should be considered a privilege rather than a right. Financial investors should recognise that when fortunes change, their original financial privilege can be revoked in favour of giving.

More socially, forgiveness of financial obligations can be understood as a sometimes-appropriate response to a change in circumstances. Financial relations are always established within a community, a community that has some members who have savings-money to offer and other members who can benefit from converting that savings-money into token-money, which then enters into the Great Exchange. The appropriate relationships of these giving and receiving members will inevitably vary. Over time, financial relationships that may have once served the common good may become socially harmful. In that case, a transition to a non-financial transfer may promote the common good more effectively. Justice will be served and the community will be stronger if investors agree to this transition with a generous spirit, by willingly offering to forgive debts that are no longer economically sensible.

9. Six confusing words

Like any specialised field, finance has a large technical vocabulary. Practitioners quickly translate any new technical development or conceptual insight into as many carefully defined terms as are needed for clarity. After many developments and insights, the results for finance are impressive. One English-language website dedicated to investments offers a glossary with fourteen thousand entries (Investopedia, ND). With such a rich verbal background, it is surprising – and significant – that some of the most basic terms of finance are used equivocally, that is with the same word carrying quite different meanings. I have already introduced the definitional ambiguity of "money". It is confusing to use the same word to describe symbol-money, which holds a variety of social and cultural meanings, token-money, which is used to modulate the Great Exchange, and savings-money, which is a repository of socially determined economic value and social-political power.

While the confusion of those three types of money is frustrating, it is understandable. They are often readily convertible into each other and they frequently take the same physical form. In addition, the borders between the types are fuzzy enough that the appropriate label may not always be clear. These excuses for not providing separate words for the different meanings of "money", though, are not applicable to any of the six important financial terms in this section. For all of these, the refusal or inability to develop a clear vocabulary reflects some mix of unnecessary intellectual confusion with not necessarily conscious ideological bias.

1. Finance

My first equivocal financial word is "finance". In the second section of this chapter I defined the practice quite narrowly, as contractual arrangements involving two-way intertemporal monetary payments, including both those that solve economic no-money-now problems and those that embody post-aristocratic arrangements which have sociological significance but no clear economic purpose. That usage of "finance", which I call pure-finance when precision is necessary to avoid confusion, is fairly intuitive, as it describes a good portion of what most people consider the financial side of the businesses of banks.

What I call general-finance refers to any source of any kind of money, especially the source of money for a particular expense. "What is the financing for …?" The blank can be filled in with almost anything that is paid-for – that factory, this month's payroll, a trip abroad, the new highway, those shoes, or these shares. General-finance includes the various forms of pure-finance, but also many sources of money which do not have any intertemporal contractual conditions: revenues of businesses, wages of consumers, hoarded savings-money, tax receipts, newly created token-money, benefit payments, and voluntary donations. In other words, "to finance something" is simply to find money to pay for it, and the "finance" is the money itself. General-finance is the "finance" in companies' "financial accounts" and "financial analysis". Pure-finance is certainly part of general-finance, but its two-way monetary flow and inherent intertemporal-ontological uncertainty make it quite different from all the other parts. Indeed, the only common feature is the use of some kind of money.

There is another common use of "finance", or more usually "finances", which can be called potential-finance. It is found is sentences such as, "Her finances are good" or "the finances are not a problem". Here "finance" refers not only to the actual money provided in general-finance but also to token-money or savings-money that would or could be available if needed. In other words, potential-finance refers to both actual money and money that might solve a potential no-money-now problem. This broader meaning of "finance" gathers in one feature of pure-finance, its look towards the future.

Finally, "finance" or more often "financial" is often used to describe everything in the left section of the Triptych. This broad-finance includes everything connected to pure-finance, but also non-financial money-things, including the money hoarded in mattresses, bank savings accounts, land, commodities used as money-things, non-economic money-for-money transactions in currency exchanges, derivative securities, and all activity in financial markets.

Like the equivocal use of "money", the simultaneous use of "finance" for economic finance, post-aristocratic finance, general-finance, potential-finance, and broad-finance can be seen as a mere accident of history. When token-money was still linked to gold and other tangible things, pure-finance was often not obviously separate from such essentially monetary operations as creating letters of credit to serve as imperfect substitutes for scarce token-money. Also, during the long, and in some ways not yet complete, transition from aristocratic to industrial societies and economies, there was, and in some ways still is, only a limited recognition of the difference between economic solutions to no-money-now problems and sociological transfers of post-aristocratic rents.

For people who believe that money is in fact credit (the erroneous belief discussed in the last section of Chapter Two), this historical accident of language remains a happy one, because the nearly interchangeable use of "money" and "finance" explicitly supports that identification. If, however, the description provided in this book is right, then the continuing verbal confusion introduces an unnecessary analytic ambiguity. The ambiguity also gives pure-finance an undeserved air of usefulness and importance. What is at best just one of several solutions to no-money-now problems is linguistically lumped in with all of the most successful aspects of the token-money system. The connotation of success associated with "finance" helps hide both what might otherwise be considered ethically objectionable poor-to-rich transfers and some less successful parts of the "financial system". This unmerited linguistic elevation tends to undermine efforts to evaluate economic finance, post-aristocratic finance and all the parts of broad-finance, because the fiction of finance being the back-up system for everything monetary hides a much less attractive reality.

I regretfully admit that this book might reinforce the conceptual confusions surrounding finance and its relations with money and society. After all, I have combined studies of money and finance in a single volume, as if the two were naturally connected. In the next chapters I will discuss the money-things of broad-finance as a whole, without always clearly dividing the pure-financial from other objects and actions in the left section of the Triptych.

My justification for all this conceptually unhelpful blending is pragmatic. To explain what pure-finance is, I have to explain what it is not but is often thought to be – somewhere in the close vicinity of token-money. To clarify the distinction, I had to explain first what this token-money is, which requires explaining what token-money is not, that is savings-money and money-things. Only then could I explain the special money-things of finance. When the distinctions are understood, then it is clear that the money-finance system that banks create and operate mixes together all the varieties of finance and money in ways that are conceptually transgressive and practically hazardous.

However, the real world's widespread conceptual transgressions cannot be wished away for the sake of intellectual clarity. Banks and kindred institutions work in the management of the money-system and in general-finance, often including but rarely limited to pure-finance. Indeed, pure-finance is almost never separated out from other types of finance. Under these confused and confusing circumstances, I decided that the most helpful approach was to put money and finance in a single book, to describe pure-finance clearly in one chapter and then to deal with general-finance for the rest of the work.

2. Savings

When money is taken away from the Great Exchange, it becomes something different. It is no longer continuously circulating token-money, wages used to pay prices and prices used to pay wages (and taxes-benefits, premiums-pay-outs, etc.). Rather, the money becomes what I have called savings-money, existing exclusively in the left section of the Triptych. The meaning of savings-money is unambiguous: potential token-money that is currently economically inert. In everyday and standard economists' usage, however, "savings" has several meanings.

A good approach to the confusion is to consider what happens when a person chooses not to spend all her wages on consumption goods and services. She "saves money", whether she puts the unspent money in a mattress, a bank savings account. or perhaps a fund that buys shares. For her, savings and reduced consumption are almost tautologically equivalent. However, the monetary effect of her savings is ambiguous. If she invests the savings-money in newly issued shares or lends it to a company that will use the money to help pay for a new factory, then there is a near-instantaneous transfer of consumption from her to some investee. Her loss of token-money is matched by an identical gain of token-money for some other persons or organisations. The numerator of the Central

Monetary Ratio, the supply of token-money in the middle section of the Triptych, does not change. If, however, she stuffs the same amount of money into her mattress, the monetary effect is entirely different. The removal of some token-money from the Great Exchange reduces the Central Ratio's numerator. If the denominator does not change, then the Ratio itself, the overall level of prices and wages, will decline.

There is a structurally similar ambiguity when a very well remunerated executive saves all the money that he does not spend. As with the poor saver, the Central Monetary Ratio will decline if the rich saver's savings end up in a very large mattress. In both cases, the Central Ratio will be constant if the money is spent by someone else, whether the transfer involves giving or finance. However, the pattern of sacrifice is entirely different. The executive consumes all that he wants, whatever he does with the saved money, while the poor saver inevitably consumes less than she could and presumably would like to.

In sum, "savings" can refer to reductions of the saver's consumption, to transfers of token-money to investees, and to reductions of the circulating supply of token-money. Those three are quite different. As with "finance", there are historical reasons for each of the uses of "savings", and the ambiguity was not always apparent to early economists. However, it is easy enough, both in theory and in practice, to separate transfers of token-money within the middle section of the Triptych from transfers from the middle to the left sections, and most economists could easily understand that the two transfers have distinctly different monetary and consumption effects. As with "finance", the persistence of the verbal ambiguity suggests the persistence of intellectual confusion.

Once again, the most likely culprit is the banking system. People generally consider their bank account balances to be savings-money which they can change into token-money when required. For the banks, however, these deposits are liabilities that are matched with assets, loans. For borrowers from the bank, these loans are generally token-money. (For now, I am ignoring loans from one financial institution to another, which disrupt the conceptual picture, rarely for good economic, social, or monetary reasons.) In effect, the banks sit astride a cognitive dissonance – the same money that is currently outside the Great Exchange for depositors is inside that Exchange for borrowers.

That dissonance would be more obvious and easier to manage if there were a clear verbal distinction between the hoarding of money in economically sterile money-things and the transfer of money from investors to investees who are operating within the middle section of the Triptych. When both these uses of money are described as savings, the banks need only ensure that the contradiction does not become too glaring. As long as individual depositors can convert as much of their savings-money as they want to token-money at a particular time, the equivocation can be considered a banking example of what Plato called a noble lie. The dissembling helps the paid-for economy function smoothly. However, even well-intentioned lies can cause trouble when they are uncovered.

At worst, the savings-lie can lead to bank runs and financial crises. In the best of times, the savings confusion often leads to disconcerting monetary confusions. In Chapter Two, I mentioned one, the idea that billionaires could instantly eliminate poverty by liquidating their savings and giving the money to the poor. As I explained there, the addition of token-money cannot on its own create additional goods and services. I will explain in Chapters Four and Five why claims that savings do or should earn a risk-free income of token-money are equally troubling. More generally, financial arrangements that provide investors with a claim on an investee's money-flows do ensure an income for investors, always subject to the uncertainty of finance's unavoidable temporal-ontological asymmetry. In contrast, hoarded savings-money, the money in the mattress, cannot earn an income. This distinction is obvious when it is put this way, but the inability to recognise it muddles many conversations about savings, investments, and economic policy.

A careful verbal distinction between token-money and savings-money would not only expose the murky ambiguity of the banking business model. It would almost certainly lead to a separation of four operating systems related to money and finance in every economy: (i) the one that manages token-money transfers inside the Great Exchange; (ii) the one that creates and distributes new token-money; (iii) the one that allocates token-money inside the Great Exchange through pure-finance; (iv) the one that stores savings-money in various forms outside of the Great Exchange. Even before any organisational changes, though, the vocabulary of savings could be improved.

3. Bank

I have used a single mundane word, bank, to describe institutions that do many things: process token-money-flows within the middle section of the Triptych; hold hoarded savings-money in the left section; create new token-money and savings-money by making loans; make financial investments with existing savings-money; organise financial arrangements for investors, investees, or both; trade and organise trading of financial money-things; organise transactions of non-financial money-things; hold non-financial money-things on behalf of clients; mix financial operations of various sorts with pooling (insurance) operations; create para-financial derivative securities; and trade and organise trading of these derivatives.

For many centuries, laws and regulations have defined the businesses and business practices of most banks in developed economies. Unregulated and regulation-dodging banks have sprung up at various times and places, most recently to support "crypto-currencies". The new institutions sometimes claim that their freedom from constraining rules will provide great things to some group of customers, but the historical record suggests otherwise. These rebel banks have always either failed fairly quickly or have fairly quickly been absorbed into the regulated banking system. The regulations of these systems vary from country to country and over time, but few if any banks have even been allowed to operate in all the businesses that I listed. Typically, the monetary and financial activities are divided among various types of institutions, only some of which are actually called "banks". The divisions and names have varied over time and by jurisdiction. Often the names have been quite confusing. For example, at one time in the United States commercial banks were quite different from savings banks, which in turn were different from savings and loans. Sometimes the names indicate nothing about the function of the institution, for example the Raiffeisen of central Europe, named after the monetary activist Friedrich Wilhelm Raiffeisen. When functions are indicated, the title is frequently more misleading than illuminating, for example the British "building societies" that did not actually build anything or the American "trusts", which had little to do with the normal use of the word.

The vast collection of unhelpful names creates a quandary for anyone trying to write about money-handling institutions. My use of a single word to describe the whole melange of businesses might give the wrong idea about my understanding of the importance of institutional design in both the middle and left sections of the Triptych. I think there is great value in having separate types of institutions with separate regulations and institutional styles for different types of monetary and financial business. However, any assignment of existing names would be more confusing than illuminating, so I have chosen the most generic word, bank.

Financial intermediary is a plausible alternative, and has the advantage of sounding more academic, but many of the institutions that I am calling banks are more monetary than financial and many do not really intermediate anything. Financial institution is better, but it is really only appropriate for institutions that are essentially financial, without any responsibility for either token-money, non-financial money-things, or pooling arrangements. Then there are central banks, which deserve special mention because their name is so deeply inappropriate. Their roles in the monetary system are totally different from any of the numerous activities associated with banks, so they obviously and urgently need a new name: my choice is central monetary authorities.

Unlike the other verbal confusions described in this section, the difficulty of finding consistent names for different types of monetary and financial institutions is well recognised. The underlying problem – deciding how to divide the various monetary, financial, and money-thing responsibilities – has been debated for almost two centuries. However, the practical analysis is still greatly hindered by the many confusions that surround both the middle and left sections of the Triptych, as well as the relations between the two. The current collection of institutional names, in English and in other languages, is probably too plagued by unnecessary sloppiness and ambiguity ever to be of much use. A new, more economically and sociologically accurate nomenclature is needed. While waiting, a single omnibus word is the least bad solution to the problem.

4. Investments

I have used "financial investments" to describe a very specific change in monetary allocation, when an investee receives and spends token-money on labour, goods, and services. Archetypal examples include companies using token-money provided through a financial money-thing to pay for a new factory, to increase production at existing factories, to pay for inventory, or to engage in expensive research. In all of these cases, the producer-investee receives token-money from financial investors. The investees expect that the things paid for by the token-money will generate enough token-money income to pay the financial investors, the owners of the relevant money-thing, the promised financial return.

This definition of financial-investment is centred on the investee, which (or who) is always provided with money to spend inside the middle section of the Triptych. From the perspective of both the investor and the overall monetary system, however, these financial investments include two quite different arrangements. In ideal-banking, today's investees are tomorrow's investors and savings generally require sacrifices of consumption, so the transfers of money largely reflect or express clear changes of consumption within the Great Exchange: from investor to investee. The sacrificing investor consumes less than she would without the investment, and the spending investee consumes exactly the same money's worth more. In contrast, the transfers of money for financial investment in the more typical elite-finance are usually moves from savings-money in the left section of the Triptych to token-money in the middle. The financial investment does not force the affluent investor to consume less. Rather, the additional token-money imperceptibly increases the Central Monetary Ratio, so prices increase a little more than the collection of paid-for things (with 'more' understood as much conceptually as numerically). The price-adjustment reduces the total consumption of everyone except the investee by just enough to compensate for the investee's increased consumption. The tiny losses are spread so broadly that they too are imperceptible, or can be compensated for by other economic shifts.

The two meanings of financial investment, with and without direct transfer of consumption, are not too confusing as long as the distinction is not forgotten. "Investment", however, also has three economic meanings.

First, when one person purchases shares, debts or any other financial security from an existing owner, the buyer is said to be "making an investment". However, since such purchases bring no new monetary resources to investees, they have nothing in common with financial investments. This distinction is sometimes recognised by using "primary" investing to refer to genuine financial investments and "secondary" investing to refer to the transfer of a money-thing from one investor to another. Unfortunately, the use of this crucial distinction is haphazard.

Second, an "investment" in a new facility may be paid for with token-money provided by yoking current sales to future expenses. There is nothing financial in this investment. At most, if the investing enterprise is profit-seeking, there is probably an expectation that some of the revenues which the new facility generates will be sent to shareholders as dividends, even though the shareholders provided none of the money needed to build the facility. However, not-for-profit enterprises also make this sort of investment, without any plan or obligation to send money as financial payments.

Finally, a purchase of new general-purpose government debt is often described as an investment. The usage makes sense to the buyer, who expects the same sort of monetary return from a government bond as from a genuine financial investment. The government, though, is doing something quite different from any genuine economic-finance investee. It will not spend the money to build something new or use it for any specific purpose, as is the expectation for a financial investment. The borrowed money will merely be blended in with tax receipts and perhaps with newly created money from the central monetary authority. All these different types of money will be used indiscriminately for whatever governments use money for. The result of this blending and indiscriminate spending is that the returns on government debt cannot come from the fruits of the projects the debt helped pay for. The return payments will simply be paid out of the government's mix of monetary sources – borrowing, taxes, and newly created money.

In short, the word "investment" is used to describe transactions which are and are not pure-financial, which are and are not related to the Great Exchange, which are and are not specifically aimed at providing some sort of return, and which are and are not dedicated to a specific purpose. It is hard to imagine a less useful piece of vocabulary.

Since none of this ambiguity is hidden, the natural question is once again why economists have not made any serious effort to clear it up. If anything, they have perpetuated and deepened it with models that discuss the gaps between "savings" and "investments", using both terms in economically ambiguous ways. The only persuasive solution to this puzzle is that economists' operative paradigm does not clearly distinguish three distinct things – the actual economy (the Great Exchange), the parts of the monetary system that overlap with the real economy (the middle section of the Triptych) and the parts of the monetary system that do not overlap with it (the left section).

The damage created by ignoring these significant differences, which do exist, is often increased by creating a clear distinction that does not actually exist. Spending that is oriented to the future is separated radically from spending on current needs and pleasures. As I am about to explain, this division vastly oversimplifies the complex social constructions required for industrial prosperity.

5. Capital

Very roughly speaking, "capital" is the thing built up by investment. The definition has to be rough, because "capital" has as many meanings as investment – two financial and at least three in the real economy. All the meanings aim to capture the same thing, the durable assets which are relied on or made use of in the Great Exchange.

In this book, I studiously avoid using the word "capital", the concept of "durable asset", the economic description of "capitalism", and the sociological-economic category of "capitalist". I believe that all these terms are more confusing than helpful, because the capital or durable assets that they are based on cannot be defined without the use of an unrealistic and arbitrary distinction between the economic short-term and long-term. As I pointed out in introducing the Great Exchange in Chapter Two, human labour and human consumption are neither. Labour is always offered now and consumption is always taken now. The imposition of temporal distinctions – this is long-term and that is short-term – distorts this essentially instantaneous economic reality. Of course, some labours bear their consumption fruits much more quickly or directly than others, but there is more continuity than division in the varieties of human labour. Not only does all labour always participate in the same process of humanising the world, but there can never be a clear division between the building-labour commonly identified as creating capital and the operating-labour identified as creating consumption. The labour of production for immediate consumption builds long-lasting skills, communities, and trust along with tangible products and consumable services. On the other side, the labour of research or factory-building is necessarily blended with the labours that keep up current production.

In this correct, seamless understanding of the economy, there is no "capital" thing that can be clearly identified and cleanly separated from other economic things. Rather, the economy's productive base is so deeply integrated with the whole social and economic community that any attempt to define and delineate it will inevitably be more misleading than insightful. As I will show, the approach of economists to "capital" has been heading towards my seamless approach for the past few decades. However, the journey is slow, so it is worth discussing the continuing verbal confusion in a little more detail.

I will start with capital's two financial meanings, retrospective and prospective. Both are supposed to represent the value, expressed in money, of the profit-generating assets of a particular enterprise. Both are measured with spurious precision. Both are studied compulsively by buyers and sellers of financial money-things, although the retrospective one has become less popular over the last few decades.

While the backwards-looking measure is now less fashionable, it remains at the heart of corporate financial accounts. The intuition behind the idea of accounting-capital is fairly straightforward. This capital is the monetary value of the claim that financial-investors, the owners of the relevant money-thing, have on the enterprise. It is what they have paid for. In principle, the capital account starts with the original money provided by financial-investors and then adds accounting profits and subtracts accounting losses. The detailed calculations are quite complicated, as might be expected from attempts to put a single value on a disparate collection of physical, intangible, and monetary assets that have been both built up and worn down over many years and in many places. In a valiant effort to make the numbers comparable over time and among enterprises, official regulatory bodies decree uniform accounting rules for calculating this historical-capital. However, the relationship between past purchases and present operations is far too complex for any set of rules to provide a very illuminating number.

Prospective financial capital, or market-value-capital, has a different set of problems. It is the value of an enterprise's capacity to generate profits, both now and in the future. The calculation of this present value has two stages. First, financial analysis is used to estimate profits expected in the future. Then, financial theory is called upon to combine all of the future profits into a single "present value". The intelligence and energy dedicated to attaching a number to the concept of market-value-capital are often remarkable. However, the actual results are essentially silly, since neither analysis nor theory can overcome reality: the future is always largely impenetrable and the relations of present and future token-money are essentially incalculable, because token-money is an instantaneous and not an intertemporal measure.

Turning to the economic meanings, one type of capital is political-economic: the capital controlled by capitalists. For Marxists and other political radicals in the second half of the 19th century, the picture was quite clear. Contemporary history was a battle between two impersonal forces: labour and capital. The first was not the labour described in this book, people humanising the world. Rather, it was people dehumanised into a collection of man-machines. The second was a political-economic force that both was and controlled the machines, mines, and everything else on and in which labour toiled. This impersonal force of capital also was and controlled vast quantities of savings-money stored on the edge of production and all the inventories needed for production (confusingly known as working or circulating capital). Capital included commercial networks. It had privileged if not exclusive access to new money from banks, and it exercised considerable political influence. Capital was impersonal, but represented by people known as capitalists. Their economic role was to oppress labour and their social-political role was to dominate the entire economy, which for Marxists meant dominating the entire political system and every important social belief-system.

Although Marxists did not see the irony. their capitalism and the capital at its centre were themselves part of an important social belief-system. In the Marxist ideology, the economy was assumed to be controlled by capitalists through their control of capital. The moral judgement and symbolic description of this supposed capitalist system vary. Marxist and other cultural critics see capitalism, especially so-called late capitalism, as a source, manifestation, and symbol of economic dehumanisation, the soulless culture of mass production, the relentless and dignity-destroying search for profits, and various other vicious powers and spirits. Somewhat curiously, almost all sworn enemies of Marxism accept their opponents' intellectual framework of capital, capitalism, and capitalists. However, they reverse the moral judgement. These defenders of capitalism see capital as the fruitful force which dominates nature, liberates labour from toil, and improves society. For them, capitalists are the worthy servants or stewards of capital, and capitalism is the system that allows capital to flourish.

What I call productive-capital, the second economic type of capital, is more specific and more material than political-economic-capital. Productive-capital is the collection of machines, factories, railroads, roads, airports, mines, trucks, and whatever other physical things are used in the production of the goods and services which people consume. For productive-capital, ownership is not an issue. The Soviet Union had a great deal of it, with few if any capitalists. Even in the most capitalist economies, roads and other important parts of the stock of productive-capital have generally been controlled by the government or some quasi-governmental agency. Productive-capital is what is meant when it is said that most of the capital of Germany and Japan was destroyed in the Second World War.

The rapid rebuilding of those bombed factories after the war was a hint that the productive-capital was too narrow a concept to describe the durable base on which industrial prosperity is constructed. Cumulative-capital, the third type of capital, refers to the necessarily broader base. It adds to the second definition all the economically helpful aspects of what can be called a culture. These include the accumulated common technical knowledge, the skills of the workforce, logistical systems, legal arrangements, cultural values, and who knows what else. "Cumulative" is my adjective. Usually, economists focus on one aspect of it at a time. Skills and education are often referred to as intellectual or human capital. Helpful social arrangements are sometimes called social capital. Access to exploitable or sustainable natural resources is known as environmental capital. Shared ethical standards are sometimes somewhat daringly described as moral capital. As I suggested at the beginning of this description, as economists explore the full extent of all these sub-capitals, they come ever closer to merging cumulative-capital with a broad and vague social concept which might be called the social capacity for prosperity.

Some of these different meanings of capital have been marked out and separated by descriptive adjectives, but the single word "capital" is still used indifferently for many things – a sloppy measure of money aggregated over time, a precise but meaningless measure of current value of a money-thing, a political-economic and ideological label, a description of physical assets, and a general indicator of some sort of enduring social-economic strength. As before, this verbal equivocation springs from the faulty paradigm of most economists. They cannot recognise the radical difference between arbitrary monetary numbers and economic things in their human and material complexity. They are equally blind to the essential difference between the backwards-looking monetary numbers built up out of prices paid inside the Great Exchange and the hypothetical and future-looking numbers connected with money-things. Because of these conceptual blurrings, the obviously large differences in the meanings of "capital" are not considered significant enough to justify the verbal innovation that would be required to clear up, for example, the muddled discussions of investment and capital offered in (Keynes, 1973), the most thoughtful work of one of the 20th century's most insightful non-Marxist economists.

What should be done while waiting for a new paradigm to take hold? Well, capital is a word with meanings that move effortlessly but confusingly from accounting to finance, and from there to economics, and on to sociology and politics. In each of those domains, there are several meanings that can be overlapping, mutually exclusive, or even contradictory. I recognise that there is a common idea behind this morass, but I think it is much easier to banish the word than to try to pin it down.

6. Government debt

I have already discussed briefly the ambiguous relations between government debt and both taxes and the direct creation of money. In this subsection, I turn to an internal ambiguity, which I alluded to earlier in this chapter. Much as the thing called money is really two quite different things, token-money and savings-money, the thing called government debt is two essentially different things: domestic-debt and foreign-debt.

Most government debt is domestic, that is governments borrowing from their own citizens, banks, and businesses. The domestic-debt owners are full participants in the monetary economy from which the government gathers almost all its tax revenues and into which it deploys almost all its money, both newly created and gathered through taxes or debt. From the perspective of the left section of the Triptych, the domestic government debt-holders are financial investors. From a political-economic-social perspective, they are taxpayers and residents, so the money-flows that are connected with their government debt holdings are only one part of their multifaceted relationship with the government. As taxpayers, the voluntary savings-money that goes to the government and the contracted token-money returns that come from the government should not considered in isolation from the mandatory money-flow of taxes. As residents, the owners of government benefit from some collection of government token-money payments and from the panoply of goods and services that are provided directly to and indirectly for the benefit of the taxpaying governed.

In unifying the government-related money-flows, I am violating distinctions that are considered almost sacred by most economists, taxpayers, and buyers of government debt. Contractual and financial government interest payments are thought to be essentially different from economic and political government taxes and benefits. The explanation of my sacrilege is simple. This distinction between taxes and welfare, like that between taxes and government debt, may be important sociologically, legally, or in some model of economic psychology, but it has no monetary or economic significance. From the perspective of the government's sources of money, debt purchases are just one way to collect money from the governed. From the perspective of the government's distribution of token money, interest payments are just one type of welfare plan or tax credit. For owners of domestic-debt, the interest income is just one part of a package of money, goods, and services that they receive from their governments, just as the wages or savings-money used to buy government debt are one part of the token-money and savings-money transfers to the government.

In contrast, foreign-debt, government debt owned by non-taxpayers, is almost totally cut off from the borrowing government's political-economic system. Domestic-debt is essentially political and social and only incidentally or accidentally financial, while foreign-debt is essentially financial and only dimly or accidentally political and social. Foreign buyers of government debt may have some political-economic motivations for their purchases. For example, they might want to hold assets in another currency, exert pressure on borrowing governments, or influence foreign exchange markets. However, the cross-border money-flows are totally separable from any non-financial agenda.

This essential difference has four implications.

First, foreign-debt buyers will typically be more concerned than domestic-debt buyers about the return payments on these money-things. For domestic owners, the return should be put into a larger political context. If they want to maximise their income over time, they might wonder whether higher interest rates now bring an increased risk of higher tax rates later. If they want to support the common good of the nation during a crisis, they might be willing to forgo the highest possible return. If they wish to live in political peace, they might prefer the political stability that typically comes with lower interest rates. For foreign-debt holders, none of these non-financial concerns have more than marginal relevance. The debts of foreign countries are one type of money-thing among many. The debts of various governments should be evaluated as purely financial alternatives to each other, as well as to shares, other types of debt, and so forth.

Second, domestic-debt does not directly affect the overall size of the domestic paid-for economy. It is merely part of the government's activities of money creation and money-allocation. In contrast, foreign-debts, whether or not they are denominated in the currency of the borrowing country, typically create genuine cross-border transfers of resources, first inward to the borrowing country and then outward to the lending one. The first transfer comes when money that first crosses political borders to buy the government debt is spent, as it normally is, on labour and consumption goods and services. For the borrowing government, this ability to buy more is generally attractive, at least initially. It seems that the government and the citizens are getting something for almost nothing – real goods and services that are not paid for by the wages of current domestic labour. Ideally, the new things do not merely bring this temporary pleasure. Foreign-debt can be used as something like economic finance, providing token-money that is spent in ways that help create the national prosperity needed to render painless the second transfer, the return payments to the foreign-debt owner. Whatever happens, though, it is clear that domestic and foreign government borrowings have dramatically different effects on the real economy in the borrowing country.

Third, for the borrowing governments, foreign debt can easily become much more onerous than domestic-debts. With taxes and a reasonably cooperative political system, governments can fully offset the economic and allocational effects of return payments on domestic-debt. That is not possible for governments' foreign-debt. Domestic taxpayers must provide the returns and the resulting tax burden is likely to be politically unpopular. The political issues involved are often complicated, but my point is simple. The economic and political dynamics of the return payments of foreign-owned and domestic-owned government debt are substantially different.

Finally and more technically, the economic value of foreign debts in the Great Exchange can change in different ways from the value of domestic debts that initially have the same monetary value. The reason is the currency exchange rate, which does not exist for domestic debt but generally does for foreign debt. The value of the return payments changes whenever this exchange rate shifts. If the debt is denominated in the currency of the borrowing nation, then the value changes for the lending country. When the debt is in the lender's currency, then the borrowing country receives any gain or pain. When the debt is in the currency of neither country, for example if Tanzania borrows in dollars from European banks, then many divisions are possible.

The verbal confusion over government debt is simpler than the others described in this section, but it raises the same question – why does it persist? It would not take a great deal of effort to speak and write about domestic-owned government debt and foreign-owned government debt as separate things. I just did that, but I believe I am a pioneer. To be fair, foreign debt that is denominated in a foreign currency is sometimes separated out as "external". However the core distinction between domestic and foreign financial arrangements is almost never made or even noticed.

The reason for this intellectual laziness is not practical, although it might well be tricky to measure the two new categories, since the ultimate owners of the relevant financial securities are often hidden. The reason is once again conceptual, or paradigmatic. The totally non-social and non-political thinking about the essentially social and political nature of financial relationships leads to conceptual confusion. Since the money-economy system is taken as a freestanding whole, not as a socially embedded collection of arrangements, the sharp political and social differences created by different types of investors do not naturally come into focus.

10. Four conceptual confusions

The same paradigmatic weakness which creates verbal ambiguities also leads to some widespread conceptual confusions about finance. I discuss four of them in this section.

1. Compounding returns

The time has come to keep my promise, made in the first section of this chapter, to tell the true story of the compounding of wealth. Recall the tremendous claims for the phenomenon. Not only does money create money as a pear tree creates pears, as Marx put it, but the creation of additional money is exponential. The fortune of financial investors naturally increases by five or ten percent each year. At a five percent compounded return, the initial value of an investment will double in fourteen years, without any effort from the investor. The five percent number may sound high, but the "Compound Annual Growth Rate" of share price gains and "reinvested" dividends for the Standard & Poor's 500 stock index, a portfolio which includes equity shares in all the largest companies traded in the United States, was seven percent between 1990 and 2017. Such statistics are not exactly false, but they are quite deceptive. There is a significant difference between the mathematical pattern and economic reality.

Compounding or exponential growth is simple enough. Put a "power" or exponent on any number greater than one and watch it grow, remarkably fast. Insofar as money is just a number, it can increase exponentially. All the numbers of savings-money, in the left section of the Triptych, qualify as a number suitable for exponential growth. The tethers of all money-things to the middle section, with its fallible and limited humanity and its harsh physical world, are too loose to break the pattern, not for many years at least. The financial system and its owners can evolve into an ever growing, economy-swallowing monster. Similarly, the magic of compounding can work for the numerator of the Central Monetary Ratio in the Triptych's middle section. Prices, wages, taxes, and all other payments can increase without limit.

Even these magic money-trees cannot grow to the sky. Eventually, political, social, or economic considerations create obstacles. Various problems can emerge. Sometimes, the money-thing numbers can become so large relative to the token-money numbers of the middle section that the discrepancy causes border problems in one currency. Alternatively, political tensions from increasing inequality between owners and non-owners of money-things can interrupt the mathematical purity of compounding with the harsh reality of social conflicts. Politics also generally gets in the way of rapid price and wage inflation sooner or later, but not always before compound growth has made past token-money-numbers look incomprehensibly small.

Compounding's magic can never get very far in the Central Ratio's denominator. While there is no consistent or objectively correct way to quantify the jumble of goods and services that constitute what is paid for in the paid-for economy, whatever numbers are assigned cannot increase any faster than is allowed by the inherent limits of the Great Exchange. The limits have proven less constraining that pre-modern people realised. The ultimate limits to increases in population and consumption do not seem to be in sight. However, what is relevant to compounding is the reality – just as true in modern as in pre-modern economies – that that pace at which people can get better at humanising the world is limited.

Even before the money-trees tumble down, the finance-monster suggested by the high calculated rates of compounding financial returns is somewhat mythical. For a financial investor's returns actually to compound at a socially disruptive rate, none of the returns, the dividend and interest income, can ever be used as token-money. Rather, the money must all be converted into savings-money and "reinvested", also known as "put back into the market". Both wordings suggest that the use of these return payments for investment is not exactly natural. That suggestion is correct in both theory and practice. In theory, it is economically consistent to keep the token-money returns circulating in the Great Exchange. In practice, the financial investors do spend a significant portion of their returns, rather than converting them into savings-money. As a result, the actual rate of increase in the value of the money-things owned by most actual investors is well below the putative pace suggested by crude compounding calculations.

The historical statistics are not wrong. Any single investor could have enjoyed the wondrous compound rates of return. A few probably did. However, there are three reasons to mistrust the numbers. First, the automatic conversion of all token-money returns into savings-money money-things deprives the financial investor from using any of the returns to pay for consumption. Such miserly behaviour is unappealing and rare. Second, the historical rates of compounding may well be higher than future ones. Over the last few decades, the growth in the total value of money-things has been much faster than the growth in the numerator of the Central Ratio. That pattern could continue, but might well not. Finally, if too many investors decide to follow the same strategy of converting all their returns to savings-money, it becomes harder to avoid some sort of serious border problems within one country. The more that is saved, the more likely a monster explosion becomes.

In sum, high compound rates of financial returns are a very special case, not a general rule.

2. Pension and government debts

I have already discussed the illusion of pension savings. To summarise, pension savings or contributions and pension payments are each part of separate contemporaneous allocation arrangements: of money between the left and middle sections of the Triptych, of token-money within the middle section, and of the goods and services of the real economy. However, past pension contributions have no direct connection with the future consumption. The future decision to allocate more money to people who have previously saved more money is a purely social-political judgement.

In so-called defined-contribution private pensions, the judgement is made quasi-mechanically. The amount of money paid out in pensions is determined by the amount and timing of money paid-in and a collection of subsequent measurable events during the years between paying-in and paying-out: the monetary interactions of interest and dividend payments, the changing prices of money-things, the management of the portfolio of pension assets, and the actual and expected death-rates of contributors. For defined-benefit and pensions in state systems, the payments in and out are often described as related by a similar chain of interactions, but the actual decisions on how high pensions will be are almost entirely political.

In economic terms, however, the connection between the two sets of numbers, payments in and payments out, is always so tenuous as to be practically invisible. Both sets of payments can change the Central Monetary Ratio slightly, and both often change the actual allocation relative to what it would be if there were no payments and no other changes. However, the past payments-in can have almost no effect on the future resources available to generate the payments-out.

There is one ultra-thin strand of cause and effect, which is often postulated in campaigns for greater pension savings. It states as fact the pious fiction that most payments-in are used to pay for physical "investments" which increase production in the middle section of the Triptych. In reality, in modern economies most purchases of money-things have little or no effect on the amount of "investment", which is largely paid for by yoking and taxes, and, for the same reason, the amount of "investment" has little to do with the amount of money used to buy money-things. Unsurprisingly, there is no evidence that the political choice to create pension funds, rather than to make pension benefit payments out of government revenues or to expect children to take care of their parents, has any economic effect.

Long-term government debts create another popular intertemporal financial confusion. It is often stated as a fact that when governments take on long-term debts, today's citizens are putting a burden on the next generation. This is largely an economic fiction.

The discussion of government debt in the last section is relevant here. Borrowing money from foreigners is quite different from domestic borrowing. With domestic-debt, money merely changes hands among taxpayers. At the beginning, the government gets money from taxpayers who happen also to be financial investors. Whether investors send token-money or savings-money, the additional money gives the government control of a larger share of the total available economic resources than it would have otherwise. The token-money payments of financial returns flow from the government to a subset of the same group of taxpayers. Interest and Large Payments from governments to the owners of these government-connected money-things are best understood as government benefit programmes that provide money for certain people at certain times. They are essentially the same as pension or unemployment benefit programmes, providing a negative tax payment to a selected group of taxpayers.

The differences among these benefit programmes are political or sociological. In post-aristocratic circles, government payments to rentiers, the largely rich people who buy bonds instead of paying taxes, are commonly described as virtuous returns on investment, while economically identical payments to the ill or unemployed are typically considered something like charity to people who cannot take care of themselves. Conversely, in more egalitarian circles, the government's unjust enrichment of rentiers would be contrasted unfavourably with the government's just provision for those most in need. The political debate is beyond the scope of this book, but the basic fact is ideologically neutral. In domestic government borrowing, no matter for how long, there is never any sort of intergenerational transfer. The money lent now is spent now and the interest payments received later come from the taxpayers who live later. The flows of money merely create changes in current allocation, just like any other token-money flows in the middle section of the Triptych.

Foreign-debt is quite different. It can indeed be a burden on the next generation. The small and large return payments to outsiders move money and presumably economic resources from inside to outside the country, just as the original payment to purchase the debt moved money and presumably economic resources from outside to inside. If the return payments last long enough, then the debt creates a two-way intergenerational flow, first into the accounts of the parents' generation and then away from the accounts of their heirs.

There need be no injustice in this intertemporal exchange. The foreign lending to today's governments will only place a significant economic burden on future taxpayers if the original money is not used to build up economic resources that produce far more money than is required for the payments of financial income. Alternatively, the financing may create a burden, but one which the next generation is willing to take up, because the money was used to serve what is widely perceived to be a worthy national cause, for example paying for weapons that preserved political independence. However, history suggests that future taxpayers will often consider their obligations to foreign lenders to be intertemporally unjust. They believe, often with good reason, that the last generation squandered the money on their pleasures, leaving this one with only the pain of repayment. The discontent often leads to political resentment and to not keeping the terms of the original financial contract.

Such intergenerational waste and anger can be a significant issue in the financial world, but their economic importance should be kept in perspective. Government debts to foreigners do not have the finality of intergenerational transfers of use and abuse in the Great Exchange. The labour involved in providing education, construction of a road or a factory, and reducing toxic emissions are all current economic actions that can have substantial positive implications in the future, perhaps in the very distant future. Such labour of the parents will bear fruit for the children and grandchildren – more knowledge, better infrastructure, and cleaner air. This fruit cannot be devalued or erased as a monetary debt can. Conversely, if one generation leaves the next one uneducated, or laden with poorly maintained roads and polluted rivers, the unfortunate heritage is durable and sometimes even indelible. Unlike financial obligations, these real economic obligations cannot be shirked or diminished, and they can never be forgiven.

3. Two types of prices

The price of a money-thing can seem to be no different from a price inside the Great Exchange. After all, I can choose to spend the same one thousand euros on either existing equity shares or a new sofa. However, I hope it is clear by now that these transactions are economically and monetarily quite different, even though my bank balance goes down by the same amount. Economically, one is outside and the other inside the Great Exchange. The monetary difference follows directly from the economic. The shares are paid for with savings-money and the sofa with token-money.

In effect, I am using "price" equivocally, since a price inside the Exchange is substantially different from one outside. The substantial difference between the money-numbers in the left and middle sections of the Triptych leads to significant differences in the way these numbers are formed and change, and in their economic and social meanings.

I sketched out the basic difference in Chapter Two. Money-numbers directly connected to real things do not generally change very much or very fast, because they are tied more or less closely to fairly stable, real things: human labour and objects and services in the humanised world. In contrast, the prices of money-things have little or no anchor in reality. They are controlled almost entirely by two non-economic forces: human emotions and the supply of baseless money. Both of these can fluctuate quickly and dramatically. The result is that money-thing prices can also fluctuate wildly, with little or no economic reason. Here I look at three aspects of that basic difference.

First, the money-numbers inside the Great Exchange have a fundamental mutuality which is totally lacking in money-thing-prices.

I mentioned the interdependence of prices and wages briefly in Chapter Two. The after-transfer prices charged for consumption goods and services are typically related to the total after-transfer wages of the labourers who created these goods and services. Conversely, the after-transfer wages paid to labourers are typically related to the after-transfer prices charged for the fruits of their labour. This two-way flow ensures that changes in money-numbers on one side of the Exchange both reflect and influence money-numbers on the other. The intimate ties of the money-numbers with the entire complex, unified, and interwoven system of labour and consumption do not completely tame price movements or always tie prices closely to labour (the negligible prices charged for most education and healthcare in developed economies are clear examples of exceptions), but they do restrict the level of irrationality.

In contrast, the money-numbers connected with money-things are almost totally unbound to reality and thus largely unbounded. There are no theoretical limits to the price of land or collectibles, and it is not clear that there are any limits in practice. There is no upper limit to commodity prices. For financial securities, it might seem that the level of interest and dividend payments would limit how high the prices can rise, but recent history shows that financial investors will accept very low current returns (indeed they will accept "negative interest rates") for a long time. Financial theory claims to tie security prices to the expected future payments to investees, but the theory is numerical mumbo-jumbo.

Second, variations of money-numbers inside the Great Exchange usually solve economic problems, while changes in money-thing prices more often cause them. Most changes in token-money prices and wages are helpful responses to developments in the Great Exchange. Higher prices are responses to higher costs, higher quality, or greater interest from buyers. Lower prices are responses to changes in the opposite direction. In turn, higher prices at least sometimes bring fewer purchasers and stimulate rival producers, higher wages typically attract more labourers, and so forth. As I said in Chapter Two, this endless, delicate dance of monetary and real economic adjustments does not always work perfectly. Some price changes are distinctly unhelpful, for example the unjustified price increases imposed by companies as they increase their domination of the supply of particular products. Overall, however, transaction-price flexibility makes significant contributions to economic efficiency.

Economists sometimes say that changes in money-thing prices, in particular to the prices of financial securities, give helpful economic signals. They exaggerate greatly. The next sub-section discusses some of the ambitious claims about the economic information contained in debt prices and the much more modest reality. The claims about the importance of the price of equities are somewhat less ambitious but hardly any more sensible or realistic. What money-thing prices do have is the potential to disturb the real economy. Dramatic changes, which are hard to avoid, can have a significant psychological effect. Rising prices can instil foolish confidence and falls can bring unnecessarily dark fear. These price movements can also have a direct and unhelpful effect on the supply and balance of token-money in the middle section of the Triptych, through the border problems in one currency. Good monetary decisions by the central monetary authority can usually keep the money-thing system from disastrous excess, but the history of financial crises shows that such decisions are too often necessary and too rarely made.

Finally, token-money prices are generally socially unifying, while money-thing prices tend to be divisive. The unity comes from the inherent balance of the Great Exchange. Each person's earnings are divided among many goods, each producer's revenue is divided among many labourers, and each adjustment to a wage or price affects the entire community's wages and prices. The flexibility of wages and transaction prices allows problems and benefits to be spread widely across the economy. It is quite different for the wild movements of the prices of money-things. There is no communal balancing, leaving space for an endless struggle to get ahead of neighbours and rivals. The prospect of large gains for little effort often brings out a greedy desire to get there first, since the gains of one owner often come at the expense of other owners. Even when almost all money-thing prices are rising simultaneously, as they often do, there are often bitter struggles to "outperform" the average. The general price increases of money-things are generally welcomed by the owners of money-things, even by the relative losers, but their gains are socially divisive, because they always come at the expense of non-owners. Morally, the volatility, non-reality, and limited internal connections of money-thing prices are almost an invitation to the greed that I will discuss in Chapter Five.

4. The mystique of interest rates

Many economists believe that interest rates have tremendous powers of economic control. They postulate that the promised return on debts both sets the overall pace of action in the entire middle section of the Triptych and guides what is supposed to be a clear division within it, between consumption and investment. These great powers are supposed to be concentrated in the hands of the central monetary authority. This organisation sets a single master or "policy" interest rate, which I will call the "central-rate". (This rate has different names in different currencies.) Like the legendary Beijing butterfly whose flapping wings eventually unleash hurricanes across the ocean, the small twitches in the central-rate can supposedly change the direction and composition of entire economies. Unlike the chaotic forces unleashed by the unaware insect, however, central monetary authorities exercise their power carefully and consciously. In theory, they exert a precisely calibrated influence on the calculations and average thought processes of all economic actors.

I hope that notion that a single number, the central-rate, can have so much influence on the numerous and complex human interactions of a modern economy sounds like magical thinking. It mostly is.

I need to be fair. Since the financial system has an economic role, changes within the financial system will presumably do something to the economy, as will changes in any other parts of the economy. In more detail, changes in any interest rate change some prospective money-flows in the middle section of the Triptych, those changes influence other prospective money-numbers, and changed monetary prospects influence economic decisions. To the extent that the central-rate influences other interest rates, changes in that interest rate will, almost by definition, have some effect on some parts of the economy for some amount of time.

The actual economic effects of particular changes in the central-rate cannot be determined, because the interlocking and mutually influencing chains of economic causality are far too complex to be disentangled accurately. The thick fog of ignorance is almost recognised in many advanced presentations of the theory of interest rates, when it is admitted that it is difficult to predict even the direction of the economic effect of changes in the central-rate. Until recently, however, the difficulty of tying interest-rate causes to specific economic effects was usually glossed over. Lower interest rates were simply postulated as encouraging all economic activity that is largely paid for with borrowed money: most notably, expanding production and building and buying houses and cars. Confidence in this magic power diminished in the long decades of a declining trend of measured inflation rates, especially the years of ultra-low and even negative central-rates after the 2008-9 financial crisis. The almost totally unexpected return of higher reported inflation in rates has – curiously in my view – restored confidence in the importance and potential efficacy of the central-rate.

The easy revival of faith in the theory of the power of central-rates suggests that a fairly detailed critical analysis is justified. I follow the lead of some distinguished economists and critics, for example (Galbraith, 1998) but I set the theory's seven-link chain of claimed causes and effects into this book's monetary and economic model.

First claim: When banks create or allocate money by making loans, the loaned money is always used to pay for either "investments" in economic activities that create employment and consumption or for additional consumption. In other words, loaned money *always* goes to support activity in the middle section of the Triptych. If this claim is not true, then the effect of interest rate changes on the paid-for economy will definitely be diluted and might be counteracted by loans that merely create savings-money in the left section of the Triptych.

Criticism: The claim that all loans add to the token-money-supply is certainly not true. Indeed, it is totally false. In most modern economies, lower interest rates are much less likely to encourage the creation of new token-money than to encourage the creation of savings-money that remains in the left section. This unwanted outcome is logical. Money is the only raw material needed to create money-things, so cheaper savings-money clearly encourages such constructions, while money is only one of many factors influencing activity in the middle section, so the effect of cheaper token-money there is likely to be more modest.

Second claim: Loaned token-money pays for all the "investments" inside the paid-for economy. This is the converse of the first claim. It is effectively a statement that no-money-now problems in the chains of production are, actually or potentially, a crippling restraint on helpful economic activity. If this claim is not true, then there will be no necessary or simple relationship between lending and "investment".

Criticism: This claim is indeed not true. The overwhelming majority of the money spent in the middle section of the Triptych is always already there. It is all spent as desired by the people and institutions who receive it as it flows around the Great Monetary Exchange. It can be allocated to solve no-money-now problems in all the ways that do not involve finance. Most commonly, yoking allows higher selling prices on existing products to pay for new or improved equipment and knowledge throughout the chains of production. The government also solves no-money-now problems by providing new token-money to people or organisations that are not likely to convert this additional income into savings-money. Even within the finance system, new equity is generally a plausible alternative to lending. While financial theory considers equity to be a sort of quasi-debt, that claim is partly confused and almost entirely wrong (this will be explained in the Appendix).

It is likely that the availability and cost of loans may sometimes somewhat constrain some types of token-money spending, especially in the current monetary arrangement, in which most newly created money comes through the creation of loans to producers, consumers, governments, and various spending institutions. A lack of such loans can reduce economic activity in undesirable ways. However, the monetary contribution to any unwanted restraint is often less important than many other factors, including (in alphabetical order) corporate profitability, demographic shifts, financial regulation, globalisation, government policies, group psychology, labour relations, technological developments, and weather.

Third claim: Interest rates determine, or at least strongly influence, the amount of money that is borrowed. The lower the interest rate is, the more that is borrowed, and the relationship between interest rate and quantity of borrowing is fairly regular.

Criticism: The interest expense associated with loans is only one of many factors involved in lending and borrowing decisions. Regulations on financial institutions, the judgements of lenders and borrowers about the likeliness of default, lenders' desperation to earn interest income, borrowers' desperation to obtain money, borrowers' judgements about the availability of attractive uses of borrowed money, and potential borrowers' ability to obtain desired money without borrowing can all be as important as the actual interest rate paid in deciding whether a loan will be made.

Fourth claim: There is a "correct" central-rate, the interest rate at which the amount of money that is created minimises unwanted unemployment (the lack of paid-for labour), sets the best balance between "consumption" and "investment", and does not substantially change the Central Monetary Ratio. In practice, there is always enough imbalance in the money-system and the economy that the correct central-rate is always changing, but in most versions of the theory there is or should be at all times in each currency an ideal, "natural", "neutral" or "(long-term) equilibrium" central-rate. This is the rate of interest that the financial system would settle on if money and the economy were in perfect balance. In that happy equilibrium, the natural rate and the central-rate would be identical. The monetary authorities, rather like the vanguard revolutionary parties of Marxist theory, set the central-rate above or below the natural rate in an effort to push history forward towards its goal of money-economy balance. Some macroeconomists claim not to believe in the existence of a natural interest rate, but it or something much like it is needed for the rest of the theory to hold together.

Criticism: The claim that there is always a correct central-rate is an intellectual disaster area. First, it is unverifiable, since the supposed natural rate is both unknown and assumed to change over time. Since the central-rate is always set in some sort of juxtaposition to this elusive natural rate, the correctness of any central rate cannot be tested. Second, the claim relies on an erroneous understanding of disequilibrium in the monetary Great Exchange. The different variables have no fixed connection with each other and each is typically more or less balanced. Clear errors of the sort that could be fixed with the "right" central-rate are rare. Third, the model of cause and effect is absurdly simplistic, since interest rates are only one of many influences on spending, "investing", and savings. Fourth, actual interest rates, the ones that might influence monetary decisions, are often quite distant from the central-rate. To move from the central to the actual rates requires making adjustments to take into account, among other things, the costs of gathering and lending money, possible losses on loans, and the desperation of potential borrowers. The adjustments often change enough to overwhelm changes in the central-rate. Fifth, the entire approach is hopelessly incomplete, since it simply ignores the role of the left section of the Triptych in the monetary system. Sixth and conversely, the approach manages also to be structurally redundant, since the relations of money and the paid-for economy can be analysed without any reference to interest rates.

Fifth claim: Without some guidance from a central monetary authority, the interest rates set by the agreements of borrowers and lenders will often be "wrong". They may end up creating too much or too little money, sometimes leading to undesired price changes and sometimes to unexploited economic opportunities.

Criticism: The supply of token-money probably often is "wrong" in at least some of the ways the interest-rate theory suggests. However, while the effect part of this link in the theoretical chain is sensible, the causal part is quite doubtful. Interest rates, both agreed and imposed, have only an indirect, generally unclear, and almost always modest effect on the actual supply of token-money. They have an even more indirect, less clear, and much smaller effect on the disposition of labour and "capital".

Sixth claim: The "monetary policy" of central monetary authorities can potentially right the wrongs created by agreed interest rates. The exact constituents and broad intellectual framework of this monetary policy have changed over the decades, but the central-rate has been considered crucial throughout.

Criticism: Since the transmission mechanism is extremely inefficient, the effect of changes in the central-rate on actual interest rates is at best modest. Since the economic importance of actual interest rates is also modest, the potential economic importance of central-rates is doubly modest. Since so much lending takes place entirely in the left section of the Triptych, with uncertain effects on the actual Great Exchange, the effects of changes in central interest rates on the middle section are also uncertain. A triple modesty is order. At most, changes in central rates presumably have some influence on lending in the middle section of the Triptych and on cross-border monetary activity, both within the relevant economy and between currencies influenced by different central rates.

Seventh claim: Central monetary authorities can actually gather enough information about the economic situation to be able to set the central-rate at a close-to-correct level. There may well be errors, but these are, or can be, recognised quickly and fairly easily corrected.

Criticism: There are two problems with this final claim. First, it is probably wrong empirically. The necessary amount of information simply cannot be gathered, because unknowable future events have a significant influence in the determination of the most correct current central-rate. For example, one central-rate is probably appropriate now if there will be a financial crisis next year, and another is appropriate now if regulators can prevent such a crisis. This indeterminacy, which is a manifestation of the temporal-ontological asymmetry inherent to finance, creates an insoluble problem. Second, the claim gives a misleading impression of the importance of getting the central-rate "right". That unreachable goal might well be worthy, but the monetary and economic authorities have several tools that are more powerful than the central rate for keeping the money-supply at economically appropriate levels. These include finding the "right" size and direction of government spending and the right adjustments to the regulation of the token-money system in the central section of the Triptych, of the savings-money system in the left section, and of the monetary boundary between the two sections.

In sum, interest rates simply do not, should not, and cannot play the monetary and economic balancing role which has given them such a fine mystique in macroeconomic theory. What interest rates as a whole do not accomplish, the central-rate accomplishes even less.

Chapter 4. Financial unreality

I discussed the relations between token-money and the real economy in the fifth section of Chapter Two. My conclusion was mixed. On the negative side, actual money-numbers are essentially unrealistic, simply because economic activity is not realistically quantifiable and thus not suitable to any sort of commensurability. On the positive side, there is a strong non-quantitative correlation between token-money transactions and actual human activity in the Great Exchange, both at the fundamental level of labour and consumption and through the long intermediate chains of production. Even when the relationship is not very direct, for example in transactions with the government and in transfers of tiny amounts of token-money, the money-numbers generally come with a fairly clear economic meaning.

There were certainly subtleties in that discussion, but it was relatively straightforward. Token-money is not very complicated, as long as it is shorn of both all tints of the precisionist-consistency fallacy and all its economically irrelevant symbolic meanings. The relations of finance with reality are much more complicated, so much so that the questions concerning the reality of finance deserve not just a section, but a full, although brief, chapter.

One problem is that the meaning of reality-distance is less clear for finance than for token-money. The reality that token-money is or is not close to is quite easy to describe – the paid-for portion of the Great Exchange of labour and consumption. The token-money system can express more or less realistically both what is physically happening on the two sides of that exchange and the social values placed on the various types of labour and consumption. The economic reality that finance is or is not close to is more complex. At some scale, the relations of financial arrangements with the economy can, at least hypothetically, be evaluated as more or less realistic – more or less in accord with actual economic conditions – but the correct scale is subject to debate. While each financial arrangement is paired with a specific narrow sliver of total economy for a limited time, much wider slivers of both space and time may often be more relevant. For example, the terms of a loan to a farmer to help him through a tractor-problem for one year may be realistically aligned to the borrowing farmer's income for the period of borrowing and repayment, but may look much less realistic when compared to the money-flows of the entire farming community over many years. In the following discussion, I try to look at reality-distance at both narrow and wide scales.

The debate over the reality-closeness of financial arrangements will inevitably be more heated when the reality in question is social than when it is strictly economic. The main problem is that unlike token-money, which can only express, more or less accurately or realistically, the values that society dictates, financial arrangements are both an independent expression of underlying social judgements of values and a fairly significant element in the establishment of those judgements. In particular, post-aristocratic finance is a realistic expression of social power-relations, as I will discuss in the first section of this chapter, but it also reinforces and to some extent creates those relations. It is hard to say that finance is reality-close when it is a key part of the reality it might be close to. In this chapter, my response to this ambiguity is to dodge the question. I try to avoid the value-judgements needed to discuss finance's social reality-closeness.

This chapter has five sections. The first is conceptual. It describes three habits of thinking in the contemporary approach to finance that seem to favour reality-distance over reality-closeness. I provide some examples, but the discussion is fairly general. After that, things get more technical, as I turn to specific financial arrangements. Fortunately for the purposes of analysis, these contracts do not come in many varieties or have an unlimited collection of distinct features. Rather, as discussed in Chapter Three, in practice there are only two basic types of financial securities, equity and debt. I discuss the reality-closeness and reality-distance of each, in the second and third sections of this Chapter respectively. Then I become even more technical, pointing out 12 features, practices, and expectations which lead various types of general-finance away from reality. The last section is a broader discussion of why reality-distant finance is economically, and also socially, dangerous.

1. Three sources of unreality

Financial money sits firmly in the left section of the Triptych. Streams of token-money returns provide some tie to the middle section, but it is easy for financial arrangements to drift leftward, further from the actual economy. The basic problem is simple. Their prices, denominated in savings-money, have no necessary relationship with their token-money income flows. That problem is amplified by the factors discussed in this section.

1. Temporal-ontological tensions

Because finance is built on promises, which are not only always easier to make than to keep but which can change their economic meanings over time, the initially agreed terms of any money-thing can easily become reality-distant. In particular, agreed interest payments that represented realistic claims on the investee's expected money-flow when the money-thing was constructed might become unrealistically high or low, because prices and wages might rise more or less than expected, or because the later economic situation of the borrower or lender might significantly alter the originally agreed economic "meaning" of the specified terms. For example, the rise in inflation rates in many countries in the 1960s and 1970s left owners of long-term debt money-things with far less "spending power" than any investor would have realistically agreed to accept when the debts were first contracted. Similarly, agreed Large Payments may have been expected to be reality-close when the terms of a loan were set, but are actually reality-distant at the time the Large Payment is due, because at the key moment the investee might have less savings-money than expected, or a new loan might not be available.

As I will discuss later, financial securities can be, and sometimes are, designed to stay reality-close. Most notably, reality is closer when the initial agreement covers only the *criteria* for determining when and what money is to be paid by the investee to the investor, not the exact monetary *quantity* of future payments. Equities do exactly that. However, it is worth noting that both the investors and investees of equities often resist taking full advantage of these money-things' reality-closeness. They insist on regular dividends and especially resist dividend reductions. This reluctance to mitigate temporal uncertainty is quite typical of finance, for example in the widespread preference for fixed income arrangements over equities. Within the debt world, it is also seen in the very limited success of inflation-linked bonds, which have future-determined payments based on officially published price indexes. Similarly, practical proposals to tie return payments to trends in the Gross Domestic Product (Benford et al, 2018) have been almost entirely ignored.

Why do users of finance show such a strong preference for numerical constancy or consistency over economic reality? A common answer is something like, "People just want to be sure how much money they will pay and receive". This "money illusion" rests on the consistency side of the precisionist-consistency fallacy. More profoundly, it must rest on some type of symbol-money, since even the briefest reflection on the working of token-money and savings-money will make it obvious that constant monetary quantities do not imply anything like constant economic values. As I explained in Chapter Two, reality-distant symbols can be more powerful than anything in the real world.

2. Intrinsically unrealistic finance-numbers

In Chapter Two I also mentioned the genuine but necessarily imprecise connections between money-numbers and the reality of the Great Exchange. In Chapter Three I pointed out that the overall prices of money-things are far more influenced by the strength of the waves of savings-money and the shifting winds of people's moods than by any direct connections with the real economy. In other words, these finance-numbers have no clear relationship whatsoever with economic reality.

Economists fairly often dispute that conclusion. As I mentioned in Chapter Three, they sometimes go so far as to argue that the current price of any money-thing is always the best available estimation of the current savings-money value of the expected total future flow of token-money from the investee to the investor. Several implausible assumptions are required to move this "efficient market hypothesis" from the tautological (the current market price is by definition the best current price that the actual participants in the relevant financial or quasi-financial market can come up with) to the economically realistic. Considering the theory's intellectual vacuity, its widespread acceptance looks like an effort to get over a latent discomfort with the hard-to-deny distance between money-thing prices and reality.

The inherent difficulty of connecting money-thing prices to the reality of economic activity or even to the reality of token-money-flows might have encouraged financiers and their regulators to be cautious about developing instruments that serve none of the helpful economic purposes listed in the sixth section of Chapter Three. After all, there is no good reason to construct a money-thing that is both reality-distant by default and serves no good purpose. If there are no good reasons, there must be bad ones, since there has in fact been a steady trend to develop money-things that try to satisfy the reality-distant – indeed, reality-hostile – desire of financial investors for a steady income in either savings-money or token-money under any and all real economic conditions, as well as money-things that provide speculators with new ways to gamble.

Many of the latter type of reality-distant securities are far more exciting and potentially lucrative than traditional debt and equity. The dividend and interest income of old-fashioned financial investors was generally a transfer of token-money within the middle section of the Triptych, but there are much larger potential financial gains and losses on the left side of the left section of the Triptych, where token-money can only be seen hazily in the distance. In that realm of pure savings-money, it is easy to accumulate and multiply tiny changes in the prices of money-things. There speculators can happily play with each other, sometimes using financial leverage to reap large gains. The speculators sometimes suffer large losses, but clever product design can concentrate the gains among speculators and spread the losses widely among the less well-informed investors who often inadvertently provide them with savings-money to play with.

Group-thinking can also increase the reality-distance of financial numbers. The comparison with token-money-numbers is typical. Mutually reinforcing emotions can sometimes have a big effect on a few money-numbers in the middle section of the Triptych, for example when a hit toy is sold on the black market at multiples of its standard retail price. However, the constraints of reality and the complex mutual dependency of many labourers and consumers sharply limit the mob-effects of moods. Those constraints do not exist in the left section of the Triptych, so it is all too easy for a conforming, over-excited and volatile mob to fall into excesses of fear or hope. When this happens, the prices of one, several, or a large class of money-things can rise or fall spectacularly, with little or no immediate cause in the real economy.

3. Hidden power relations

In Chapter Three, I claimed that modern financial systems overall reinforce the economic, social, and political power of the already privileged. Whether this tendency is judged to be good, ethically neutral, a necessary evil, or just plain reprehensible, it often encourages a double unreality in financial arrangements: the psychological unreality of the non-recognition of the economic unreality of finance. In other words, those who gain from finance are both powerful enough to direct the system towards arrangements which tend to serve them rather than to reflect the actual economy of the Great Exchange and blind enough not to recognise what they are doing. Outside observers see a pattern of economically unrealistic reinforcements of privilege in financial arrangements, but the privileged themselves sincerely believe the system is fair and realistic. Here are three examples.

I have already mentioned the first one, the claim that some money-things can and should generate a steady "risk-free" return of token-money in all economic conditions. The economists who make this claim have a theoretical justification that is based on unrealistic understandings of how token-money is related to savings-money, of how savings-money is related to financial arrangements, and of how financial arrangements are related to the activity in the real economy. The cumulative effect of these misunderstandings is to claim that rich people should be rewarded for their effortless non-consumption by receiving a steady stream of token-money in all economic circumstances. At best, the acceptance of this claim increases the burden of financial "tribute" in bad times. At worst, it creates instruments that make punitively unrealistic economic demands on those tribute-payers. The economists who promote these risk-free returns never seem to notice either the weaknesses of their argument or the sociological effects of the arrangements they are persuaded are just.

Second, one of the leading arguments against governments creating new money directly is that governments' need to find buyers for its debt money-things gives financial investors an economically helpful power. They can discipline governments that borrow excessively by simply refusing to buy their debt or by demanding such punitively high returns that these governments will be provoked to mend their irresponsible ways. The argument is based on what looks from the outside like a wilful refusal to note that financial investors are always far too weak to change the course of a determined government. In reality, all governments have the power to force banks to create money to lend to them, so loans provide no more of a restraint than supposedly independent central monetary authorities. The defence of the economic value of private investors working as government "bond vigilantes" also shows a similar, seemingly wilful refusal to notice that there are almost no examples of such discipline in action. However, this curious blindness allows the financial-investors who own government debt to receive a steady income flow from taxpayers. 'It is difficult to get a man to understand something when his salary depends upon his not understanding it', as the writer Upton Sinclair wrote (Ratcliffe, 2016). For the beneficiaries of the current system of deficit finance, economic reality is easily misunderstood.

Third, lenders are generally reluctant to forgive loans which realistically should never have been made, for example to poor and poorly managed countries. In practice, such loans are often "written down" eventually, but usually long after full payment become incompatible with the economic reality of the investee and only after long disputes and negotiations that worsen the borrowers' already weak economic position. Lenders can cite the moral principle that debts are contracts which should be honoured. However, they could and should also recognise that irresponsible lending deserves to be penalised and that troubled borrowers need help far more than they need punishment. The obtuseness may be blamed on lenders' faulty economic analysis, but a sociologist would be likely to suggest that richer investors are merely using reality-distance as a shield to cover up their unjust use of their social and economic power over poorer investees.

2. Semi-realistic finance: shares

In Chapter Three, I expressed doubts about the wisdom, from the perspective of political economy, of treating the owners of equity ("shareholders") in a company as the owners of the entire company. Companies are many things: communities of labour, physical systems of production, repositories and users of knowledge and skills, servants to and guides of customers and societies, and in principle always dedicated to the common good. The ownership of shares, or indeed any primarily monetary arrangement, is a sociologically unrealistic base for governing such multifaceted and socially embedded entities. This social reality-distance deserves careful attention, but is irrelevant to the topic of this chapter. What is relevant is the reality-closeness of equities, considered only as money-things, to the token-money-flows of the relevant companies. In that respect, that is as far as the two-way monetary flows are concerned, shares are economically quite realistic, at least when the companies that issue them are new.

My justification of this claim starts with a reminder of what these equity shares are. Conceptually, they are a possible solution for a particular no-money-now problem, the one faced by people who need token-money to engage in an economic activity that is expected eventually to be profitable. The profitability is crucial, because profits are the source of the equity investors' return. More technically, the no-money-now problem is, so to speak, confined within a legally isolated structure, the corporation. This is the investee of the financial arrangement. The investors who solve the no-money-now problem are shareholders. The investee is said to issue equity or shares to the investors. Generally the shareholders exchange money for shares, but shares are sometimes issued to people or organisations that provide something else of value: patents, labour that is not fully rewarded with wages, or some sort of political or cultural support. Actually, in most jurisdictions, there is no need for any contribution from shareholders. The directors who have legal control over the corporations can issue shares for any reason or none, and at any price. The legal references are important. Corporations do not obey any natural laws of economics or finance. Their rules, including the rights and duties of shareholders, are established through the law and regulation of the corporation's home jurisdiction. In all jurisdictions, shares have some sort of a legal claim on what legally certified accountants identify as profits available for shareholders. The shareholders' claim is normally satisfied through the payment of dividends. The prospect of receiving future token-money dividends is the primary source of the shares' savings-money value.

When a corporation is new, there is generally a fairly close, causal relationship between the contributions made by shareholders to a corporation and the dividends these shareholders receive. In other words, the money and other things that come *from* the shareholders into the corporation have made a substantial and direct contribution to the operations that generate the dividends that are sent out of the corporation *to* the shareholders. This investment-dividend exchange can reasonably be described as reality-close. Also, the dividend paid out in any year typically has a fairly close relationship with the current or recent actual profits being earned. In other words, the timing and level of dividends is also reality-close.

There are many exceptions to both types of reality-closeness. Sometimes the shareholders' money and talents play a relatively minor role in the generation of profits. For example, in a business that earns high profits primarily from "packaging" the labour of skilled employees earning just wages, the relationship of dividends to the shareholders' contributions of money is quite reality-distant from the start, although that distance can be reduced by issuing most of the shares to the profit-generating employees. In Chapter Five, I will argue that the gap between a realistic monetary evaluation of the shareholders' contribution to profits and the dividends that shareholders typically receive systematically widens as successful corporations age.

As for the reality-closeness of the timing and quantity of dividends, reality-distant dividends are actually fairly common. Companies sometimes pay unrealistically high dividends, relative to the money needed for long-term corporate flourishing. They sometimes pay unrealistically low dividends, relative to their ability to spend wisely the shareholders' profits that are not paid out as dividends (retained profits).

The determination of the reality-closeness of dividends relies on, among other things, the ability of financial accounts to measure shareholders' profits in a reasonably realistic way. Overall, the edifice of accounting standards is usually solid enough for "reported profits" to be a reasonably realistic starting place for calculating appropriate dividends. However, no profit-number can be more than a rough approximation of the quantity of token-money truly and durably available for shareholders. The qualifications are substantial. The precisionist-consistency fallacy limits the possible accuracy of any numbers, because the incommensurability of money-numbers calculated at different times and places both makes precision impossible and ensures that even rough consistency among companies and over time will be an ambitious goal. The inclusion of many financial money-numbers (interest expense and income, speculative gains and losses, the financial element of lease payments) in the calculations of the financial money-number "profits for shareholders" further increases the economic inaccuracy. Also, the accountants who set and apply the rules are influenced by the desire of shareholders and managers for high reported profits.

3. Unrealistic finance: debt

The first corporations with shares were created in the 17th century, and the modern corporate economy started no more than two centuries ago. In contrast, almost all modern forms of debt money-things date back millennia. I have already made scattered references to the reality-distant features of these fixed income obligations. This section is more comprehensive. It consists of a list of nine ways in which debt tends to be economically unrealistic, followed by some speculation about the reasons for the enduring popularity of these deeply flawed money-things.

1. Arbitrary interest rates

In financial theory, interest rates are, or at least might be, reality-close. Any actual interest rate can be decomposed into components, each of which can be estimated and each of which corresponds to some part of economic or monetary reality. The theory starts with a natural rate of interest, which, in some versions of the theory, turns out to be equal to the expected rate of growth of real GDP, a reality-close objective number by the low standards of finance. This natural rate is then adjusted to compensate for various costs and potential losses, including those created by current labour and future monetary changes. In reality, though, the adjustments are only a hodgepodge of largely arbitrary estimations of the likely effect of overlapping, mostly hidden, and mutually interacting posited factors that can provide only a *post hoc* justification of actual interest rates. The theory is implausible in general, impossible in detail, and so far from verifiable that the numbers which emerge are in practice reality-distant. (There are more details in the Appendix.)

Indeed, actual interest rates have no particular relationship with economic reality. They do not have any clear relationship to any economic gains provided by the invested money or even to general economic conditions. Still, like the money-numbers in the middle section of the Triptych, these financial-numbers are not random. Various factors may be at play. Something like mutual consent is certain – the interest rate is agreed by the lender and the borrower. The policies of the monetary authorities usually have some influence, as do lenders' judgements of how likely the borrower is to default on the agreed terms. For some loans, the interest rate is set or modified by a government that is less concerned with financial returns than with some economic or political agenda. That is a particular sort of power relationship: the government's agenda overpowers other concerns and calculations. In other situations, the power is somewhat less uneven, but needy borrowers are often forced to pay interest rates that they should consider unacceptably high and desperate savings-money holders are sometimes forced to accept returns which they should consider undesirably low. The complex real causality of particular rates is interesting, but my interest here is narrower. What debt lacks totally is the fairly close tie of equity dividends to the actual results of the investee.

2. Inflation non-recognition

I mentioned the limited interest in "inflation-linked" debt money-things in the previous section. Considering that generalised price changes have been one of the most consistent features of the middle section of the Triptych for the last century, the reluctance to develop and use such money-things amounts to a conscious vote against tying them to reality.

The economic effects of this non-attachment to reality can be quite significant, even after taking into account the crudeness of any measures of changes in the Central Monetary Ratio (changes in the overall price level expressed as rates of inflation). When that ratio was increasing steadily, as it did for most of the 1960s and 1970s, the token-money received by lenders consistently paid for far fewer economic resources in the middle section of the Triptych than these investors expected when they agreed on the terms. In the subsequent decades, it has been the borrowers who have been disappointed.

3. Bubbles

While almost all equity is fairly closely related to activity in the Great Exchange (shares in banks are the leading partial exception), much debt is financial, located almost entirely in the left section of the Triptych. It is easy and common to used borrowed money to buy land or some other money-thing. A sort of no-money-now problem is solved in such "leveraged" arrangements: the lack of the savings-money needed to buy a thing which is priced in savings-money. However, the logic is basically crazed. The point of money-things is to hold savings-money and in modern economies the money-thing is always held with at least the vague intention of eventually converting savings-money into token-money. The use of additional savings-money which belongs to someone else to buy a money-thing can only confuse the already often tenuous connection of the money-thing with any part of the economic reality of the middle section of the Triptych.

As more savings-money is made available to pay for particular money-things, the prices of those things almost automatically increase. As prices rise, would-be owners confidently borrow savings-money to buy these things, both hoping for and encouraging further price increases. Banks are happy to create new savings-money to support the trend, because they are confident that the rising prices of the money-things will protect the value of their loans. As prices rise further, both borrowers and lenders become more confident that savings-money gains will keep flowing. Fundamentally, they are happy because their thinking is reality-distant. They are wilfully unaware of their own monetary solipsism. Such self-reinforcing price increases are sometimes called bubbles, in honour of both their rapid expansion and their lack of durable reality. Something like reality does eventually pop such bubbles. When some sort of setback leads to sales of these money-things at lower prices, savings-money is destroyed and the price spiral can reverse into a "bust". The withdrawal and destruction of savings-money lead to price declines of the relevant money-things, which lead to further withdrawals, more savings-money destruction, and continued price declines.

At the centre of this toxic pattern is the financial support of finance, loans that are totally detached from economic reality. This financial finance is not always clearly harmful, but it is always reality-distant. It is so embedded in debt practices and thinking that its existence is often not noticed. However, reality-close loans that transfer token-money, create token-money, or convert savings-money into token-money are economically totally different from the reality-distant loans that create or transfer savings-money entirely in the left section of the Triptych.

4. Fixed interest payments

While dividend payments vary with shareholders' profits, payments on fixed income instruments are, as the name suggests, fixed from the beginning. I have already discussed the economic unreality of this arrangement relative to the effects of general price changes. Even if prices remained reasonably constant, however, the practice of constant payments ignores the temporal-ontological asymmetry inherent to all financial arrangements. In short, the real world is certain to change, so any promise of financial constancy is intrinsically reality-distant. The monetary resources of the borrower and the realistic monetary expectations of the lender will change over the length of the loan, so what is a realistic payment at the beginning can easily become unrealistic as time goes on. The economic unreality of interest payments is sometimes mitigated by "floating" interest rates or "resets". In these arrangements, the rate is adjusted at regular or irregular intervals to reflect some change, whether in current prevailing interest rates or in the will and whim of the lender. The existence but limited use of such practices only emphasises the widespread enthusiasm for reality-distance in the financial system.

5. Short maturities

Short maturities are another reality-distant feature of many debt money-things. To be fair, the actual interest rate on a loan which lasts only "overnight", a few days, or a few months is likely to stay quite realistic until repayment, so such money-things avoid the reality-distance that comes with changes in the relevant environment that are not reflected in the interest rate. However, the reality of the interest rates is often more than compensated for by the unreality of these money-things' fictional maturities. In economic finance, investees need time to earn substantial returns, so to the extent that short-maturity loans are economic finance, they always have to be "rolled over" or "refinanced", that is exchanged for another loan rather than cancelled through a Large Payment. The investees in post-aristocratic financial loans are almost as likely to require refinancing. The reasoning behind the specific reliance on pseudo-maturities is both too technical and of too little economic importance for me to discuss here. Suffice it to say that while the roll-over system is usually unproblematic, there are exceptions. These generally come at times of economic stress, when a strong financial system is most needed. Instead, the financial pressure created by the reality-distant inability to roll over debts can worsen the economic situation.

6. Full "repayment" on maturity

Roll-overs are necessary because the Large Payment on debt money-things (the repayment of the nominal principal value) is inherently reality-distant. A reality-close payment would be "in kind" – for example, the factory that the borrowed money paid for. However, debts are in the left section of the Triptych, so lenders want savings-money. This can be provided if some of the profits generated by the invested money are steadily hoarded (a once popular system known as a "sinking fund"). More typically, the debts are rolled over or exchanged for other finance money-things.

As is typical in debt money-things, less unrealistic arrangements are readily available. "Perpetual bonds", without any Large Payment, are very rare, but "amortising" mortgage loans are common in many housing "markets". These money-things retain the reality-distance of fixed payments but eliminate the reality-distance of Large Payments. Considering the common preference for reality-distance, it might be surprising that these amortising loans are so common, but it is not surprising that they have not spread more widely or that their reality has increasingly been undermined by "equity loans", "re-mortgaging", and "interest-only" mortgages, which all make demands for final Large Payments on mortgages more likely.

7. The noble lie of banking

I have already discussed the basic economic reality-distance of most banking, including the noble lie that allows the money that depositors think of as *their* savings-money to be the same money that borrowers think of as *their* token-money. The deception sometimes serves the good purpose of expanding the token-money-supply to keep the Central Monetary Ratio fairly steady. However, like many lies, the noble lie of banking leads to further untruths, in this case greater reality-distance. Regulators sometimes allow and sometimes require money to be moved around from bank to bank or between banks and central monetary authorities. Sometimes the goal is to ensure that enough but not too many loans are made, and sometimes it is to balance the quantity of loans with some measure of the bank's ability to keep their promises to depositors if the noble lie is caught out by insufficient payments from borrowers. Some of these movements of money correspond to some real transfer of economic resources, but they often have no clear or direct relationship with reality. Even when these money-movements reduce the risk inherent to the double-counting of money that is at the heart of the banking system, they also tend to encourage bank managers to focus their time and attention on the risk that this reality-distant system will go badly wrong. The whole financial system's lack of interest in reducing reality-distance is so great that no serious consideration is ever given to the possibility of creating a banking system that is reality-closer than the current one.

8. Awkward defaults

Reality interrupts the planned pattern of payments in debt instruments when borrowers cannot, or sometimes when they will not, deliver the agreed returns. However, in the conflict of reality with unreality, unreality often clings on. Rather than adjust the financial arrangement to match reality, lenders often impose new reality-distant terms. The direction of unreality varies. Sometimes borrowers are able to "walk away" with little or no future obligation, sometimes even when their economic positions are strong enough to allow some payments. Probably more often, replacement loans are agreed with conditions that remain onerous relative to the borrowers' likely future economic and monetary resources.

To be fair, default is quite often a moment of truth, and reality does indeed often enter into the subsequent financial arrangements. When full forgiveness is appropriate, it is sometimes granted. Debt money-things are sometimes converted into equity money-things or restructured on terms that are both flexible and realistic. Even when such happy results are obtained, however, there is usually an intermediate period of tense negotiations. For the managers involved, financial arrangements often become "more real" than everyday business operations, a sort of triumph of an artificially constructed unreality over the economic reality of making, paying, and selling in the Great Exchange. Businesses often require money to get through the period of waiting, which is provided through "debtor in possession" financing. The additional money temporarily increases the unreality of the financial arrangements, but is typically consolidated into the more or less realistic "restructuring" of the debts.

9. Uncertainly distributed defaults

Finally, there is a structural unreality in the portion of interest rates that can be considered an insurance premium against default. I mentioned earlier in this section that this premium cannot actually be calculated, because it cannot be separated from other adjustments to the central-rate. However, the premium undoubtedly exists – banks' high-risk loans carry higher interest rates than lower-risk ones. I also mentioned the inevitable circularity of this practice – the additional interest expense increases the chance of default. The unreality, which is shared with many pooling arrangements, is perhaps more subtle. It comes from the imposition of probabilistic calculations on individuals. The reality is binary – each borrower either will or will not pay according to the agreed terms. It is also variable, since the quantity of non-payment, unlike the agreed payments, is not fixed. For a particular borrower, a realistic interest rate on each loan would provide the lender with an adequate return, after taking actual non-payments on that loan into account. Because the future is unknown, such an exact allocation is impossible. The best that can be managed is a probabilistic pooling, in which the borrowers that do not default pay an unrealistically high interest rate while the future defaulters pay an unrealistically low rate.

This sort of reality-distance is not intrinsically unjust. The differentiation of pooled risks is a reasonable way of coping with the partial predictability, or probabilistic knowledge, of fortune. For example, it seems fair that a 75-year-old should pay more for a year's life insurance coverage than a healthy 30-year-old, even though most 75-year-olds will live to celebrate their 76th birthday. However, even just practices can be reality-distant, and this one is. In finance, it can place heavy burdens on businesses which would be better able to serve the common good with lighter ones.

It is easy to explain why reality-distant debt finance was common in pre-modern and early modern economies. Loans were more easily manageable than economically sounder money-things. Broadly owned equities simply cannot work without something like corporate legal structures, comprehensive accounting records, and trustworthy legal authorities. Adjustments for changes in overall prices require a quantity of measurements and a sophistication of statistical technique which were inconceivable until the 20th century. (Historians have reconstructed various numerical monetary and economic indexes for earlier eras, but they are far less comprehensive and far more flawed than today's statistics.) The historical story is similar for other possible financial tethers to reality, for example money-thing returns that are calculated proportions of the borrower's wages or income. Such arrangements require levels of social organisation, social trust, mathematical sophistication, and readily available information which no society had until well into the modern era.

However, as I pointed out in Chapter One, the tenacity of outmoded techniques is a peculiarity of finance in the modern economy. Societies gave up on hand spinning when faster and more accurate machines were invented. They gave up on ledger books when computers came along. History cannot explain, let alone justify, the decision to cling to the economic unreality of fixed interest rates and fixed maturities.

I have alluded to three reasons for the persistent reliance on reality-distant debt arrangements, even when reality-closer arrangements are readily available. The first is institutional. The operations of the middle section of the Triptych depend on the firmly entrenched and deeply interlocking bank-money-debt system. The rewards from change might not appear to be great enough to justify taking on its difficulties and dangers.

The second block to change is psychological, the lure of the precisionist-consistency fallacy. People would rather not recognise just how reality-distant – both in precision and in likely economic meaning – the many future-dependent numbers of finance actually are. The comfort from pretending can be significant, so the arguments in favour of reality-distance in finance are often more potent because they are, rather than in spite of being, empirically ridiculous.

The final reason is political. The precise, agreed numbers give an appearance of clarity and justice to arrangements that might otherwise be condemned as unjust post-aristocratic finance. In other words, there is a sort of sociological-political mystification at the heart of debt instruments, much like the pious praise of the quasi-mystical value of "property rights" that obscures the poor-to-rich transfer of rents.

There may well be other factors which help protect the pre-eminence of unrealistic debt in the financial system. In any case, the reasons are not strong enough to justify the practice.

4. Unrealistic finance: "dis-economising"

Historians and social psychologists often note how rarely people question either the need or the justice of the most basic facts of their surroundings. I just mentioned one such blind acceptance, of the dominance of debt in financial arrangements. Similarly but more profoundly, the whole financial system is generally accepted blindly and as a whole. It is simply taken as given, part of the economy and the society. There are certainly reformers, who are especially vocal whenever parts of the financial system fail badly. However, the fairly well-set terms of the debate on possible improvements do not include discussions of the distinction between reality-close and reality-distant arrangements. In the financial world, it is rarely argued that it is generally better to keep financial arrangements reality-close or that the desirability of any reality-distant arrangement should automatically be questioned, so it is almost never asked what aspects of economic reality finance should be close to.

The result of this lack of interest is a sort of default drift toward reality-distance in finance, because reality-distant arrangements often serve the convenience and desires of the financial community, at least in the short term. In this section I will show that tendency in action, by listing a full dozen inherently reality-distant financial practices and attitudes. In the following section, I will explain why this trend encourages the failures that make the financial system such a problem in modern economies.

Before going into what will inevitably be a series of somewhat technical details, a simple summary might be helpful, especially for readers who have had the blessing of limited dealings with the financial world. I think that "a piece of paper", a phrase which used to be common in the financial markets, provides a helpful hermeneutic key. When financial agreements have a clear tie to the Great Exchange, they are not merely pieces of paper (which these days are actually data entries). Rather, these money-things summarise intertemporal transfers of genuine economic resources – token-money which can buy roughly *this* much labour and consumer goods and serves now is exchanged for later token-money payments which will buy roughly *that* much economic stuff. The "this" and "that" are necessarily imprecise, because money is an imprecise tool dealing with essentially non-quantitative economic activity, but the intertemporal transfer of control of economic resources is quite real. However, as finance moves leftward in the Triptych, away from reality, the money-things become increasingly distorted mirrors of any economic activity. At the extreme, which is reached all too often, they lose touch with reality altogether. They become numerical commitments, quasi-tokens which have only the most distant and tenuous ties with labour and consumption: nothing more than pieces-of-paper. What follows is a list of reality-distant attributes that are attractive in such pieces-of-paper.

1. Liquidity

A money-thing is considered liquid if the savings-money it holds can easily be taken out of it. For example, publicly listed shares are generally considered liquid because large quantities of them can usually be sold very quickly. Conversely, a savings account from which withdrawals are only allowed with, say, three months' notice, is not very liquid. Houses and valuable paintings are extremely illiquid – it often takes months to sell them, or longer if there is a dispute about the price.

Within the financial world, liquidity is considered an obvious good. Owners of money-things are anxious for the freedom to sell, because without that the freedom to buy is meaningless. A great effort is made to satisfy this desire. Banks rarely put tight restrictions on withdrawals from savings accounts. Various intermediaries "provide" liquidity – they promise to buy financial securities. Others will create financial debts, lending owners most of the amount of money that various money-things could be sold for.

In the real economy, of course, there is almost nothing like financial liquidity. Shares in a factory may be disposed of, but the factory cannot be un-built or divided. A shareholder can decide to stop living with the consequences of a corporation's bad decision, but the people affected by the decision do not have that freedom. In other words, liquidity is inherently reality-distant. The distance is not necessarily bad. There may sometimes be good social or economic reasons to tolerate this sort of unreality. For example, society probably benefits when a retired person can easily sell financial investments to a person who is saving for retirement, or when an ill person can easily sell to make up for an unexpected loss of income. (Arguably, yoking or taxes could be still better solutions to these no-money-now problems than liquid financial money-things.) However, as with all types of financial reality-distance, any praise of liquidity should be set against the dangers that flow from unreal finance.

2. Maturity transformation

Debts generally come to an end with a Large Payment. Equities are almost always perpetual, without any end or "maturity". However, if an equity can be sold immediately in a liquid stock market, then it can be treated as having the shortest possible maturity. This change from an infinite to an infinitesimally small lifespan of a financial arrangement is an extreme example of what is known as "maturity transformation".

Less dramatic shortenings are at the core of conventional banks' noble lie, discussed in the previous section. The banks transform deposits that have a short maturity, often no more than a few hours and rarely more than few years, into loans that mature in several years in theory and in the indefinite future when the practical need for roll-overs is taken into account. This "maturity mismatch" is generally a source of profit for banks, because the long-term interest rates they receive are usually higher than the short-term ones they pay out. Conflicting desires to share, protect, and manage the profits from changing maturities lie behind many of the sophisticated banking products – for example swaps, interest rate options, and wholesale funding – developed in the last few decades.

Like liquidity, the ability to transform maturities is widely praised inside the financial system. However, it is, like liquidity, quite reality-distant, although liquidity is distant from the real economy while maturity transformations are mostly distant from the reality of the money-finance system. The transformations can only shift the division of interest payments when things go well and losses when things go badly.

3. Arbitrage

Although the prices of most money-things are almost arbitrary, the relations between the prices of different money-things are not. Logically, identical money-things should have identical prices at any time and similar money-things should have similar prices. In liquid markets, traders can limit any deviation from the appropriate identities and similarities by buying relatively under-priced money-things, purchases that tend to push their prices up, and selling relatively overpriced ones, purchases that tend to push their prices down. These transactions continue until the gap between actual and appropriate prices is too small for traders to gain from further transactions. The whole process of correcting clear or perceived pricing errors is known as "arbitrage".

The simplest arbitrage involves buying some money-thing in one market (say the New York Stock Exchange) and selling it at a very slightly higher price in another (say the London Stock Exchange). The most complex arbitrages involve anticipations of price trends in the short period between buying and selling and estimations of the appropriate price differences for similar money-things, for example houses in the same neighbourhood or otherwise identical bonds with different maturities. The trading decisions of professionals are often based on variations of the arbitrage principle, trying to exploit discrepancies between the actual price of one or more money-things and the price suggested as fair by calculations that are based on more or less sophisticated financial theory.

Within the logic of financial markets, all varieties of arbitrage are considered almost hygienic, as they clean up pricing "inefficiencies". From the outside, however, such activities look like the efforts of insiders to take advantage of less sophisticated players in financial and other money-thing markets. In any case, all of these gains and losses from arbitrage are reality-distant. The search for them reflects an interest in financial markets that is at best tangentially related to the real economy.

4. Financial gambling

The human urge to gamble is strong, as is the confidence of gamblers and their interest in both improving their odds and limiting their possible losses. From its beginning and especially in the last half-century or so, the financial industry has been happy not only to satisfy but to encourage this urge. Bankers have developed many new types of pieces-of-paper to take advantage of gamblers' tendency to believe in their superior ability, to find ways to make financial gamblers believe that they have superior odds, and to provide gambler-clients with roughly the desired level of thrill. Money-things can be very good instruments for skilled gambling. Like the performance of horses in a race, the future price of a piece-of-paper falls in the gambler-pleasing range between predictable and obviously random. Unlike racing horses, however, there are ties between the money-things prices and the middle section of the Triptych. However the ties of financial gambling to any underlying economic reality are distant indeed.

Derivative securities (generally known simply as derivatives) give the financial gamblers especially reality-distant games to play. Each derivative money-thing is a combination of another money-thing, a particular price for that thing, and a particular time or time-range. The derivative money-thing either forces or allows one gambler to buy or sell the other, underlying money-thing at the particular price at the particular time. The price of the derivative is derived from the gap between the current and the expected future price of the other, "underlying" money-thing. Because the prices of these para-financial pieces-of-paper vary with changes in any of the variables, they tend to be very volatile.

The frequent changes make them particularly attractive to financial gamblers, who are politely referred to as "speculators" or even "investors". These money-things allow them to speculate about the results of speculation on money-things. It is like placing bets on how much different punters at the racetrack will win or lose on a certain day. The reality of the Great Exchange is a distant speck on the horizon. The finance industry, which profits greatly from serving as the casino "house" in arranging the derivative business, has found, and often funded, economic justifications for these trades. They are claimed to stabilise markets and spread risks. As might be expected from a business that mostly appeals to gamblers and has only the thinnest ties to reality, derivatives have tended more to have the opposite effect: destabilising prices and concentrating risks.

Commodity futures are reality-closer than the dominant financial derivatives. Genuine farmers and other actual producers agree to sell their crops and other products (from wheat and hogs to lumber and iron ore) to gambler-speculators months before the actual production or delivery. The gambler-speculators then trade this promise to deliver products. The futures' prices rise and fall, often quite dramatically, based on a steady drip of new information about supply and demand for the relevant commodity. Although the production is quite real, the price volatility of the future is very distant from the economic reality of the production in the Great Exchange of labour and consumption and generally somewhat distant from the reality of the final price in the middle section of the Triptych. If further reality-distance and resulting gambling thrills are desired, banks will happily and profitably (for them) construct derivatives of futures.

5. Artificial money-things

In Chapter Three, I discussed pooling as a solution to no-money-now problems. In finance, two other sorts of pooling are very common. In both, people buy interests in collections of money-things. One type of collection is reality-close and the other reality-distant.

Ideal-banking is based on reality-close pooling. The institutional tie between loans and deposits gives each depositor a tiny interest in and income from thousands or millions of different loans, each of which provides an investee with token-money. Similarly, when equity owners create portfolios of shares in a wide variety of different corporations, the arrangements are reasonably close to a large section of the paid-for economy. Such pooled investments are quite reasonable arrangements for financial investors who bring no particular economic expertise to their investments.

Before the 2008 financial crisis, money-things based on the other, reality-distant type of pooling became popular. Their popularity is rebounding as I write. In these pools, a large number of money-things are first collected, and then re-divided into new money-things that are expected to be more appealing to financial investors or to speculators. The new money-things have various financial qualities. The most common arrangement involves creating a chain of debt money-things of decreasing riskiness. Loan losses first reduce the value of the riskiest "tranche". When that security has lost all its value, subsequent losses fall on the next riskiest tranche, and so forth. There are many other permutations, including combinations of debts and equity derivatives.

These money-things show the all too common financial pattern of ingenious design and unclear but clearly distant relationships with the Great Exchange. Some of the pooled money-things created before the financial crisis suffered unrealistically high losses during the crisis. Others, although connected to the same money-things, had unrealistically low losses. For the division and extent of losses, the design of the money-things often proved to be more significant than the developments in the real economy, and almost as significant as developments in the prices of money-things. Almost everything about that pattern is very reality-distant.

The success in selling such pooled investments can be traced to the orientation of the banks that created them. Their primary mission is neither to keep finance close to reality nor to serve the common economic good. Their mission is to serve themselves, which they do by gaining revenues from their financial investor customers. That purpose is rarely served by creating simple, reality-close instruments. It is served by developing complex products that put distance between the investors and reality.

6. The mess of foreign exchange

In the discussion of border problems across currencies in Chapter Two, I mentioned the banks that sometimes own money-things that are priced in foreign currencies. There I was discussing the gains available from supporting trade imbalances, but cross-currency general-finance offers other temptations: to profit from differences and changes in various national interest rates and to create and profit from changes in currency exchange rates. In addition, the relatively lightly regulated "no man's land" between currencies is such a good home for large-scale speculation that foreign exchange markets (also known as currency markets) have become virtual palaces of unreality. In effect, financial gamblers have learned how to treat one currency as a special sort of money-thing, a container for another currency. Since exchange rates change all the time, in large part because speculators are always buying and selling, this sort of speculation is especially alluring to thrill-seeking gamblers.

There is no need for all this reality-distance. Currency exchanges which accompany real economic changes are reality-close by nature. Consider two tourists visiting New York, one from St Louis and one from Stuttgart. When they pay dollars for their hotels, meals, and visits to the Statue of Liberty, they are equally close to the reality of the Great Exchange. The German tourist's need to exchange euros for dollars does not increase that distance.

Whether the actual number of dollars the German received in exchange for her euros is reality-close is another matter. Even without any speculation, the exchange rates and their changes would be shaped by necessarily unknown interactions of undoubtedly inaccurate expectations for several relevant factors: relative price levels, relative inflation rates, relative economic prospects, and the monetary balance of buying and selling between the two countries. With the speculation of today's currency markets, in which the financial flows are about 15 times larger than the cross-border token-money flows linked to the Great Exchange, the current exchange rate is certain to be speculator-close and very likely to be reality-distant. Indeed, the imbalance of speculation and economic reality in currency markets is so great that speculatively-driven changes in exchange rates are at least as likely to influence economic reality as reality is to influence the rates. For the most part, however, these exchange values do not even achieve that slightly perverse reality-closeness. The exchange rate trends just entertain gamblers and enrich intermediaries.

7. Financial debts

In the discussion of financialisation in Chapter Three I introduced financial debts, that is the borrowing of savings-money to help pay for a money-thing. These financial arrangements are totally reality-distant, as they have no connection to the middle section of the Triptych. On the contrary, by increasing the savings-money price of money-things, individual financial debts move those things further away from the paid-for economy. Increases in the total quantity of financial debts, a category that arguably includes most government debts, increase the reality-distance of the Triptych's entire left section, while increasing the chances of one-currency border problems (between savings-money and token-money).

The lack of economic anchors of financial debts makes them, like foreign currencies, ideal material for reality-distant manoeuvres. For example, companies sometimes choose to use borrowed money to pay dividends to shareholders. (This is a common practice in so-called leveraged buyouts and the underlying transaction in many so-called share buybacks.) This financial choice can increase shareholders' returns, especially in the short run, but it could hardly be more distant from any concern for the reality of labour, production, consumption, or the common good. Similarly, when property speculators take on large mortgages with the intention of selling quickly with large gains, they are operating at a vast distance from the economic reality of the consumption of housing. Indeed, their desire to increase house prices and their indifference to the good of any occupants suggests a distance that is almost as hostile as it is great.

8. Corporate leverage

Corporations have borrowed money for as long as there have been corporations. Indeed, long before there were corporations, merchants and craftsmen often borrowed money to pay for their inventories and raw materials. That type of borrowing was often reality-close. The sales of the things acquired or processed with the help of the borrowed money provided the revenues needed for both interest payments and Large Payments. The Large Payment ("repayment") was generally scheduled to occur when the things the loaned money paid for were all sold, so that the loaned money, which was no longer tied up in the inventories it paid for, could be returned, as least if there was no need or desire to replenish the inventory. Even if the business continued in operations, arguably new loans would pay for new inventories, continuing a cycle of reality-close loans and repayments. In other words, even the Large Payment was arguably reality-close for these inventory-related money-things.

The economic reality is quite different in large modern corporations. Corporations are social entities that are financially defined by equity. Inventories and accounts receivable are not conceptually different from other parts of the operations, so there is no good reason for them to be associated with non-equity money-things. When corporations have no-money-now problems, new equity is the only reality-close financial solution. Debt always adds a reality-distant complexity to the corporation's natural monetary structure.

The regular use of debt, however, appeals to many shareholders, because it creates leverage. For reasonably successful companies in times of fairly low interest rates, a greater use of debt leads to higher shareholders' profits and thus higher potential dividends for each share. The calculations of those gains are extremely familiar to financial professionals both inside and outside of the corporations, as is the awareness that this leverage can work against shareholders if profits are too low or interest rates are too high. In recent years, hope and greed have been much more powerful than fear, so the use of leverage in corporations has been increasing. The debt-favouring financial illiteracy of most tax codes has encouraged this reality-distant trend.

9. Demanded short-term returns

Like the idea that companies should normally rely on both debt and equity to solve their no-money-now problems, the idea that any kind of money should be exempt from the ravages, or even the effects, of time is so well established that its strangeness is rarely noticed. Actually, this idea is far closer to symbol-money than to the reality of the Great Exchange. While God, beauty, or love may be unchanging, everything in the middle section of the Triptych is firmly stuck in the world of generation and decay. To expect the value of savings-money to hold through all time and every circumstance is to think in a reality-distant way. Even more reality-distant is the commonly made claim that the real value of hoarded savings-money should actually increase – always, automatically, and without any chance of reversal. The saver should not have to do anything at all to garner this "risk-free return". The earning is the responsibility of whatever entity is responsible for managing the hoarded money.

There is a complicated argument from financial theory to explain why a positive risk-free return is a natural part of the financial world. There is also a simple argument from the political science of power: post-aristocratic finance demands it. Whatever the justifications, the economic reality is that nothing in this life is or can be expected to be "risk-free", nothing about the nature of savings-money or money-things would require a mandatory return, and nothing in the economy mandates one. To portray a social choice to provide such a return as a law of finance is to stand reality on its head.

10. Demanded long term returns

While any mandated risk-free return on savings is obviously economically unrealistic, it is far more difficult to judge just what level of returns on riskier and longer-term investments is in accord with economic reality. Financial theory has an answer, or at least a technique which claims to frame the argument. Unfortunately, the technique is so riddled with confusions that it offers little insight. Still, the question is worth asking. Return expectations that are unrealistically high, relative to the real social-economic situation and to financial investors' real economic contributions, are likely to make either the financial or political system unstable. Conceivably, returns on finance that are unrealistically low by the same standards could make the economy less stable.

I will discuss unjustly high returns in Chapter Five. Besides justice, political-economic reality imposes limits. Financial investors cannot realistically expect to keep on receiving more token-money payments than renters, borrowers, customers, taxpayers and whoever else ultimately provides the money are willing, or can be compelled, to offer. The reality-limit will vary over time and across societies. Aristocratic social arrangements often supported tremendous luxury for the very few while leaving the mass of rent-paying peasants in desperate poverty. Such an immiserating level of direct extraction would probably be unacceptable today almost everywhere. The actual current limits are harder to discern, but in my judgement, the level of returns expected within the financial system is often much higher than the level considered socially acceptable by most people outside of the system. In other words, financial return expectations are politically or socially reality-distant.

11. Price changes in money-things

I have mentioned several times that the price of land, shares, fixed income instruments, derivatives, gold, and any other money-thing rises or falls along with both the supply of savings-money in the left section of the Triptych and the shifts in financial investors' emotions and judgements. In a social analysis, even dramatic price moves can perhaps be considered realistic, but economically most of the moves are necessarily reality-distant, because the changes are so thoroughly detached from the reality of the Great Exchange.

12. Expectations

Banks can and sometimes do show and encourage reality-close thinking. To the extent that something like ideal-banks still exist, those institutions are in a reasonably realistic relationship with the Great Exchange. Although they do typically promise a risk-free return to savers, their loans are closely related to real economic activity. Some contemporary sellers of equity "index funds" have a similarly realistic approach.

However, in most financial markets, and in many less community-oriented banks, reality-distance is necessary for survival, let alone success. Most customers seem to prefer quasi-magical promises of huge gains to much more modest and realistic expectations. This preference creates a symbiosis of unreality. Customers want higher returns than any politically acceptable financial system can realistically provide for long periods. Banks often try to design products or find specific money-things that will meet those unrealistic expectations. However, that effort will most often prove vain, leaving financial investors to believe or try to believe that "next time will be different". The banks' reality-distant efforts to please are both reactions to and encouragements of the customers' reality-distant demands for high returns. The distance from reality increases along with the proportion of the promised returns that is supposed to come from gains on financial speculation.

Employees of banks are often well rewarded for their promotion of unreality. Indeed, the very high prices and salaries in finance are best understood as something like a bribe made in hope. If the banker is well rewarded, the thinking seems to go, then her promises are more likely to come true. The combination of wealth, accompanying social power, and structural reality-distance sounds socially toxic. It may or may not be good for social leaders to be ambitious, but it is never good for them to be fantasists, and success in the operation of reality-distant finance almost always requires some embrace of fantastical hopes and promises.

5. The danger of reality-distance

By now, it should be clear that somewhere between much and most of broad-finance is reality-distant. Just as finance has a systemic bias in favour of post-aristocratic monetary relations, it has a systemic bias against closeness to the realities and limits of the Great Exchange. This fact raises three questions – why, with what good results, and with what bad results? The first has no simple answer, the second has an unfortunately easy answer and the third requires a daunting list. I will discuss them in turn.

1. Why?

Social causality is never clear and almost always contested. In my discussion of the various varieties of reality-distance in finance I have hinted at several causes from various domains. There is tradition – we have always done it that way. There are the patterns of human psychology that encourage a desire for numerical certainty and certainty across time, even when such certainty is actually impossible. There is the political and economic power of financial investors, which allows them to establish or preserve reality-distant financial arrangements that tend to be beneficial to them. There is the ambition of the owners of money-things, a character flaw which leads them to expect unrealistically large gains. There is intellectual incompetence, the inability to think realistically about those large gains, which encourages unrealistic expectations in financial markets, both over time and from frequent trading. Finally, there are the various symbolic meanings of finance, many of which lead to financial arrangements that are very far from the Great Exchange.

That is my list, but some items on it may be disputed and there may well be many other equally good or better explanations for the frequent preference for reality-distance in finance. However, all of these motivations seem to act predominantly below the level of consciousness, so perhaps reality-distance thrives in part simply because it is not noticed, as I suggested earlier in this section.

It is clear, though, that much of what is considered good within the financial world is reality-distant. A list of the financial system's goals compiled by financiers, rentiers, and professional investors would be likely to include one reality-close item, the provision of economy-building financial investments, and many reality-distant objectives: liquidity, risk-reduction for financial investors, efficient arbitrage for financial investors, debt-based financial structures, maximal performance for financial investors, and ease of speculation.

2. What goods does reality-distant finance promote?

I can think of four possible goods that reality-distance in finance might promote.

First, enthusiasts for strong and largely inherited economic hierarchies can point out that some types of reality-distant finance protect the desired social order. Liquidity, risk-free returns, maturity transformations, and the acceptance of quite high long-term returns all benefit the rich more than the poor and help ensure that savings-money fortunes lead to ample consumption and social power in the next generation.

Second, enthusiasts for do-gooding foundations, not-for-profit educational and medical organisations, other charitable institutions, and private pensions systems can say that reality-distance in finance helps these organisations support the common good. The arguments are the same as the pro-inherited hierarchy ones, but these virtuous organisations and systems can be supported without endorsing any sort of social hierarchy.

Third, without the reality-distance of financial speculation, the world might be a duller and perhaps a more dangerous place. As a variety of gambling, reality-distant speculation is certainly lively. It is arguably less socially disruptive than casinos and less addictive than online play. It is also legal and closely regulated.

Finally, reality-distant finance could be better in many ways than the available alternatives. For example, investors might be less willing to provide money for useful economic purposes if the only available arrangements were less lucrative, less liquid, and more obviously insecure than the current reality-distant collection.

I do not find any of these arguments very persuasive. First, anti-egalitarians should recognise that today's economic hierarchies rely more on wages than finance. In any case, reality-distance adds little to the support that reality-closer finance would provide to hierarchical economies. Second, it is not obviously better for organisations and individuals to be supported by financial income than by current contributions. Even if this financial income is considered good, the benefits from reality-distance do not obviously outweigh the costs I will describe in the following subsection. Third, gambling is at best a vice to be tolerated. There is no good reason to think that there is anything particularly tolerable about financial speculation's large quantities of money, high chances of doing significant economic harm, and inevitable exploitation of unwilling and unknowing participants in financial markets. Fourth, it is implausible that less reality-distant finance would discourage any economically and socially helpful form of finance. Even if some useful economic finance was discouraged, there are generally other, equally effective solutions to the relevant no-money-now problems.

3. What harm does reality-distant finance do?

While all claimed good effects of financial reality-distance are some combination of trivial and dubious, the bad ones are all too evident. Various sorts of reality-distance cause or worsen several types of problem.

Monetary imbalances: Large, reality-distant changes in the prices of money-things tend to destabilise the left section of the Triptych, an instability that tends to create one-currency border problems. For example, when house prices rise and many owners take out "second mortgages" to turn some of the gains into consumption, the infusion of token-money can disrupt the balances of the paid-for economy. The additional supply will increase the numerator of the Central Monetary Ratio. If nothing happens to the denominator, the result will be undesired price inflation, or unwanted pressure on currency borders.

Similarly, the reality-distance in foreign exchange markets increases the possibility and likely severity of border problems in two currencies. Large, reality-distant inflows of savings-money from foreign countries distort banking systems and provide support for ultimately untenable patterns of production and consumption. Equally reality-distant outflows introduce new distortions in banking and major disruptions in production and consumption. Reality-distant changes in exchange rates disrupt cross-currency trade and create financial strains when there is substantial cross-currency borrowing.

Poor allocation of economic resources: Unrealistic terms and prices of money-things can lead to the inefficient use or unjust distribution of economic resources. Unrealistic signals from the left section of the Triptych can encourage spending too much or too little money in different parts of the middle section. In particular, high share prices in one sector, for example some new technology, often encourage a rush of spending by new and old competitors, while unrealistically low interest rates sometimes spur unhelpful activity in sectors that are partly regulated by the cost or availability of borrowed money, for example housing construction in the United States. Also, reality-distant financial speculation amplifies changes in the prices of commodities, which often disrupt the economic behaviour of users and producers.

Post-aristocratic financial tendencies: For social egalitarians, post-aristocratic finance is simultaneously reality-distant and undesirable. It is reality-distant because its poor-rich transfers have no clear or just relation to the economic reality of labour and consumption. It is undesirable because it solidifies, magnifies, and increases the social effects of already unjust economic hierarchies. People with more mixed judgements of economic hierarchies might condemn only some reality-distant aspects of post-aristocratic finance. For example, they might consider the ability to pass financial income to heirs to be reality-distant, because the heirs have no just claim on the savings-money and the income that it provides. Alternatively, they might condemn only the expanding fortunes in the left side of the Triptych, which entrench the position of the rich with little connection to the reality of economic activity in the middle section.

Speculative waste: Reality-distant financial speculation is a destructive and parasitic imposition on banks and economic finance. The confusion and mixing of gambling with financial investing endangers and weakens the latter process. The economic damage done by the bubbles and busts of reality-distant speculation is sometimes great and always unnecessary.

Too much finance: The most visible distortion of resource use encouraged by reality-distant finance is found in the financial sector itself. Compared to realistic assessment of the sector's potential for supporting the economic good, the finance business is much too large and its workers are too skilled and too well paid. The excesses, only enhanced by financialisation, seem largely to reflect a social fixation with the high-class gambling that finance makes possible.

Greed: The next chapter is dedicated to greed and finance. Here I will only point out that reality-distant financial debts and corporate leverage serve no economic purpose, and no other purpose than the satisfaction of greedy desires. They can do no good, but they can do significant harm by distorting economic decision-making and creating or amplifying pointless social tensions.

Chapter 5. Greed in finance

If the political, economic, and thought leaders of modern societies had studied the problems of the monetary and financial systems with dispassionate reason, all of them would probably have been addressed reasonably successfully long ago. After all, as I pointed out in Chapter One, the history of the modern economy includes both the creation and solution of a great many practical difficulties. Such accomplishments as fairly safe and healthy urban life for more than a billion people, well organised global enterprises employing as many as a million people, and universal free-to-user education required remarkable persistence, imagination, ambition, and openness to dramatic change. If all those virtues had been put to use in the domain of money and especially in finance, these systems would by now be more loyal and reliable servants of the common good. In fact, though, all efforts at reform of money-finance have been limited, so much so that today's global financial system has many of the key features – and weaknesses – of the various national systems at the beginning of the era of paper money in the late 19th century. Financial systems have even retained much of their post-aristocratic entrenchment of privilege, a sharp contrast with the at least partially successful efforts at egalitarianism in healthcare, education, infrastructure, and even food and clothing.

Why has so little been done? Some possible explanations can be rejected. Stupidity is out of the question – money and especially finance have long attracted the attention of some of the canniest people in any society. In the last two centuries, many intelligent and thoughtful scholars have also studied them. A shortage of competent "human resources" is also not a plausible explanation. Many experts in the hard sciences, the social sciences, and the humanities have worked in or on the finance industry or studied parts of the money-finance system in numerous universities, government and quasi-government agencies, and other organisations.

Ignorance is a more plausible explanation for the inaction. As I explained in Chapter Two, the empirical reality that currencies were tied to precious metals hid the baseless essence of money until well after baseless money had actually supplanted the "gold-backed" variety. The resulting misunderstandings about money undoubtedly made clear thinking about finance more difficult. Similarly, it might have been easy to miss the post-aristocratic social role of finance before the development of large money-based economies, some type of national accounts, and the development of socialist economics. Still, all excuses for ignorance melted away at least a century ago, and there have been enough financial crises and struggles over the subsequent years to have focused minds on what could have been learned. Also, ignorance created by past confusions cannot explain why economic finance was rarely if ever put in the appropriate economic context, as one of several potential solutions to no-money-now problems. It looks like financial reform has been held back by forces that are harder to cure than ignorance.

Another possible explanation is the weight of tradition. Perhaps people are so attached to old ways or so afraid of the disruption that changing to new ones might cause that they will not or cannot believe that they should or even can make fundamental changes. This argument makes no sense for money, which in fact has changed almost beyond recognition from the archaic systems that were based on treasure-money to today's arrangements, based on token-money. Contemporary finance arrangements are, as I mentioned in Chapter Three, remarkably close to those of past generations, but the persistence only raises the question of why tradition could weigh heavily in a domain that is technically easy to change. After all, financial contracts can be created and destroyed without any physical changes in labour, consumption, or social organisation.

There may be other inadequate explanations for inaction, but rather than search for and then discredit them, it is best to turn to something wider, in this case to the penumbra of symbolic meanings which surrounds both money and finance. I provided long lists at the beginnings of Chapters Two and Three, explaining, among many other things, that these tokens, indicators, relationships, and practices have a deep and lasting connection with greed. It is now time to address the practical effects of this moral or ethical association on the money and finance systems.

My claim is simple. Greed is a harmful passion which threatens the social and economic order whenever money is counted, whether in the left or middle sections of the Triptych. Distracted by greed, individuals, organisations, and societies have been unwilling to strive hard to promote safety and justice in their money and finance systems. It is literally the besetting sin of finance. In particular, it is largely responsible, either directly or indirectly, for four serious weaknesses. First, the greed for money encourages the individualistic and precisionist errors of monetary analysis, because greed leads people to keep jealous count of exactly how much – how much things cost, how much people are paid, how much money they have, and how much more or less money they have than their neighbours. Second, greed is the fundamental reason that many banks and bankers are so often untrustworthy. Third, greed explains why already relatively rich people are so dedicated to the continuation of post-aristocratic finance. Fourth, greed is the only persuasive explanation for the social tolerance of the numerous excesses of financial activity.

What is this greed to which I am so opposed? In a rough way, greed is easy to understand. All people are familiar with it, from their roles as parents, workers, friends, and political observers. We often chastise others for being greedy, while we often reject any accusations that we are ourselves being greedy. However, the concept of greed is alien to all the leading contemporary academic models of behaviour. The moral frameworks in which greed is at home have largely been banished from sociology, psychology, history, and anthropology. The thought-structures of academic economics, as I will explain in more detail later, are particularly hostile to any conscious debate about any sort of good and evil, including the evil of greed. I cannot even turn to mainstream contemporary philosophy. While the objectively good moral life was a central philosophical topic from Plato's days until not that long ago, over the last few generations the traditional distinctions of virtue and vice have largely been abandoned. Fortunately, there is an intellectual remnant that continues to work in these traditions, made up of some explicitly religious thinkers and some secular proponents of "virtue ethics". With some help from these thinkers, I will try to provide a clear philosophical-psychological explanation of what monetary-financial greed is and why it is wrong. That discussion takes up the first six sections of this chapter. The final six sections explain in some detail just what greed does in finance, including some of the ways in which greedy desires cloud or confuse judgements.

1. The moral life

Some readers may be scandalised, or at least baffled, by the nature of my claim. How can the persistent dysfunctions of a significant part of contemporary economies be explained by something as moral, private, and old-fashioned as greed?

The first doubt, about morality, is based on a traditional understanding that economics is a purely descriptive discipline – moral judgements are excluded by definition. Most economists now recognise that this narrow view is intellectually incoherent. Ethical judgements are obviously and inevitably a central part of any purposeful human activity, including economic activity. For economists to claim that they can or should avoid discussing such judgements shows, at best, that they do not understand what they are doing. As worst, it demonstrates a desire to avoid the serious professional responsibility to discuss the economic good.

The second doubt is less implausible. Economics is typically concerned primarily with the behaviour and desires of groups, while greed is obviously individual and not obviously social. It seems normal for left-wing economists to speak about the moral and obviously social evils of oppression and for libertarians to discuss the moral and equally obviously social evils of domineering governments, but both groups of economists would probably agree that as professionals they should shun all discussions about the effects of these social forces on individuals' moral habits and choices. That approach to economics, however, is too exclusively social. In reality, there is always a two-way flow. Individual judgements always help shape common moral or ethical standards and those common standards help shape individual moral judgements and practices. If greed is a problem among people labouring or participating in finance, as I claim, then it will be reinforced socially: by the rules and expectations of all the financially relevant bureaucracies, by the financial aspirations that are considered respectable for politicians and members of other social elites, and by the financial lessons given to children. Equally and reciprocally, to the extent that greed flourishes in financial organisations and the broader society, financial greed will flourish in the behaviour and desires of many individuals, and will cause few qualms in these individuals' consciences. A full discussion of financial greed must include its individual as well as its social causes and manifestations.

My reliance on traditional morality creates the third potential scandal. When economists do speak of morality – although they usually refer to less judgemental-sounding categories such as "ethics" or "values" – their judgements are likely to be veiled in science-y terminology such as "misled by poor incentive structures" or "unconscious bias". In contrast, Christians traditionally included greed on a list of seven deadly sins that was rational and direct but not at all science-y. Greed, like such peers as lust, pride, and sloth, seems out of place in a serious 21st century study of anything other than, perhaps, moral theology. Such cultural judgements are hard to argue with, but I hope to show that a familiar manifestation of this old-fashioned vice provides a clear explanation of the frequent failings of finance.

Some familiarity with my modified, modernised, and simplified version of Aristotelian-Thomistic ethics might help make the following discussion of greed more comprehensible and persuasive. Many readers will recognise my moral framing, but others might benefit from a brief and broad outline.

To start, there is (such a thing as) good and bad behaviour. We should expect good behaviour from ourselves and from others, and it should be rewarded. Bad behaviour should be discouraged and punished. There are also good desires, which should be encouraged, and bad ones, which should be discouraged. These simple dualities are not psychologically symmetrical. Rather (philosophers in the Thomistic tradition would say), people always perceive the good to be more desirable than the bad. They always want to have good rather bad things. They generally want other people, especially those close to them, to be good and to want the good. People try to help their children, friends, neighbours, and leaders to cultivate good desires and to find and follow good paths in life.

Virtue requires intellectual and emotional effort, because human desires are often morally confused. What seems to be good at the moment of desire may actually be bad. Sometimes people are punished directly for acting on bad desires, when the desired thing causes them some sort of harm. Often, however, the bad desire or act has no obvious deleterious effect on the person who wishes or acts badly, but does some other harm: to the ultimate good of the individual, the shared good of some group of people, the common good of a whole society or the whole human community, or the always good divine will.

Sometimes people recognise their moral mistakes, perhaps after acquiring more knowledge, giving the matter more thought, or simply calming down and abandoning some of the distortions of judgement that misdirected emotions can cause. Sometimes, however, people never manage to understand that a decision to try to satisfy a particular desire was actually wrong. Indeed, people often persistently fail to recognise or accept the objectively bad nature of some of their desires, judgements, and actions. For example, as I hope to show, financial greed often passes unrecognised, un-admitted, and completely un-repented.

People always live in some degree of moral doubt and tension. They frequently struggle to know what is good, and then they struggle actually to do what they know or think is good. In practice, people all sometimes want the wrong things and sometimes act badly. The moral life consists in the unending struggle to define, find, and strive for the good, while resisting the ever-present temptations to turn away from the good and towards the bad and disordered. This moral struggle, with its mix of successes and failures, is inescapably personal – I make my own choices. The struggle is also inescapably communal, since any organisation's values, rules, and structures always have moral characteristics. Further, as I pointed out at the beginning of this section, the personal and the communal influence each other. My own decisions are in part shaped by the standards which I receive from the various communities I belong to, while a collection of personal decisions influences the standards of surrounding communities.

Just like individuals and communities, entire societies struggle to get everything right, and just like their members, societies inevitably fail some of the time. The social struggle always involves customs, laws, and standards of practices. Some of these social markers enjoin virtue, but are sometimes or often disobeyed. Other markers are ethically flawed. They might entrench injustice, promote vice, or in some other way ease the path to bad individual desires and actions.

Our moral rules and standards come partly from tradition ("this is what my parents and teachers told me"), partly from authority ("this is what God/the Gods/the Church/the King/the law tells me), and partly from reasoned judgements ("this choice is guided by these reasons"). The moral life is lived through a mixture of decisions made with consciously considered arguments and decisions made by habit, that is by the developed practice of almost unthinking evaluations of what is right and wrong in a certain type of situation.

The degree of universality of moral rules is a contested topic. People and peoples have different enough ideas of what is desirable, permissible, undesirable, and deeply wrong that it is possible to argue for an exclusively or largely individual, cultural, or social understanding of morality. However, people and peoples also have similar enough moral standards that it is possible to argue for some sort of universal "natural law" of morality which is in some way part of human nature. The advent of Christianity and other "spiritual" doctrines has complicated this debate, since such doctrines typically encourage a reversal of what otherwise seem obvious moral standards – poverty and humility, not wealth and grandeur, are good; it is better to suffer than to do evil; it is better to give than to receive.

The debate on moral universals is quite relevant to the discussion of greed. On one side, different behaviour is considered greedy in different cultures. For example, a rich person today would likely be judged extremely greedy if she expected the poor to provide her with what in a pre-modern society would have been judged a normal and non-greedy level of tribute. On the other side, there is something universal about the condemnation of excessive desires. Every culture seems to condemn behaviours and desires that can reasonably be called greedy. I will provide what I hope is a generally acceptable contemporary definition of financial greed later in this chapter.

What kind of thing is the objectionable thing that we call greed? I have described it as a sin, a word that has the advantage of being a clear and direct way to describe behaviour and desires that should be rejected. For some of the scandalised secular readers I mentioned earlier, the terminology of sin and virtue has the disadvantage of a close association with the Christianity that they reject as absurd or meaningless. Such readers do not have to give up on my argument. While I think that the Christian moral framing provides the clearest description of the foundation of the financial exception, there are several alternative, Christian-distant vocabularies.

Such readers can follow Aristotle's portrayal of ethical errors as departures, either excess or a deficiency, from an appropriate moderation. The Greek philosopher says that greed is an excessive desire for material things, which should be desired only moderately (Balot, 2002: 22-57). Alternatively, these readers could substitute some more Platonic model of human nature, taking greed as a sign that disordered desires have overcome clear-sighted reason. There are also the Freudians, who have their own vocabulary that tries to capture the connection between greed and other self-destructive or antisocial desires. Finally, social anthropology and early sociology treat greed as a socially unacceptable level of desire. In whatever way greed is described, it is dangerous, both to the greedy person and to the society which does not hold her desires in check. The bad effects damage the heart and soul of the greedy person – the Christian framing makes this particularly clear – and lead to various types of social tension and disorder.

2. Understanding greed

I have presented the conclusion, that greed is bad, before describing exactly what I mean by greed in the money-financial system. As the preceding discussion suggests, there is no point in searching for a universal definition of greed which can be translated easily into monetary and financial terms. There is no number or formula that marks – truly, always, and everywhere

– the boundary between greedy and fair or just. Rather, monetary and financial greed can always and everywhere be understood only in their social and cultural contexts. I am most interested in the developed economies where most financial activity takes place. There the understanding of greed must be set in the context of an economy of historically unprecedented complexity, a society of historically unprecedented prosperity, money-issuing governments of historically unprecedented social scope and economic influence, a dominant political ideology which praises some sorts of egalitarian practices, and a social reality which reinforces some sorts of social privilege. More specifically, the understanding of greed must be set in the context of the benefits of economic finance, the realistic economic alternatives to that finance, the social attitudes towards post-aristocratic finance, and the importance of finance in the economy. That list may sound daunting, but I hope to show that in the relevant societies there is a broadly shared understanding of the contours of a greedy approach to savings-money and, especially, to finance.

My description of financial greed in this time and part of the world will come in the next section of this chapter. In this one, I will provide a short list of the leading elements of the symbolic penumbra which surrounds greed. As I did for money in Chapter Two and finance in Chapter Three, I want to separate out the emotional, psychological, and sociological "thick description" of greed from the narrower, more mundane, and more practical understanding that will help me evaluate the greed in current financial arrangements. This list has a different form from the previous ones, because greed is more psychological than conceptual or tangible. There are five basic approaches to greed, a term which I am using as equivalent to avarice, cupidity, acquisitiveness, and covetousness. The first four are basically distractions from the financially relevant understanding of greed, while the fifth, the calculating and maximising approach to life, provides a good background to the more detailed analysis in the rest of the chapter.

One introductory comment might be helpful. Some philosophers limit greed to the desire for money and others to the desire for both money and the things that money can buy. My discussion in most of the chapter largely follows this restricted understanding, but in this section a broader approach is appropriate. As an element in the human response to the world, greed is a fairly general disorder. It is a way of seeing, wanting, worrying, and enjoying which can be applied widely – to all sorts of things, to people, and even to divine favours. In the various versions of the Faust legend, for example, the scholar signed his pact with the devil because he was greedy for power, for deep knowledge, or for new experiences. The desire varies with the telling of the story, but the gnawing and compelling emotion that can be called greed is common to all.

Greed is:

1. *A disease of the soul*: Ebenezer Scrooge, the hero of Charles Dickens's *A Christmas Carol*, allowed his desire for Gain to become a 'master-passion' that destroys all his previous 'nobler aspirations'. The well-known tale develops one of the basic psychological pictures and practical trajectories of extreme greed. The greedy person thinks that the desire for security in the world, to be 'beyond the chance of its sordid reproach', is 'wiser' than to be concerned with other people (Dickens, 2018: Stave 2). Such a monomania leads directly to cruelty, as the greedy person does not care about the welfare of others, only about his own desire. This desire is both superficially reasonable – to be a 'good man of business' (Dickens, 2018: Stave 1) – and madly unlimited: it can never be satisfied.

Scrooge's greed is miserly. He wants to spend as little of his accumulated money as possible. In the modern world, this concept of greed as a disease of endless and all-encompassing desire is often attached to quite different approaches to disbursement. Many greedy people are spendthrifts who justify their greed as necessary to keep up the consumption patterns needed to prevent social reproach or to have a good life. Then again, some greedy people are neither miserly nor extravagant. They live in a moderate way, other than in their submission to an unquenchable desire for more.

The extremism of this simple greed makes for good literature, but it is not a helpful way of thinking about greed in finance. While no amount of financial gain is enough for a few people, the moral problem is usually subtler. Greedy people steadily both want and think that they deserve more than it is just for them to have. Their self-justifications are based on a false understanding of justice and moderation, rather than on an inaccurate appraisal of their wild desire for security and control.

2. *A source of social disorder*: Friedrich Engels, the co-founder of Marxism, identified greed as the driving force of the modern economy. The economy has worked wonders, '[b]ut it achieved them by setting in motion the lowest instincts and passions in man and developing them at the expense of all his other abilities. From its first day to this, sheer greed was the driving spirit of civilization; wealth and again wealth and once more wealth, wealth, not of society, but of the single scurvy individual – here was its one and final aim' (Engels, 2021: Chapter 9). In other words, the massive desire which Dickens described was let loose on a massive scale, and became a revolutionary social force.

The idea of greed as a social power is not exclusively Marxist or socialist. I will explain in the next section that extreme self-described capitalists sometimes claim that "greed is good" exactly because it has such social power. In both versions of this narrative, greed is socially disruptive. The versions differ only in their evaluation of the greed-driven demolition of the previous order and the quality of the greed-powered leadership of the new one.

Other explanations of the great social power of greed start from a quite different understanding of social relations. Greed is sometimes portrayed as powerfully antisocial, because it encourages people not to share, thus breaking the communal bonds that are crucial for social flourishing. This autarkic greed is thought to lead rich people to refuse to serve the nation or to pay their fair share of taxes, and even to prefer national servitude or mass wretchedness to the thwarting of their own greedy desires. A more technical accusation was common before baseless-money was well established, when the difference between token-money and savings-money was not well understood. Physiocrat economists and other less organised thinkers concluded that greed encouraged the hoarding of money. This reduced the amount of money in circulation and as a result, they thought, the amount of economic activity.

Like the extreme portrayals of the deformities caused by individual greed, all of these extreme descriptions of the social effects of untrammelled greed are exciting, and quite possibly sometimes true. However, none of them is very helpful for understanding the subtle effects of financial greed. In finance, I will argue, greed is distressingly untrammelled, but, as I pointed out in Chapter Three, finance actually plays a fairly minor role in society, especially when the money-financial system is working as its participants think it should. If this were not so, and if financial greed were as disruptive as these dramatic social models assume, then finance would be a massive economic and social drag all the time. Since the financial system is usually no worse than somewhat inefficient and usually introduces only relatively modest injustices, those models must be exaggerated. I am confident that a less greed-infested system would be more stable, besides being more just, but I do not think that financial greed can be seen as anything like a driving force of history.

3. *A lack of emotional control*: In *The Psychopathology of Everyday Life,* Sigmund Freud described 'the primitive greed of the suckling, which wishes to seize every object'. The father of psychoanalysis believed that this greed is only 'only imperfectly subdued through culture and training' (Freud, 1914: Chapter 7). In other words, as civilised adults, we want but never fully manage to control fully our primal greed. The model of destructive passions that triumph when we cannot control them is not exclusively Freudian. It can be seen as early as Plato's *Phaedrus* and as recently as the latest hot-blooded murder or cold-hearted Wall Street scandal.

In psychological models of this sort, to give free rein to greed (the chariot image is Plato's) is to abandon not only self-control but the hard-won moral habit of prudence and the intellectual virtue of rational analysis. Greed always brings out something desperate, irrational, and animalistic in our nature. In the throes of greed, our instincts and habits go all wrong and we are unable to think straight. We want to have more, but like little children coveting their playmate's toys just to have them rather than to use them, the desire becomes almost detached from any judgement about the good of possessing these objects of desire.

Once again, this model is sometimes relevant to financial greed, but does not describe the phenomenon as a whole very well. Some speculators are basically gambling addicts who might well be described as out of control. However, the greed I will soon start to describe is mostly under very good control. It is rational – most decisions in finance have always been fairly carefully measured. It is also rationalised. Finance has articulate defenders, some of whom deny that financial greed exists and some of whom explain that greed is either good in itself or something unfortunately necessary for finance to work well. The combination of rationality and rationalisation, with some precisionist thinking thrown in, can be seen in such flourishing little industries as "compensation consultants", which justify and quantify the greedy desires of senior executives (not only in finance), and "investment consulting" which does much the same thing for financial investors.

4. *Lack of sound judgement*: The fourth approach to greed is the Aristotelian one I mentioned earlier. Greed is literally a disorder, the desire for more than the right, moderate amount of whatever is wanted. In this understanding, there is a correct order to human desires and actions. To do or want more or less than the correct amount is disordered. The error comes in two parts. The first is ignorance, not to know what is right to want or to do. Ignorance can be corrected fairly easily by instruction. The more serious disorder is in the will, rather than the intelligence: not to be able to control one's emotions and choices, despite knowing what is right. This too can be corrected, but only imperfectly and with difficulty, for the will is much more resistant to training than the intellect.

In this model, a sound and ordered judgement is always in accord with the natural order of the world. In the Aristotelian understanding, which is also the predominant pre-modern Christian understanding, everything in the world has a natural order, so greed is a desire which is unnatural, in some understanding of human and cosmic nature. It is basically greedy to want more of anything than is just, to prefer lower things to higher ones, and to cultivate the talents and skills that help satisfy these base desires, such as for money, things, and power, while neglecting those that could be used to search for noble things such as wisdom, love, and beauty. Greed is opposed to just moderation in desires. Because greed pulls the will towards taking, it also tends to be opposed to the virtue of generosity, which requires giving. Modern Aristotelians are likely to see greed as tending to be opposed to the social virtues of collaboration and solidarity.

This understanding of greed captures the way that greediness becomes a habit, an unthinking way of reacting to the world. It also starts from a plausible understanding of the deep connection between the social and moral orders. However, the full Aristotelian worldview, which assumes that everything is comprehensively ordered, is not actually required to study financial greed. All that is needed is an acceptance that the world of money-numbers – wages and prices in the Great Exchange, money-thing prices and interest rates outside of the Exchange, the terms and conditions which surround the numbers – can be judged as just or unjust in a particular social and economic context.

Also, in finance, it will turn out that Aristotle's hierarchy of difficulty is backwards. It is relatively easy for most people to limit their monetary desires to what they think or are told is just. It turns out to be extremely difficult to think clearly about what desires are actually just.

5. *Calculating and cold-hearted*: The final image is closest to the greed which, as I will argue in the rest of this chapter, frames the most commonly accepted attitude towards both savings-money and most of the standard practices of finance. This is the greed that is cold, grasping, self-assured, and always calculating. In this greed, there is no desperation or depravity, just a clear understanding that more is always better than less, and that there is nothing wrong with working as hard as possible to get more, as long as laws are not broken. Everything else, from traditions to respect, can be sacrificed for the sake of the always incomplete satisfaction of this desire. However, in this sort of greed, everything else does not have to be jettisoned. The greed is not a master-passion like Scrooge's, just an approach to certain important parts of life. Indeed, the greedy person assumes that in these parts of life – perhaps the job or the shopping, definitely everything connected to savings-money and money-things – such a more-is-better-than-less approach is natural and appropriate. To optimise and maximise is considered "rational". The calculations of this greed are ubiquitous and often numerical, but they can also take the form

of more conceptual balances of gain and loss. The calculations are necessarily self-centred and impersonal – the good of the other and the good of the community have no role. Numbers are generally seen as helpful, perhaps because they are so impersonal.

This greed is found most clearly and purely in the utilitarian desire simply to maximise, without much thought about the true value of whatever is to be accumulated. Calculating greed also fits with the scientific rationality that judges all things by some numerical standards, and with any egotistical philosophies that "look out for number one" or that doubt the reality or seriousness of obligations to other people.

This idea of greed is the most subtle. It is often missed because it is quite different from the other types I have described. Unlike the first image in this section, this sort of greed is rarely seen as psychologically disordered. Rather, it is usually considered normal, unobjectionable, and almost unavoidable. Similarly, it is almost the opposite of the second image of greed as socially disordered. This cold-hearted greed thrives in and supports existing institutions in contemporary society. Like the third image, this greed is emotionally uncontrolled, but in the opposite way from the wildly accumulating desires of the incontinent greed for all things. It is cold and measured. Unlike the fourth image, this greed does not recognise the possibility of moderation, for it is based entirely on maximisation.

3. Monetary and financial greed

It is almost time to define monetary and financial greed. First, though, I need to make two basic distinctions.

Thing-greed vs. monetary-greed

In Chapter 2, I defined the token-money as an instantaneous (or short-lived) token that facilitates the Great Exchange of labour with its fruits. In this strictly pragmatic role, money cannot inspire greed. Any desire for more token-money is not really a desire for money but is entirely thing-greed, a craving for what the money could buy. Of course, the immediate thing-greed may be expressed in terms of token-money – "I wish I had another million dollars to buy a yacht" or "I would buy so many cool things if I had a million euros". However, the substance of the disordered desire – "I wish I could have a luxurious yacht" or "I wish I had a million-euro-worth collection of cool things" – is not monetary. It cannot be, because baseless token-money has no real substance. For the sake of convenience, however, I will include the excessive craving for the things token-money can buy in the category of monetary greed.

The principal element in that category, though, is savings-money greed. My fundamental argument is that this greed, which is connected to the savings-money in the left section of the Triptych, explains the financial exception discussed in Chapter One. Its exclusion from most discussions of finance is a crippling error, something like ignoring mortality, love, or knowledge when considering the human condition.

Monetary greed can be divided between token-money greed, more precisely greed for what-token-money-can-buy, and savings-money greed. In turn, savings-money greed has two different aspects. When savings-money is taken to represent hoped-for future consumption, coveting it is a sort of temporal extension of token-money greed: the desire to consume more things later as well as now. In today's more prosperous economies, however, the other aspect is usually more prevalent. Savings-money greed is primarily for the savings-money itself, rather than for what it will eventually buy. What is desired most of all is what the savings-money signifies: its social, psychological, and cultural values.

The difference between token-money greed and savings-money greed is essential. Token-money greed is intrinsically finite, limited by the physical limits of the human body and of the natural world. I can consume only so much food, clothing, or any other material thing. There are only so many hours during which I can be served or entertained by other people's labours. There is even a practical limit, although admittedly a very high one, to the amount of hospitality, luxury, and opulence that I can personally offer or use. These limits ensure that while actual consumption can certainly be excessive, it cannot be infinite. What is true for consumption is true for the token-money that procures it. There is no point in having or craving more token-money than I can use. It is entirely different in the realms of monetary storage and symbol. Savings-money testifies to social standing and class membership. It provides political power and protection. There is effectively no limit to the desire for any of these perceived goods. I can desire enough savings-money to protect me against the most unlikely calamity, enough to keep my children living in luxury, enough for my great-great-grandchildren to remain billionaires, enough to pay for hundreds of years of masses offered to lessen my sufferings in Purgatory, enough to show my neighbours how rich I am, enough to buy a title of nobility or a dictatorship, or simply enough to demonstrate my true worth conclusively to myself or to God. The last quantity is especially infinite, so to speak, since money can never buy or show true worth.

Just as there is no limit to the potential demand for savings-money, there is no limit to the potential supply. Any money-thing in the Triptych's left section can always become more valuable and in that unreal domain more savings-money can always be created – all without any direct effect on the labour, buying, making, selling, and consumption in the Triptych's middle section. This potential infinity easily encourages a mutually reinforcing momentum of greed. If the greedy craving of person-one for X amount of savings-money is gratified, then person-two will urgently and greedily request the creation of twice-X savings-money to get ahead of her rival, and so on, to infinity or a financial crisis, whichever comes first.

A psychological note might be helpful here. The social and symbolic nature of much money-greed helps explain why it has often been associated with miserly behaviour, which is the literal opposite of thing-greed. One of the psychological reasons to crave savings-money is to store up some sort of power over or protection against the world and its harshness. Of course, neither the earthly treasures of savings-money nor the goods and services bought with token-money can ever really protect us from the profound sadnesses of the human condition: despair, disease, and death. Once greed sets in, though, the inevitable but impossible-to-accept failure of money to buy what is desired only increases the desire for more, in particular for more of the protective savings-money. With that mindset, current consumption can merely dissipate the sense of future security, so misers convert as much token-money as possible into less obviously ineffective savings-money.

Savings-money greed vs. finance-greed

Finance-greed is a variety of savings-money greed. It includes greed for everything in general-finance that is more complex than hoarded savings-money, including greed connected with speculation and with money-things such as collectibles and commodities. While simple savings-money greed can be expressed as a single desire, for a higher quantity of savings-money, finance-greed encompasses many desires, including cravings for higher returns, more protection from losses, triumphs in speculation, and the ownership of exclusive money-things. Basically, greedy financial investors crave arrangements in which they will always do well and are never hurt by finance's temporal-ontological asymmetry. The greedy financial story starts with their initial claim on the future, which is as high as possible. If the future turns out to be better than was anticipated when the original arrangement was agreed, greedy financial investors expect a higher return. When the future turns out worse, they expect the original terms to be maintained. When there is some money-thing that seems particularly well placed to gain from the future, they crave participation in it.

While financial greed can be seen as largely an extension and expansion of savings-money-greed, the prevalence of post-aristocratic finance creates an important sociological difference between them. Savings-money greed does implicitly favour the relatively rich, who have a good supply of savings-money, over the relatively poor, who have little or none. However, indulging this greed does not in itself change the economic relationship between the two groups. The rich get richer in the left section of the Triptych, but their share of consumption in the middle section of the Triptych does not necessarily increase. When finance-greed is indulged, however, there is a clear change. The poor-to-rich transfers of post-aristocratic finance are amplified, so, the rich get richer *because and as* the poor get poorer.

A definition of monetary greed

There are many reasonable ways to describe monetary greed, many of which have already been mentioned or alluded to. The greed can be a preference for money and what it can buy above other, higher things. It can be the treatment of savings-money as an end and goal rather than a means to other ends. It might be the immoderate love of savings-money or of what token-money can buy. It might be, in a financial mode, the love of promises of money in the future. In a more social register, it might be the desire for money which is not deemed to be appropriate for a member of a particular caste, class, or group.

None of these definitions is wrong, and all of them will colour the following discussion. However, for the purposes of understanding the disorders of finance, the best definition of savings-money and financial greed emerges from the calculating image of greed discussed in the last section. Monetary greed is *the desire for more money (token and savings) than is enough, natural, reasonable, merited, just or good.* All of these words are hard to define, because they all (even "natural") are socially determined or influenced, but none of them is ever meaningless.

What is "enough"? The philosophical answer to the question is debatable, but the sociological response is fairly clear. A person or family is not greedy if she or they want only enough money to acquire what is deemed suitable to them. The "deemed suitable", the actual amount of goods and services that is "enough", varies with the people's social, economic, and psychological positions. Whatever that sufficient collection is, it is greedy to want to buy more than that, and it is greedy to want to collect more savings-money or money-things than will be needed to ensure, under normal circumstances, this sufficiency.

Of course, any particular judgement of what constitutes "enough" will be controversial, as will be the degree of uncertainty that finance should protect against, and indeed the personal responsibility to provide for the consumption of heirs, friends, and members of various communities. It is certainly possible, indeed likely, that the desire for what is considered merely "enough" within a particularly rich society would be considered greedily excessive in a poorer one, or by some universal standard. I will discuss these interpretative difficulties shortly, when I go over the other adjectives in my definition of greed. The difficulties are serious, but they do not invalidate the definition. Rather, they help frame the moral debates that are necessary for both the good life and solid economies. In such discussions, it is crucial to start with the right question. My definition suggests that for financial greed, a good first question is whether the person desires more than is enough for him or her, now and in this place.

"Natural" is a tribute to the idea that our economic life should be ordered for the goods which we need to live out well our human nature, both as individuals and as communities. The coming of industrial prosperity has changed the understanding of what it is natural to desire. It might have been greedy for a peasant to want clean running water two centuries ago. Until less than a century ago, greed would have reached surreal or even demonic levels when someone coveted flying thousands of kilometres in a few hours. Now such desires can be judged natural. Along with greater prosperity, the coming of greater social equality has changed what is natural to expect from our communities. It is natural, and not greedy, to expect universal education and uniformly high-quality healthcare. Conversely, it now may be socially unnatural, and thus greedy, for members of the elite to expect to live isolated from all socially unstructured encounters with common people, a desire that was completely natural in most aristocratic societies.

"Reasonable" refers to judgements made after a thoughtful and thorough analysis of needs and desires. This approach is necessary because the standards given by family or community may permit greedy desires. For example, the widespread approval for post-aristocratic finance, or at least the general lack of active criticism of it, does not indicate that such poor-to-rich transfers are reasonable. Since the standard of reasonableness is not set by current social mores, it often points to changes in the expectations permitted by those mores. When social rules and standards tolerate or reinforce greed, they should be changed.

"Merited" refers to one of the basic criteria for social and economic judgement – what we deserve. I have already referred to the pre-modern merit assigned to familial social position. This was the widespread belief that aristocrats deserved their large allocations of consumption goods and services, just for who they or their parents were. There were also geographic and ethnic standards – in France, the "French natives" deserved more and the Roma less, just for being who they were. (The Roma may not have liked that standard, but even the losers in this sort of allocation system often accepted it as the ways things are.) In more egalitarian modern societies, merit is more usually associated with effort or accomplishment. It is generally not considered greedy to expect some reward for working hard, even if not much is produced by the toil. Similarly, it is not considered greedy to expect some reward for getting something done, even if the accomplishment did not require much toil. However, it is greedy to desire more than such efforts or accomplishments are thought to deserve.

"Just" and "good" are big philosophical words, far too profound to be captured in a brief explanation. However difficult they may be, they are necessary for any full understanding of greed, or indeed of anything in the economy. Justice, the right order of the individual soul and of any society, is an all-encompassing standard of judgement of anything in the human condition. Goodness is more than all-encompassing, as it brings in something beyond the human condition, the transcendental excellence which religious believers ascribe to God or the divine. To be truly good is to transcend the limits and travails of the human condition, to live in accord with a perfection that is somehow both forever out of reach and also a reliable guide to our direction in life. Paradoxically, it is not at all greedy to desire with the greatest intensity this definitionally impossible goodness. On the contrary, it is usually just as greedy to turn firmly away from the highest Good, which transcends and transforms my personal wishes, as it is to desire to violate the standards of purely worldly justice.

Three standards of judgement for monetary greed

What is the standard for deciding whether a monetary desire is greedy? That question is crucial to the practical task of evaluating current and possible financial practices and attitudes. My approach to answering the question for any particular monetary desire is to consider three standards of moral judgement: subjective, objective, and social. I will discuss each of these in some detail in the ninth section of this chapter, after I have gone into the place of greed in the real economies of the past and present, in the imagination of economists, and in the left section of the Triptych. In anticipation of that, brief descriptions of each might be helpful.

Desires are greedy according to the *subjective standard* when they harm the character or soul of the desiring person (the subject). The harm can come in various forms. The desired objects of rewards may be undeserved because the desiring person has not made an effort or sacrifice that would merit them. Alternatively, the desired objects or rewards may simply be too luxurious for *any* person to enjoy without falling into moral decadence. More subtly, the objects may be too grand for the good of this particular person who has this particular social position in this particular society.

The *objective standard* of monetary greed relies on what a financial investment has actually accomplished. Monetary desires are objectively greedy when they are for rewards that are excessive relative to the desiring person's objective or actual contribution to a particular project or to the common good, however little or much was subjectively sacrificed. When a person's contribution is relatively unimportant, or could easily and willingly have been made by many other people, the objectively just reward is relatively small, however great the subjective sacrifice. For greed in contemporary economic finance, the objective standard leads immediately to the question of what portion of the success of economic enterprises can be credited to purely financial investment, as compared to other contributors to success and profitability, most notably the skill and toil of the labourers directly involved and the more indirect support of the various elements of the common economic patrimony.

Finally, the *social standard* of financial greed starts with an assessment of whether financial returns are in accord with the common good. Even if a desire is not greedy either subjectively or objectively, it might disrupt the social balance in a significant and inappropriate way. As an extreme example, consider the construction of a factory producing luxury food for cats at a time when children in the community are starving. The subjective enthusiasm for feline health may not be harmful to the character of the financial investors, the financial investors may be willing to sacrifice their own comfort for the sake of their pets' comfort, and the reward, helping animals thrive, may be objectively good. However, the desire for a financial return from this project is still greedy in the particular social context, because it comes at the expense of human life, which is intrinsically more valuable than animal life.

As a more realistic example, consider societies in which a fairly large degree of economic equality is widely considered to be a social good. This is the stated political standard in every contemporary affluent society. In such polities, desires that would add significantly to inequality must be considered greedy. This consideration is highly relevant when considering the justice of post-aristocratic finance. Indeed, if a more egalitarian society is always considered to be socially just, than all post-aristocratic finance is socially greedy.

4. Four tricky terms

In the ninth section of Chapter Three I discussed six words that are used to mean quite different things. The discussion of greed also runs into some ambiguities of vocabulary, but the underlying problem is somewhat different. In finance, the central issue was the unwillingness to recognise that the left and middle sections of the Triptych are fundamentally different. For greed, the prime issue is legitimisation – two words which carry clear moral overtones, usury and miserliness, have largely been banished from financial discourse and two terms that are used in that discourse, cost of capital and imperfect competition, are defined in ways that hide their moral connotations.

Usury

Usury is best understood as the greedy practice of finance. More technically, it is the demand for returns on financial investment that fail some standard of justice. Using my three-part practical definition of greed, returns are usurious when they are subjectively unjust (higher than needed to compensate for any sacrifice by the investor), objectively unjust (an unjustly high compensation for the contribution of the invested money to the investee's monetary gains), or socially unjust (leading to an unjust distribution of token-money in the economy or of savings-money in the society). Although the concept of usury is usually associated with debt and not equity – in so-called Islamic finance, equity is explicitly excluded from the condemnation of usury – desired equity returns can certainly be greedy.

The exclusion of equity from usury reflects the gradual loss of the concept's once tremendous cultural resonance. By the mid-19th century, when equity finance was starting to become central to the industrial portions of advanced economies, interest payments were accepted as a normal part of commerce and industry, lenders and borrowers were mostly trusted to find financial arrangements that were mutually beneficial, and this low standard of commutative justice was considered enough to avoid usury. Even the Catholic Church, which had always treated usury as a great sin, largely relented. Its condemnations were firm in words and solid in concept, but in practice the bishops accepted that most business loans were not morally suspect.

As money increasingly became defined as a form of credit, and even more as financial theory took shape, returns that were once considered usurious have come to be considered necessary for the effective functioning of the economy. The theories ignore post-aristocratic finance and do not approach economic finance as I did in Chapter Three, as an optional and often problematic solution to no-money-now problems. Rather, they assumed that financial returns determined by "the market" are central to the successful functioning of the money system and the economy. That assumption leaves little if any space for the concept of usury.

In particular, financial theory, which I will discuss in modest detail in the Appendix, is not simply amoral. It explicitly justifies all actual, market-determined interest rates on quasi-psychological grounds. The threshold of usury can never be crossed if investors have to be compensated for both possible losses and the distress which the prospect of those losses may cause them. This model of financial behaviour effectively jettisons the concepts that are needed even to discuss the possibility of greed. Unsurprisingly, as the theory developed, the word "usury" first lost much of its meaning and then almost disappeared from use.

Miserliness

I have already mentioned miserliness several times, as a Freudian fear of giving to the outside world, an antisocial hoarding of token-money (especially before baseless money became common), and one possible manifestation of the deranged passion of greed. Even that modest interest is unusual these days. The once popular word and concept have gone out of fashion, for a good reason and a bad one. The good reason is that it has become harder to be miserly as economies have become more prosperous. In pre-modern economies, hoarding money almost always led to significant sacrifices of consumption, the traditional essence of miserliness. The practice was obvious to all, especially when the quantity of hoarded money was large relative to the money spent on everyday life. In today's developed economies, it is possible for most people to save a significant share of their income without anything like painful sacrifices. For today's middle class in developed economies, few if any sacrifices are needed to create a significant hoard of savings-money over a few years or decades. At most, all that is required is often a slightly smaller house than could be afforded, less extravagant holidays, and fewer meals out. Conversely, an almost surreal degree of self-denial is required to behave like an old-fashioned miser – sitting in the cold rather than spending on heat, eating rotten food because it is cheaper, and wearing rags to save on clothing.

The bad reason for forgetting misers is that savings-money-greed is no longer considered problematic. If greed is bad, then it is miserly for someone who has savings-money in excess of likely needs to hoard the surplus rather than spend it or give it away, even if the excess saver's actual lifestyle is not particularly frugal. The easy acceptance of endless accumulation as ethically neutral or even good is a sign of moral confusion. Miserly greed about not spending or not donating does not affect the financial system in the way that my principal topic, greed about financial arrangements, does. However, it is still greed, and deserves to be analysed and condemned.

Indeed, the disappearance of the picturesque misers of old should not have impoverished the moral debate about the appropriate quantity of savings-money for different people. There is a strong argument that what might be called neo-miserly behaviour – saving too much relative to need instead of relative to consumption – is extremely common among the rich. It is neo-miserly to maintain savings-money balances that are larger than necessary to deal with age and adversity, and perhaps to leave a reasonable inheritance. The quantification of non-miserly savings depends on the plausible available alternatives. If I can count on friends, family, the community, or the government to help me out, then the threshold for neo-miserly greed will be lower than if I am truly on my own whatever happens. For people who can take advantage of universal basic services and the protective economic cocoons of welfare states, the line separating prudence from neo-miserly hoarding should probably be set at a fairly low level.

Cost of capital

The cost of capital is a variable in financial theory. The details of its calculation are mind-numbing in their pseudo-sophistication and unreality, but the basic idea is simple. Some return is required to entice financial investment and the required level of that required return is not determined by any standard of justice. Rather, a bold series of assumptions are thrown together that supposedly demonstrate that investors will not and should not bring savings money to any project or enterprise that is expected to provide anything less than a certain level of return. In the theory, this minimum required return is roughly the cost of capital. Economists often consider the provision of this return to financial investors to be a necessary cost of doing business for investees. Revenues should be sufficient for this mandatory payment to equity investors, just as they should be high enough to pay wages. In this model of corporate life, the required return is not really a profit. Indeed, the phrase "economic profit" is used to describe any money left over after deducting the money supposedly owed to financial investors for the use of their money.

The corporate costs of capital that emerge from the calculations have recently been around 10%, if not higher. This was bizarre, as the returns on alternative uses of savings money were little above zero and sometimes negative for more than a decade. The comparison with financial alternatives is not even the most disconcerting one. Financial returns should be compared to other solutions of no-money-now problems. As I have pointed out, most factories, roads and other long-term projects are actually built without providing any direct financial-style return. Taxpayers and customers are compelled to pay, whether or not they will eventually benefit from the spending. In sum, the calculated cost of capital is far out of line with economic reality.

Looking at these implausibly high numbers, a cynic might suggest that the main purpose of the mathematical mystification of financial theory is to recast financial greed as an economic necessity so as to avoid criticism. I believe this accusation is somewhat unfair. None of the people who developed the theory and few if any of the people who teach or use it would admit to such a base intention. Their conscious motivations are, if anything, almost the reverse: to provide a rigorous and scientific model to describe what might otherwise seem like random interest rates and returns which appeared to be wildly inconsistent over time and between investments. Their unconscious motivations might be different, but even without discussing such murky matters, it can be said that the results of the theory would be quite acceptable if its purpose had in fact been to justify greedy returns.

The concept of a cost of capital is not totally fallacious. In a particular economic and social environment, investors may well refuse to provide money unless a particular return is offered or aimed at. However, monetary situations and expectations are never simply determined by some unchangeable facts of human nature or economic reality. On the contrary, savings-money arrangements are always constructed in ways that reflect or reinforce several factors, including social power structures, ideals of justice, fears of social disorder, and, at least sometimes, economic efficiency. The idea of a cost of capital is best understood in such complex terms, rather than simply accepted as a replacement for moral analyses.

Imperfect competition

Imperfect competition is an idea from economics, not finance, but it provides an almost mechanical and definitely non-moral way of describing some morally suspect monetary and financial arrangements. The basic idea is that financial investors in companies can often expect even higher returns than the cost-of-capital calculations suggest, because the companies' profits are not greatly constrained by competition from rival enterprises. A full discussion of the relevant model of corporate activity and its great distance from the reality of technology, commerce, and consumer behaviour would take me far from the topic of this book. However, there is a relevant psychological assumption which underlies all models of "competition": companies naturally seek to maximise profits. An alternative formulation of the assumption is that the concept of a "fair" level of profits is meaningless. If imperfect competition permits high returns, then the nature of corporations necessarily leads them to search for such competition and to collect those high returns. As shareholders are considered "owners" of corporations, most of the gains from imperfect competition accrue to them.

It is not only producers that are spurred on by the relentless pressure of the theory of imperfect competition. Banks also strive to create and exploit "pricing power" and any "informational advantages" that they have over their customers. The result of this orientation is interest rates on their loans which are expected to lead to profits far higher than even the most generous estimate of their cost of capital. As I pointed out in Chapter One, the actual returns have often been lower, because banks have intermittently been unable to resist the temptations of unnecessarily reckless behaviour. However, the high costs of recklessness are in part the result of the unrestrained and usually successful pursuit of very high returns.

Standard economic theory holds that close-to-perfect competition, perhaps supplemented by regulation, usually keeps profits from rising too high above the cost of capital. In the current economic reality, however, competition tends to be quite limited. The only restraints on the flourishing of greed are often socially enforced moral standards and expectations. I will argue later in this chapter that those ethical restraints are especially weak in finance.

5. Can monetary-financial greed be good?

In the next section I will describe many of the bad effects of savings-money greed. In this one, I will briefly mention the contrary claim, that some or all varieties of monetary greed are good in some way or ways. This claim comes in several varieties. Some thinkers have argued that some of what is called "greed" is really a sensible and morally unobjectionable self-interest. While true greed may well be evil, this false-greed is good for the economy and society. Other thinkers accept both the standard definition and the badness of greed, but claim that this admittedly undesirable greed is inextricably connected with the dispositions that create a strong modern economy: helpful ambition, energy, curiosity, a will to control nature, practical imagination, socially revolutionary fervour, and evangelical self-confidence. A further group sees greed as having much more modest and ambiguous good effects, for example in the jobs created by the rich person's greedy desires for luxuries. Yet another set of people reject all moral criticism of greed, claiming that it is simply a good form of self-expression with no adverse economic effects. Finally, there are those who admit that greed is a vice, but defend it as less harmful, either to the vicious person or to the community, than such rival sins as lust, anger, and the unmeasured thirst for military glory.

A full discussion of all of these arguments would take me into domains far from money and finance. In particular, I would have to engage with some basic puzzles of moral philosophy: how to evaluate the morality of particular actions and desires; whether bad intentions can produce good results; if so, whether this relationship justifies encouraging bad intentions. I would also have to draw something like a moral map of the mind, to describe how greed fits in with reasoning, with other desires, and with the human drives to cooperate, love, compete, and so forth. I will not even start down that path, because I believe that the philosophically simple definition of monetary greed in a previous section and the description of some of its many bad effects in the next section provide a sufficiently strong case for the evil of greed, without the need for more sophisticated analysis. I will only make four brief observations.

First, greed is by definition – by my definition at least – a vice, sin, or disorder. It is always a deviation from something good, whether the goodness is individual or social. This understanding of greed can be denied, of course, but only with some difficulty. As any parent can testify, "too much" is a category that children have no trouble understanding, and children must learn to control their desires to function well in the world. In adult life, the badness of greed is also considered common sense – people will often deny being greedy, but they will almost never say, other than in a self-mocking tone, that they are in fact greedy and that they have and should have no problem with it. I do not deny the possibility that some morally good or morally neutral emotional or psychological states resemble greed in some ways. For example, both a person dedicated to helping humanity and a greedy one might found a company and hope for its rapid success. However, the motives and approach of the two founders would be quite different. In reality, most founders have a mix of motivations, often including both great generosity and grand greed.

Second, even when or if monetary greed is an unavoidable part of the moral mix in some part of the money-economy Triptych, its presence is always regrettable. For example, it may well be true that all successful entrepreneurs and financial investors are somewhat motivated by greed and it is conceivably true that greed sometimes helps concentrate their minds and sharpen their judgements. Still, it is undoubtedly true that greed will also have bad effects on their character, attention span, relations with other people, and understanding of their responsibility to the community. As I will explain in the next section, fundamentally, the more that people favour their greedy desires over other desires and concerns, the less they are able to inspire and feel the trust that is necessary to bind together any human venture.

Third, this social binding is far more important to the modern economy than anything which can possibly be promoted by greed. This statement contradicts two claims of many theorists of "free and competitive markets": first that greed helps competition serve the common good and second that modern economies are best described as "competitive market economies". I just said that it is far from certain that greed actually sharpens competition in any socially helpful way, but even if the first claim is true, the second one is false. Competitive markets, although most often not very competitive, undoubtedly play a role in modern economies, but they are less significant by most standards than such features as rule-based bureaucracies, the many laws, regulations and agencies of governments, largely non-market and non-competitive institutions such as schools, hospitals, and labour unions, the numerous communities of knowledge and expertise, and monopolistic, oligopolistic, and monopsonic commercial arrangements. Individual greed is harmful to all of these institutions. What might be called institutional greed, the members' shared desire for unmerited revenues and social status, is harmful to the economy and the society in which it is set. Also, as I will discuss in the seventh section of this chapter, there are significant constraints on greed in the real economy.

Finally, financial greed is especially unlikely to be helpful for the economy. As I have explained, greed comes easily in the left section of the Triptych, because there are no limits to the quantities of savings-money that can be accumulated and because the numerical nature of money encourages comparisons, which encourage even more intense desires to gain more, especially as numerically measured greed blends into the prideful search for social status. There is no way that this easy greed in the left section can have a good effect on the middle section, but there is ample historical evidence of bad effects from the untrammelled desire of money-thing owners for more money – both higher payments of token-money and gains of savings-money from various sorts of speculation.

6. What monetary greed does

In the human condition, one disorder tends to lead to others. Wars breed resentment, which breeds further wars. Unmerited fear stimulates aggression, which generates more fear and ill-will. Sexual infidelity causes pain and mistrust, which can coalesce into a cycle of cruelty and revenge. The disorder of monetary greed – the greed for more of what token-money can buy and for more savings-money and more and more valuable money-things – is no exception to this pattern. Its effects ripple through the character and behaviour of the greedy person, the whole society, and especially the economy. I will discuss each in turn.

Character and behaviour: Greed *distorts judgements*. Because greed is recognised as bad and people do not want to be bad, the savings-money-greedy person always relies on some necessarily fallacious reasoning to explain why she is not actually being greedy. She might exaggerate her merit, overestimate the amount of money needed for security, or even twist her motivations to claim she wants more solely so she can give more away in a generous spirit. When thinking about the gains from post-aristocratic finance, she might rely on an exaggerated respect for tradition or contracts.

Unfortunately, the misjudgements are not likely to be limited to the topic at hand. The unwillingness to question one set of emotions and desires supports a worldview which distorts many responses and judgements. My greed-stained perspective will lead me systematically to devalue the concerns of other people and to minimise the value of any argument that might threaten to expose my greed. In other words, I will become more selfish and less rational.

In particular, *greed reduces generosity*. Generosity is not necessarily incompatible with wealth: owning much property and many money-things. Aristotle even argues that wealth is a prerequisite for generosity, since only wealthy people have enough to give away. For Christians, it is more complicated. Jesus says that a poor widow who gives a small amount from her meagre supply is more generous than a rich man who gives much more without any sacrifice of consumption (Luke 21.1-4). Whether the greedy person is rich or poor, however, the presence of greed will always tend to reduce generosity. It does not matter whether the amount that could be given away is large or small, nor whether or not it is large enough to reduce the donor's own consumption. In all cases, the logic of greed leads me to be more reluctant to give, share, spend generously, and otherwise make my money serve the common good.

Excessive material and savings-money desires *distract attention from more important desires*. This effect is traditionally explained in transcendental terms. To paraphrase Jesus (Mark 8.36), the man who wishes to own the whole world pays no attention to his immortal soul. At a less elevated level, the greedy person is often too worried about getting more money to exercise his nobler responsibilities and aspirations. He slights love, duty, honour, wisdom, and beauty, as well as religious piety. In the economic life, greed tends to distract attention away from justice and social responsibility. It frequently leads to a preference for more profits soon over the potential profits which would come from more expensive commitments to future excellence. In the financial life, greed leads to the preference for gains from doing as little economic work as possible, through speculation and leverage, over gains from the hard slog of factory-building and other activities paid for by pure-finance.

Society: Vices and virtues are ultimately personal, but they are also social. Our standards for greed are in large part set for an entire society, and each member's individual standards cannot help but be influenced by those of their communities, both large and small. As a result of these close connections, greed *encourages further greed*. Following the metaphor of disease, greed tends to be contagious. If my respected mentors or professional colleagues happily engage in financial speculation, expect high financial returns, or demand risk-free returns, then I am very likely to consider such behaviour acceptable, and unlikely even to consider whether it might be greedy. Indeed, if my unworthy office rival's wage is five million euros, I am far more likely to think I deserve six million euros than to criticise him for being greedy. The spread of greed can be rapid. Once some degree of monetary greed is established as acceptable in one profession or one financial practice, the acceptability tends to spread into related professions and similar practices.

Greed *disrupts commutative justice*. I explained in Chapter Two that there can be no objectively true money-numbers. Each price, wage, tax, and so forth is established through conscious, half-conscious, and unconscious estimations and calculations. The lack of a firm anchor of objective truth leaves all money-numbers vulnerable to the influence of emotions, inclinations, and the uncontrolled desires of greed. Greed on one side of a transaction is likely to be matched by greed on the other, and the more powerful party is likely to get her greedy way. Savings-money, which has almost no anchor in the economy and no objective truth whatsoever, is even more vulnerable than token-money to uncontrolled desires, giving the people on the more powerful side of transactions even more ability to get their greedy way. The greed of economic power and the power of savings-money greed are not limited to individuals. Organisations such as banks, companies, and government agencies can also adopt a greedy worldview in their transactions. I have suggested that the supposedly definitional and non-moral corporate dedication to shareholder profits is in fact structurally greedy. If the corporations are powerful enough, and they often are, this greedy disposition leads to systemically greedy high prices, low wages, and low tax payments.

The greed of the powerful brings disorder not only to individual economic choices and money-things. It also *disrupts social justice*. Any divisions between the weak and the strong in the social fabric are widened by the greater ability of the strong to turn their monetary greed into more savings-money. The poor-to-rich transfers of post-aristocratic finance add injury to insult, as the relatively poor are forced to pay a sort of tribute to the relatively rich.

Also, *communities are divided by monetary greed*. In the central section of the Triptych, greed over wages divides one group of workers from another. More subtly, the greed of consumers about prices sets them against the workers whose wages are largely paid from the revenues created by those prices. The greed of taxpayers and of the recipients of benefits creates strains in government finances, often setting the relatively rich against the relatively poor. Greed about profits divides workers from employers and managers from shareholders. In the left section of the Triptych, greed about housing values encourages various sorts of segregation and exclusivity. The greed of financial investors and especially of speculators encourages division between the world of finance and the real economy.

Economy: Greed *disorients economic effort*. It distracts managers from their communal responsibilities. It lures financial investors in economic finance into the economically useless search for speculative gains. It encourages the unmerited tributes of post-aristocratic finance. More technically, in recent years the financially greedy practice of substituting debt for equity in leveraged buyouts has discouraged long-term commitments to business excellence. Also rather technically, the greed-motivated flows of money from one currency to another without any economic purpose has led to much economically foolish lending and several unnecessary financial crises.

Monetary greed *encourages economic neglect*. In a reasonably just economy without any greed, problems would be addressed merely because they are serious and opportunities would be exploited merely because of a commitment to the common good. The moral weakness of human nature renders such a utopia impossible, but economies can be further or closer to this ideal. The presence of monetary greed inevitably pulls them further away. Many problems simply do not have greed-friendly solutions and many opportunities cannot be grasped, or at least grasped well, in greed-friendly ways. Financial greed not only encourages a preference for financial solutions to no-money-now problems that may have better, non-financial solutions. It also leads to reduced effort to solve all sorts of problems for which no financial solution can be found. Savings-money greed can also lead to solutions which are greed-friendly but hostile to the common good. For example, restrictions on housing construction in many cities around the world satisfy greedy owners and would-be owners by helping to support the prices of these money-things (more precisely the price of the land connected with the housing), but the restrictions do not support the common good of universal decent housing.

Finally, monetary greed *aggravates economic conflicts*. The modern economy is made up of numerous complex entities tied together in numerous multifaceted relationships. Even without greed, it is difficult to create and maintain cooperation, because the various groups have different goals and standards of excellence. Sympathetic negotiations and respectful compromises are required to minimise disputes. Greedy people and enterprises, however, are often too interested in their own monetary gains to allow much sympathy or respect. When greed distorts the vision of all sides of a negotiation, the best possible result is a mistrustful balance of unrighteous indignation. The combination of financial greed and post-aristocratic finance is especially toxic. It creates a very basic conflict between those who pay and those who receive these payments of social tribute.

7. Greed, economists, and the actual economy

Economists and greed

Up to now, I have judged greed but not discussed its prevalence in real economies. In this section, I fill that gap with an argument that is likely to be unfamiliar to readers who are used to the standard presentation of "free market" economies. My claim is that while greed can certainly be found in complex and sophisticated modern economies, it is generally considered more bad than good and is restrained to a significant extent. The forces of restraint are both external – laws, regulations, and customs – and internal – the moral beliefs of most economic actors and the cultures of most economic organisations, including many parts of profit-seeking corporations.

My argument is unfamiliar because many economists and commentators on the economy see far more greed than I do in the economy. In my judgement, what they see when they look at the economy is distorted by what they expect to see. They are pre-persuaded that "competitive markets" are the dominant organisational form in modern economies. This market model of the economy can be described as greed-friendly, because all market actors are thought to be guided solely by a "self-interest" that has no moral qualities or limits. On the contrary, what the self is assumed always to be interested in is gaining more token-money and savings-money, however much the market participant might already have. With this economic view, the economy must be greed-friendly. Indeed, the idea of disordered excess, which is the central idea of monetary greed, is meaningless or at least incomprehensible in this model, which takes the goodness of some sort of material maximisation as an unquestionable truth.

That greed-friendly vision is very unrealistic. To start, it vastly exaggerates the role of competitive markets and competition in general in the lives of labour in developed modern economies. At the scale of organisations, non-market and not very competitive government agencies, healthcare providers, educational institutions, and various not-for-profit institutions employ close to half the paid labour. More significant, the overwhelming majority of employees in organisations that are oriented towards competitive striving are not primarily working in markets. They work in bureaucracies and in communities of labour in which the psychology of competition, while often present, is generally secondary to both the psychology of cooperation and the non-competitive pursuit of excellence.

Of course, greed can flourish without either competition or markets. However, in the actual economy – excluding finance – greed is almost never nurtured or exalted. More often it is discouraged, disapproved of, and, at worst, tolerated. That treatment should hardly be surprising, considering the already mentioned social rejection of greedy attitudes: parents' strong disapproval of greed in their children, the general unwillingness to admit to being truly (as compared to ironically or in some controlled way) greedy, and the acceptance that "greedy" is always an insulting description (except in a comparative metaphor such as "he is not greedy for things but is greedy for knowledge" or "holiness").

The negative judgement of and response to greed is found in the rules, regulations, and expectations that institutionalise the middle section of the Triptych. Wages and prices are generally expected to be reasonably fair and just. Employers, employees, producers, and customers are all expected to avoid greedy disregard of the needs of and harms to other people and groups. They are not supposed to allow greed to lead them to make contracts that are too exploitative, products that are too shoddy, and advertising that is too deceptive. All these practices are generally prohibited – strictly in theory and somewhat effectively in practice.

The anti-greed moral standards could certainly be higher and more diligently enforced, but almost no leaders of industry, commerce, government, healthcare, education, unions, leisure, or entertainment would dare to say publicly – or be likely to think privately – that greed is good. Even millionaires and billionaires generally seem to feel duty-bound to deny that their wealth is a sign of individual greed or a result of greedy behaviour. Remarkably high wages suggest that these men and women are often actually somewhat hypocritical in their professions of service to customers, shareholders, workers, the common good, or some other noble end. However, hypocrisy is the tribute that vice pays to virtue. The rich recognise that they should not admit to greed, largely because they agree with the consensus judgement that greed is bad for them and for the economy. I believe that this judgement is correct. Although I cannot provide quantitative evidence, I am confident that a comparative study would show that the more successful the economy is by almost any standard, the more effective is its resistance to greed.

Seven ways greed is restrained

If the starting assumption is that economies – excluding finance – are not greed-friendly, the evidence to support that assumption is not hard to find. I identify seven greed-limiting factors that are commonly found in contemporary economies.

1. *Competition*: In the market model, the pressure from actual or potential competition limits the damage done by participants' greed. The model has some validity. The threat of lower priced rivals does sometimes restrain producers' greed in setting prices and the threat of losing a job or an employee may reduce greed in demanding higher wages or offering lower ones. However, the greed-dampening effect is generally modest. There is limited competition in large parts of modern economies. Where competition seems to be present, it is often and fairly easily thwarted by actual monopolies or the monopolistic behaviour created through formal or informal collusion. Even when the potential arrival of less greedy new rivals could provide some anti-greed discipline, incumbent producers can often purchase potential challengers or use their market power and regulatory connections to crush them.

2. *Profit regulation*: Regulation is a much more substantial barrier to greed than competition. For more than a century, government agencies in almost all jurisdictions have restricted the scope of greed in many industries, including those which are run as monopolies or near-monopolies and those deemed especially important. The regulations have most often focused on mandating maximum prices to avoid "gouging" – easily recognised as a manifestation of greed. Also, companies are sometimes forced to subsidise some groups of customers or to spend money on activities that serve the common good but will not bring in revenues, let alone profits. Regulators that expect their charges to be "good corporate citizens" almost always consider greedy behaviour a sign of bad citizenship.

3. *Industrial regulation*: Profits are directly regulated at relatively few companies, but industrial regulation envelops all enterprises in developed economies in a thick net of detailed rules on many aspects of business life, including product safety, product labelling, workplace safety, wages and

terms of employment, noxious emissions, land use, various kinds of discrimination, and the fair treatment of customers. In almost every case, the regulations restrain greed. When greedy behaviour in any domain becomes too flagrant, new regulations are generally established to limit the abuse. The web of limits, protections, requirements, and disclosures constrains all companies to establish cultures of compliance, in which greed is explicitly considered a hazard to sound practice. When greed causes this culture to fail, as it did when car air bag tests were faked or when a system in an aircraft upgrade was not thoroughly tested or documented, the monetary and reputational damage is often severe. The possibility of things going so badly wrong generally dampens greedy optimism among senior executives.

4. *Extensive public service*: A substantial minority of employees in modern economies work in organisations that have an ethos that is structurally hostile to greed. The list includes most parts of the public administration, public schools, publicly funded healthcare, public welfare systems, the military, emergency services, private charities, and religious groups. Of course, no organisation is totally exempt from the damage done by greedy individuals or greedy institutional cultures and sub-cultures. There will be a temptation to monetary greed whenever money changes hands and whenever savings-money can be accumulated. However, when an organisation's "mission" is service of the common good, that temptation is constrained by the organisation's operational and aspirational orientation. Greedy civil servants, medical professionals, and so forth are generally disliked by their colleagues and often despised by the general public – a disdain which discourages greed. All together, these greed-hostile sectors are large enough to influence the overall culture of the economy. People who are trained in them or pass through them are likely to show some resistance to greedy impulses even when they work in more greed-tolerant organisations.

5. *Bureaucracy*: The 20th century construction of the compliance culture around regulation only reinforced the basic organisational structure of the modern economy developed in the 19th century – not a competitive struggle of battling commercial armies but a collection of hierarchical, rule-based bureaucracies. Each organisation's bureaucracy is typically both largely

self-sufficient and in close, mostly cooperative relations with the comparable bureaucracies of related organisations, including those of supposed rivals. For most people working in the middle section of the Triptych, the greed-friendly competitive markets of economists have little direct effect. For them, the wages and privileges of labour are largely set by the job description, with a few pre-calibrated adjustments for special situations. The rules are almost always hostile to greed, because it is considered a disruptive force to bureaucratic organisations. Even when greed is tolerated, for example among partners at leading law firms or among various sorts of celebrities, procedures are in place that sometimes modulate it and a pretence of impartiality and equity is almost always maintained.

6. *Popular and professional pressure*: Economic development in most countries has often been matched by the expansion of a civil society that provides reasonably effective monitoring and pressure for reform. Journalists, labour unions, whistle-blowers, lawyers, and now social media discover, publicise, and try to punish and change many sorts of bad behaviour, including various manifestations of greed. The pressure has often been intermittent and inadequate, but an informed public certainly discourages greed. The public, it should be noted, rarely sympathises with greedy behaviour in business. Greed, especially when it harms some common good, creates a bad reputation. No one ever says, "You can't blame Executive X too much for buying ingredients that poisoned customers. His goal was worthy: maximising his own income by boosting his company's profits".

7. *Ideas and ideals*: The widespread public dislike of economic greed springs from a collection of not always consistent and often indistinctly articulated principles. While the principles supporting competitive markets are essentially greed-friendly, most of the other guiding notions of the contemporary economy retain the nearly universal pre-modern opprobrium of greed. There is little or no room for greed in the Enlightenment praise of reason and science, the universalism of the Enlightenment political tradition, the efficiency and rationality of effective bureaucracy, or the secularised recasting of the Christian culture of service.

All of these have had enough effect on the economy to give greed a bad name, which has restrained its flowering.

The weakening defences against greed

The presence of these seven elements supports my claim that greedy behaviour is basically discouraged in the non-financial economy. However, I share the belief of many social critics that the rejection has become less wholehearted over the last three or four decades. The reasons for the shift are disputed – suggestions include changes in leading ideas, popular sentiment, social power structures, and economic arrangements. Whatever the underlying disease, the symptoms are fairly clear. The enthusiasms for "deregulation", the "Washington Consensus", smaller governments, and reliance on "markets" are all at least in part signs of a greater acceptance of greedy behaviour. The rise of financialisation presumably reflects and certainly encourages the greater economic acceptance of greed. Quite significantly, economic actors feel less shame about appearing greedy now than they did fifty years ago.

The extremely rapid rise in executive pay, relative to the typical pay of underlings, provides an instructive example of the increased social respectability of greed in the mainstream economy. From the 1930s until the 1980s, the dominant corporate culture in Western economies ensured restraint in the level of pay for top bosses. The standard proposed by early management guru Peter Drucker was 20 or 25 times the average of employees (Drucker Institute, 2011). Such limits were widely considered morally right, and the ethical arguments were buttressed by the fear of godless, oppressive Communism, and a social consensus that companies' "chief executives" were more executives than chiefs. High marginal tax rates (as high as 90% in the United States) reinforced the message (Saez and Zucman, 2019).

All these expectations, arguments, and policies produced the desired effect. Executive pay did not increase any faster than average pay during the period. The anti-greed consensus was so strong that bosses rarely complained that they were underpaid. Indeed, they were so firmly stuck inside a greed-resistant worldview that they were often only dimly aware of how much their potential greed was being suppressed. The extent of that suppression only became clear when the cultural expectations changed. Then bosses started to increase their own rewards at a vertiginous rate. As is typical with greed, they found justifications, most notably the claim that higher pay advanced "shareholder value". Of course, such reasoning does not stand up to even superficial analysis – the goal is mistaken, the measures are wrong, and high executive pay does not have any relation to the poor measures of the foolish goal. However, neither stronger logic nor popular disgust stopped the greed, presumably because the social mood had changed. The ratio of top to average pay is now in triple digits at most big companies. The lamentable change demonstrates both the previous success and its fragility. As with all moral struggles, in the fight against greed the victories can pass almost unnoticed and success is easily lost.

I should add a caveat to the argument in this section. My broad generalisations of both historical and current social attitudes towards greed in the economy cannot be proven, simply because social attitudes are never uniform or unanimous. In any society, some people endorse greed more or less consciously, and more people practice it with more or less self-righteousness. In comparing societies, there can only be more or less social tolerance, more or less social shame, greater or lesser restrictions on greedy behaviour. Still, despite all the unavoidable epistemological uncertainty, I think it is possible to make a meaningful and illuminating comparison between the social attitudes towards greed in the economy as a whole and those in financial activity. My judgement is that greed has been and remains far more tolerated in finance than in the rest of the economy.

8. Greed in finance: historical overview

Throughout history, thinkers and societies have more often than not considered greed to be a necessary accompaniment to finance. At the beginning of the Western intellectual tradition, Aristotle argued that the desire for money to make more money is inherently disordered, because money does not increase by nature. This disordered desire can be described as greed. (I am simplifying an argument that is, in my judgement, largely faulty.) Throughout the pre-modern West, a similar, almost visceral distaste for the morals of finance has been common among the general populace, the aristocratic elite, and religious teachers. Financial practices were generally seen as grasping and base – that is greedy – by nature. It was generally expected that moneylenders, the professional ancestors of modern bankers, would be greedy people. That expectation was often self-fulfilling, as the people who choose to be involved in such a morally suspect profession were very likely to be unusually greedy to begin with.

The pre-modern tradition of greedy finance was largely reinforced in the early decades of the industrial era, when there was more economic finance for greed to feed on. The expansion of finance had two main causes. First, the rapid expansion of new industrial enterprises led to an expansion of the sort of no-money-now problems that economic finance was particularly well suited to solve. Second, and more important, the general inability to recognise that money is a baseless token led to a greater reliance on financial arrangements. With paid-for production increasing and governments unwilling to create money that was not connected to gold and silver, the supply of officially sanctioned token-money was consistently too small to keep prices constant. Businesses turned to banks to close the token-money gap. The banks' "letters of credit", which allowed bills to be paid through the long "now" of production, were eventually standardised and unofficially sanctioned as token-money.

The rise of what I have called ideal-banking shows that this early financialisation could nurture less greedy approaches to finance. However, in practice the new industrial finance and the expanded trading finance mostly retained the traditional financial culture of greedy lenders, while adding an ever-thicker layer of particularly greedy financial speculation on new ventures. Banking gradually became a somewhat more respectable profession, but through the 19th century much of it remained in the hands of socially ostracised groups – Jews everywhere, Protestants in Catholic countries, and non-conformists in Britain. As in pre-industrial economies, the outsider financiers were expected to be greedy, and they often were so in their professional dealings. The frequent philanthropic use of some of the greedily acquired savings-money does not negate the financial greed.

However, as the rise of ideal-banks and the expiatory benevolence of financiers suggest, finance and greed do not automatically go together.

Alongside the dominant expectation and tradition of unrestrained greed in finance are longstanding authoritative social demands for moral restraint in finance. The Old Testament condemns some lending with returns and demands routine forgiveness of debts. The anti-greed tradition that led to the ideal-banks started with the 15th century *monte di pietà*, which aimed to offer poor borrowers less unjust terms than standard moneylenders. Usury was theoretically prohibited throughout the Christian centuries and the condemnation of unjust financial returns remained a common social theme as Christendom declined.

In addition, and quite significantly for the purposes of this book, it became easier for financiers to be less greedy as the reality of financial arrangements changed. Subjective, objective, and social greed were all hard to avoid in pre-industrial economies, where loans were mostly to labourers heading towards debt slavery and to kings whose military ambitions outstripped their tax-raising ability. The development of trade and manufacturing provided normal banks and ideal-banks with more opportunities to avoid greed by offering fair monetary returns to depositors, fair interest rates and general support for borrowers, and active attention to the common good of society. The competition from ideal-banks probably restrained greed at their less public-spirited rivals.

While the continuing social opprobrium for financial excess may also have restrained financial greed well into the 20th century, the social attitude towards greed changed in the last decades of that century. One sign of the shift was the decline of ideal-banking. In almost every country, these institutions changed their legal structures, business goals, and corporate cultures so that they could emulate their commercial rivals in promoting greed among customers and employees. More generally, the businesses and cultures of the profit-seeking banks became more dominated by the greediest domains of finance: speculation and trading. Smaller banks increasingly merged into larger institutions, reducing the close, greed-discouraging ties of banks to particular communities. Regulators, increasingly controlled by past or future bank employees, mostly encouraged the shift. Laws against usury were repealed or gutted. In the United States and Britain, private pension funds expanded and came to rely increasingly on financial gains for providing pensioners with their promised income. Speculation on home prices spread through many developed economies. Criticisms of greed, which had been standard fare in religious exhortation and cultural jeremiads for millennia, became rare and were often muted.

This shift in the social response to greed in finance matches, both chronologically and conceptually, the weakening of the social condemnation of greed and the increasing financialisation in the real economy. In this new era, the near-collapse of the global financial system in 2008, largely caused by an array of irresponsible greedy financial practices, inspired no lasting anti-greed rhetoric and almost no punishments of the greedy culprits, either individual or corporate.

9. Greed in finance: a typology

I hope that the discussion of various aspects of monetary greed has brought some familiarity with this unavoidable but somewhat controllable part of economic and social reality. More ambitiously, I also hope that familiarity has made readers desire a paradigm of finance which includes greed in its analytic framework. In any case, such a paradigm is what the rest of this chapter will explore. To start this analysis, I will discuss some financial aspects of the three types of monetary greed introduced earlier: subjective, objective, and social.

Subjective greed

Subjective financial greed is ultimately individual and inherently psychological. There is enough commonality in individual situations and attitudes to allow for helpful generalisation, but the judgement of subjective greed requires what might be described as looking with clear eyes deep into the soul of the potentially greedy person. The most appropriate object of this moral gaze is the person we see in the mirror. The search for subjective financial greed requires what contemporary Marxists sometimes call autocritique and Christians an examination of conscience. I need to ask myself some hard questions. Are my desires concerning savings-money and money-things excessive? Will satisfying these desires make me more unjust? Over time, will my current approach to monetary desires create or support bad habits? Will I start to assume that I need and deserve excessively high financial returns?

These are questions which people generally avoid asking about themselves and which no human can answer definitively for someone else. However, two externally available standards can help spur on and advance the necessary moral inquiry about subjective greed, both individually and, in a tentative way, throughout the financial system.

First, anyone's desired returns can be compared to the *sacrifices* required to receive them. At least arguably, it is always subjectively greedy to think that I deserve to gain something without experiencing a loss of at least equal value in exchange: a proportionate effort, pain, or renunciation. As humans who always live in mutual dependence with other people, we cannot truly deserve "something for nothing". In Chapter Two, I described the Great Exchange as constituted by gifts, but these gifts are always in some way reciprocal. It is greedy to wish to stand outside of that generous exchange.

In discussions of subjective greed, the common language of finance points in the wrong moral direction. Financial investments do not earn returns in the same natural way that labour earns consumption. In any society with egalitarian pretensions, financial returns that are not paired with some sort of sacrifice are more likely to be judged as greedy than as merited or earned. What sort of sacrifices are morally relevant? Rather arbitrarily, I divide the sacrifices involved in financial investment into three categories, each with its own level of non-greedy returns.

In the *ideal-savings* that lies behind ideal-banking, the financial returns of the relatively poor investors can be assumed to be received in direct exchange for ethically significant sacrifices of consumption. As it was often said when this form of finance was flourishing, the savings-money for the loans made by these institutions were collected from "the pennies of the poor". It is not subjectively greedy for such investors to expect fairly high returns. To use a rough analogy, these financial investors walked so that their investees could use a car. It is fair to ask the drivers to reimburse the pedestrians for their trouble.

Ideal-savings have almost disappeared in developed economies, where the financial debts of the poorest quarter of the population generally outweigh any savings-money nest-eggs. The middle classes that have replaced so much of the proletariat and working class engage in what might be called *middle-class finance*. These fairly well-off investors make some sacrifices, but not substantial ones. The savers might have a less comfortable house or a less luxurious holiday than would have been available if they had consumed all of their token-money income. Continuing the analogy, these financial investors drive to work in an older, smaller car, so that the investee can have the car he needs. A modest return does not sound like a greedy recompense for such a modest sacrifice.

In contemporary economies, middle-class finance provides a much higher proportion of the savings-money for financial investments than what is left of ideal-savings. However, the bulk of newly created savings-money (excluding that involved in governments' money-creation) comes from what might be called *painless investments*. This is savings-money that was obtained or created, and could be destroyed completely, without any meaningful effect on the owner's past, current, and, in many cases, distant future consumption. The financial investments of very highly paid executives, business owners, and entertainers are all painless, as are those of the heirs to substantial collections of money-things. For these privileged people, the desire to acquire and hold onto so much savings-money might well be subjectively greedy in the first place. The desire to have that money produce returns, let alone high returns, is even more morally suspect. It is like having 20 cars and no need of money, but charging your poor tenant for borrowing one vehicle to take her child to the doctor.

The dominant psychological patterns in developed economies are an inversion of my moral recommendations: richer people are more covetous of high financial returns than their poorer neighbours and compatriots. The business model of many ideal-banks relied on the renunciation of subjective greed. They offered member-savers relatively low returns on their savings and member-borrowers relatively low interest rates on their loans. One reason that the mix worked was that the investors and investees were basically the same people at different times in their lives. More ethically, these financial investors could be persuaded to eschew subjectively greedy desires. In stark contrast. the richest financial investors typically employ private bankers or wealth managers to search out the highest possible returns for their painless investments. Paying someone from your abundant funds to help you become even richer without any effort on your part *may* not be subjectively greedy, but the burden of proof surely rests on those rich investors.

Second, subjective financial greed may be judged by the fairly constant standards of *human nature and economic organisations*. In every social-economic situation, there is some maximum morally acceptable ratio of token-money returns to savings-money invested. It is always subjectively greedy to expect or even to accept more than that. Similarly, there is some degree of certainty and constancy of return that it is subjectively greedy to demand in uncertain economies, and all economies are uncertain.

I have already discussed the unreality of what I consider to be the most galling example of this sort of subjective greed: the claim that all savings-money, including hoarded savings-money, merits a risk-free return. There is no economic or psychological justification for exempting any investments from the pains of any economic bad times. I will discuss the objective and social greed of demanding risk-free returns in the next sub-sections.

Some other examples of this absolute subjective greed will be provided later. The list includes the desire for ever-rising prices of various types of money-things, the desire that financial investments provide gains that are disproportionately large relative to any plausible losses, and the assumption that the sole or overriding purpose of corporations should be to provide as high a financial return as possible to shareholders.

That list encompasses most of the desires, and some of the simple expectations, of a large number of individual and professional financial investors. For example, it suggests that homeowners are greedy whenever they want their land to make them richer just because they own it – to make money while sleeping in their own beds. To anyone who has not undertaken the examination of financial conscience recommended at the beginning of this section, such a wide condemnation is likely to be shocking. I am claiming that many of the normal working practices of middle-class life around the world are actually greedy. What is wrong, a critic might ask, with wanting gains from property, a safe income from investments, and strong stock markets? Are those not all things that we should expect to find in prosperous, well-ordered societies? Are they not the just rewards of prudence or of a reasonable moderation in consumption?

My answer to all of these questions is a resounding "No". Those desires are wrong, simply because it is subjectively greedy – fundamentally and unequivocally – to ask the financial system to give anyone more, either in rewards and in certainty, than the paid-for economy can justly provide. Greed is not always punished in this life (some would say that it is rarely punished), but these widespread manifestations of financial greed intermittently cause quite practical problems. They are significant contributors to the financial exception to the general resilience of the economy. When people – not just the lords of finance and the captains of industry, but ordinary people – expect finance to work unjust wonders in the left section of the Triptych, they invite serious trouble in the middle section.

Objective greed

Objective greed refers to the desire for economic rewards that are disproportionately large relative to the economic or social contributions that are being rewarded. Continuing with my automotive analogy, it is greedy for the person who only opens the garage door to expect to be paid for providing the vehicle.

The concept of objective financial greed is problematic but unavoidable. It is problematic because all judgements about how much some individual's financial investment has contributed to the relevant common good will be highly controversial, as will any judgement of the appropriate rewards for particular objective contributions. The concept is unavoidable because it is based on one aspect of the universal concept of commutative economic justice: we should be paid for the good that our labour actually does. Doctors who cure deserve higher wages than peers who do not, even if the less successful ones work just as hard and have just as much education, experience, and support. Such clear comparisons are rarely available in our heavily interconnected economies. The actual contributions of any individual's labour – and of any particular financial investments – cannot be determined with any precision. Still, it is up to chief executives who are paid 300 times as much as the average employee of their companies to show that desiring such wages is not objectively greedy. It is also up to early-stage equity investors in a successful start-up to defend the justice of multiplying the savings-money value of their original investments a thousand-fold, or even just five-fold. They need to explain how that money actually contributed so much to the corporate success that their willingness to consider such gains is not objectively greedy.

It is always possible to quibble over numbers – if five-fold returns are objectively greedy, what about four-fold? It may be more fruitful to consider types of financial investments and structures of returns. I will give some examples, starting with the rather specialised case of financial investments that support hugely destructive modern wars. Since plunder and reparations can almost never compensate for the losses of fighting, there can be no plausible hope of a direct monetary return from financial investing in military ventures. Such financial investors are basically using their savings-money to promote destruction. Is there enough objective good in that outcome for any desire of token-money rewards not to be considered objectively greedy? Perhaps any returns on "war bonds" are a form of ethically unacceptable "war profiteering", so finance should have no role in paying for wars. (That would certainly be an historical novelty.)

Wars are rare, but modern economies include several much more common activities that have similar mixes of no-money-now problems and no clear way to generate obvious monetary profits. Healthcare and education are the pre-eminent examples. Together, they account for about one fifth of the wages paid in most developed economies. The overwhelming majority of those wages are paid through national tax-benefit systems. Token-money taxes pay for most of the things that economic finance is particularly good at supporting: expensive new buildings and equipment, and the training of skilled professionals. When finance is used to pay for some of these economic-things, any returns to the financial investors are effectively provided or at least mediated by governments. For those returns not to be objectively greedy, the presences of financial investors and financial obligations must provide otherwise unavailable objective contributions to the excellence in the provision of healthcare and education. In some countries, the judgement that the insistence on finance is superfluous and greedy is reinforced by the availability of another alternative to finance, giving, to solve no-money-now problems in education and health. Private schools, universities, and healthcare facilities can rely on donors while waiting for revenue from students and patients.

Equities are my last, and possibly most controversial, example of possible systemic objective financial greed. The fundamental problem is that the return structure on these money-things has changed much less than the objective importance of financial investors' contribution to corporate profits. The bankers and other backers of 19th and early 20th century ventures provided token-money that was often not readily available in those less monetised and less flexible economies. Also, these financial investors often provided valuable contacts, political protection, and organisational expertise. For the investee enterprises, the confidence demonstrated by knowledgeable professionals could be a commercially important asset. The venture capital firms that offer something similar today can make a good argument that they can desire fairly high returns without being objectively greedy. However, most of the savings-money that supports new ventures comes from banks or people that will provide little or nothing other than money. Any claim for more than quite modest returns on this sort of money-alone financial investment is likely to be objectively greedy.

One qualification is needed here. Like any financial investor, the buyers of new equities are not objectively greedy to ask for returns on successful financial investments that are high enough to compensate for the possibility of low returns and losses on other promising but ultimately unsuccessful investments. However, greed can easily lurk in the definition of "promising", because it is objectively greedy to want to be compensated for taking reckless risks in financial investments. Calculations of "high enough to compensate" returns are also ethically problematic. Financial theory sometimes claims that these financial investors deserve compensation not only for likely or actual losses, but for the psychological tension created by "risk-taking". That sort of theory certainly sounds like a science-y excuse for objective greed.

The probability of objective greed among equity investors increases greatly once the initial investors have earned their initial, possibly justly high returns. Since today's companies typically rely far more on yoking than on finance for their healthy operation and expansion, the early monetary support has an ever-diminishing connection with later corporate success. Financial investments, especially equity investments, do start the ball rolling, so to speak. By the time a fair return has been earned, however, the inertial flow of token-money from customers keeps the ball in motion. This inertia can come to dominate quite quickly. Successful companies that depend more on human skills than expensive equipment often earn enough profits in the first decade of operations to provide a non-greedy return to all financial investors, including a Large Payment for debt investors and enough money to "extinguish" equity investors' non-greedy financial claims. From that point forward, any return demanded by the already fairly rewarded financial investors is very likely to be objectively greedy.

Social greed

Financial desires and expectations are socially greedy when they disrupt the common good, whether or not they are either subjectively or objectively greedy. The concept of social greed is closely related to the political notion of social injustice and the more religious idea of social "structures of sin". All three of these types of large-scale ethical disorders are philosophically challenging, since the moral quality of greed can only be attributed to individual people, not to groups. However, for the last few centuries, social and economic reformers have persuasively argued that particular social arrangements can broadly enable and encourage morally disordered individual desires and persistently unjust allocations of goods and evils to groups within a society. In these circumstances, such philosophically loose talk is not merely excusable but enlightening. It is helpful to say that slavery is unjust to enslaved persons, war is unjust to civilians, the lack of universal healthcare or education may be unjust to the poor, and that certain financial practices may strongly encourage greed. The injustice of unjust social structures is likely to be particularly invidious, because the greed-encouraging practices and arrangements are almost by definition deeply embedded in the "way things are". They are easily accepted without any ethical questioning.

I mentioned the possible social greed of post-aristocratic finance when I introduced the concept earlier in this chapter. In some ways, the practice of poor-to-rich financial transfers certainly fits the description of social greed. The ethical rightness of these transfers is taken for granted by the relevant financial investors and rarely questioned in an articulate way by the poorer people who provide the token-money for the returns. Also, the practices might be socially wrong without any subjective greed and without any standard of accomplishment to judge objective greediness. However, the final judgement of social greed depends on a judgement of the justice of both the hierarchical economic order of contemporary societies and the use of financial arrangements to support this order. The dominant egalitarian rhetoric points to social greed being at the ethical heart of post-aristocratic finance, but many other social patterns, including the arrangements of wages, housing, and elite education, suggest that post-aristocratic finance is broadly in accord with the dominant sense of social justice. Since this is not a book of normative political philosophy, I will neither simply condemn the practice as greedy nor defend it as just or as socially beneficial. I will merely say that post-aristocratic finance is clearly greedy according to most egalitarian understandings of social justice. (The combination of condemning greed in finance and accepting the possible justice of non-egalitarian social thinking is unusual in the current discourse, but it was certainly common in the early decades of the Industrial Revolution.)

Even the most hierarchy-friendly social thinkers might worry about the tendency of reality-distant finance to promote social greed. One leading result of the toleration of reality-distance is the promotion of a class of professional financial speculators whose most important professional goal is to be somewhat better than their clients at gratifying their equally greedy desires. The existence of this class seems to be socially greedy. Another result is the enrichment of a small group of successful financial speculators at the expense of the larger group of unsuccessful peers. That result too seems like social greed, albeit at a smaller scale.

Financialisation is my last example of possible social financial greed. The tendency to think of business and society primarily in terms of returns on monetary investments could conceivably promote moderation, if the desired returns were modest. In practice, however, financialisation is intimately connected with the desire to maximise returns. The spread of this sort of financial thinking inevitably encourages the spread of greedy expectations in businesses and to some extent throughout the economy and the society in which the economy is embedded.

Greedy investees

Throughout the discussion of greed in finance, I have focussed almost entirely on the greed of financial investors. This choice is, so to speak, reality-close. Financial arrangements are negotiated contracts, but the investors normally negotiate from a much stronger position than the investees. The greed of the powerful generally excludes or overpowers the greed of the weak.

There is, however, no reason to think that investees are any less greedy than investors, in either their current desires or their potential actions. On the contrary, investors and investees share the moral weaknesses of human nature and operate in the same greed-welcoming financial system, so they are likely to be roughly equal in their susceptibility to greed. Particular social and economic circumstances, just like particular personalities, may be more or less conducive to greed, but greed will flourish almost everywhere and in almost everyone within a supportive or even a neutral social environment. People with very strong moral characters might respond to the experience of being squeezed by the greedy by not squeezing back when they can. For the rest of us, greed inspires counter-greed. In general, the behaviour of investees who are also, or who become, investors supports the hypothesis of ethical uniformity.

Investees do sometimes have a chance to show their greed, most notably in housing markets. Home-buyers who take out mortgage loans are simultaneously buyers of a money-thing and financial investees. As investors, any greed takes the form of desiring increases in the savings-money price of their land money-thing. As investees, the greed shows up in the desire to magnify their gains by borrowing as much savings-money as possible. Of course, investee greed is not limited to housing. Its presence, although usually more potential than actual, helps explain many of the manifestations of greed that I will discuss in the following two sections.

10. Greed in finance: details

With this tripartite typology in the background, I will now list some standard presuppositions in financial arrangements that are greedy by one or more of the three standards. Many of them have been mentioned already, but I think it is helpful to bring them together in one place.

Risk-free returns

In finance, greed basically takes two forms, the desire for unjustly high monetary returns and the desire to take on inappropriately little risk of monetary loss. The second, epitomised in the assumption that savings-money should earn a guaranteed "risk-free" positive return, is always subjectively, objectively, and socially greedy. The demand is subjectively greedy because it unjustly claims that investors should be granted an exemption to the inherent temporal-ontological uncertainly of finance, in other words that they should not be subject to the unavoidable vagaries of fortune. The greed of this ultimatum is clear when it is taken to extremes, for example demanding a risk-free return on a loan to the government after the nation has been devasted by war. In normal times, the subjective greed is less outstanding, but no less present.

To understand why the expectation of risk-free returns is objectively greedy requires understanding how this return is supposed to be generated. The "guaranteed" return can be offered by a bank to some of its depositors or investors. Alternatively, it can be offered directly by a "risk-free" government. In either case, a risk-free return in an inevitably risky world necessarily implies a transfer of risk, because someone has to take on the risk from which the risk-free holders are exempt. For banks, the risk-bearers are borrowers and fee-payers. For governments, taxpayers ultimately pay the return to the risk-exempt holders of government debt. There is no objective justification for this transfer, so the demander of risk-free return is objectively greedy.

This claim might be countered by the observation that risk-free returns are set to be lower than expected risk-bearing returns, a relationship that might demonstrate some objective recognition of what is going on. However, the counter-claim misses the essential point – while it is not necessarily greedy to transfer away some risks and returns, it is always greedy to assume, against reality, that *all* risks should be avoided.

The demand for risk-free returns is socially greedy because the provision of such returns is socially divisive, almost by nature. The qualification of "almost" is necessary because the availability of risk-free financial investments would not necessarily be socially unjust in a financially egalitarian society where all financial investors had the same amount of savings-money to invest. In the reality of hierarchical and unequal economies, however, guaranteed risk-free returns reinforce the advantages of post-aristocratic investors. In effect, they push the already rich to become richer at the expense of the poor. The demand for such economic advantage is socially greedy by any but the most extremely hierarchical moral standards. In developing economies where no-money-now problems are endemic, the demand for a risk-free return is especially socially greedy, because it increases the returns demanded from the riskier borrowers, investees whose spending is overall more likely to promote the common, social good than the financial investments of risk-shy investors.

Economists sometimes describe the denial of risk-free returns as a variety of "financial repression": governments or powerful financial cartels prohibit investors from earning the supposedly normal returns that would be available in an unimpeded financial market. The simplest form of this repression is limiting returns to levels that economists judge to be unjustly low, or, if the economists want to keep a pretence of amorality, returns that are lower than they would be in an unconstrained financial market. Any claim of ethical neutrality is undermined by the use of "repression", a word which almost never comes with positive ethical connotations. The economists' moral judgement is real but erroneous. Financial markets are not trustworthy moral guides, and risk-free returns have no place in a just economy.

Excessive reliance on savings-money

For the first centuries of industrialisation, increasing urbanisation and production brought a steadily increasing need for token-money, but the supply of gold and truly gold-backed money was often inadequate for the economy's needs. Savings-money helped meet this token-monetary need, as banks "discounted" and standardised claims on loans to businesses, turning the near-money of promises of future token-money payments by individual businesses into what might be called the nearer-money of promises by presumably more monetarily sound banks. The system was much better than nothing, but it was cumbersome to operate and prone to easily spreading collapses in monetary confidence, when it turned out that some banks were not monetarily sound.

Those weaknesses were great enough that the reliance of the token-money system on savings-money should have disappeared as soon as governments could take over management of the token-money-supply. Such a takeover was not practicable until certain conditions were met. First and foremost, governments had to understand that token-money does not need any savings-money backing. More technically but still significantly, the authorities needed to have enough information about current economic conditions to be able to manage a centralised token-money system well. Also required was a money-transfer system that easily and cheaply distributed token-money throughout the economy. Even in the most advanced economies, those conditions were not all satisfied until after the great governmental expansions of the Second World War. However, they were certainly in place well before the 2008 global financial crisis, when the paid-for economies' excessive reliance on savings-money led to yet another economic crisis. If not before then after that debacle, it should have been painfully clear that savings-money was neither a necessary nor a helpful tool for managing the supply of token-money.

Why, then, does savings-money still play such a prominent role in token-money-creation? The most common answer to that question from economists is roughly that the current system is still less bad than the alternative of direct governmental monetary control. The argument is that savings-money intermediation can ward off the spectre of governments' unchecked monetary power leading to economically disastrous increases in the Central Monetary Ratio. Financial investors, the economists declare, will refuse to lend to too reckless governments. The problem with this belief is not that the spectre is imaginary. It is real enough. The problem is that the presence of savings-money in the middle of the process of creating token-money is not a ghostbuster. Reckless governments have demonstrated time and time again that they can force banks to lend to them, or just drop the savings-money tie as desired. The savings-money intermediation enriches bankers, but it does not impede unwanted inflation.

This enrichment suggests a better explanation for the insistence on keeping savings-money in the money-creation system: social greed. Economists, many of whom have worked for and with banks, are comfortable with a system that provides the banking system with both easy profits and social respect for being the source of monetary stability. Without much awareness or any ill intent, economists can easily rationalise their opposition to an alternative. Social greed influences intellectual analysis as well as emotions and actions.

A more greed-intolerant financial system would bring a lesser reliance on savings-money in many other areas. Without greed-blindness, governments that wanted former university students to "pay for their education" would turn to the tax system, not to loans. Lending to consumers would mostly be replaced by change (higher wages) and by pooling (steady small payments into a pool in exchange for larger emergency payments and for the intermittent distribution of housing, cars, and other expensive durable items). Tax codes and laws of corporations would discourage instead of encourage extensive financial arrangements for businesses. The left side of the Triptych would only be called on reluctantly, only after seriously considered simpler alternative ways to solve no-money-now problems and to promote the common good.

Unlimited returns

The investors' effort to maximise financial returns without any limit is socially and objectively greedy.

Socially, investees will only be willing to provide very high returns under duress. High payments on loans to pay for life-saving surgery exploit desperation, similar loans to keep poor people from misery exploit social injustice, and high interest rates on payday loans often exploit ignorance and poor character. The returns earned by taking advantage of such weaknesses are greedy. Conceivably, the only financial solution to some no-money-now problem involves very high returns. That is not a justification for this arrangement. It is an argument for finding a non-financial solution to the problem. The unwillingness to search for such solutions and the willingness to search for or to accept exploitative financial returns demonstrate social greed.

Finance-provided money can never be crucial in an economy with baseless money. It is always realistic to create new money to solve a no-money-now problem, and it is usually realistic to find ways to gather or transfer existing money which do not require a financial arrangement. Since these alternatives are readily available, the equitable rewards for providing money through finance will be either quite modest or objectively greedy. Even when finance is a morally and economically reasonable solution for a no-money-now problem, for example when setting up a new company, financial investors are objectively greedy if they do not limit their desired returns in accord with the objective limit to the possible contribution of financial investors to the success of a particular venture.

This judgement of the social and objective greediness of maximal desires may sound extreme. It is certainly unusual. Like the normalcy of expecting returns that do not compensate for any effort or sacrifice (discussed in the previous section), the normalcy of the unlimited maximisation of financial desires is usually accepted without question. However, in not only questioning but condemning this approach, I am not engaging in some utopian or quixotic effort to reform human nature. I am merely calling for the imposition of the same sort of limits to greed that continue to be imposed in non-financial economic arrangements, limits which have played a crucial role in the building up of complex, collaborative, and tremendously productive modern economies.

The social share

The demand for overall returns that increase the financial investors' share of token-money income within an economy is objectively greedy. This demand is built into many social-economic arrangements, even after correcting for the confusions of compound interest discussed in Chapter Three. The pattern was painfully clear in some pre-industrial economies. A desperate peasant would borrow on punitive terms, because a loan was his only hope of keeping alive until the next harvest. Unable to meet those punitive terms, he would continue to borrow more and more, until most of what he could claim as the fruits of his labour were owed to his creditors. In many societies, in the natural course of things – that is barring revolt or ethical injunctions for debt forgiveness – he would eventually be reduced to debt-slavery. The Old Testament's Deuteronomic code enjoins regular society-wide debt forgiveness, presumably to change the nature of things and limit the extent of debt slavery.

The patterns are less dire in today's industrial economies. Debtors can often default without ending up in servitude, so cycles of rising payments can be broken. Nonetheless, in many countries a combination of post-aristocratic finance, new financialisation, and old social-economic arrangements that favour expensive financial commitments has recently led to an increasing ratio of financial payments to wages. The increase is a sign of objective greed. Since financial investors' contribution to the common good is not increasing, they are greedy to want an increasing share of the common income. Individual investors may need to do some research and engage in some moral analysis to understand their participation in social greed, but just as avoidable ignorance of the laws is no excuse for disobedience, avoidable intellectual indolence is not an excuse for not trying to find and fight against this form of objective financial greed. Such moral sloth is particularly difficult to excuse in today's well-informed and carefully measured economies.

Financial isolation

Any durable separation of returns from trends in the overall economy is socially greedy. Debt instruments were created before "the economy" was anything like a coherent concept, let alone one that could be put into anything like numerical terms. However, even then, it was possible to tie finance, as well as the proto-finance of feudal tributes, to what would later be identified as the economy. If the harvest was bad or in the face of invasion or a borrower's serious illness, it was greedy for lenders not to relax the terms of debts. Of course, lenders often were greedy.

In modern economies, everything in the middle section of the Triptych is measured regularly. Small armies of experts follow trends in the whole and in parts of the token-money-economy. Trends in real quantities, from kilometres travelled by car to litres of beer brewed, are carefully measured and correlated with trends in money-numbers. When finance is reality-close, the terms of the arrangements take advantage of some of this available information. The obvious example is equity dividends. Leaving aside the overall justice of the unending claim on profits, the payment of a fairly constant proportion of an enterprise's financial accounting profits to shareholders can be part of a non-greedy distribution of revenues. When shareholders insist on the same dividend in good times and bad, they are socially greedy, because they are favouring their own desire for a steady income over the common good of everyone connected to the company.

In reality, much contemporary finance involves exactly that sort of greed. The financial system takes almost no advantage of the vast array of economic indicators. Debt could be issued with flexible or reality-close payments, but rarely is. This reality-distant obliviousness shows investors treating themselves as socially separated from the economy. In other words, they are socially greedy.

Once again, this moral judgement effectively condemns some current normal and widespread financial practices. Reality-distant debt is as accepted and respectable in contemporary economies and societies as various forms of slavery were in most pre-modern communities. The analogy is imprecise, though, because slavery was generally quite well integrated into the prevailing understanding of good or necessary social arrangements while fixed-income financial arrangements can only seem normal with a willing suspension of the ethical and practical standards applied to the rest of the economy.

The preference for financial solutions

The assumption that finance is a preferred solution to no-money-now problems is subjectively greedy. The need for and possibility of questioning that assumption has expanded greatly, along with the increasing technical capabilities and greater flows of timely information in modern economies. For much of history, debt finance was often either the only or clearly the best tool for addressing no-money-now problems. Governments were not strong enough to provide tax-based solutions, trust was not widespread enough to create equities or large and long-lasting monetary pools, few people were rich enough for giving to be realistic on a large scale, and societies were not well ordered enough to create many open-ended yoking arrangements.

All those limits have disappeared. Governments run huge and effective tax-benefit systems. Laws, customs, and greater ambient wealth support numerous non-financial solutions to no-money-now problems. Finance, even when it is reality-close and not especially greedy, tends to be less attractive socially than any of these alternatives. After all, finance is the only one of these solutions that always brings intertemporal tension. Also, it requires the most complex policing and it fits most uneasily with the instantaneous nature of the Great Exchange.

With so much going against it, finance should rarely be the first choice for solving no-money-now problems. Subjective greed lurks when finance is favoured unthinkingly and when alternatives are dismissed without good reasons. The arguments of potential financial investors and of the experts whom they pay are almost inevitably biased, often unconsciously, by the greedy prospect of financial returns that are almost always acquired without necessity and generally without the merit of sacrifice.

The greed-friendly practices are deeply embedded in economic and social laws and customs. Non-greedy people are often constrained to adopt subjectively and socially greedy financial solutions, even if they can or could see ethically and even practically superior alternatives. A corporate executive, for example, might well prefer to eliminate her profitable company's equity, abandon the use of debt, or pay for expansion by charging higher prices (instead of turning to finance). However, corporate law, tax rules, and competitive conditions can make all these preferences totally unrealistic. It is not individual greed but socially greedy rules and customs that effectively force her to turn to finance. Similarly, charitable organisations and pensioners might prefer to avoid depending on finance and the sale of money-things, but they are socially constrained.

Financial lending and leverage

The desire to magnify returns through financial leverage is objectively and subjectively greedy. It is certainly appropriate to debate where to set the boundary between non-greedy and greedy for a particular financial arrangement or a particular set of such arrangements. That boundary may well vary by place and over time, to reflect the significant differences among the economies and societies in which the unchanging defining principles of greed are to be applied. However, in a particular situation the border itself is fixed. It is greedy to try to get around this limit by "juicing up" returns through the use of leverage. It is much like the small child who, having reached the limit of allowed chocolates, decides that it is now fine to gorge on ice cream. It is subjectively greedy to take advantage of the possibility of such possibilities.

With so much greed involved, it is not surprising that the social effects of financial lending and leverage are often unjust. For example, the financial investors in highly leveraged companies often gain mightily, while the workers typically struggle.

Three conclusions

I hope that the list of greedy financial practices is long enough to show how vulnerable financial arrangements are to the distortions which greed creates. Before turning to more specific examples of financial greed, I have three summary comments.

First, in contemporary economies, financial greed is widespread. An arrangement is greedy if it is greedy according to any of the three standards, and many commonly accepted financial practices are indeed greedy by one or more of them.

- Subjectively, when financial activity requires little or no sacrifice or effort from an investor, it is greedy for that investor to demand more than minimal returns. Since many investors today are rich enough to invest without much sacrifice or effort, greed certainly seems to be present.

- Objectively, the money of financial investors is rarely either very scarce or hugely important for the success of economic ventures, so it is greedy to demand financial returns which suggest more than a modest contribution from the provision of this money. The desired returns of some debt investors may not be objectively greedy, but few if any equity investors make appropriately modest demands.

- Also objectively, finance is often not the best method for solving no-money-now problems, so the insistence on using finance when better methods are available is greedy. Many of the manifestations of financialisation involve exactly such an insistence.

- Socially, post-aristocratic finance is structurally greedy by one prevalent ethical standard, and many financial arrangements have post-aristocratic elements.

Second, the evidence of widespread financial greed is hard to miss. Neither a refined moral sensibility nor detailed technical knowledge is required to see that greed permeates many common financial arrangements. Indeed, I am confident that anyone applying the sort of moral approach that is regularly used to identify and restrain greedy behaviour in the middle section of the Triptych would come to much the same conclusions that I have.

- Anyone not used to the financial world is likely to feel there is something morally "off" about wanting to "get rich while sleeping".

- Anyone with more than the most meagre social conscience is likely to feel uneasy about a system that helps the rich get richer without any significant effort on their part and often at the expense of the poor.

The third comment follows from the first two. Morality-free finance seems to be, or to have become, completely acceptable. Financial arrangements are treated by most people involved in them as if some of the normal rules of good and fair conduct do not apply. Following the standards endorsed by the whole society, they unquestioningly accept behaviour that would be condemned as blatantly greedy in their labour or consumption. Even taxes are usually approached with less greed than stock market investing or "getting on the housing ladder". This enthusiastic social acceptance is the subject of the next section.

11. Greed in finance: social acceptance

The extent of social acceptance of financial greed is striking. In Chapter One, I mentioned the inability to integrate anti-greed policies into the financial reforms enacted after the 2008 global financial crisis. That is an extreme example of an almost universal response. Obviously greedy desires are commonly ignored, supported, or excused. More subtle manifestations of greed escape moral analysis entirely. Even when critics of financial arrangements do attack greed, their rhetoric is rarely connected to coherent analysis or concrete proposals. Outside of anarchist and other culturally revolutionary circles, criticism of normal financial practices and expectations as greedy are almost never heard. Almost no one complains about the spread of greed-friendly "financial literacy" and the even more greed-friendly theory of finance.

I can only speculate on the reasons for this tolerance. It may have something to do with some of the many symbolic meanings of money discussed in Chapter Two, or with the symbolic meanings of finance discussed in Chapter Three. It may be related to the prevalence of the ideology of unenlightened self-interest which is used to defend the goodness of greed. It may be a historical legacy, a residue of the traditional condemnation of finance as inherently greedy, but with the condemnation part left out. Marxists can make a case for the not always conscious manipulation of public opinion by the financial elite. The many widespread intellectual confusions that surround the nature of money and finance undoubtedly play a role, but they seem to be as much effect as cause of the tolerance of greed.

Whatever the reasons, the problem is widespread. Here I bring together some mostly already mentioned examples of widely tolerated or rewarded financial greed.

House prices

The integration of housing into the Great Exchange will always be challenging. A large sum of token-money is needed to construct any sort of housing in the first place, followed by relatively small sums to keep existing housing in good condition. In a reality-close system, there would be a close connection between the token-money that people actually pay for their own housing (whether as a single sum, a supposedly limited series of mortgage payments, or a supposedly unlimited series of rental payments) and the actual token-money paid to provide the good of housing to all the people within some housing-community (a neighbourhood, region, or nation, or even the entire world). In current practice, however, only a small proportion of the actual flow of money from housing consumers – payments to former owners, banks, landlords, and builders – is unequivocally dedicated to maintenance and new construction. It would also be reality-close to make a clear distinction between the savings-money used to pay for land and the token-money used to pay for the labour of building and maintaining housing. That division almost never occurs outside of economists' models.

In short, the housing money-system is reality-distant. Such reality-distance is almost as sure an invitation to greed as leaving crumbs on the floor is an invitation to mice. And the greed-mice have indeed made themselves at home in the monetary economy of housing. Some governments and employers sometimes provide housing with reasonably reality-close flows of money, but residences are often and increasingly treated as money-things. Owners and non-owners alike expect the savings-money value of housing to increase. Potential owners often use financial leverage to become owners and actual owners add financial leverage in the hope of increasing their own gains from any increase in the price of the housing money-things that they own. They can barely comprehend the possibility that the financial returns of landlords and the quasi-financial returns of owners might be excessive.

This standard housing-finance is inherently greedy: often subjectively, almost always objectively, and almost certainly socially. If greed were considered an evil to be countered, something would be done to ensure that housing-related greed was thwarted as much as possible. Instead, restrictions on mortgage lending, the source of financial leverage, are minimal, and taxes on capital gains from housing, the manifestation of quasi-financial gains, are almost always modest. The results of this social and regulatory indifference are what would be expected from my moral analysis of greed and the nature of prices in the left section of the Triptych. There are numerous housing-price booms, generally followed by busts. Even when there are no booms, the price of land often increases over time, and potential owners of housing almost always greedily expect these ill-gotten gains.

I am often struck by the social acceptability of housing greed in developed economies. Only when price changes are very turbulent is there any criticism of housing-market greed, and moral condemnations seem to be forgotten rapidly. Few social commentators note the social greed that is deeply embedded in the desire for rising housing prices. At most, some attention is paid to one effect of satisfying that greed, the gap in social authority and savings-money between owners and renters. House-price chatter in rich countries almost never rises to being an ethical debate. Even people who think of themselves as anti-capitalist will often talk fervently about buying and selling at advantageous prices.

The stock market

Companies play a major role in the modern economy and their legal, corporate form is almost always based on the financial concept of equity shares. As late as the end of the 19th century, the price of these shares rarely diverged greatly from the "book value", the accountants' calculation of the current value of the corporation's machines, land, inventories, and other material objects, adjusted for monetary and financial claims and obligations. At most, the share price might include a fairly modest adjustment for the fairly narrowly defined "goodwill" of customers. Few companies had shares which were traded freely. Many owners of both traded and untraded shares were presumably greedy, but there were relatively few equity-related opportunities for their greed to flourish.

Now, however, there are numerous opportunities. Investors who freely and rapidly buy and sell shares own a substantial portion of all equity, share prices rise and fall quickly, and a very broadly defined goodwill usually accounts for a major portion of the share price. Few shareholders take more than a cursory interest in the actual operations of companies. These financial investors are largely motivated by savings-money hopes, that all share prices will rise and that the prices of the shares they currently own will rise more than most. The interest in stock market gains has become a topic of such common interest that changes in the "market indexes" which standardise a collection of share prices are regularly reported as significant news. The reports never suggest that there is anything greedy about the holder of a money-thing wishing for its potential sale price to increase without having done anything to merit this return.

The equity owners' combination of gambling and hope amounts to an intoxicated mix of subjective, objective, and social greed. In the passion for higher share prices, the social nature of companies and their array of economic purposes are generally forgotten entirely. A rising share price is simply considered a good thing. It does not matter whether the increase reflects the company's increased contributions to the common good, gains for shareholders at the expense of other, quite possibly more deserving groups, or an increased reality-distance in the savings-money price of the money-thing. In my experience, both professional and amateur stock market investors typically meet the claim that this lack of discrimination is subjectively and socially greedy with incomprehension. Even people who describe themselves as socialists or social democrats often treat the stock market as a largely morality-free zone.

Total returns for investment portfolios

With the help of some doubtful financial theory (to be discussed in the Appendix), the rough greed of wanting "the stock market to go up" and rejoicing when "the value of my portfolio has increased" has been refined into a complex collection of measurements. Financial investors, many of whom are better described as speculators, attentively compare the "performance" of particular investments, portfolios (groups of investments), or financial price indexes over many different chosen periods. The calculations of performance require many careful decisions about how to count what. Difficulties include reconciling investments denominated in different currencies, combining price changes for often dissimilar money-things, denominated in savings-money, with token-money payments of interest and dividends, comparing performance over different time periods and adjusting for flows of money in and out of portfolios. When actual portfolios are compared with hypothetical "paper" portfolios, there are problems calculating the full costs of hypothetical sales and purchases and adjusting for the expenses of managing the actual portfolio. If that were not enough, all of the performance data is often "adjusted for risk", which actually involves a series of arbitrary adjustments based on tendentious calculations of the past volatility and correlations of the prices of the various money-things in a particular portfolio.

The work involved is meticulous and extensive. However, if greed were not distorting the judgements of investment professionals, the pointlessness of such measures would be obvious. First, they are pointless because they rely on artificial and falsifying temporal assumptions. In particular, the measurements of current prices of money-things that are not currently being sold have no particular bearing on the actual savings-money and potential token-money that will be received when the sale takes place. Second, they are pointless because actual token-money-numbers are not really comparable with semi-fictional savings-money-numbers. Third, they are pointless because adjustments for something that might be called risk are necessary to compare results honestly, but the actual riskiness can only be determined in retrospect. Fourth, they are pointless because they have no predictive value, since both "the markets" and "the managers" always change in unpredictable ways. Fifth, they are pointless because monetary precision is always a false hope. There is no economic meaning in the precise calculations of total returns to a tenth of a percent.

Since greed does distort judgements, the widespread blindness to the pointlessness should not be surprising. I have already mentioned the primary moral disorder in investment management, the refusal to question whether looking for "good" performance is actually good or is actually greedy by one or more of the three standards. The search for relative performance, that is better performance than peers or than some paper portfolio over some arbitrary period, adds a hint of desperation to any investor greed. Not only does the investor probably want to gain higher returns than she deserves – usually subjectively, objectively, and socially – but she wants to gain higher returns than her equally greedy peers in a process which is, over time, largely random. The secondary greedy disorder is the desire for numbers that do not exist – refined calculations to see who has really won this or that financial race to perform best and by exactly how much, and also adjusted for risk. Like the sophisticated gamblers on horses who consider track conditions and equine health reports, professional investment managers surround their primal greed with something like science.

Among a select group of afficionados, the scientifically refined greed receives at least as much social approval as the crude greed of less sophisticated stock market "players". The provision of performance measurement has become a fairly significant industry, employing skilled professionals at dedicated consulting firms and making use of extensive and expensive databases. Almost never do these professionals look up from their spreadsheets and reports long enough to worry that they might be supporting structures of greed.

The promotion of debt

I discussed the many ways in which debt is more reality-distant than equity in Chapter Four, where I also discussed the overwhelmingly negative economic and social role of financial leverage in the left section of the Triptych and of corporate leverage in the central section. At various points, I have suggested that domestic government debt is almost always inferior to either taxes or the direct creation of money and that foreign (cross-border) government debt is more often than not a bad idea politically and economically. I have also discussed the greed expressed in agreed interest rates that are too high to be economically realistic. The implication of these arguments is simple and strong – debt tends to be greedy as well as economically unhelpful.

If greed were not distorting the judgements of the economists, politicians, and regulators concerned with the economic helpfulness of finance, the relevant rules would be set to discourage the use of debt. There could be fees, limits, changes in the management of the money-supply, new roles for banks and central monetary authorities, and anti-debt education. At the very least, anyone whose vision was not confused by greed would be anxious to eliminate any rules which *favour* debt over equity or over alternative solutions to no-money-now problems.

In reality, though, the political-intellectual distortion-field of greed is remarkably powerful. In most jurisdictions, corporate and financial leverage are strongly encouraged by the tax deductibility of interest payments. Bank regulators effectively favour increased lending by almost never considering the relationship of lending to actual economic activity. Legislators force governments to use loans to cover fiscal deficits, while central monetary authorities work almost entirely with debts, so that their monetary policy is biased in favour of increasing the issuance of debts.

Venture capital and leveraged buy-outs

I suggested in the last section that the economy is so much a common effort and money is so readily available that it is objectively greedy to demand high returns for simply providing money to solve the no-money-now problems of almost all companies. The tolerance of legal structures and economic customs that allow people who do no more than that to satisfy some extraordinarily greedy desires is a sign of the social tolerance, not to say encouragement, of objective greed. Two types of such greed-oriented structures are currently widespread. Unsurprisingly, both have become significant only during the recent period of financialisation, financial dis-economising, and increasing tolerance for financial greed. Both provide a pretext for money-providers, along with a few insiders, to claim that their extractions make economic as well as legal sense.

The first are venture capital firms, organisations which buy shares in new companies. Along with token-money, they often provide valuable economic services such as accounting expertise, contacts with experienced managers, and strategic advice. However, even taking these para-monetary contributions into account, their typical expectations of returns generally seem unjustly high. Venture capitalists often develop complex financial structures to increase their rewards if the companies they provide money for are successful, while using the tax system to minimise their effective losses if the companies do badly. They promise potential senior executives their own vast rewards to lure them from existing companies that would often be more economically sensible providers of money and expertise for new ventures. To a significant extent, the much praised "start-up culture" of Silicon Valley and other "hotbeds of innovation" represents a largely successful effort to introduce unnecessarily large and necessarily greedy financial arrangements into parts of the middle section of the Triptych.

Far from being described as greedy, or even as unnecessarily greedy, venture capital is commonly lauded, especially in the United States, as a source of cherished "entrepreneurial" energy. Only extreme anti-capitalists have the temerity to suggest that larger existing enterprises, universities, and government agencies could provide the same innovations with equal, if perhaps somewhat different, excellence and with far less money going to financial investors. The greed is always tolerated and sometimes encouraged, following one of the arguments that greed is good (listed in the third section of this chapter). Most often, it seems not even to be noticed. Gargantuan returns for successful venture capital investors and at worst modest losses for unsuccessful rivals are simply accepted as the way of the world, without any ethical debate.

The second greed-supporting structure is known as leveraged buy-outs or, rather misleadingly, as private equity (it is "private" in a special financial sense, but its basic strategy is to replace equity with debt). These firms typically buy all the shares of existing companies, paying mostly with borrowed savings-money. Once taken over, the strategies of the investee companies are usually changed to increase immediate profits, frequently at the expense of durable excellence. The debts that now surround the company – most of the money borrowed by the new owners is turned into debts of the purchased company itself – put particular pressure on the enterprises whenever revenues decline or mistakes are made. The new owners also generally extract high fees and dividends, further reducing the money available for workers and increasing prices for customers.

It is hard even to imagine a corporate monetary arrangement which would offer less economic good and support more types of greed than leveraged buyouts. Governments lose from the exemption of debt from taxes, while workers, customers, communities, and the future lose from the short-term pressure for profits. Almost always, these profits serve largely to satisfy the greedy desires of the small groups of already rich people who impose post-aristocratic finance on a supine community. Their greed is often criticised, but it is also tolerated. Efforts to make even the most modest reductions in the returns for buyout investors have been defeated by political lobbying based on specious claims of economic contributions.

Speculation and trading

That gambling involves monetary greed is rarely denied. The gambler hopes for exactly the type of unmerited and unjust return which I have defined as greedy, both objectively and subjectively. However, gambling is quite distant from the pure-finance I discussed in Chapter Three, because gambling has nothing to do with solving a no-money-now problem. On the contrary, gambling often creates such problems, when people lose the money that they need to keep up their expected level of consumption.

That some kinds of general-finance are basically gambling, and thus essentially greedy, used to be almost universally accepted. This truth was hard to deny, since until well into the 20th century most of the "players" in stock markets and in the bonds of troubled companies and governments had little information, less technique for estimating true value, and no moral scruples. They were basically "rolling the dice". As might be expected for any variety of gambling, most of the speculators lost money. The "insiders" who promoted bad investments could do well by providing the raw material for the frenzied search for those elusive unmerited returns. Although some of the losers in "the markets" were and are themselves rich, overall, financial speculation then and now favours those with more information, greater savings-money reserves to bear temporary losses, and a great deal of time to spend learning how to outsmart the opposition. In other words, speculation often ends up becoming a somewhat veiled but especially greedy version of post-aristocratic finance.

The desire to "play" again and again is central to the gambling psychology. The small wins encourage more action and the ease of betting again encourages perseverance after losses. In financial markets, the rapid repetition of bets is known as trading and the ease of making new bets is called liquidity. I mentioned in Chapter Four that both trading and liquidity are reality-distant. They are also both gambling-friendly. Again, until well into the 20th century, it was understood that liquidity and rapid trading were occasions for gambling. Many jurisdictions tried to discourage both, by imposing high taxes on the "short-term" gains from trading and by charging high fees for each transaction.

Over the last half-century, such restrictions have almost all fallen away, presumably at least in part because financial gambling, and the greed which motivates it, have become increasingly respectable. The result is that the playing in and management of this economically pointless gambling has become a major part of the professional investment business. This development is exemplified and reinforced by the financial theory I will discuss in the Appendix, by the flourishing of derivatives, foreign exchange markets and other financial securities that are basically designed for gambling, by the vast intellectual efforts dedicated to "beating the market", and by the elaborate theoretical defences of the economic value of financial gambling. Of course, none of this changes the monetary and moral facts. As with any form of gambling, winning is almost impossible without privileged information. However, subjective greed motivates the gamblers to keep trying.

By now, gambling is so deeply set into the operations of financial markets that frequent trading is considered normal, even for professionals who are charged with managing portfolios that will not be "cashed in" (changed from savings-money to token-money) for many years. "Performance" is measured daily. Even "high frequency trading", in which shares are held for small fractions of a second, is referred to as a sort of investment. I suppose that there is a way of seeing something good in the unwillingness to admit either that most "trading" in financial markets amounts to economically pointless "speculation" or that most speculation is in no significant way different from gambling. The denial of reality can be interpreted as a sign that participants in these markets would like to be free from any taint of greed. However, that is extremely modest praise. The social willingness to allow greed to dominate what could be an important system in managing the economy is better interpreted as a sign of a morally disordered social-economic vision.

Uncritical thinking about money-things

It should be obvious that there can be nothing good in the unbridled increase in the prices of any type of money-things. At best, shifts that have little or no relationship with the real economy are likely to create social tensions. At worst, when price changes on unanchored money-things lead to money being pulled across the border between the left and middle sections of the Triptych, there can be significant disruptions in the Central Monetary Ratio – and thus unwanted and unhelpful disruptions of real economic activity.

It should also be obvious that winning competitions for the best "performance" among owners of money-things is a meagre accomplishment of no economic value. The list of reasons is daunting. Technically, the calculations are spurious because the mix of token-money and savings-money creates insurmountable measurement problems. Besides, the starting times and end-points for comparisons are totally arbitrary, but have a major effect on the reported results. Economically, what happens in the world of pieces-of-paper "investing" has almost nothing to do with the pure-finance of providing token-money to solve no-money-now problems. Morally, there is almost never any goodness in winning such a contest, since it is subjectively and objectively greedy to desire gains from merely trading money-things, especially when the traders have neither made any personal sacrifices or provided much token-money to economically worthy investees.

Yet again, it should be obvious that when money-things do not directly create anything in the real economy, as they often do not, increased prices can have no economic value. If the price of land (or of the buildings placed on it) rises, the owner's subjective greed may be assuaged. However, there is nothing to interest students of the real economy, because the price increase in the left section of the Triptych changes nothing in the middle section. It is the same for prices of existing equity shares. It is almost the same when the prices of debt money-things change because of changes in the predominant interest rates. There is only the modest economic effect that comes from interest payments being made in token-money, so their changes can affect the real economy.

Overall, it should be obvious that popular interest in share prices is pointless and that popular interest in interest rates is likely to be confused. Prices of existing shares are only loosely connected to the real economy, and interest rates can only be understood in the context of inflation rates, economic growth, and social tensions. Business news reports should pay almost no attention to the stock market, while investors who outperform other investors should be classed with successful gamblers and magicians, or with crafty practitioners of the dubious arts of persuasion. Their labour certainly does not make them experts on the economy, since almost everything they work with and everything they try to accomplish is at best reality-distant, typically reality-distorting, and at worst reality-damaging.

Yet, none of these obvious truths is widely accepted by most economists, or if they do understand and accept any of them, they are fairly discreet about it. Among the general public, these obvious truths are almost unknown. Rather than think critically about money-things, experts and amateurs often demonstrate an apparently endless fascination with the prices of money-things and the rivalries of leading professional investors. The most successful of these professionals are often described as geniuses and sometimes consulted as economic sages. Their fortunes are widely accepted as merited rewards for their professional excellence. The interest and approval resemble the genial fascination with sporting events and the high rewards provided to the best athletes. However, the financial fiction is different, because it starts with the intellectual distortions created by greed and it is a powerful expression of the socially approved greed that permeates finance.

Corporate governance

It should be obvious that companies are complex human organisations with complex, overlapping, and sometimes contradictory goals and excellences. In the economy, they should support flourishing on both sides of the Great Exchange, providing worthy labour and worthy consumption goods and services. They always have a responsibility to the humanised world and sometimes must do their own humanisation. They operate in at least one society, and they both use and support many physical, psychological, and cultural networks and excellences. They are constructions of the law, both subject to and influencing the political authorities and, in case of crisis, expected to abandon everything to serve some higher or more urgent aspect of the common good.

Indeed, it should be obvious that profit-centred, essentially monetary entities would be high on the list of the things that corporations essentially should *not* be. While token-money is one of the systems that guide these social entities and tie them to the rest of society, token-money is never more than an ethically neutral means to whatever the entity's ethical ends may be. The money flows can and should be adjusted – by changing prices, wages, taxes, and fees – to ensure that, for example, the products are of the right quality or the wages are at the right level. Not only is token-money clearly a poor guide to corporate excellence, but token-money profits, especially in their precisionist incarnation as financial accounting profits, are clearly a poor guide to monetary efficiency. Very high profits may sometimes be just rewards for the shareholders of companies that are serving the common good, but more often they are a sign that something is going wrong in the complex and shifting assignment of money-numbers on the two sides of the Great Exchange. It is literally absurd to imagine that "maximising profits", if such an instantaneous concept can even be applied in a meaningful way to a continuing social entity, could be a helpful guide to decisions within and about companies.

This modest position of profits in the hierarchy of corporate goods is obvious to most workers, customers, and unbiased outsiders. It is reflected in at least some laws and in the folk wisdom of sayings such as "profits can be good servants but are never good masters". Outside of the financial world, almost no one assumes that high profits should be the central goal of all corporations. It is only some shareholders, people whose thinking is likely to be influenced by their unenlightened self-interest in high profits, who routinely, rigorously, and falsely claim that more profits are by definition better than less profits, and that all the other interests in a corporation are always secondary to theirs. Their conviction is often sincere, and always objectively greedy.

The socially tolerated objective greed of shareholders has created an opportunity for the flourishing of straightforward monetary greed among senior corporate executives. They have somehow managed to persuade the boards of directors, which are supposed to control them, that "shareholder value" justifies ridiculously high wages. The logic, needless to say, is faulty by any standard, but when greed is tolerated, minds are distorted and logic is discarded.

Unreformed banks

My final example of the social tolerance of greed is the most subtle, but probably the most damaging to the real economy. Some decades ago, the excuse of ignorance about the nature of banking was taken away from the regulators who set rules for banks and the academic economists who advise them. By now, any informed person should be able to see that the current, greed-friendly structure of banks is totally out of accord with the nature of money and of pure finance.

To fuse the economically vital business of managing payments with the economically important business of creating enough money to keep the middle section of the Triptych working smoothly is bad enough. To add the often speculative business of lending money, especially financial lending, is an invitation to greed. The vital and important roles of banks limit the constraints on lending and encourage governments to protect banks from damage caused by their own greedy excesses in lending.

As discussed in Chapter One, almost every economic downturn for more than a century can be traced to greedy behaviour in banks (using my broad definition of "banks"), and at the core of the banks' malfunctioning are economic structures that cannot help but tolerate greedy lending practices. Detailed regulations are supposed to prevent banks from being reckless, but thousands of pages of rules and thousands of calculations are unlikely to keep hysterical, greed-inspired optimism away forever from every large bank. In any case, it is far simpler to reduce risk and greed by separating businesses and removing banks from money-creation than by regulating lending and trading. The mental distortions created by greed have undoubtedly played a significant role in the maintenance of structures that are both unnecessary and incontrovertibly hazardous.

These varieties of social toleration of financial greed that I have just listed are often mutually reinforcing. For example, individuals are supported in their greedy desires for unmerited returns from owning money-things by observing that regulators encourage or at least do not block banks' greedy search for gains. The toxic circle is closed when banks offer financial leverage to the money-thing owners, both encouraging and developing greed all around. The thick net of accepted greed creates the great financial exception in the list of reasonably stable and responsive contemporary social-economic organisations.

12. Greed in finance: summary

The argument presented in this long chapter has probably been unfamiliar to many readers, since serious moral analysis of contemporary finance is rare. As a conclusion, I thought it might be helpful to restate the argument more succinctly and with some polemical fervour.

The nature of the problem

The problem of monetary greed starts with human nature – greed, like all other disordered desires, is always a temptation for all people. Greed spreads, so it can eventually distort the moral judgements of entire groups, for example of financial investors. For this book, the relevant monetary greed is for the money-things and the savings-money in the left section of the Triptych. Greed comes easily in that reality-distant region, because there are no constraints on the quantity of savings-money that can be created, and thus desired. Financial arrangements add an intertemporal dimension to greed. They extend the excesses of desire into the future, including not only the desire to multiply money but also to be protected from declines in the value of money-things. In sum, finance serves as a sort of fertiliser for greed, transforming the simple moral weed of individual monetary greed into a plant with roots that spread widely, damaging otherwise healthier plants in the economy and society.

My argument in this chapter is that the crux of the problem of financial greed is not the greed itself, which cannot be eradicated, but the morally flaccid social response to it. For non-financial greed, the overall social response is the equivalent of a fairly effective pesticide. Parents chastise greedy children, students and workers shun and mock greedy peers, potential lovers are repelled by displays of greed, greedy politicians are despised, and so forth. In the economy, laws, rules, and customs generally restrain the greed of landlords, bosses, corporations, unions, and pretty much everyone who has the power to grab more than her, his, or its fair share. At best, economic greed is tolerated as a necessary evil, or overlooked as long as it does not obviously harm other people. Even then, greedy executives, workers, and consumers, like greedy children, lovers, and politicians, at least half-know that their behaviour could get them into trouble, and they might even quarter-know that if that happens, they will rightly be judged harshly by a greed-hostile society. It is not like that for financial greed. Far from it. This greed is pervasive, promoted, and pernicious.

Pervasive

Financial greed is so pervasive that it often escapes notice. Only the greed of workers in financial institutions has come under much public scrutiny, and that scrutiny has been intermittent and incoherent. The moral rot is certainly not limited to the flamboyant bankers I will discuss in the next section.

Rather, financial greed is present whenever and wherever financial investors wish for returns which are subjectively, objectively, or socially greedy. These greedy demands are found in most financial arrangements in prosperous economies and in virtually all of them when the investors are already economically privileged. They are built into the organisation and terms of all sorts of money-things – debt and equity, land and commodities, derivatives and speculation, bank accounts and collectibles, publicly traded and privately held investments, liquid and illiquid ones.

Greed oozes out of finance into corporate life whenever and wherever the managers of companies try to grant the greedy wishes of shareholders, and whenever and wherever the writers of tax codes magnify or merely fail to expropriate greed-tainted returns. This financial greed pushes directly against the overall good of the communities in which the companies operate, including the good of the company's own employees and customers. Financial greed is deeply embedded in almost all companies quoted on stock exchanges and in many which are not.

Greed sets the moral tone whenever and wherever the basic human good and necessity of shelter is turned into a money-thing, a property which the owner expects to increase in money-value simply because it is there. The housing greed is so great and so widespread that in many jurisdictions greedy worries about "property values" limit the construction of new housing and set owners against each other and especially against non-owners. The housing greed is so great that the sensible and just idea of taxing away all "unearned" returns on land – the expression used by followers of the 19th century economist Henry George to describe what I am calling objective greed – has received little attention.

Just as financial greed distorts the basic human good of shelter, it can distort the basic human relationship of children to their parents, or of a society to their older members. Greed poisons this last type of love and duty whenever and wherever financial returns are used to help determine the income of the elderly. The old who depend directly on the goodwill of their children or of the next generation as a whole are likely to be rewarded for their generosity and service to their children while they were growing up. The old people who depend on distributions from pension funds are rewarded for favouring their own financial returns at the expense of the younger people who provide them. Financial greed converts the responsibility of the young to the old from a source of intergenerational unity into a wedge of division.

Financial greed has been around since the beginning of finance, but in recent years it has become more pervasive. Over the last half-century, more companies have been more guided by "shareholder value", which converts companies from servants of the common good to servants of financial greed. More attention has been paid to financial theory, which could have been developed to justify the greedy desires of everyday investors and the even greedier desires of speculators and promoters of private equity.

More recently, the floods of new savings-money created by central monetary authorities after the 2008-9 financial crisis and 2020 anti-Covid-19 economic restrictions have stimulated additional greed throughout the left section of the Triptych. As the supply of savings-money increased, the price of money-things rose while the cost of obtaining savings-money, the interest rate of government debt, fell to zero or even a little less. Neither the price increases nor the yield declines reduced greed. On the contrary, they inspired a frenzied search for higher yields in riskier financial arrangements.

Promoted

Perhaps the strangest thing about financial greed is the enthusiasm which surrounds it. This positive response to moral disorder is very unusual. It is common for bad behaviour to be condemned in principle but tolerated in practice. The abuse of drugs and alcohol and the use of prostitutes have typically been ensconced in this sort of moral-social ambiguity. It is also fairly common for vices to be condemned in principle and practice, but not very effectively. All sorts of concupiscence – lust and gluttony as well as greed – are generally not accepted and very grudgingly tolerated in limited quantities. Then there are emotions and desires which are recognised as wrong but very hard to control. Anger and jealousy fit into this category. They are often discouraged or channelled into controlled directions and rituals, but they are not expected to disappear.

Financial greed is different, in our economies and societies. Behaviour that is clearly greedy is considered normal, even praiseworthy. Good citizens routinely recommend education in "financial literacy" which includes injunctions to try to get as high returns as possible on financial investments. "Private bankers" fall over themselves to promise higher returns to the people whose existing wealth makes such returns the most subjectively greedy. Successful investment managers are warmly praised and richly rewarded for satisfying their customers' greed. "Financial engineering" is often criticised for adding needless complexity or structural weakness to the financial system, but rarely for its prime purpose – satisfying the greed of financial investors. Professional investors are trained to look for higher returns without any attention to the economic effect of their choices. In other words, they are trained to satisfy objective greed. Senior corporate executives justify their greedy pay settlements by referring to their responsibility for satisfying the greed of equity investors.

It is fair to say that greed is promoted throughout the financial system. Almost never do either investors or investees receive messages from professional advisors, personal teachers, or political authorities encouraging moderation or reminding them of the importance of any sort of social justice or personal virtue. On the contrary, it is assumed and expected that they will play by the rules of the game, which always call for them to crave more, without any attention to the moral order. They are sometimes even legally or professionally required to follow the counsels of excess. For example, corporate directors and managers are not allowed to suggest that shareholders should want less. A professional financial advisor whose goals included protecting the client from their greedy desires would be fired for gross misconduct.

Charitable organisations that strive for moral excellence in their principal endeavours often endorse financial greed when it comes to the performance of their endowment funds. It has become fashionable for such virtue-oriented groups to instruct portfolio managers to filter investments on ethical grounds. Trustees do not wish to be associated with the gains from causing global warming or taking money from gamblers. However, the portfolio managers are almost never told to avoid greedy financial gambling in their own portfolios, or to lobby companies to reduce their greedy profit margins, because the current level only supports the shareholders' greed. It is almost the reverse. The managers of charity funds are told to search for as high returns as possible from the investments which their consciences allow.

This promotion of greed is quite active, but there is also more passive encouragement, in the normalisation and absence of criticism of greedy desires and behaviour. This passive promotion has become stronger in recent decades. Ideal-banks have declined so much that the most viable model of non-greedy financial arrangements has almost disappeared (with some notable exceptions in Germany). The end of usury laws has removed one of the few critical standards which blocked or shamed greedy behaviour.

Pernicious

The acceptance of greed has encouraged the creation and perpetuation of a structurally unjust, economically unhelpful, and inherently unstable financial system.

The financial greed which blinds financial investors to moral and social responsibilities is certainly not the only cause of undesired (at least rhetorically) income inequality and morally insensitive economic and social arrangements, but it is an aggravating factor. Resentment against the privileges of the prosperous has contributed to the recent rise of popular political discontent. Financial greed, especially when combined with post-aristocratic finance, certainly increases those privileges.

Most significantly, financial greed is the principal source of the financial exception. The greed itself leads to unsustainable excesses, and the distorting effects of that greed on people's thinking prevents reforms that would make finance more stable. Thanks to financial greed, the financial system is unnecessarily large, companies and banks are unnecessarily fragile, the balance of token-money and savings-money is unnecessarily fluid, and financial demands are unnecessarily large and rigid. The financial system's reality-distance is tolerated largely because it is fertile ground for greedy speculative behaviour.

The evil effects of the flourishing of financial greed over the last few decades have spread quite widely. Corporate leaders often say that they avoid investments that do not promise a high enough return, but greedy financial thinking often leads them to set a standard of "high enough" that harms the overall economic common good. Housing greed has not only created booms and busts, it has left many people unable to afford to move, whether to a new city that offers better economic prospects or simply out of their parents' home. The blindness to the moral danger of finance has probably encouraged the inappropriate use of financial arrangements to avoid dealing directly with politically sensitive problems. Pensions, payday loans, student loans, and much housing finance come to mind.

Perhaps the greatest danger caused by the increased normalisation of financial greed is its spread throughout the economy. The long-established consensus that economic greed should not be welcomed seems to be fraying. Of course, the direction of causality in this dire trend is uncertain. Finance may just have been the first sector in which a new, less moral approach to all sorts of economic greed was able to gain acceptance. As the most susceptible part of the economy to greed, it would naturally have the weakest resistance to this rising new idea. Still, whether financial greed is itself the disease or just a symptom of one, its spread is socially unwelcome.

Curable

The current moral blindness about financial greed is neither inevitable nor ineradicable. While the battles against economic greed are never over – fights against sin never are – the battle over finance is especially important. It is the least tamed frontier in the struggle to moralise the economy, or perhaps now it is the vanguard of the campaign to legitimise economic greed. Either way, defenders of untrammelled financial greed among investors, speculators, and home-owners are wrong to claim that this disordered desire is a prerequisite for a flourishing economy. They are equally wrong to claim that financial relations cannot avoid encouraging greed. There is a better way. More precisely, there are many better ways, some of which I have already hinted at. The details, though, are less important than the principle: financial greed is worth fighting against. We cannot know how well that battle will go, because we have not yet accepted the need to fight.

A six-point summary of my argument

Before closing, it might be helpful to summarise the key points of this book.

1. My analysis is based on what I call the Triptych. Its three sections show the relationship of the various things called money to the economy: in the right is the economy without money, in the middle the economy with money, and on the left money outside of the economy. The money in the left section is savings-money, while the money in the middle is token-money. In this picture, money-things are either entirely or largely in the left section.

2. Token-money is a very useful tool for organising the economy, which *is* the Great Exchange of labour and consumption within the humanised world. Money works as the Exchange works, paying people for their labour and allowing people to pay for their consumption. The numbers attached to money are the key to its success, as they allow labour to be divided, combined, and congealed in specific prices.

3. Money is *not* a lot of things that people have thought it is. It is not necessarily dehumanising or antisocial. It is not backed by the value of some commodity. Money-numbers do not indicate anything very significant about "values", whether absolute or relative, genuine or social. Money is not really a store of value. Most important for understanding finance, token-money does not represent intertemporal debts.

4. Financial arrangements are only one of several possible solutions to no-money-now problems. In economic terms, the intertemporal commitments of finance and the reliance on money-things in the left section of the Triptych are not attractive features. From that perspective, solutions such as taxation and "yoking" are often superior to finance. Also, post-aristocratic finance, which transfers token-money from many relatively poor people to a much smaller number of relatively rich people, is very common but hard to justify in hypothetically egalitarian societies.

5. Many financial arrangements are reality-distant. Their money flows do not correspond well with other monetary action in the economy or with any clear relationship of economic cause and effect. The reality-distance leaves the financial system vulnerable to economic and non-economic disruptions. In particular, reality-distant finance both encourages and is encouraged by greed.

6. Greed in the financial system is pervasive, promoted, and pernicious. The social tolerance for greed is much greater in finance than in other parts of the economy. Greed is not only widely accepted in the financial system, but much of that system is designed to encourage or satisfy greedy expectations.

Overall, then, the money system now works pretty well, although it would work much better with direct governmental money creation. There is, though, a serious problem of people taking money and money-numbers too seriously. In contrast, finance is in severe need of a major rethink.

The future: In the Preface, I briefly mentioned the past existence of a sixth chapter that presented my own monetary and financial rethinking in some detail. The chapter has been omitted, largely to avoid my being dismissed as a financial fantasist. The thrust of the proposed changes, though, would come as no surprise to readers of this chapter. To end the financial exception, the monetary system needs to be detached from the financial system and the latter needs new rules, organisations, and practices.

However, my principal recommendation is not technical. In line with the title of this chapter and with the economic paradigm that I am presenting, it is moral. No combination of technical changes, no matter how profound, will keep financial collapses away, unless the changes reflect and fortify a firm social and shared personal intention to renounce and reject greed in finance. The financial injustices and crises will continue until and unless there is a critical mass of people – among homeowners, bankers, financial investors, politicians, economists, philosophers, parents raising children, executives planning for retirement, teachers, and every other group in society – who seriously intend both not to be greedy themselves and not to approve of other people's greed. I am not asking for perfection of character, just for the removal of the special moral – really immoral – status that finance has too long enjoyed in the hearts, minds, and rules of modern societies. As and when that change of moral mood begins, a good debate on exactly how to create greed-resistant finance will inevitably follow. Perhaps then my proposals for a new financial order would or will seem obvious and even realistic.

Appendix

In this main text of this book, I have tried to avoid discussions of matters that are more complicated than they are interesting, that is interesting to readers who have little or no experience of how today's financial institutions actually work in practice and who have had the good fortune not to be exposed to financial theory. For them, discussions of the detailed workings and justifications of the current financial system would only be an unhelpful distraction. However, I recognise some readers might have the relevant experience and bad luck. They might find an ethical approach to these matters interesting and not too complicated. The appendix is aimed at this more immersed audience, although I do try to explain the specialised vocabulary well enough that curious neophytes will have some idea of what is going on.

Banks

As an introductory note, it is perhaps worth repeating that I am using "bank" to describe all institutions that do business in money, general-finance, or both. I focus on the different businesses, which are fairly constant, rather than on the institutional boundaries, which shift. Indeed, the current structure of lending-and-deposit banks is basically a historical accident. There is no economic reason to put the data processing business of managing money-flows in the same organisation as money creation, hoarding savings-money, registering the ownership of money-things, and anything to do with financial investing. On the contrary, without greed-induced distortions of thinking, it would be clear that the economy would be well served by a fairly strict separation of token-money flow-management from everything else that banks do, and that there would be strong arguments for further separations of businesses.

In theory, banks do not have to be stained with greed. The organisational cultures and the workers could be like those of most other businesses in the generally greed-hostile economy. They could focus on efficient operations and look for only reasonable profits and fair wages. Banks perhaps could be like that, but outside of the remains of ideal banking they not. Most banks and banking businesses are deeply stained with greed.

Before going into details, a social comment might be helpful. In my judgement, while banking greed is ample, extensive, and deeply set into institutional cultures, it is far more an effect than a cause of the general flourishing of financial greed. Greed only prospers in banks, their employees, and most of their businesses because, and as long as, their customers encourage them and the broader society does not discourage them. Certainly, like drug-dealers, these greed-dealers also encourage their customers and attempt to influence social values. The mutual amplification should not, though, be used to exculpate everyone else. Blame-shifting is all too easy, to judge by the ease with which customers complain about the greedily high costs of their greed-seeking transactions. Partly to discourage that practice (as well as to signal the more technical nature of this discussion), I have relegated banks' institutional greed to this appendix.

I start with the banking business which is economically the most important, the *management of money-flows* around the central section of the Triptych. Banks help with most physical monetary transactions and ensure the accurate recording of almost all electronic ones. (In many jurisdictions, central monetary authorities are currently planning to take on some of this responsibility.) At the level of operations, the money-moving business is essentially greed-free. Bank tellers, call centre operators, and the vast army of technology specialists are not particularly highly paid, relative to other people with jobs requiring similar skills and trustworthiness. In most of the world (the United States is a partial exception), banks have moved fairly swiftly to use more efficient technology as it became available, even when the newer arrangements brought lower potential profits (from declining "floats") along with lower costs.

Above the most technical level, however, greed permeates this business. Reality-distant pricing is used to extract high profits. In most countries, banks routinely offer misleading and greed-filled encouragement to the customers of their money-moving business to borrow money, generally at greedy interest rates. More subtly, greed leads to the refusal to think of and price the management of money-flows as a universal public service.

Next comes the responsibility for *creating new money through bank lending*. I said in Chapter Five that a truly non-greedy approach to money-creation would take the responsibility away from banks and separate it entirely from debt, removing all possibility of monetary greed. Staying within the bounds of the current system, a non-greedy approach to banks' money creation would ensure that new money is created exclusively to solve pure-finance no-money-now problems, focussing on solutions that serve the common good. Currently, however, pure-finance accounts for a relatively modest proportion of banks' money-creation, and the common good almost never enters into bankers' thought processes. Instead, they look for the widest possible "spreads", the gap between the interest rates received on loans and that paid on deposits. (From a systemic perspective, lending creates and precedes funding both temporally and conceptually, but the two are close to simultaneous from the perspective of individual institutions.) The effort to create as wide an interest-rate wedge as possible within the economy is objectively and socially greedy, and one principal result of this effort, a predominance of loans used to create or increase financial leverage, is objectively greedy.

More comprehensively, the *typical orientation of conventional deposit-and-lend banks* is greedy. Banks encourage companies to prefer debt to equity. They encourage consumers to borrow money. They lobby governments to maintain tax laws that favour debt and to discourage laws that favour or even protect less greedy ideal-finance operations. They generously reward employees who help "grow the revenue line", without any attention to the common good produced by any additional revenue. They avoid clear disclosure of their prices and they embrace misleading advertising. In the "financial management" of their own operations, they use as much financial leverage as they can get away with, even though the choice to rely on relatively small quantities of equity leaves their economically vital money-transfer business more vulnerable to serious damage from mistakes in their lending businesses. The prime motivation for all of this is subjective and objective greed – of shareholders, senior executives, and loan officers. Still, as individuals, the overwhelming majority of the people involved in lending-and-deposit banking are not especially greedy, at least not by the standard of the other banking businesses that I am about to describe. There are a few exceptionally well-paid loan-generators, but most people in these businesses work with only modestly more greed than bureaucrats in other businesses.

The *creation of new financial arrangements* (underwriting) is a business riddled with greed. The bankers involved are often paid at levels that are almost inevitably greedy, both subjectively and objectively. The prices of newly created shares are set to balance the greed of the individual or corporate investees, who wish to garner as much money as possible, with the greed of investors, who wish for as large and as fast an increase in the share price as possible. The bankers involved in the transaction try to satisfy both sides by turning the new shares into a desired luxury good, so that investors will forget whatever vestigial notions of value-for-savings-money they might have. To this end, offerings of shares are surrounded by advertising, slick presentations, and absurdly optimistic predictions from analysts who claim to be objective but who are basically paid to think positively. The bankers and the analysts expect rich rewards for their persuasive abilities. Their objective greed is unquestionable, since their objective contribution is limited to selling, work that is at best distantly supportive of investees' actual provision of employment and production.

Some bankers help *rearrange the economic and financial structures of existing companies*. They help with mergers, acquisitions, divestments, and exchanging debt for equity or equity for debt. Not all of this work is directly or primarily financial, but much of it involves changes in financial arrangements, so banks of some sort are typically closely involved. Some of the non-financial portion of this work helps the economy operate more efficiently, so it has some objective value, although doubts can be raised about the actual contribution of the resulting gains in economic efficiency, in general or in particular cases, to the common good. There can be few doubts about the lack of good of much financial rearranging: there is none. Savings-money shifts that aim only to increase profits of one group of financial investors at the expense of some other group have no or negative economic effects.

For the banks and bankers involved in these rearrangements, however, neither the total economic good nor the gains and losses of different financial investors is usually a great concern. What matters most is simply "selling the deal". If a company, or more precisely its managers and key shareholders and directors, can be persuaded to engage in a transaction that brings revenues to the arranging bank, then that bank almost definitionally perceives the transaction as good. The subjective greed in this business is tremendous. Bankers and banks take huge fees, as much as they can persuade clients to pay. The degree of objective greed is harder to determine, but it is often substantial, considering how little economic good most largely financial transactions create, and how adding financial leverage to companies, one the main effects of "deals" for almost half a century, is never good for the economy.

Stock exchanges were once imposing buildings in which a great deal of greedy trading and speculation was mixed with a very modest amount of pure-finance. Over the last half-century, there have been great changes in both the physical and institutional arrangements. The rise of computers and telecommunications has eliminated the need for buildings to trade in. The rise of yoking and venture capital as solutions to no-money-now problems have reduced the exchanges' contribution to pure-finance, while the rise of equity derivatives has both reduced the relative importance of trading "on" the now largely virtual stock exchanges and created new trading opportunities for banks. The cost of each transaction, both on and off the exchanges, has fallen significantly, but an increase in the quantity of trades has at least compensated for that decline in most countries (although the measurement techniques are subject to some dispute). In these transactions, banks sometimes merely find counterparties for their clients. Sometimes the banks, generally represented by very highly paid employees, trade with or against their clients.

Amidst all this change, one thing has remained constant: the greedy orientation of the banks and almost all the people directly involved in the business of trading. For the banks, the basic goal is always to increase buying and selling while keeping fees, commissions, and "spreads" as large as possible. The greed is objective, since the trading that is encouraged has at best infinitesimal net positive economic value. (The claimed, and dubious, positives of "price discovery" and "liquidity", have to be set against the clear and substantial costs of maintaining trading systems.) Subjective greed is also prevalent, since the incomes of many of the people involved is often too large not to qualify. Particularly in the United States, the business of "selling hope" to stock market gamblers (the phrase was first applied to cosmetics) gives many people the opportunity to satisfy some of their own greedy desires by exciting and modulating the greedy desires of their clients.

The *banks that create derivative securities* are well aware of the varieties of greed that motivate different buyers and sellers. These banks design derivative "products" that appeal to their clients' particular moral weaknesses and intellectual confusions. For example, unsophisticated clients are sold complicated products that supposedly limit the risk of loss or magnify gains, or simply products that allow easy trading. Sophisticated clients are sometimes flattered with products that usually provide steady small gains, often at the expense of the unsophisticated clients who are taking the other side of the bet. Sometimes the sophisticated clients are lured into complex derivatives that are supposed to help balance their portfolios or introduced into trading strategies that are supposed to be almost failproof.

In most cases, the bank creating the product is the only sure winner. Product designers can usually ensure that the clients bear all the risks that come with the derivatives' participation in the temporal-ontological asymmetry of finance. The bank's profitability can usually be built into any new development. However, banks do not always follow the strict injunction given to drug-dealers: don't mess with the intoxicating substance. During the 2008 financial crisis, several banks suffered huge losses because they gambled instead of keeping to the safely profitable, and hugely greedy, role of the "house" in the casino or the arranger or fixer in other types of gambling.

The markets for stock markets and derivatives are large and relatively well-known parts of the *trading system for money-things*. There are many others that are less familiar to non-specialists. I discussed one, artificial financial entities, in the fourth section of Chapter Four. These come in many varieties, with many features, including simulated or artificial securities and various types of insurance. There are also lively markets in many kinds of debt and in such money-things as interest rates swaps, commodity prices, inflation hedges, emissions permits, and crypto-currencies. Many, many kinds of derivatives are traded. The underlying securities or variables include currency exchange rates, crop prices, energy prices, metal prices, all sorts of interest rates, default rates on loans, and inflation rates.

In every case, gambling is the prime interest of the banks' clients. The banks, acting as exchanges and organisers ("clearing houses"), take the safest and usually most profitable role of "the house". These banks can sometimes also trade profitably, by taking advantage of their knowledge of customers' intentions and desires. In every case, the banks' traders and product designers do not merely facilitate their customers' greed. They actively encourage it, through friendly patter and careful design. In general, there is little hypocrisy in this encouragement. The facilitators of trading are institutions and people who fully subscribe to the greedy culture that is fundamental to reality-distant financial markets.

Earlier in this Appendix I mentioned the greedy orientation that is typical of banks oriented to taking deposits and making loans. Their institutional cultures are much less greedy, however, than those of the *banks involved primarily in trading the money-things of general-finance*. The gap is hardly surprising. For deposit-and-lending banks, some portion of loans serve pure-finance, which often solves genuine economic no-money-now problems, some portion of deposits represent genuine sacrifices of consumption, and another, overlapping portion of deposits represent prudent reserves against disaster. Some trading-banks do help pure-finance by arranging the sale of new shares, but, as pointed out a little earlier, that business is permeated with greed, despite its helpful economic purpose. For the rest, almost everything that the trading-banks do serves to facilitate and increase the subjective greed of customers. With no economic goal to serve, it is almost inevitable that the customers' greed permeates the banks' culture.

Sometimes the culture of greed is expressed crudely, as in the banks known as "bucket shops". The banks buy money-things at one price and sell them at a much higher one to subjectively very greedy and economically very unsophisticated customers. Often, the culture of greed is much more decorous. Suave bankers can encourage rich, subjectively greedy individuals to pay large fees for professional investment management, to trade frequently, and to buy more sophisticated products that are highly profitable for the bank. There are also professional cultures of greed, found in institutions such as pension and mutual funds. Trading-banks dedicated to doing business with these clients are adept at hiding greed behind and within apparently innocuous and even helpful activities such as offering expertise on possible investments and strategies and providing and explaining complex financial products. Within the trading-banks, it is understood that the rhetoric is always about serving clients but the reality is the search for arguments that persuade clients to trade more and to participate more in markets that offer higher profits for the banks.

The shareholders of trading-banks receive some of the profits from the institutional greed, but most of it is distributed to employees. The *greed of general-finance bankers* is rightly legendary. Since most of what they are paid to do serves no economic purpose, their high salaries are objectively greedy. Subjective greed is harder to demonstrate, but most people who have spent time with successful bankers would say their desires for rewards are vastly in excess of any standard of personal contribution, merit, or sacrifice. Many successful broad-finance bankers are also, or even primarily, financial investors or managers of financial investment organisations. For example, hedge funds frequently blend the money of managers and clients, and sometimes act as intermediaries, as well as clients, of trading-banks. However, while the institutional boundaries are often fluid and confusing, the greed is constant. Hedge funds typically receive enormous management fees.

Finally, the *banks are surrounded by a large penumbra* of greed-filled businesses. The lawyers, public relations firms, consultants, accountants, and journalists who deal with banks are generally less greedy than the banks and bankers that pay them, but the industry's culture of greedy extravagance seeps outward and is hard to resist. The desire of these service-organisations to retain and gain business leads to endorsements, support, and encouragement of greed-motivated products and actions. In most of these businesses, the fees charged to financial clients and the wages that they generate are higher than for comparable non-financial business. Inevitably, the lure of more pay for the same sort of work both encourages the greed of the people involved and attracts already quite greedy people to join in.

None of the greedy cultures within and around banks would thrive if banks operated entirely in the middle section of the Triptych. The reality of the paid-for economy provides a monetary anchor and its moral standards at least sometimes restrain greed. Banks, however, mostly operate in the left section. The resulting distance from the Great Exchange limits the economic damage done by the greed of banks and bankers. Unfortunately, there is enough greed and enough overlap with the middle section of the Triptych for the bankers' moral disorder to make significant contributions to the financial exception.

Financial theory

Financial arrangements were made in many societies for many centuries without any theory to describe them. Indeed, before well into the 19th century, many professionals of finance were unfamiliar with calculations that are now considered elementary. For example, the technique for comparing interest rates on fixed income instruments with different maturities and stated interest rates was not perfected until the beginning of the 20th century (Homer, 2005). The theory that claims to provide a mathematically coherent psychological, economic, and monetary explanation of money-thing prices and their changes was developed only during the second half of that century (Perold, 2004) (Parker, 1968).

The long absence of a rigorous mathematical model for finance should not be surprising. To start, numbers are not exactly natural for either the sharing of effort and rewards, the basic social principle behind the returns of pure-finance, or the continuing social obligation of the poor to the rich, the social principle behind post-aristocratic finance. These notions are so non-quantitative that both types of relations were part of the social-economic structures of moneyless societies. The introduction of money obviously added numbers, but the idea of a uniform quantification of finance, which is money over time, was literally inconceivable until the beginning of the scientific age. However, once modern ideas about the uniformity of measurements of things over time became widely enough accepted to penetrate the merchant class, it was probably only a matter of time until a full theory of finance would be developed. In fact, quite a bit of time was needed, because the current theory of finance had to wait for both the neoclassical model of economic psychology, which was only formalised in the late 19th century, and a familiarity with statistical reasoning, which only became widespread among non-specialists after the Second World War.

Financial theory may be relatively recent, but it is now quite sophisticated. It fully models the interrelated problems of determining, interpreting, and comparing the prices of various financial securities. The comparisons are with both other, more or less similar securities and with some sort of postulated or calculated "true" value. The theory is quite influential. It is used, or claimed to be used, by investors when they study their portfolios, by banks when they create new financial securities, by traders as they participate in the often hyperactive financial markets, and by corporate executives when they evaluate potential projects.

I have alluded to this theory's many basic conceptual problems several times already, and will mention others in this section, but my interest here is primarily moral. I want to show that both the psychological foundation of the theoretical edifice and the intellectual choices made in many of the details of quantification serve to promote or at least to tolerate greedy expectations. Speaking roughly, the theory makes three morally disastrous assumptions. First, financial investors should and basically do always want as high returns as they can possibly obtain. Second, financial investors should and basically can decide themselves how high returns should be under various conditions. Third, people working in the economy can know enough about the future to use financial calculations as a base for economic decisions. This first assumption ratifies greed, the second hides it, and the third fertilises it by giving an excuse for greedy behaviour. Parts of the theory do not support greed. They are often ignored.

I will now discuss the moral implications of seven parts of financial theory, doing my best to minimise the use of technical terminology. However, the lack of equations and formulas in what follows is not merely an effort to help readers who are not mathematically inclined. I am trying to show the generally greed-friendly assumptions that are easily forgotten when they are expressed in the amoral notation of mathematics.

Time value of money

Financial theory does not start with the possible justice of an investee paying an investor for the temporary use of her money. Nor does it start with the possible justice of the investor sharing in the fruits of the investee's labour, labour which the financial investment made more productive. Although both those plausible arguments stand in the background, the actual theory relies on a bizarre psychological claim: always and everywhere, all people consider token-money to be more valuable when they have it now than when they will have it in the future.

The notion is absurd, even before the additional claim of a precisionist quantification, measured in tenths of a percent per year, of the supposed preference. There is no theoretical case, empirical pattern, or objective possibility that this claim is valid. Theoretically, token-money does not store value and cannot provide comparisons of value across time or place. A quantity of token-money, which by definition exists only in a particular here-and-now of the Great Exchange, can have no regular "value" relationship with the same quantity of token-money in some other here-and-now. Empirically, people's desire for money varies with their temperaments and the circumstances of their lives. They might want money more now, because they feel poor, have an urgent need, crave some luxury, or see a promising opportunity. However, they might well want money more later, when it is then and not now that desire, poverty, needs, and opportunities are felt to be present and pressing. Objectively, the degree to which a quantity of money supports the individual and common good is totally independent of time. Money may do more good now or it may do more good later.

Why adopt a clearly false psychological premise? As far I can tell, the only motivation, which I do not think is a conscious one, is that this unattractive portrait of human nature – always the grasshopper and never the ant – leads smoothly into a precise and greed-friendly justification of financial returns. Because the supposed pain of not currently having money is assumed to be constant over time, the premise justifies a constant return. Because the pain is assumed to be a universal feature of human nature, it justifies a universal "required rate of return" on all financial investments, starting with a risk-free rate. Because the time-preference is presented as an unavoidable fact of human nature, it cannot be judged morally. Greed is not a relevant concept.

The assumption that there is a psychologically determined risk-free rate has two greed-friendly effects. First, the reliance on subjective psychology effectively delegates the determination of this rate to investors. They decide how much reward they need for delaying satisfaction. In practice, there is an important limit to how greedy investors are allowed to be. The central monetary authority's central-rate establishes, or at least influences, the risk-free rate, overruling the will of investors and investees. Since the 2008 financial crisis, the central-rate has been far lower than most investors think a risk-free rate should be. However, that check is not intentional. In principle, the central monetary authorities generally have no moral problem with greedily high central-rates. Second, the amoral psychology of financial theory excludes any debate on the moral sociology of post-aristocratic finance. After all, the rich have the same need as the poor to be compensated for having money later instead of now.

Quantification of risk

The next step in financial theory is to claim that the risk-free rate is nowhere near high enough to compensate financial investors in non-risk-free money-things for the many risks they take on.

The first and largest risk is that the money-things might provide a negative or even an unduly low return (the investments "lose money" or "do not earn their cost of capital"). In a non-greedy system, this quite genuine risk would be dealt with fully by pooling large numbers of structurally similar loans (for example to companies in the same regions or industry). The lenders to the pool would receive regular premiums from the borrowers, with the size of each premium determined by the recent patterns of promise-breaking by the pool's members. This equity-like system would support commutative justice between financial investors and some group of investees.

The actual, greed-friendly system does not work like that. Financial theory teaches that interest rates on loans include a "default risk premium", which is set in advance. The arrangement is just to the extent that the bulk of interest payments actually compensate for the minority of actual non-payments. However, financial theory adds the claim that investors need to be compensated not only for actual losses, but for the possibility that the actual losses are more than expected. In other words, it assumes that investors deserve a quite handsome reward for simply accepting the possibility of unsatisfactory returns. The additional reward is typically generous enough that financial investors in portfolios of risky financial securities generally earn far higher returns overall than investors in risk-free securities. There is much greed and no justice in that result.

The theory also claims that investors in debts should earn a premium for taking on "inflation risk", the possibility that rising prices and interest rates will erode the value of a financial security. The more distant the maturity of the fixed income security, the greater is the risk that the actual rate of inflation will differ from the expected rate that is "priced in" to the original interest rate. The theory kindly explains – kind to the financial investors – that the lenders require an additional risk premium for inflation uncertainty. Without the blinding effect of greed, it would be clear that a more reality-close inclusion of some sort of regular adjustment for past and current inflation rates would provide compensation with much more justice and no greed. However, the theory ignores this possibility, so greedy lenders can ask for a high inflation uncertainty premium while hoping for unexpectedly low inflation rates, while greedy borrowers negotiate with the opposite motivations.

Theory further introduces a "time premium" to compensate for the supposed additional risks of non-payment and inflation that come with longer maturities. It should hardly be surprising that once economic, price, and time risk have all been fully compensated, the calculated total risk premium provides investors with a return that is almost always objectively greedy and is usually subjectively and socially greedy.

In practice, the returns to investors have sometimes been much less than the theory tells them they deserve. Such occasional "disappointments" are generally caused by economic and especially financial crises, which bring large losses on financial investments. In financial theory, the losses, which are mostly caused by the mutually reinforcing greed of financial investors and investees, are used as evidence of the need for greedily high-risk premiums. There is an irony here. The theory explains why greedy financial investors should end up not only compensated but rewarded for creating and continuing the financial exception.

Discount rate

The theoretical justification of a high "risk-adjusted" return on fixed-income money-things is mirrored and amplified in the theory of "required returns", "cost of equity capital", and "discount rate" on equities. The three phrases refer to slightly different aspects of the same basic idea, the minimum acceptable level of a particular ratio: the numerator is either the reported profits or the money available for dividends and the denominator is either an original monetary investment or the accounting value attributed to that investment after some years ("book value"). Theory teaches that for any company this "return on equity", or its close relatives "return on investment" and "cash flow return on equity", should be high enough to provide the original equity investors with an appropriate return on their financial investment.

The flurry of terms should not obscure the reality-distance and greed of the calculations that are involved. It is assumed that equities are risker than debts, so equity investors deserve an "equity risk premium", in addition to all the premiums over the risk-free rate which investors in risky debt are assumed to require. This assumption of greater equity riskiness is totally unmerited, since equities are protected from unexpected increases in inflation rates while fixed income debts are not, and over time the unending participation of equities in the success of both companies (which I described as objectively greedy in Chapter Five) and overall economies more than compensates for the relatively rare losses suffered when companies are unable to pay dividends but can make interest payments.

Equities do have a liquidity risk: sellers might not like the available price at the time they want to sell. Of course, the desire for ready liquidity of money-things is itself greedily reality-distant. In addition, the same financial investors' greedy hopes and fears greatly magnify the inherent volatility of the prices of money-things, creating another greedy irony. The greater and more disruptive the financial investors' greed is, the higher will be the reward they expect for their bad behaviour.

The required rate of return might sometimes be relevant to some investees. Arguably, managers could set prices high enough to provide financial investors with the profits and dividends that they expect. However, in reality, future prices and profits are rarely under the control of these managers. Besides, the complexity and ambiguity of profit calculations adds an aura of fantasy to the mathematical precision that usually surrounds the calculations of discount rates. There is even less justification for company managers using discount rates in discussions of possible major spending plans, for example on new factories or marketing a new product. The introduction of a largely arbitrary discount rate adds no useful information to the necessarily inaccurate estimations of future profits. In addition, the whole issue of returns to equity investors on incremental investment is economically irrelevant to a company that can and mostly does solve its no-money-now problems with yoking rather than finance.

The calculated required returns and discount rates are almost always absurdly high. That is not a disadvantage for the managers and shareholders who want to justify their own desire for greedy returns. They can say, "I am not greedy to demand this level of profits. I am just following the science of finance". For any functioning economy, however, the calculated costs of capital are often so bizarre that they have to be ignored. If a company has a cost of capital of, say, ten percent, then financial investors will only provide one dollar if the company can give the investor $1.10 a year from now. A simple calculation shows that with this 10% cost of capital a company would only be unwilling to pay more than $6 now for something that would be worth $100 in 30 years. With that perspective, it is hardly worth worrying about the possible good and bad events a generation from now. For example, the current or present value of the revenues from trees that will be ready to harvest some decades hence is not worth considering, nor are the expenses of decommissioning a nuclear power plant a generation from now. So, financial theory tells lumber companies not to replace cut trees and power generators to spend now without worrying about what happens to radioactive waste. Fortunately, the greed supported by the financial theory of required returns rarely overrules common economic sense. Managers of lumber producers and regulators of nuclear power producers generally find ways to ignore the faulty theory.

Efficient prices of money-things

The part of financial theory known as the efficient market hypothesis claims that for any money-thing traded in financial markets, the current price is the best available estimate of its true value. The claim is problematic at the highest theoretical level, because the meaning of "true value" is unclear. Prices of all sorts, and especially of money-things, can have no clear relationship with the subjective, objective, or social value of the things paid for, since that value is human and human values are not quantifiable, and since the relation of money-things to any human value is indirect at best. At a lower but still elevated level, the idea of a true monetary value for a money-thing is almost incoherent, because of the temporal-ontological asymmetry. There is no current price that can objectively be considered equal to a collection of monetary payments to be received in the future, and no adjustment to the current price can assign a monetary value to the uncertainty of those payments. The best that can be managed is an equivalence under some set of agreed rules both for summarising guesses about the future and for converting a range of possible numbers into a single number.

More empirically, the history of financial markets does not really support the intuitive idea behind market efficiency. The crowds that determine the prices of money-things are sometimes prescient, but greed tends to damage judgement, spread easily, and increase as it spreads. The numerous bubbles and busts and the rapid gyrations of prices in financial markets suggest that the mesh of greed and mass psychology makes these markets quite inefficient.

Still, the evidence does mostly support the efficient market hypothesis at the most trivial level. Individual financial investors rarely "outperform" for long periods. More technically, their "total return", as measured by generally accepted conventions, is rarely greater than that generated, again as measured by generally accepted conventions, by the indexes that summarise the overall changes in the relevant financial markets. The scarcity of superiority suggests that it is hard, perhaps impossible, to have consistently better judgements about most of the determinants of future money-thing prices. The recognition of this likely inability has actually reduced one sort of financial greed. Over the last decade, more investors have chosen "passive" funds, which are managed only to match the overall ups and downs of indexes.

The efficient market hypothesis does not only encourage restraint, however. Like the rest of financial theory, it encourages greed, although in this case the connection is unusually subtle. It goes like this. The implicit suggestion that money-thing prices hold some information about the likely future encourages paying more attention to them. This attention supports corporate managers who argue that they should be rewarded for presiding over a rising share price. More generally, the assumption that the price of a money-thing speaks as much truth as is available discourages any desire to question the role of greed in establishing that price.

Such efficient-price thinking is confused. While it is possible that a high or rising share price corresponds with a positive or improving multidimensional evaluation of corporate excellence, it certainly need not do so, and often does not. All too frequently, high share prices merely reflect some combination of the quite possibly temporary success of some socially greedy business practice with the subjectively greedy enthusiasm of buyers of those shares. Rising share prices gratify and encourage both varieties of greed, while the morally blind encouragement of high share prices is itself a reflection and encouragement of a greedy financial orientation.

The meaning of money-thing numbers

I have mentioned several times the reality-distance of both the prices and the changes in the prices of money-things. Since both the levels and the changes have no clear or uniform causal relationship with anything going on in the middle section of the Triptych, their irrationality is hardly surprising. They are, as they say, features not bugs of the financial system. Both types of irrationality are clearly invitations to greed. The lack of an upper bound to a money-thing price removes the possibility of a practical limit to greedy hopes. The lack of a clear or necessary tie of the money-thing's price to economic reality precludes any logical limit. Further, since prices can move around rapidly and without any clear or predictable pattern or discernible causal relationship, reality provides almost no constraint to the greedy hope of winning at short-term financial gambling.

Financial theory is not needed to incite speculative greed about money-thing prices, but it does provide a sort of intellectual cover. Gambling, after all, has a poor reputation. If playing the financial markets is no more "gentlemanly" than handicapping horseraces, then it is a shady business at best, since cheating is the most, and perhaps the only, effective way to beat the odds consistently on the track. Mathematically informed gamblers can win in some games of chance, but they generally consider their labour more of a hobby than a dignified profession. "Playing the markets" in finance once attracted similar social disdain, including a suspicion that success often came from some underhand arrangement. Financial theory has helped remove this stigma, by providing what sound like rational explanations for both price levels and price changes.

I have already introduced the ingredients for the rationalisation of prices, the time value of money, and risk premiums. These are combined with a forecast of future payments from the investee to the investor to create a bold but meaningless equivalence. The current price, in savings-money, is said to be equal to the "risk-adjusted present value" (or the "discounted future value" or simply the "net present value") of the "expected future cash flows" to the investor. This is a bad idea on three levels. The first is the failure to worry about the equivalence of two different types of money, token-money payments to financial investors and the savings-money price of a money-thing. Not noticing the problems with assuming the two are convertible can be excused, since the idea that "money" is used equivocally is very unfamiliar. The second problem is the greed-friendly assumptions behind the calculations.

The third problem with understanding money-thing prices as net present values is the total intellectual vacuity of combining two long series of totally unknown numbers, future cash flows and future interest rates. It is senseless to hope that a large collection of numbers that by definition cannot be known can help determine the true value of a thing here and now, even before adjusting those unknown numbers by a reality-distant discount factor. If there were no speculation on these prices, there would be little or no interest in finding a true value. However, there is a great deal of speculation and the idea that speculators are searching for or helping to establish a true value provides an intellectual justification for it. In other words, the calculations of net present value, no matter how flimsy the logic behind them is, dress up the greedy hope to win at gambling with some respectable clothing: the intellectual pursuit of accurate and "efficient" valuations.

Financial theory's approach to price changes of money-things is far less ridiculous than its approach to price levels. Indeed, the theory's principal conclusion about these changes, that in the short term most of them are random, is quite sensible. The evidence largely supports the claim of a "random walk" of prices, although the judgement depends to some extent on how randomness is defined and calculated and how long the short term is. Like the efficient market hypothesis, the random-walk hypothesis basically discourages greed in trading, since it teaches that only trading based on superior information obtained at a relatively low cost can possibly satisfy traders' greedy desires. The random-walk theory subtly encourages greed, by providing scientific categories for analysing price changes. Indeed, many traders happily play with the techniques used by theoreticians to test for randomness. The traders hope, generally but not always in vain, that classifying reams of historical data with mildly sophisticated mathematical techniques will allow them to satisfy their greedy desires to do what the theory says is almost impossible.

Debt-equity equivalence

Economists often assume that differences in price can accurately quantify almost any differences in quality or qualities. If one peach is juicier and tastier but less fresh than another, the relative prices should and can express all of those differences. This claim is wrong, as discussed in Chapter One, but useful, as discussed in Chapter Two. Here, I am interested in financial theory's monetary-meaning overreach: the claim that savings-money-numbers can consistently "price in" *all* the qualities and future quantities of structurally different money-things. I have already discussed the long list of assumptions needed to provide supposedly consistent prices for all kinds of debt, and I could have discussed similar difficulties in comparing the prices of equity shares in companies with very different qualities.

The largest tension between financial theory and the rather peculiar reality of the left section of the Triptych comes in the even more ambitious claim that relative prices can capture the many differences between debt and equity. The two types of money-thing differ fundamentally in several dimensions: potential maximum returns, the timing and structure of potential losses, their susceptibility to changes in inflation, and their relationship to developments in both the overall economy and the particular investee. Financial theory claims to price all this in.

For pragmatic and historical reasons, the theory starts with debt as the standard financial arrangement. It treats equity as debt-plus: debt plus variable returns, additional possible gains, greater protection against unexpected changes in inflation rates, and greater vulnerability to economic disappointments. If realism were the goal, the presentation would have been equity-minus, since equities are far closer than any debt to the realities of the paid-for economy. However, the principal flaw is not with the method of creating the equivalence but with the assumption that one can be created. Debt and equity work too differently over time for there to be a correct way to use relative prices to make these different types of money-things interchangeable.

Fortunately, the inability to price debt in terms of equity, or vice versa, has no economic importance. Relative prices within the middle section of the Triptych have limited economic meaning, and relative prices in the reality-distant left section have even less. However, the theory does provide some intellectual cover for various types of greedy behaviour. The greedy and reality-distant preference for debt over equity financing can be defended as theoretically justified and morally neutral "balance sheet optimisation". The theory's analytic techniques – the alphas and betas of risk and return, the "efficient frontiers" of portfolios, the "Sharpe ratios" and "covariance" studies – can occupy financial investors in search of a greedy, reality-distant return.

Executive compensation and "alignment" with shareholders

Financial theory is mostly about finance. Indeed, for the most part it reduces the actual economy to a supposedly tractable set of exogenous influences on financial markets' efficient but volatile trading and price-setting. When dealing with "pieces of paper", the "underlying" companies whose financial securities are being traded is reduced to a "discounted cash flow model". Theorists will admit that the numbers are gross oversimplifications that are certainly wrong, but they assert almost absent-mindedly that they are the best available estimates. They equally breezily dismiss the complaint of undue volatility of outputs from models in which small changes in variables produce implausibly large differences in "fair values". This intellectual violence only makes sense because everyone involved knows that what really matters is not the underlying companies but the trading.

While financial theory as a whole is intellectually embarrassing, neither the antics in the left side of the Triptych nor their flimsy intellectual justifications have much relevance to what happens in the middle section. There is one significant exception. The financial assumption that the maximisation of the share price is necessarily the overriding goal of all corporate managers is economically harmful. The financial assumption relies on two claims made by some economists: shareholders' interests have absolute priority over those of other corporate stakeholders and shareholders want only to maximise the share price. Many other economists reject one or both of these claims, but financial theory simply takes profit-maximising companies as an input into the share price model. The one-dimensional enterprise is just one more unrealistic assumption, made with the same casual indifference as all the other unrealistic economic and psychological assumptions.

I discussed the damage done by greed-infested "shareholder capitalism" earlier in this chapter – the reduction of useful spending, the lack of consideration of the common good, and the absurd salaries paid to senior executives. The contribution of financial theory to this damaging practice is secondary to the machinations of the economic and social elite, but it does contribute. Its presence in the ideologically charged debate provides a good example of how the apparently neutral notions of financial theory serve to support structures of greed, in the economy as well as in the financial world.

Greed by numbers

In this book, I have used numbers as little as possible. That abstinence may seem strange. Token-money is a quantification of part of the economy, money-numbers are the principal raw material for finance-numbers, and finance is nothing if not numerical. However, the lack of numbers, which goes along with a paucity of algebraic formulas, is in accord with one of my starting principles: the essentially non-quantitative nature of economic activity. The Great Exchange of labour and consumption is the interaction of basically unmeasurable and always incommensurate human activities. Anthropology, sociology, psychology, organisational behaviour, law, and moral philosophy provide more insight into the economy than any numerical analysis possibly can.

What is true of economics is also true of finance – actual numbers and generalised equations introduce a false precision that inhibits understanding. Specific numbers, equations and formulas seem to float away from their non-quantitative social and economic background. In isolation, these quantity-things cannot provide much insight into either what is going on in specific financial arrangements or the overall social approach to finance.

I discussed why specific token-money-numbers deserve little attention in Chapter Two. The basic problem is that individual and relative prices reflect too many factors, from social status through scarcity value to labour-hours, to provide much economic insight. I could have made a similar analysis of the near-meaninglessness of specific measures of the Central Monetary Ratio. The prices of the money-things of finance deserve even less respect, since they are barely anchored to anything in the real economy.

Interest rates and other measures of financial returns might be different. Certainly, both theologians and lawmakers have often thought so. Over the centuries, specific interest rates have been set as the limit above which financial arrangements were definitionally usurious. The theology has largely been abandoned and the laws repealed, but the temptation lives on in a modified form. In Thomas Piketty's 2014 bestseller *Capital in the 21st Century*, the French economist set an effective limit for acceptable returns with his algebraic inequality of "r>g" (Piketty, 2014). It is only a slight simplification to say that he defined investment returns (r) that were higher than the rate of economic growth (g) in the relevant economy as being socially greedy.

Such purely numerical and algebraic definitions of financial greed are inherently faulty. The justice of a particular return-number cannot be determined without considering essentially non-numerical factors – subjective, objective, and social. A full discussion of morally, socially, and economically appropriate financial returns, both expected and actual, also requires careful thought about general economic flourishing, specific economic structures, trends in the Central Monetary Ratio (inflation), the relative sizes of the left and middle sections of the Triptych, and the organisation of the tax system. A full ethical debate of return-numbers would also take into account questions of social cohesion and stratification, the availability and desirability of non-financial solutions to no-money-now problems, and the type of financial arrangement under study. Finally, the threshold for greed may be different in post-aristocratic, government-related, and factory-building finance. R>g may be a catchy slogan for nerds and neo-Marxists – for a while it was emblazoned on T-shirts – but even if it is good economics (I have severe doubts), it is inadequate for serious ethical analysis.

There is another problem with any simple moral judgements of particular financial numbers. The temporal-ontological uncertainty of finance makes those numbers remarkably hard to interpret. In the late 1970s, the measured annual rate of price inflation in many developed countries was higher than 10%, and the terms of debt securities reflected the expectation that the inflation rate would not decline greatly for many years. With that expectation, an interest rate of 11% on a bond maturing in thirty years would probably not have seemed objectively greedy. However, inflation rates then fell steadily for decades, so anyone who purchased such a bond would probably have ended up with a return that was high enough to suggest both objective and subjective greed. The sudden increase in inflation rates in 2022 created similar changes in the opposite direction.

Actual return-numbers are confusing in two dimensions: meaning and morals. In terms of meaning, it is not easy to put any collection of numbers into a single, intellectually coherent system. Such a unification is only possible through the liberal use of financial theories, but there is much less order and reason in the financial world than the theory assumes. Money-numbers are never precise or consistent indicators of true value. The return-numbers of finance, which are effectively money-numbers with prospective or retrospective temporal uncertainty and inconsistency added in, inherently have substantially more imprecision and inconstancy than money-numbers, so they will give little true information, whether they are considered individually or grouped together.

That practical confusion spills over into the second, moral dimension. The numbers simply do not make enough economic sense to have a clear moral meaning on their own, without any social and economic context. Since the avoidance of greed is not a consideration in determining these numbers – if anything, they are set by maximising the available satisfaction of the stronger party's greedy desires – it is quite likely that many of them are in fact greedy by one or more standards. However, the bare return-numbers tell no moral tales. At most, they can emit some desperate cries. For example, the triple-digit return-numbers (hundreds of percent annually) demanded from "payday" loan borrowers cry out, "Greedy lenders" and the multiple digit returns received by initial equity investors in successful technology companies scream, "Excess". For the most part, though, financial greed is best analysed by looking at the expectations (for maximising or for fairness), structures, reality-distance, and social relations that lie behind them, not at the raw numbers themselves.

Because finance is usually analysed exactly as I suggest it should not be, with numbers, there are several commonly discussed topics that deserve a brief moral analysis. The first is *usury*, discussed in Chapter Five. It has often been condemned, but rarely well defined. I have expressed some regret at the disappearance of laws against usury and moral condemnations of it, but what I miss is the laws' moral stance, not their numerical specifications. There cannot be anything like a clear numerical border, valid for all times and under all conditions, between usurious and non-usurious arrangements. The word and the concept are well worth reviving, but only if they are used as part of a fairly sophisticated analytic framework.

Taxes can affect the greed involved in financial arrangements. For example, a buyer of a bond which promises a 10% return would be judged less subjectively greedy if he plausibly expects his interest income to be taxed at a 50% or a 100% rate than if he expects to pay no taxes on that income. Of course, the highly taxed arrangement might still be objectively or socially greedy. More generally, the tax system can be used as a social weapon against investors' greed. High tax rates, whether on financial income, the value or changes of value of money-things, or speculative income, almost automatically reduce the scope of all sorts of greed.

I have alluded to what are known as *"real interest rates"* on several occasions, although I have avoided the commonly used adjective, since (as mentioned in the discussion of "real" incomes and production in Chapter Two) it is misleading to use "real" to describe numbers which are entirely the product of arbitrary and only partly consistent adjustments to actual money-numbers and return-numbers. Despite the bad choice of wording, there is a good idea behind the "real" adjustment. Financial returns that do not take into account the losses of "purchasing power" caused by overall inflation (or gains from deflation) are reality-distant. Of course, the calculations of those losses (or gains) are necessarily imprecise. Money is a crude tool, and aggregating money-numbers can increase the roughness of the measure. Still, in trying to evaluate the greed in particular arrangements, it is certainly better to adjust numbers to make them less misleading, which the "real" adjustments basically do.

Corporate *returns on equity* are calculations rather than actual payments. That difference is not recognised in financial theory, where the ratio of the profits to "equity capital" (or "shareholders' capital") is treated as identical to the interest rate of a loan. The claim of equivalence is unrealistic. Equity return-numbers are not really comparable with the debt ones. The debt ratios are problematic, since they falsely postulate a comparability of money-numbers over time, but their falseness is minimal in comparison to that of profits and corporate equity.

Both accounting constructions, of profits and equity capital, make use of token-money values that have been assigned consistently but not meaningfully. Both calculations require the addition and subtraction of various money-numbers that describe, with the usual monetary imprecision, all of the company's relationships that fall, at least in part, in the left section of the Triptych. The equity capital calculations also include some, but by no means all, of the things which keep the company in steady operation. Neither calculation includes adjustments for the effects of changing prices. Overall, the profit numbers are not as much of a hodgepodge as the equity numbers, but the ratio of the two is not a reliable guide to anything. The incomparability of the debt and equity numbers explains part of the wide divergence between current interest rates and expected returns for shareholders, although the greater greed of shareholders probably plays a larger part.

Negative interest rates are one of the more remarkable developments of the last few years. The intentional setting of the central rate below the measured rate of inflation ("negative real rates") has been common enough to acquire a technical description, financial repression, but economists had long assumed that actual negative interest rates would be unacceptable to professional investors and the general public. However, in the long effort to repair finance-economy relations after the 2008 global financial crisis, many central monetary authorities set very slightly negative central-rates. These were not passed on to the general public, but professional investors did not seem to be bothered by the slow erosion of the nominal value of their hoarded savings-money.

Can it be greedy to receive a negative interest rate? Certainly, the guarantee of a loss in nominal value and, when there is any price inflation, a near-certainty of a loss in "real" value reduce the scope for greediness in the investors who take up these negative rates. However, a financial and social context is needed to judge the overall greediness. The negative rates are basically part of a policy of several years of "quantitative easing", which expanded the quantity of savings-money in the left section of the Triptych. This expansion probably encouraged much more subjective, objective, and social greed than could have been discouraged by negative rates.

– End –

Index

thrift, 129-30, 150-1

time: concept of, xvii, 148; finance and, 151, 163, 179, 190-1, 206, 262-3, 264, 267, 275; in financial theory (time value of money), 397-8, 399, 404-6; in the Great Exchange, 60-2, 64; and labour, 4, 47, 49, 55, 58-9, 86, 114, 146; land and, 363; savings-money and, 148-9, 191, 204, 289, 312; token-money and, 13, 16, 19-21, 39, 85, 118, 123, 152-60, 215, 271

tractor problem 126-8, 172, 175-6, 202-3, 211

trading (money-things), 197, 234, 283, 292, 340, 369-71, 372, 391-4; and financial theory, 405, 407

truck (and barter), 63-4, 74, 104

trust: in credit-money, 154; in the economy, 1, 192, 239; in finance, 166, 197-8, 278, 299, 320, 353, 358; and token-money, 15, 63, 117-20, 143, 189

United States, 5, 86, 132, 204, 234-5, 247, 295, 338, 340, 368, 388, 392

usury, 207, 319-20, 340

utilitarian philosophy, xvii, 11, 21, 114, 116, 311

Veronese (painter) 28

venture capital, 347, 368-9

wars, 9, 184-6, 225, 327, 340, 346, 349, 351; First World War, 70, 136; as labour, 46, 223; profiteering, 346; Russia-Ukraine, 4, 6, 137; Second World War, 5, 6, 136, 242, 353, 396

Wordsworth, William, 17

World Economic Forum, 169, 210

yoking (alternative to finance), 171, 173-4, 190, 195, 199-201, 237, 281; and equity greed, 348, 391, 401; and government, 177; history, 358; and pensions, 250

Zimbabwe, 136

Bibliography

Adorno, T. and Horkheimer, M. (2002). *Dialectic of enlightenment*. Stanford CA: Stanford University Press.

Agamben, G. (2016). Capitalism as religion. In: McLoughlin, D. ed. *Agamben and radical politics*, Edinburgh: Edinburgh University Press, pp. 18-24.

Airport Industry Review. (2020). Berlin Brandenburg airport: a construction timeline [online]. Available from: https://airport. nridigital.com/air_feb21/berlin_brandenburg_airport_construction [accessed 24 June 2022].

Anderson, Gary A. (2009). *Sin: a history*. New Haven: Yale University Press.

Appleby, J. O. (1976). Locke, liberalism and the natural law of money. *Past & Present*, 71 (May), pp. 43-69. Available from: https://www.jstor.org/ stable/pdf/650353.pdf [accessed 24 June 2022].

Aquinas T. (1920). *Summa theologicae*. London: Sheed & Ward.

Arestis, P. and Sawyer, M. (2003). On the effectiveness of monetary policy and fiscal policy. *Levy Economics Institute of Bard College Working Paper*, 369. Available from: https://www.levyinstitute.org/publications/on-the-effectiveness-of-monetary-policy-and-fiscal-policy [accessed 24 June 2022].

Aristotle (1984). *Politics*. In: Barnes, J. ed. *The complete works of Aristotle*, vol. 2, pp. 1986-2129. Princeton: Princeton University Press.

Backhouse, R. and Boianovsky, M. (2012). *Transforming modern macroeconomics: exploring disequilibrium microfoundations, 1956–2003*. Cambridge: Cambridge University Press. Available from: doi:10.1017/CBO9781139150859 [accessed 26 June 2022].

Balot, R. K. (2002). *Greed and injustice in classical Athens*. Princeton: Princeton University Press.

Bandelj, N., Wherry, F., and Zelizer, V. eds. *Money talks: explaining how money really works*. Princeton: Princeton University Press.

bankmycell (2022). How many smartphones are in the world? Available from: https://www.bankmycell.com/blog/how-many-phones-are-in-the-world# [accessed 22 June 2022].

Benedict XVI (2009). *Caritas in veritate*. Available from: https://www.vatican.va/content/benedict-xvi/en/encyclicals/documents/hf_ben-xvi_enc_20090629_caritas-in-veritate.html [accessed 27 June 2022].

Benford, J., Ostry, J. D., and Shiller, R. eds. (2018). *Sovereign GDP-linked bonds: rationale and design*. London: CEPR. Available from: https://voxeu.org/article/sovereign-gdp-linked-bonds-rationale-and-design [accessed 27 June 2022].

Bloch, M. (1954). *Esquisse d'une histoire monétaire de l'Europe*. Paris: A. Colin.

Borio, C. and Hofmann, B. (2017). Is monetary policy less effective when interest rates are persistently low? In: Hambur, J. and Simon, J. eds. *Monetary policy and financial stability in a world of low interest rates: proceedings of a conference* pp. 59-87. Sydney: Reserve Bank of Australia. Available from: https://www.rba.gov.au/publications/confs/2017/pdf/rba-conference-volume-2017-borio-hofmann.pdf [accessed 27 June 2022].

Borio, C. and Zabai, A. (2016). Unconventional monetary policies: a re-appraisal. *Bank for International Settlements Working Paper*, 570. Available from: https://www.bis.org/publ/work570.htm [accessed 27 June 2022].

Boulding, K. (1969). Economics as a moral science. *The American Economic Review* 59(1), pp. 1-12. Available from: https://www.jstor.org/stable/1811088 [accessed 27 June 2022].

Bryan, W. J. 1896. William Jennings Bryan cross of gold speech July 8, 1896. Available from: http://www.let.rug.nl/usa/documents/1876-1900/william-jennings-bryan-cross-of-gold-speech-july-8-1896.php [accessed 27 June 2022].

Burton, N. 2020. Is greed good? The psychology and philosophy of greed. *Psychology Today* [online] https://www.psychologytoday.com/gb/blog/hide-and-seek/201410/is-greed-good [accessed 27 June 2022].

Cameron, R. ed. (1972). *Banking and economic development: some lessons of history*. New York: Oxford University Press.

Clarke, S. (2006). Crisis theory. Available from: https://homepages.warwick.ac.uk/~syrbe/pubs/Crisistheory.pdf [accessed 26 June 2022].

Cohen, N. (2021). How Britain paid for war: bond holders in the Great War 1914-32. *Bank Underground* [online] https://bankunderground.co.uk/2021/01/18/how-britain-paid-for-war-bond-holders-in-the-great-war-1914-32/ [accessed 27 June 2022].

Coyle, D. (2016). *GDP: a brief but affectionate history - revised and expanded edition*. Princeton: Princeton University Press.

Davis, J., Fuenzalida C., and Taylor, A. (2021). The natural rate puzzle: global macro trends and the market-implied r*. *NBER Working* Paper, 26560. Available from: https://www.nber.org/papers/w26560 [accessed 25 June 2022].

Desan, C. (2014). Making money: coin, currency, and the coming of capitalism. Oxford: Oxford University Press.

Desrosières, A. (2000). *Politique des grands nombres: histoire de la raison statistique*. Paris: Éditions La Découverte.

Dickens, C. (2018). *A Christmas carol*. Available from https://www.gutenberg.org/files/46/46-h/46-h.htm [accessed 25 June 2022].

Dodd, N. (2014). *The social life of money*. Princeton: Princeton University Press.

Douglas, M. and Isherwood B. (1978). *The world of goods*. London: Basic Books.

Douglas, M. (2002). *Purity and danger: an analysis of concept of pollution and taboo*. 2nd ed. London: Routledge.

Douglas, M. (2002). Introduction. In Mauss, M., *The gift*. London: Routledge. Available from: https://files.libcom.org/files/Mauss%20-%20The%20Gift.pdf [accessed 28 June 2022].

Drucker Institute (2011). Letter to Chairwoman Mary Schapiro. Available from: https://www.sec.gov/comments/df-title-ix/executive-compensation/executivecompensation-60.pdf [accessed 25 June 2022].

Eatwell, J., Milgate, M., and Newmann, P. eds. (1987). *The new Palgrave: money*, London: Macmillan.

Eichengreen, B., Hausmann, R., and Panizza, U. (2002). Original sin: the pain, the mystery and the road to redemption. Available from https://repository.graduateinstitute.ch/record/286974/?ln=en [accessed 28 June 2022].

Eichengreen B. and Ritschl, A. Understanding West German economic growth in the 1950s. SFB 649 Discussion Paper 2008-068. Available from shttps://edoc.hu-berlin.de/bitstream/handle/18452/4812/68.pdf?sequence=1&isAllowed=y [accessed 28 June 2022].

Einaudi, L. (2000). From the franc to the 'Europe': the attempted transformation of the Latin monetary union into a European monetary union, 1865-1873. *The Economic History Review, New Series*, 53(2) pp. 284-308.

Engels, F. (2010). Origin of the family, private property, and the state. Available from: https://www.marxists.org/archive/marx/works/download/pdf/origin_family.pdf [accessed 25 June 2022].

Federal Reserve History (2013). Nixon ends convertibility of u.s. dollars to gold and announces wage/price controls. Available from https://www. federalreservehistory.org/essays/gold-convertibility-ends [accessed 28 June 2022].

Ferguson, S. (2018). *Declarations of dependence: money, aesthetics, and the politics of care.* Lincoln NE: University of Nebraska Press.

Folbre, N. (2001). *The invisible heart: economics and family values.* New York: Free Press.

Folbre, N. (2009). *Greed, lust and gender: a history of economic ideas.* New York: Oxford University Press.

Franks, A. (2019). John Paul II's Labor on Marx. *Church Life Journal* [online], 19 August 2019. Available from: https://churchlifejournal.nd.edu/ articles/jp2s-labor-on-marx/ [accessed 28 June 2022].

Freud, S. (1914). *Psychopathology of everyday life.* London: T. Fisher Unwin. Available from https://psychclassics.yorku.ca/Freud/Psycho/ [accessed 28 June 2022].

Friedman, M. (1961). The lag in effect of monetary policy. *Journal of Political Economy*, 69(5), pp. 447-466.

Fullwiler, S. (2009). What If the government just prints money? *New Economic Perspectives* [online], 22 November 2009. Available from: http://neweconomicperspectives.org/2009/11/what-if-government-just-prints-money.html [accessed 28 June 2022].

Garber, P. (1990). Famous first bubbles. *Journal of Economic Perspectives*, 4(2), pp. 35-54. Available from https://pubs.aeaweb.org/doi/pdf/10.1257/ jep.4.2.35 [accessed 26 June 2022].

Geertz, C. (1973). Thick description: toward an interpretive theory of culture. In: *Selected Essays.* 1st ed. New York, NY: Basic Books, pp. 3-30.

Godelier, M. (1996). *L'Enigme du don.* Paris: Fayard.

Goetzmann, W. and Rowenhorst, K. G. eds. (2005). *The origins of value: the financial innovations that created modern capital markets*. Oxford: Oxford University Press.

Goodhart, C. (1998). The two concepts of money: implications for the analysis of optimal currency areas. *European Journal of Political Economy*, 14(3), pp. 407-432. Available from https://www.sciencedirect.com/ science/article/abs/pii/S0176268098000159 [accessed 25 June 2022].

Graeber, D. *Debt, the first 5000 years*, 2nd ed. Brooklyn: Melville House.

Gross, M. and Siebenbrunner, C. (2019). Money creation in fiat and digital currency systems. *IMF Working Paper*, 2019/285. Available from: https://www.imf.org/en/Publications/WP/Issues/2019/12/20/Money-Creation-in-Fiat-and-Digital-Currency-Systems-48843 [accessed 25 June 2022].

Hadas, E. (2007). *Human goods, economic evils: a moral look at the dismal science*. Wilmington DE: ISI Books.

Hadas, E. (2021). *Counsels of imperfection: thinking through catholic social teaching*. Washington: Catholic University of America Press.

Hanke, S. and Krus, N. (2013). World hyperinflations. In: Parker R. and Whaples, R., *The handbook of major events in economic history*, pp 367-377. London: Routledge.

Hayek, F. 1945. The use of knowledge in society. *American Economic Review*, 35(4), pp. 519-30. Available from: https://www.cato.org/sites/cato.org/ files/articles/hayek-use-knowledge-society.pdf [accessed 25 June 2022].

Hegel G. W. F. (1975). *Hegel's Logic: being part one of the encyclopaedia of the philosophical sciences*. Oxford: Oxford University Press.

Hegel, G. W. F. (1967). *Hegel's Philosophy of right*. Oxford: Oxford University Press.

Heidegger, M. (1977). Letter on humanism. In: *Basic writings*. New York: Harper & Row, pp. 193-242.

Hilt, E., Jaremski, M. and Rahn, W. (2021). Wall Street: Liberty Bonds and the transformation of American finance. *NBER Working Paper*, 27703. Available from: https://www.nber.org/papers/w27703 [accessed 25 June 2022].

Hockett, R. and Omarova, S. (2017). The finance franchise. *Cornell Law Review* 102, pp. 1143-1218. Available from: https://scholarship.law.cornell.edu/cgi/viewcontent.cgi?article=2660&context=facpub [accessed 25 June 2022].

Homer, S. and Sylla, R. (2005). *History of interest rates*, 4th ed. Hoboken, NJ: Wiley.

Hudson, M. (1999). The use and abuse of mathematical economics. *Michael Hudson on finance, real estate and the powers of neoliberalism*, 24 September 1999. Available from: https://michael-hudson.com/1999/09/the-use-and-abuse-of-mathematical-economics-2/ [accessed 25 June 2022].

Hudson, M. (2018). *...and forgive them their debts: lending, foreclosure and redemption from bronze age finance to the Jubilee Year*. Dresden: ISLET.

IDC (2022). Global smartphone shipments expected to decline 3.5% in 2022, amidst global uncertainty and weaker demand, according to IDC, 1 June 2022. Available from https://www.idc.com/getdoc.jsp?containerId=prUS49226922 [accessed 28 June 2022].

Ingham, G. (2004). *The nature of money*. Cambridge: Polity.

Ingham, G. (2020). *Money*. Cambridge: Polity.

Ingrao, B. (2022). The alchemy of money: money as a standard of value. In: Resina, J. R. ed. *Cultures of currencies: literature and the symbolic foundation of money*. New York: Routledge, pp. 179-205.

Investopedia (ND). *About us*. Available from: https://www.investopedia.com/about-us-5093223 [accessed 25 June 2022].

Jespersen, J. (2009). *Keynes's lost distinction between industrial and financial circulation of money*, 7 November 2009. Available from jesperj@ruc.dk

https://www.postkeynesian.net/downloads/working-papers/PKWP
0905.pdf [accessed 25 June 2022].

John Paul II (1981). *Laborem Exercens*. Available from https://www.
vatican.va/content/john-paul-ii/en/encyclicals/documents/hf_jp-ii_enc_
14091981_laborem-exercens.html [accessed 25 June 2022].

Jordà, Ò., Schularick, M., Taylor, A., and Ward, F. (2018). Global financial
cycles and risk premiums. *NBER Working Paper*, 24677. Available at
https://www.nber.org/papers/w24677 [accessed 25 June 2022].

Jordà, Ò., Knoll, K., Kuvshinov, D., Schularick, M., and Taylor, A. (2019).
The rate of return on everything, 1870–2015. *The Quarterly Journal of
Economics*, 134(3), pp. 1225-1298. Available from https://doi.org/
10.1093/qje/qjz012 [accessed 25 June 2022].

Jordà, Ò., Singh, S., and Taylor, A. (2020). The long-run effects of monetary
policy. *Federal Reserve Bank of San Francisco Working Paper*, 2020-01.
Available from https://doi.org/10.24148/wp2020-01 [accessed 25 June
2022].

Kant, I. (2012). *Groundwork of the metaphysics of morals*. Cambridge:
Cambridge University Press.

Keynes, J. M. (1973). *The general theory of employment, interest and money*.
London: Macmillan.

Kindleberger, C. (1993). *A financial history of western Europe*, 2nd ed.
London: Routledge.

Kindleberger C. (1995). *The world economy and national finance in historical
perspective*. Ann Arbor MI: University of Michigan Press.

Klein, J. (1968). *Greek mathematical thought and origin of algebra*. Cambridge
MA: MIT Press.

Knafo, S. (2013). *The making of modern finance: liberal governance and the gold
standard*. London: Routledge.

Kohl, S. (2018). More mortgages, more homes? The effect of housing financialization on homeownership in historical perspective. *Politics & Society*, 46(2), pp. 177-203. Available from https://doi.org/10.1177/0032329218755750 [accessed 25 June 2022].

Komlosy, A. (2018). *Work: the last 1,000 years*. London: Verso.

Konings, Martijn, 2015. *The emotional logic of capitalism: what progressives have missed*. Stanford CA: Stanford University Press.

Kuhn, T. (1970). *The structure of scientific revolutions, 2nd ed*. Chicago: University of Chicago Press.

Lee, K. and Werner, R. (2018). Reconsidering monetary policy: an empirical examination of the relationship between interest rates and nominal gdp growth in the U.S., U.K., Germany and Japan. *Ecological Economics*, 146(April), pp. 26-34. Available from https://www.sciencedirect.com/science/article/pii/S0921800916307510 [accessed 28 June 2022].

Lee, K. and Werner, R. (2022). Are lower interest rates really associated with higher growth? New empirical evidence on the interest rate thesis from 19 countries. *International Journal of Finance and Economics* (preprint). Available from https://onlinelibrary.wiley.com/doi/10.1002/ijfe.2630 [accessed 25 June 2022].

Lerner, A. (1983). Functional finance and the federal debt. *Social Research*, 10. In: Colander C. ed., *Selected Economic Writing of Abba P. Lerner*. New York: New York University Press, pp. 297-310.

Levine, R. (2005). Finance and growth: theory and evidence. In: Aghion, P. and Durlauf, S., *Handbook of economic growth, volume 1A*. Amsterdam: Elsevier, pp 866-934. Available from http://faculty.haas.berkeley.edu/ross_levine/Papers/Forth_Book_Durlauf_FinNGrowth.pdf [accessed 25 June 2022].

Locke, J. (2021). *Second treatise of government*. Available from https://www.gutenberg.org/files/7370/7370-h/7370-h.htm [accessed 25 June 2022].

Long, S. and Sievers, B. eds. (2012). *Towards a socioanalysis of money, finance and capitalism: beneath the surface of the financial industry.* Abingdon: Routledge.

MacIntyre, A. (1990). *Three rival versions of moral enquiry: encyclopaedia, genealogy and tradition.* London: Bloomsbury.

MacIntyre A. (1988). *Whose justice? Which rationality?* Notre Dame IN: Notre Dame Press.

Macy, M. (1988). Value theory and the "golden eggs": appropriating the magic of accumulation. *Sociological Theory* 6(2) pp. 131-52. Available from https://doi.org/10.2307/202112 [accessed 28 June 2022].

Marx, K. (1977). *Capital,* Vol 1. New York: Vintage.

Marx, K. (1894). *Capital,* Vol 3. Available from https://www.marxists .org/archive/marx/works/1894-c3/index.htm [accessed 25 June 2022].

Marx, K. (1978). Manifesto of the Communist Party. In Tucker, R. ed., *The Marx-Engels Reader,* 2nd ed. New York: Norton.

Marx, K. (2009). *A contribution to the critique of political economy.* Available from https://www.marxists.org/archive/marx/works/1859/critique-pol-economy/ [accessed 25 June 2022].

McLeay, M., Radia, A. and Thomas, R. (2014). Money creation in the modern economy. *Bank of England Quarterly Bulletin,* Q1, pp 14-27. Available from https://www.bankofengland.co.uk/-/media/boe/files/quarterly-bulletin/2014/money-creation-in-the-modern-economy.pdf [accessed 25 June 2022].

Meikle, S. (1994). Aristotle on money. *Phronesis* 39(1), pp. 26-44. Available from http://www.jstor.org/stable/4182455. [accessed 25 June 2022].

Meikle, S., 1995. *Aristotle's economic thought.* Oxford: Oxford University Press.

Meikle, S. (2020). The switch from agency to causation in Marx. In: Róna, P., Zsolnai, L. eds. *Agency and Causal Explanation in Economics. Virtues and Economics*, vol. 5, pp. 125-136. Cham: Springer. Available at https://doi.org/10.1007/978-3-030-26114-6_8 [accessed 25 June 2022].

Milonakis, D. (2017). Formalising economics: social change, values, mechanics and mathematics in economic discourse. *Cambridge Journal of Economics*, 41(5) pp. 1367-1390. Available from https://doi.org/ 10.1093/cje/bex045 [accessed 25 June 2022].

Morningstar (ND). The magic of compounding. Available from: http://news.morningstar.com/classroom2/course.asp?docId=142858&p age=1&CN [accessed 25 June 2022].

New Economics Foundation (2017). *Making money from making money: seignorage in the modern economy*. Available from https://neweconomics .org/uploads/files/NEF_MAKING-MONEY-OUT-OF-MONEY_amend ment_E.pdf [accessed 28 June 2022].

Noonan, J. (1957). *The scholastic analysis of usury*. Cambridge MA: Harvard University Press.

Oaks, J. (2018). François Viète's revolution in algebra. *Archive for History of Exact Sciences*, 72(3), pp. 245-302. Available from https://link.springer .com/article/10.1007/s00407-018-0208-0 [accessed 28 June 2022].

Ovid (2020). *Metamorphoses*. Available from http://johnstoniatexts .x10host.com/ovid/ovidtofc.html [accessed 25 June 2022].

Parker, R. (1968). Discounted cash flow in historical perspective. *Journal of Accounting Research*, 6(1) pp. 58-71. Available from https://www. jstor.org/stable/2490123?origin=crossref&seq=1 [accessed 25 June 2022].

Peacock, M. (2017). The ontology of money. *Cambridge Journal of Economics*, 41(5), pp. 1471-1487. Available from https://doi.org/10.1093/cje/bex012 [accessed 25 June 2022].

Péguy, Charles, 2019. *Notes on Bergson and Descartes: philosophy, Christianity, and modernity in contestation*. Eugene, OR: Wipf & Stock. Cited in Martin J., The annunciation of the flesh: bodily mediation in the work of Charles Péguy. *Communio International Catholic Review*, 48(1) pp. 30-51.

Perold, A. (2004). The capital asset pricing model. *Journal of Economic Perspectives*, 18(3), pp. 3-24. Available from https://pubs.aeaweb.org/doi/pdfplus/10.1257/0895330042162340 [accessed 28 June 2022].

Piketty, T. (2013). *Capital in the twenty-first century*. Cambridge MA: Harvard University Press.

Polanyi, K. (2001). *The great transformation: the political and economic origins of our time*. Boston: Beacon Press.

Poley, J. (2016). *The devil's riches: a modern history of greed*. Oxford: Berghahn.

Pringle, R. (2019). *The power of money: how ideas about money shaped the modern world*. London: Palgrave Macmillan.

Quinn, S. (2019). *American bonds: how credit markets shaped a nation*. Princeton: Princeton University Press.

Ratcliff, S. ed. (2018). *Oxford essential quotations*, 6th ed. Oxford: Oxford University Press. Available at https://www.oxfordreference.com/view/10.1093/acref/9780191866692.001.0001/acref-9780191866692 [accessed 28 June 2022].

Rendahl, P. and Freund, L. (2019). Banks do not create money out of thin air. *Vox EU* (14 December 2019) Available at https://voxeu.org/article/banks-do-not-create-money-out-thin-air#.XfSi0yf9Ixc.twitter [accessed 28 June 2022].

Robertson, A. (2011). *Greed: gut feelings, growth, and history*. Cambridge: Polity.

Rosanvallon, P. (1989). *Le libéralisme économique*. Paris: Éditions de Seuil.

Saez, E. and Zucman, G. (2019). *The triumph of injustice: how the rich dodge taxes and how to make them pay.* New York: Norton.

Sanders, J. (2020). Jubilee in the Bible. *Biblical Theology Bulletin* 50(1), pp. 4-6. Available from https://journals.sagepub.com/doi/pdf/10.1177/014610 7919892838 [accessed 28 June 2022].

Searle, J. (2017). Money: ontology and deception. *Cambridge Journal of Economics* 41(5), pp. 1453-1470. Available from https://doi.org/ 10.1093/cje/bex034 [accessed 28 June 2022].

Selby, P. (2014). *Grace and mortgage: an idol unmasked.* London: Darton, Longman and Todd.

Simmel, G. (1990). *The philosophy of money*, 2nd ed. London: Routledge.

Simons, H. (1948). *Economic policy for a free society.* Chicago: University of Chicago Press.

Smith, A. (2003). *The wealth of nations.* New York: Bantam Dell.

Smithin, J. ed. (2000). *What is money?* London: Routledge.

Söffner, J. What does money signify? The "transvaluation of values" taking place in the relation between currency and language. In Resina, J. R. ed., *Cultures of currencies: literature and the symbolic foundation of money.* New York: Routledge, pp. 18-35

Spang, R. (2010). Money, money, money. *History Workshop Journal,* 69(Spring), pp. 225-233.

Sparkes, R. (2006). From mortmain to corporate social responsibility. In: Allouche, J. ed., *Corporate Social Responsibility,* Vol 1. Basingstoke: Palgrave Macmillan, pp. 38-72.

Storck, T. (2009). Is usury still a sin? *Communio: International Catholic Review,* 36(Fall), pp. 447-474.

Studwell, J. (2014). *How Asia works: success and failure in the world's most dynamic region.* New York: Grove Atlantic.

Syrquin, M. (2016). A review essay on "GDP: a brief but affectionate history" by Diane Coyle. *Journal of Economic Literature.* 54(2) pp. 573-588. Available from https://www.jstor.org/stable/43966745. [accessed 28 June 2022].

Tymoigne, É. (2003). Keynes and Commons on money. *Journal of Economic Issues.* 37(3), pp. 527-545. Available from https://www.jstor.org/stable/4227920?seq=1#page_scan_tab_contents [accessed 28 June 2022].

Urban, J. and Pürckhauer, A. (2016). Feminist economics. *Exploring Economics* [online] https://www.exploring-economics.org/en/orientation/feminist-economics/ [accessed 26 June 2022].

Volf, M. (1991). *Work in the spirit: toward a theology of work.* New York: Oxford University Press.

White, M. (2002). Doctoring Adam Smith: the fable of the diamonds and water paradox. *History of Political Economy,* 34(4), pp. 659-683.

Woodin, T., Crook D., and Carpentier, V. (2010). Community and mutual ownership: A historical review. *Joseph Rowntree Foundation* [online]. https://www.jrf.org.uk/sites/default/files/jrf/migrated/files/community-mutual-ownership-full.pdf [accessed 26 June 2022].

Wordsworth, W. (1802). *The world is too much with us.* Available from https://poets.org/poem/world-too-much-us [accessed 26 June 2022].

Zelizer, V. (1997). *The social meaning of money.* Princeton, NJ: Princeton University Press.

Zelmanovitz, L. (2016). *The ontology and function of money: the philosophical fundamentals of monetary institutions.* Lanham MD: Lexington Books.

Zuckert, M. (2007). The fullness of being: Thomas Aquinas and the modern critique of natural law. *The Review of Politics,* 69(1), pp. 28-47. Available at https://www.jstor.org/stable/20452850?seq=1 [accessed 26 June 2022].